TRUST, DISTRUST, AND MISTRUST
IN MULTINATIONAL DEMOCRACIES

DEMOCRACY, DIVERSITY, AND CITIZEN ENGAGEMENT SERIES

Series editor: Alain-G. Gagnon

With the twenty-first-century world struggling to address various forms of conflict and new types of political and cultural claims, the Democracy, Diversity, and Citizen Engagement Series revitalizes research in the fields of nationalism, federalism, and cosmopolitanism, and examines the interactions between ethnicity, identity, and politics. Works published in this series are concerned with the theme of representation – of citizens and of interests – and how these ideas are defended at local and global levels that are increasingly converging. Further, the series advances and advocates new public policies and social projects with a view to creating change and accommodating diversity in its many expressions. In doing so, the series instills democratic practices in meaningful new ways by studying key subjects such as the mobilization of citizens, groups, communities, and nations, and the advancement of social justice and political stability.

Under the leadership of the Interdisciplinary Research Centre on Diversity and Democracy, this series creates a forum where current research on democracy, diversity, and citizen engagement can be examined within the context of the study of nations as well as of nations divided by state frontiers.

Trust, Distrust, and Mistrust in Multinational Democracies

Comparative Perspectives

Edited by

DIMITRIOS KARMIS
AND FRANÇOIS ROCHER

McGill-Queen's University Press
Montreal & Kingston · London · Chicago

© McGill-Queen's University Press 2018

ISBN 978-0-7735-5342-2 (cloth)
ISBN 978-0-7735-5343-9 (paper)
ISBN 978-0-7735-5433-7 (ePDF)
ISBN 978-0-7735-5434-4 (ePUB)

Legal deposit second quarter 2018
Bibliothèque nationale du Québec

Printed in Canada on acid-free paper that is 100% ancient forest free
(100% post-consumer recycled), processed chlorine free

Funded by the   Financé par le
Government   gouvernement   Canadä   Canada Council   Conseil des arts
of Canada   du Canada   for the Arts   du Canada

We acknowledge the support of the Canada Council for the Arts, which
last year invested $153 million to bring the arts to Canadians throughout
the country.

Nous remercions le Conseil des arts du Canada de son soutien. L'an dernier,
le Conseil a investi 153 millions de dollars pour mettre de l'art dans la vie
des Canadiennes et des Canadiens de tout le pays.

Library and Archives Canada Cataloguing in Publication

Trust, distrust, and mistrust in multinational democracies: comparative
perspectives / edited by Dimitrios Karmis and François Rocher.

(Democracy, diversity, and citizen engagement series; 4)
Includes bibliographical references and index.
Issued in print and electronic formats.
ISBN 978-0-7735-5342-2 (cloth). – ISBN 978-0-7735-5343-9 (paper). –
ISBN 978-0-7735-5433-7 (ePDF). – ISBN 978-0-7735-5434-4 (ePUB)

1. Political participation – Cross-cultural studies. 2. Democracy – Public
opinion – Cross-cultural studies. 3. Trust – Political aspects – Cross-cultural
studies. 4. Political alienation – Cross-cultural studies. 5. Comparative
government. I. Karmis, Dimitrios, 1964–, editor II. Rocher, François, editor
III. Series: Democracy, diversity, and citizen engagement series; 4

JF799.T78 2018   323'.042   C2018-901336-2
                                          C2018-901337-0

This book was typeset by Marquis Interscript in 10.5/13 Sabon.

Contents

Tables and Figures

TRUST, DISTRUST, AND MISTRUST
IN MULTINATIONAL DEMOCRACIES

The Language of Trust, Distrust, and Mistrust in Multinational Democracies

Dimitrios Karmis
in Collaboration with François Rocher

In the past thirty years, much has been said about the decline of trust in democracies, and intense debates have occurred about the nature and complexity of the relationship between trust and democracy (Zmerli and Hooghe 2011; Rosanvallon 2006, 2008; Lenard 2008, 2005; Andrain and Smith 2006; Hetherington 2005, 1998; Pharr and Putnam 2000; Putnam 2000, 1995; Warren 1999; Nye, Zelikow, and King 1997; Fukuyama 1995). In this literature, political trust is understood as trust towards political institutions (including trust towards political actors who inhabit the institutions), trust between citizens, and to a lesser extent, trust between groups. However, surprisingly enough, the literature on trust has given no special attention to the issue of trust between minority and majority nations in multinational democracies. While there has been a growing interest in trust among scholars of multinational democracies (Kymlicka and Banting 2006; Festenstein 2005; Harty and Murphy 2005), the present volume, which is part of the work of the Groupe de recherche sur les sociétés plurinationales (GRSP), is the first collaborative, critical, historical, and comparative survey of the dynamics of trust, distrust, and mistrust in multinational democracies.

For several years now, the GRSP has emphasized that multinational democracy is "a new and distinctive type of political association that is coming into prominence at the dawn of the twenty-first century" (Tully 2001: 1). As Charles Taylor pointed out, this emerging type of democracy arises primarily from the "constitutive tensions" of

democratic societies: as they become more and more diverse, democratic societies "require a new kind of unity" in order to maintain
their legitimacy (Taylor 2001: xiii). According to James Tully, multinational democracies share four major characteristics that break with
the model of "single-nation democracies (which are often presumed
to be the norm)" (2001: 2). First, they are "constitutional associations that contain two or more nations or peoples. The members of
the nations are, or aspire to be, recognized as self-governing peoples
with the right of self-determination" (2). Second, on the institutional
level, citizens of the various national political communities – most
often territorially based – have their own self-governing institutions,
while participating in the self-governing multination as well. This
means that multinational democracies exhibit various sorts of federal
or federal-like arrangements. Third – in contrast with the conventional equation of democracy, a single state, and single nationhood
– both "the nations and the composite multination are constitutional
democracies" (3). Fourth, in the context of the population movements and identity awakening of the late twentieth and early twenty-
first centuries, "multinational democracies are also multicultural,"
which means that they have to supplement "the procedures and
institutions for the reconciliation of their multinational diversity"
with procedures and institutions for the reconciliation of their multicultural diversity (3–4).

The aim of this introduction is to present some of the main concepts
and issues pertaining to the dynamics of trust, distrust, and mistrust
in multinational democracies, and to briefly indicate some of the
chapters' main contributions to these topics.

THEORETICAL AND METHODOLOGICAL CONSIDERATIONS

Over the years, studies on trust have increasingly emphasized its challenging theoretical and methodological complexity. From various
disciplines and perspectives, the contributors to the present volume
propose different ways to account for the complex, multifaceted
nature of trust. Taken together, their writings help to broaden the
scope of the literature on trust in at least three ways.

First, some chapters argue for the combination rather than the
opposition of the main theoretical accounts of trust. While past schol-
arship has spent considerable effort in opposing strategic calculative

accounts of trust (e.g., Hardin 2002, 2006) to normative non-calculative ones (e.g., Uslaner 2002), several contributions to this volume suggest that the understanding of a complex, multifaceted phenomenon like trust may often benefit from a more oecumenical and pragmatic approach. For example, in chapter 1, Dario Castiglione's comparative survey of the terms capturing "what we normally mean by 'trust'" in Romance and Germanic languages reveals both their family resemblances and the wide range of meanings and nuances conveyed by the idea of trust. These meanings can be divided into four clusters and placed "in a partly overlapping sequence of *beliefs*, *expectations*, and *attitudes of faith* and *hope*." This constitutes "a broad but somewhat continuous spectrum of meanings of trust ... contained within two polarities defined by cognitive and moral conceptions of trust, while in between them we find more behaviourally inclined conceptions." For Castiglione, this cognitive/moral or calculative/non-calculative polarity of the various meanings we give to trust suggests that "the *problem* of trust concerns *both* our cognitive and moral expectations about others and others' actions, and that a combination of approaches may be the best way "to understand how [trust] works in relation to social cohesion" – especially in "divided" or multinational societies. Similarly, in chapter 4 on "representative trust," Patti Tamara Lenard maintains that the trust citizens extend (or not) to their representatives is based both on probabilistic calculations and "on the affective or emotional cues that guide us in extending our trust 'intuitively.'"

Second, the present collection stands out for its particular focus on the dynamics of trust, distrust, and mistrust. Beliefs, attitudes, practices, and relations of trust, distrust, and mistrust are *situated*, *interacting*, and *coexisting* phenomena. As will be discussed in the following sections of this introduction, in multinational democracies, these phenomena are *situated* into particular historical and institutional power relations between minority and majority nations – relations that produce their own dynamics over time. Through such situated dynamics, trust, distrust, and mistrust *interact* closely and in numerous ways. If "the twin of trust is betrayal" (Dunn 1990: 34), a breach of trust is often the beginning of distrust. By contrast, in some situations, extending trust may contribute to the generation of trustworthiness and, ultimately, may help to break down a dynamic of distrust. Finally, while trust, distrust, and mistrust are often considered to be incompatible, mutually exclusive phenomena, they may *coexist* in various and more or less subtle ways, especially if we distinguish mistrust from distrust and if we accept that there are different types and degrees of trust, mistrust, and distrust. For instance, we routinely trust people to carry out activities they were trained for, but not activities for which they have no credentials. In other words, we both trust them to carry out certain activities and distrust them to carry out others. We may even show a high level of trust in the former case, and a high level of distrust in the latter. Various typologies of trust and distrust have developed over the years. Moreover, in recent years, some authors have developed a key, systematic distinction between distrust and mistrust (e.g. Rosanvallon 2006; Lenard 2008). Despite some differences, they usually emphasize that generalized distrust is a problem for democracy, while various forms of mistrust – especially vigilance – are central to democracy and can be compatible with trust. Other authors have made a similar point by simply distinguishing between different types of trust and distrust (e.g. Warren 2017).

Dynamics of distrust have been characteristic of multinational democracies. The "constitutive tensions" of such deeply diverse democracies are particularly challenging for the establishment of relations of trust. In chapter 3, from the perspective of analytical philosophy, David Robichaud examines how such diversity-related tensions can give rise to dynamics of distrust. First, he shows how distrust can occur at two levels: (1) the collective reputations of groups and communities; and (2) direct, face-to-face interactions between individuals belonging to separate communities. In the former case, our disposition to trust individuals belonging to communities different from our own is structured by negative collective ideas that we have about such communities (beliefs about their trustworthiness, but also about their disposition to consider us trustworthy). In the latter case, our tendency to trust is more influenced by the greater difficulty we have in identifying, in direct interpersonal relations with individuals belonging to communities different from our own, our interlocutor's disposition to behave in a manner favourable to us. Here, what is at issue is our "capacity to *read* another person" rather than the reputation of her community. Second, Robichaud argues that these sources of distrust can combine into three types of dynamics of distrust that are difficult to alter, and which represent a major threat to solidarity in deeply diverse democracies. As we will see in the next section, other chapters study specific dynamics of distrust in multinational democracies.

Important questions are raised by the view that mistrust – and especially vigilance – is distinct from distrust, is central to democracy, and is compatible with trust. In what sense is vigilance key to multi-national democracy? In what form is it reconcilable with trust? To what extent is it context dependent? In chapter 5, Dimitrios Karmis and Darren O'Toole address these questions through a critical reading of Philip Pettit's influential *Republicanism: A Theory of Freedom and Government* (1997). Karmis and O'Toole contend that despite several merits, Pettit's conceptual framework needs significant revisions. Using examples from the history of Canada-Québec relations, they argue that such a framework seriously underestimates the depth of the tension between vigilance and trust. They also show how Pettit's unconditional "overtures of trust" are imprudent and risky in the context of significantly asymmetrical power relations between a minority nation and a majority nation.

Third, most of the chapters in this collection contribute to the still-nascent comparative literature on trust, distrust, and mistrust in multinational democracies. Two chapters are fully comparative, while the others provide case studies with comparative lessons. In chapter 11, Philip Resnick gives a broad comparative overview of the dynamics of trust and distrust between minority and majority nations in Belgium, Canada, Spain, and the United Kingdom. In chapter 12, Réjean Pelletier and Jérôme Couture compare the impact of national identity – single or double – on trust in central political institutions and in the minority nation's institutions in Catalonia and Québec. Chapters 5 through 10 – by Karmis and O'Toole, Peter H. Russell, François Rocher, Jeremy Webber, Jean Leclair, and Alexandre Pelletier and Richard Simeon – study different aspects of the dynamics of trust, distrust, and mistrust in Canada. Chapters 13 (Kris Deschouwer) and 14 (Dave Sinardet and Niels Morsink) focus on the case of Belgium.

TIME, INSTITUTIONS, AND POWER

The situatedness of trust, distrust, and mistrust calls for contextual analysis. Several chapters focus on how defining institutional moments and power differentials affect trust in the relations between minority and majority nations.

In *Democracy in America*, in what might look like a prefiguration of path dependency analysis, Tocqueville emphasized the importance of the "starting point," the foundational moments of political entities,[1] arguing that political entities "all bear some marks of their origins," that "the circumstances that accompanied their birth and contributed to their development affected the whole term of their being" (Tocqueville 1990: 26–7). In an era dominated by the (single) nation-state model, multinational polities have usually emerged from compromise rather than choice. In chapter 6, Peter H. Russell sums it up well when he refers to Canada's multinational character as the result of two "incomplete conquests" of pre-existing nations: on one hand, the Indigenous Peoples, through the Royal Proclamation (1763) and the Treaty of Niagara (1764); on the other, the Canadiens, through the Quebec Act (1774). Following Hardin's views on "trust as encapsulated interests" and "power differentials as an obstacle to trust" (Hardin 2006), Russell argues that "a rough equality of power between the parties," at least at the time, made it in everyone's interest to find common ground. In other words, Canada's foundation rests on a political relationship of trust as encapsulated interests – rather than on a shared vision of common values – between the British, the Canadiens, and the Indigenous Peoples. Then, looking at subsequent defining institutional moments in the history of Canada, Russell contends that shifts in power towards the English-speaking majority largely explain the rise of mistrust and distrust among minority nations. This is especially true of the relationships of Canadian to Indigenous political authorities, characterized by broken promises, violations of agreements, disparagement, and subordination, if not outright state deception. It is worth noting that Russell emphasizes the cumulative temporal effects of such breaches of trust – coloured by colonialism and racism – despite several recent Supreme Court of Canada rulings and significant political developments in favour of Indigenous Peoples. Indigenous distrust towards Canada is especially strong and pervasive when it comes to land and governance issues. According to Russell, the history of the relationship between the Canadiens/Québec and Canada was different, and the betrayals experienced by the former were never as deep as those suffered by Indigenous Peoples. The adoption of a federal form of government, court decisions, and the electoral weight of Québec made it possible to exert some influence over federal policy so as to enforce respect for Québec's interests and ensure that the majority would be less hostile towards them.

In chapter 7, François Rocher provides a significantly different interpretation of the Québec-Canada dynamics of trust, distrust, and mistrust since the confederation debates. Although he shares with Russell a Hardin-inspired conception of trust, Rocher puts more emphasis on the original and subsequent power differentials between the parties, as well as the sequences and cumulative path-dependent effects of defining institutional moments characterized by distrust and vigilance. Following his typology of trust (considerable and moderate) and distrust (moderate and radical) in multinational contexts marked by asymmetry between communities, Rocher emphasizes the importance of the post-Confederation infringements of rights of French Catholic minorities: first in New Brunswick, then in Manitoba after the contested conviction of Louis Riel, and finally in Ontario following the 1912 adoption of Regulation 17. This sequence of infringements significantly upset the relative balance of power negotiated in 1867, illustrating the fact that the 1867 federation rested on a misunderstanding of the union's purposes, provoked a rapid shift from moderate trust to moderate distrust among the French Canadian elite, and set the path towards a mostly unilingual Canada. In the end, the accumulation of negative experiences, the asymmetry of power, and the many disagreements about the shared purposes of the union strengthened feelings of distrust that culminated in the events leading to the 1982 repatriation of the Constitution. For Rocher, the sequence of defining constitutional moments that took place in the 1980s and 1990s gave a final blow to the dualist principle at the core of Québec's historical understanding of the initial compromise. In short, unlike Russell, Rocher emphasizes a "strong trend" towards "the deterioration of Québec's negotiating power within the federation," increasing Québec's (sometimes radical) distrust and mistrust towards the rest of Canada.

Compared to Canada, in the past fifty years, Belgium has been more successful at reforming its constitution on the basis of mutual compromises. This may in part be due to the bipolar and consociative nature of the political system, which favours a more even balance of power between the parties. In chapter 13, Kris Deschouwer shows that such apparent successes do not tell the whole story. While they required a certain amount of trust to occur, they have not generated steady and lasting increases in trust, either from citizens and political elites towards the political system, or shared between Flemish-speaking and French-speaking elites. Along with the four constitutional reforms (in 1970, 1980, 1987, and 1993) that made Belgium a federation, the successive scissions of the three main political parties along linguistic lines – the

Christian-Democrats in 1968, the Liberals in 1972, and the Socialists in 1978 – appear to be key institutional moments in the bipolarization of the Belgian political system. With political parties addressing and seeking election from separate groups of voters, there are fewer incentives for moderation in electoral promises, it is harder to form stable government coalitions, and it is particularly difficult to fulfil the contradictory expectations of separate groups of voters. In a way, this is the paradox of the federalization of Belgium: it has helped the country to solve major crises, while in the long run it has made compromises more difficult to achieve and more precarious to maintain.

In chapter 11, Philip Resnick argues that the dynamics of trust and distrust between minority and majority nations in Belgium, Canada, Spain, and the United Kingdom depend heavily on contingent factors. In other words, path dependency, power asymmetry, and contingency are all important for the comparative historical analysis of the institutions affecting trust.

INSTITUTIONS, ELITES, AND CIVIL SOCIETY

The dynamics of trust, distrust, and mistrust between minority and majority nations are also shaped by the political elites within political institutions, as well as by the intellectual elites who report and analyze their activities. In chapter 8, taking the 1990s failure of the Meech Lake Accord in Canada as a case in point, Jeremy Webber argues that constitutional negotiations and constitutional amendments should not be the observers' only focus when they examine trust between minority and majority nations. While the rejection of the Meech Lake Accord certainly undermined the trust of many Québécois in the willingness of Canadians outside Québec to share their vision of Canada, the Canadian political class proposed a series of measures (other than amendments to the constitutional text itself) so inspired by the defunct accord that the latter's principles now guide the practice of Canadian federalism. According to Webber, "the approach to the Canadian federation reflected in Meech scored a belated victory." For example, the Canadian Charter of Rights and Freedoms has been interpreted in such a way as to reflect the distinct society principle contrary to the homogenization fears expressed when the Charter was adopted. The courts have accepted the principle of cultural diversity and the institutional consequences that flow from it, in particular with respect to the interpretation of language rights. In the same way, the House of Commons has adopted a series of resolutions that recognize Québec as a distinct society (1995), and the Québécois as a nation within a united Canada (2006). Webber does not argue against constitutional amendments, as he recognizes that they have undeniable advantages in comparison with changes generated by federal practices. He instead argues "against the fetishization of the word – the tendency to assume that the constitutional text defines who we are as a country, or to try to make it do so." He invites students of Canada to look at the purpose of trust, namely the Québécois' practical capacity to exercise self-determination. Put differently, he invites them to consider the living constitution rather than what is explicitly written, since "what matters, in the end, is how we are able to live under constitutional arrangements, not what they say."

In chapter 9, Jean Leclair stresses that such fetishization of the written constitution is one of the key characteristics (along with the confusion between state, nation, and society; the nation as a subjective entity; monism; and a totalizing conception of culture) of the methodological nationalism underlying many studies of multinational federalism. Based on examples from studies of Canadian federalism, Leclair argues that "methodological nationalism contributes to cultivating a feeling of distrust by providing only a partial glimpse (although I am not saying an erroneous one) of Canada's federal dynamics." By contrast, Leclair maintains that the combination of methodological and liberal federalism provides a different and often neglected picture of Canadian federalism. With its "emphasis on federalism as a limit on power," it may not be a substitute for trust, but it can help citizens to see low trust in a different light: namely, as resulting in part from the institutionalization of a healthy mistrust that comes with federation and federalism.

While Deschouwer's chapter emphasizes that Belgium's constitutional compromises have had paradoxical effects and that the successive scissions of the main political parties along linguistic lines were key institutional moments in the bipolarization of the political system, Dave Sinardet and Niels Morsink reach similar conclusions by focusing on the dynamic of trust, distrust, and mistrust between the elites of political parties. In chapter 14, Sinardet and Morsink argue that the importance of trust between the political elites of a consociative federation should not be underestimated. The authors distinguish relational trust from structural trust. Relational trust places the accent on the proximity and repetition of interactions between elites, thus enabling them to understand the positions and preferences of their partners. Structural trust is related to the roles played by the elites rather than to the individuals themselves. In some circumstances, weakened structural trust can be compensated for by increased relational trust. To the question of whether the duty of political elites to obtain institutionalized consensus makes trust superfluous, Sinardet and Morsink answer that there has to be a minimum degree of trust in the other party's desire to cooperate before negotiations begin, and that consociative mechanisms, such as the right to veto and guaranteed representation, cannot replace it. On the contrary, consociative mechanisms in the absence of trust can lead to institutional paralysis. The case of Belgium shows that consociative mechanisms based on dissuasion or the obligation to reach a compromise can favour the emergence of relational trust. This helped Belgium to adopt four constitutional reforms in twenty-five years, avoiding conflicts through the transfer of disputed jurisdictions to regions and communities. However, this centrifugal dynamic has prevented trust from taking a structural form, since it has not favoured the development of a vision based on intercommunity collective interest and a feeling of loyalty to the federation. The partisan elites have begun doubting the federal loyalty of their counterparts and defending the exclusive interests of their own communities.

Despite such work on the dynamics of trust, distrust, and mistrust between the partisan elites in Belgium, the issue of trust in multinational civil societies has been little explored. In chapter 10, Alexandre Pelletier and Richard Simeon study various patterns of interaction between trust, accommodation, and cooperation in Canadian voluntary associations. For the authors, the concepts of trust and cooperation are distinct and should be treated as ordinal variables. More (or less) substantive trust affects the model and associative structure adopted by linguistic groups in their relationships, and makes more (or less) meaningful cooperation possible.

MULTINATIONAL DEMOCRACY AND IDENTITY

The single-nation democracy model largely relies on the assumption that the trust needed for modern democratic citizenship requires a shared national identity. Yet, as we saw at the outset of the present introduction, the rejection of such a shared national identity is part of the *raison d'être* of multinational democracies: they are "constitutional associations that contain two or more nations or peoples"

(Tully 2001: 2) and "require a new kind of unity" (Taylor 2001: xiii). What does this mean for trust and identity in such democratic polities?

In chapter 2, Geneviève Nootens relies on Charles Tilly's conception of trust as a social mechanism in order to criticize the liberal nationalist account of trust in modern democratic politics. In her view, the problem with such an account does not lie in its defence of the normative value of national belonging. Instead, it lies in a too-simple understanding of trust in democratic politics, with interpersonal trust rooted in a shared national identity acting as a substitute for relations of proximity – something which is particularly problematic for understanding democratization mechanisms and processes in plurinational societies and at the global level. Among other things, the liberal nationalist view of trust underestimates the part played by power relationships and, following Tilly's terms, "the (partial) integration of the networks that embody trust relationships between individuals and groups into public politics."

In chapter 12, Réjean Pelletier and Jérôme Couture discuss whether different types of national identity have an impact on political trust defined as trust in political institutions. More precisely, they ask the following question: "Among members of the minority nations of Québec and Catalonia, does the way one defines oneself – by a single or double identity – have an impact on trust in central political institutions and in the minority nation's institutions?" Data on Canada and Québec comes from Pelletier and Couture's own surveys, and they are compared to data from similar surveys done in Spain and Catalonia. It turns out that trust in central institutions is lower among those who identify themselves exclusively with the minority nation, both in Québec and Catalonia. "Double identity" incorporates the greatest number of people in the two minority nations, and individuals who reported double identity resemble those who identified themselves uniquely with the majority nation. They seemed satisfied both with their double belonging and with the central and regional political institutions. In sum, in the cases of Catalonia and Québec, double identity is a source of trust in the political institutions of multinational democracies.

NOTE

1 Tocqueville uses successively the terms "nations," "peoples," and "states" (1990: 26–7).

REFERENCES

Andrain, Charles F., and James T. Smith. 2006. *Political Democracy, Trust, and Social Justice*. Boston: Northeastern University Press.

Dunn, John. 1990. "Trust and Political Agency." In *Interpreting Political Responsibility: Essays 1981–1989*, 26–44. Cambridge: Polity Press.

Festenstein, Matthew. 2005. *Negotiating Diversity: Culture, Deliberation, Trust*. Cambridge: Polity Press.

Fukuyama, Francis. 1995. *Trust: The Social Virtues and the Creation of Prosperity*. New York: Free Press.

Hardin, Russell. 2002. *Trust and Trustworthiness*. New York: Russell Sage Foundation.

– 2006. *Trust*. Cambridge: Polity Press.

Harty, Siobhan, and Michael Murphy. 2005. *In Defence of Multinational Citizenship*. Vancouver: University of British Columbia Press.

Hetherington, Marc J. 1998. "The Political Relevance of Trust." *American Political Science Review* 92, no. 4: 791–808.

– 2005. *Why Trust Matters: Declining Political Trust and the Demise of American Liberalism*. Princeton: Princeton University Press.

Kymlicka, Will, and Keith Banting, eds. 2006. *Multiculturalism and the Welfare State: Recognition and Redistribution in Contemporary Democracies*. Oxford: Oxford University Press.

Lenard, Patti Tamara. 2005. "The Decline of Trust, The Decline of Democracy?" *Critical Review of International Social and Political Philosophy* 8: 363–78.

– 2008. "Trust Your Compatriots, but Count Your Change: The Roles of Trust, Mistrust, and Distrust in Democracy." *Political Studies* 56: 312–32.

Nye, Joseph S., Philip D. Zelikow, and David C. King, eds. 1997. *Why People Don't Trust Government?* Cambridge: Cambridge University Press.

Pettit, Philip. 1997. *Republicanism: A Theory of Freedom and Government*. Oxford: Oxford University Press.

Pharr, Susan J., and Robert D. Putnam, eds. 2000. *Disaffected Democracies: What's Troubling the Trilateral Democracies*. Princeton: Princeton University Press.

Putnam, Robert. 1995. "Bowling Alone: America's Declining Social Capital." *Journal of Democracy* 6: 65–78.

– 2000. *Bowling Alone: The Collapse and Revival of American Community*. New York: Simon and Schuster.

Rosanvallon, Pierre. 2006. *La contre-démocratie: La politique à l'âge de la défiance*. Paris: Seuil.

– 2008. *Counter-Democracy: Politics in an Age of Distrust*. Cambridge: Cambridge University Press.

Taylor, Charles. 2001. "Foreword." In *Multinational Democracies*, edited by Alain-G. Gagnon and James Tully, xiii–xv. Cambridge: Cambridge University Press.

Tocqueville, Alexis de. 1990 [1835]. *Democracy in America*. Volume 1. New York: Vintage.

Tully, James. 2001. "Introduction." In *Multinational Democracies*, edited by Alain-G. Gagnon and James Tully, 1–33. Cambridge: Cambridge University Press.

Uslaner, Eric M. 2002. *The Moral Foundations of Trust*. Cambridge: Cambridge University Press.

Warren, Mark E., ed. 1999. *Democracy and Trust*. Cambridge: Cambridge University Press.

– 2017. "What Kind of Trust Does a Democracy Need? Trust from the Perspective of Democratic Theory." In *Handbook on Political Trust*, edited by Sonja Zmerli and Tom W.G. van der Meer, 33–52. Cheltenham: Edward Elgar Publishing.

Zmerli, Sonja, and Marc Hooghe, eds. 2011. *Political Trust: Why Context Matters*. Colchester: ECPR Press.

PART ONE

Theoretical Debates

Conceptions of Trust:
From Social Mechanism
to Normative Principle

Dario Castiglione

Trust offers a normatively and philosophically attractive way of conceiving the social order. Normatively, the reasons for such attractiveness lie in the way that trust downplays the role of force and external sanctions as the explanation of why we get along with each other. Philosophically, trust identifies an intriguing way in which people understand and relate to one another. As we shall see, both aspects of this relation count. Though the meaning of "trust" is not easy to fathom, this should not deter us from taking trust seriously in social and moral discourses. Being attentive to the different meanings we attribute to trust in common language is a way of understanding the role that trust plays in our society, and even more so in societies that are "divided" or multinational in character. Such attentiveness is analytically fruitful, for it helps to reveal some of the mechanisms that bind people together. It may also suggest, programmatically through the facets of our uses of trust, the kind of policies, institutions, characters, and attitudes we may wish to promote in society. This paper cannot cover all aspects of this discussion, nor deal with any single one in detail. The literature on trust is already rich and complex, and much of what I want to argue here comes with no pretension to great originality. More modestly, I wish to suggest that there is some mileage to be gained from combining the variety of ways in which trust is both used and theorized, in order to understand how it works in relation to social cohesion. In the following, I wish to draw attention to three elements: the first is the family of words that in several languages capture what we normally mean by "trust"; the second is the tension between "predictive" and "normative" conceptions, and how this tension captures issues central to our conception of the social order; the third is how we can use trust as a normative principle for civil society – something that may be relevant for mobilizing the resources of trust in divided societies. In my discussion, I also hope to show that different conceptions and different uses of "trust" are partly defined by the complementary, though not always symmetric, ways in which it relates to "distrust" and/or "mistrust." In most circumstances, trust is characterized by the way in which its "contours" are determined. To explore the exact nature of these relationships is not the main scope of this paper, but I aim to show that it is an avenue worth exploring, as it helps make sense of what trust does and what the extent of its social value may be.

FAMILY RESEMBLANCES

There is a surprisingly rich vein of meanings and nuances conveyed by the idea of trust. This is true across languages – something that is, if anything, reinforced by the overlap of semantic fields that one finds when translating "trust" and other cognate terms from one language to another. Although analytic simplification is necessary when we define a concept that we wish to use for either empirical or normative purposes, there is also something to be said for the simple lexical exercise of mapping out the meanings that a concept may take in ordinary language. In our case, I shall limit myself to a simple catalogue of cognate terms, which, at least in the Romance and Germanic languages, have strong family resemblances. I leave it to readers to explore in their own minds the multifarious ways in which these words are interconnected in ordinary language. In English, we have: trust, trustworthy; distrust, mistrust; confidence, confident (related to faith); and credit, credible, credibility (implying reputation). In French: *confiance*; *défiance, méfiance, méfiant*; *crédit, crédibilité*, and *crédible (réputation)*. In Italian: *fiducia (fede)*; *sfiducia, sfiduciáto* (or "*senza speranza*" – without hope); *diffidenza*; *credito*, and *credibile (considerazione, reputazione)*. In German: *vertrauen, trauen*; *mistrauen, misstrauisch*; *glaube(n), glaubwürdigkeit*, and *glaublich*.

Keeping these terms and their interlacing meanings in mind, and without any pretention of being systematic, it is possible to suggest that there are four main clusters of meanings for the idea of trust. In one sense, "trust" expresses a *belief* in other people's actions and motivations. In this first meaning, to trust is to believe, in the sense of being cognizant of the favourable intentions that others have towards us, or being aware that their behaviour will have a favourable effect on us or our interests. In a second sense, closely related to the first one, "trust" expresses an *expectation* about future events, based on either a prediction of the actions of others or an insight into their motivations. Trust as expectation is a particular form of belief about others, but one that does not always follow from reasoned calculation, thus partly distinguishing it from the first meaning, and in some way bringing it closer to the other two senses. These other two meanings of "trust" consist of two related, but distinguishable *attitudes* – of faith, on the one hand, and of hope and confidence, on the other – that are manifested when we trust other people. Such an attitude more properly regards the actions and intentions of others, but it can also characterize our relation to the world at large.

Each of these senses of "trust" involves a view of others as *trustworthy*, but the mechanisms through which we arrive at such a conclusion differ significantly from meaning to meaning, as does the relative importance that each of these meanings gives to the assessment of trustworthiness. The way in which we express our trust comes with many different connotations which accompany our beliefs, expectations, and attitudes. They may express an assessment of others, a confidence in or reliance upon others, or a dependency on others. Trusting in others may come from shrewd calculation, a somewhat fideistic attitude, or a more or less well-founded optimism. The relational aspect of trust – the way in which trust configures the relationship between us and the other(s) – is crucial, for it determines what we *do* in trusting. It also explains the role that trust plays as part of a causal chain of events, considering also the possibility that it may figure as part of a circular relationship, appearing both as cause and effect.

CALCULATIVE AND MORAL CONCEPTIONS OF TRUST

In a rather impressionistic manner, I have so far suggested that there are four partly overlapping clusters of meanings of "trust," and that these can also be captured by the way in which ideas of trust combine with a series of cognate terms. However, by placing the various clusters in a partly overlapping sequence of *beliefs*, *expectations*, and *attitudes of faith* and *hope*, I have implicitly argued that there is a broad but somewhat continuous spectrum of meanings of trust. These are contained within two polarities defined by cognitive and moral conceptions of trust, while in between them we find more behaviourally inclined conceptions. Here are some possible distinctions, which also reflect some recent theories of trust. First, we have the cluster of cognitive meanings that rest on different assessments of the trustworthiness of others. Russell Hardin's (2002) theory of "encapsulated interest," for instance, bases trust primarily on our belief about the interests of others, and how such interests can be trusted (in a predictive sense) to produce a kind of behaviour that may be favourable to us, and which therefore we can trust (in a more generic sense). But, equally, we can trust others on the basis of beliefs regarding their character disposition or their moral commitment, which we might assume guides their action towards us in certain circumstances, regardless of where their particular interests lie.

The second cluster of meanings, located in the middle of the cognitive-moral polarity, comprises those senses that equate trust with behavioural factors, rather than cognition or moral attitudinal factors. Here, trust is treated either as mere expectation, or ungrounded faith, or as a kind of personal attitude towards others (see, for instance, Williamson 1996: 272–3). The senses of trust as faith or as an attitude spill over into the third cluster, positioned at the moral end of the spectrum. Here, trust is regarded as a kind of optimistic attitude, based on a sense of openness and goodwill towards others (Uslaner 2002). In a related sense, trust is conceived as a way of "lowering one's guard" or making oneself vulnerable to others (Elster 2007: 344–52; Baier 1994, 2010); and by extending this sense towards a more collective perspective, trust can be understood as a form of inter-dependence based on non-calculative motivations.

I believe that taking on board, and trying to accommodate, various meanings and theories of trust is both profitable and correct. Hardin (2002) has made a convincing case for restricting trust to a purely cognitive level. It nevertheless seems to me that the *problem* of trust concerns *both* our cognitive and moral expectations about others and others' actions. The need to take trust to be both calculative and moral is well illustrated by Martin Hollis when he talks about two varieties of trust: "Firstly, we trust one another to behave predictably in a sense which applies equally to the natural world as well … Secondly, we trust one another to do what is right" (1998: 10). Hollis shows how these two meanings of trust bring forward two different ways in which we *expect* things to happen. In the former sense, trust consists in the expectation *that* someone would do something, but in the latter sense, trust is the expectation *of* someone doing something (11). I shall return to this distinction later on to show that, as Hollis himself remarks, there is a further distinction hidden in the moral expectation *of* someone doing the right thing. For the time being, I wish to note that it is because of this ambiguity that "expectations" can be located in the middle of the cognitive-moral polarity that I suggested above.

Since I think the *problem* of trust is *both* cognitive and moral, I would like to briefly sketch both of its sides before returning to how they interconnect. In dealing with the cognitive side, one can profitably use Hardin's own analysis of "encapsulated trust," without necessarily endorsing his conclusion that trust is exclusively cognitive in nature. Hardin defines trust as a three-part relation: A trusts B to do X. For him, "generalized trust" and "trust in general" are elliptic forms of trust, for they simply elide the specific context in which A trusts B. Because of the particular knowledge that grounds the operation of A trusting B, Hardin maintains that trust depends on a cognitive assessment made by A that his or her interests are encapsulated in what B will predictably do. Thus, "I trust you" ultimately means: I believe you are trustworthy in relation to action X (see Hardin 2002: 1–10). Hardin insists that "trusting" is wholly cognitive, and that therefore it is not an "action." This makes it possible, according to him, to put a wedge between the cognitive judgement we make and the action we undertake on its basis. Thus, I may trust you with respect to X, but decide nonetheless not to take the risk; or conversely, I may not trust you, in the sense that I do not believe that you are trustworthy, but decide to take the risk nonetheless, which is a form of exchange or cooperation without trust. According to this meaning, "trust" is the result of rational assessment, and as part of this rational assessment, I can also decide to *trust* you in those situations where rational calculation (or backward induction) may advise me against it.

The last sentence, however, shows the difficulty of the cognitive position in terms of giving an account of ordinary-language usages of "trust." If "trust" consists in a cognitive assessment, how can I decide to trust without contradicting myself? At least according to this theory, the second use of "trust" marked above in italics is, therefore, improper because it clearly indicates an action. The point has implicitly been raised by Oliver Williamson (1996), who suggests that the calculative understanding of trust can ultimately be reduced to the language of risk, and that it would be better to drop the language of trust altogether when talking of it in calculative terms. Hardin's paradox of trusting without trusting could therefore be rendered more economical with the statement that if we do not regard someone as being trustworthy, we may still be inclined to *take the risk* of engaging in exchanges or cooperating with them. As a form of calculation, this may not be entirely irrational on the part of the risk-taker, partly because it might depend on particular circumstances. It could also depend on trustworthiness, or a reputation for trustworthiness, as something that within the parameters of the calculative paradigm can operate both as a predictive element and as an incentive. It plays a predictive role insofar as it encourages others to cooperate with one; it may be an incentive because it helps in either gaining or keeping a reputation, which has value for one to the extent that it facilitates the engagement in cooperative and profitable ventures with others.

Williamson's suggestion of doing away with the language of trust in the cognitive sense may have some merit in game theoretic contexts, or in calculative discourses at large, but like Hardin's position, it may also fail to make sense of ordinary language usage. The very idea of trustworthiness, which is so central to Hardin's analysis of encapsulated interest, would be meaningless if we replaced trust with risk. Trustworthiness requires someone to act in such a way that one is (or is regarded to be) *worthy* of trust. But, once re-worded in the language of risk, this would imply acting in a way in which the *other* should take a greater risk. It may be that when we translate the two formulations in practical terms the same type of action applies, though it can be seen from different perspectives, and this may not be without significance. Indeed, my suggestion is that the cognitive sense of trust is not wholly independent from its moral sense, and that this may be thought of as both an attitude and a social bond.

The moral sense of trust is normally conceived of as an action and as a character trait. In moral and behavioural conceptions, trust does not entirely depend on trustworthiness. It constitutes a kind of action: specifically, an attempt to establish a link with others or "force" an obligation upon them by making oneself dependent and vulnerable. In this sense, one is taking a conscious risk and becoming vulnerable in establishing a relationship of trust. In experimental conditions, it seems that those who willingly take such a risk are better at eliciting trustworthiness. Trust as an action establishes a kind of *link* or a *connection* (or a *bond* – a *lien, vincolo/legame, Verbindung*) with others. The link is twofold. It puts one in the hands of another (making one vulnerable), but also puts the other under some form of obligation – it is like a "gift."

By approaching trust from both a cognitive and a moral perspective, one can better understand the reasons underlying trust. These are both instrumental and moral: not trusting can be costly, and gives the wrong signal to the other. Trusting can be based on or induce trustworthiness, both in the cunning form described by Philip Pettit (1995) as trust-responsiveness – which involves gaining leverage over others by cultivating a reputation for trustworthiness – or in the more direct form of encouraging moral behaviour. The actions resulting from these two attitudes may not always be easily distinguishable and even the motivations may tend to mix, but it is only by attending to both the cognitive and moral meaning of trust that we can capture both of these processes and their full implications.

In summary, trusting consists of two parallel operations: a cognitive one that involves a type of positive belief about what the trusted person will do; and a moral action that involves an attitude towards others and a way of relating to (or linking with) them. At both a cognitive and practical level, trusting others means to treat them as reliable: trustworthy, worthy (*digne, degno*) of trust. It also means soliciting trustworthiness, either directly or indirectly, thus attempting to create a virtuous circle where trust begets trustworthiness and trustworthiness begets trust. This makes each other's action interdependent, creating the basis for a social bond.

THE SOCIAL BOND AND THE CONTOURS OF DISTRUST

So far, I have maintained that there is something to be gained if we understand trust as encompassing both calculative and moral expectations, and consisting of both beliefs and attitudes. This is how, for instance, Martin Hollis (1999) understands it. But, in his analysis, Hollis makes a further point, which I think is of some importance. The predictive part of trust does not simply work at the calculative end, but also as part of our moral expectations. In speaking of my expectation *of* you doing something, insofar as you have incurred an obligation towards me, Hollis says: "There is a bond between us and I expect you to honour it in two senses, one predictive and the other normative. On the one hand, I predict that you will. On the other, I believe that you should – or at least that you believe that you should" (1999: 11). It is this latter sense that defines the moral expectation as an expectation *of* you doing something; though this does not exclude that normative expectations have an inevitably predictive aspect, which tends to qualify our moral expectations. This may have important consequences for how we contextualize trust as a form of moral behaviour, beyond simply putting ourselves unconditionally in someone else's power.

Notice also that the "moral" expectations can be characterized as either intrinsically moral (in a more universalistic and universalizable sense), or as social norms, in a more *local* sense. These social norms can be of different kinds, and can be represented as a form of congealed trust. Alejandro Portes (1998) has synthetized them into four types of relation-based motivations, which bind people together. They are different strategies, besides self-interest, for the provision of trust. In other words, they identify stable motivational patterns that give rise to expectations that are directly dependent on how we relate to others in situations where economic rationality does not obtain (or at least does not seem to be the main motive for action). Such relation-based motivations comprise both over-socialized and instrumental (or under-socialized) motivational sources. The former consist in "value introjection" and "bounded solidarity," while the latter include "reciprocity exchanges" and "enforceable trust" (Portes 1998: 7–10). The point about these forms of moral trust and expectation is that not only are they not strictly calculative, they are not always morally defensible from a more general (or indeed, individual) perspective. This implies that *moral* trust is not always a good, even when it functions to establish social and interpersonal links upon which the social bond itself may need to rest.

If trust is not an unalloyed good even in its moral sense, we may perhaps look more closely at its opposites, distrust and mistrust, to see whether there is something that may recommend them, and in which circumstances. There is an important asymmetry here, if we consider the predictive and the more moral conceptions of trust. With regard to the former, distrust or mistrust are not very different from a lack of trust. Insofar as we *lack* trust in someone to act in a way that furthers our interests and well-being, we can say that we either distrust or mistrust this person without it carrying a meaning different from a simple absence of trust. The same applies to more general circumstances in which we refrain from acting in a certain way because we have no trust that there are conditions for us to so behave without the possibility of suffering as a consequence. So, we may refrain from walking close to a park at night because we have no trust in (or we distrust) the safety of that area at that particular time. But the relationship between lack of trust and distrust (or mistrust) is different when we move from this more cognitive and merely predictive sense to a more attitudinal and moral sense. Since distrust and mistrust are, in these cases, more than a *lack* of trust (as a mere absence), they signify more entrenched attitudes in relation to others or to a certain environment. We do not simply distrust (or mistrust) others because we believe that they may behave in certain ways or out of certain motives, but because we expect a certain behaviour *of* them. We are not just assessing what they will do, we are also judging them for what we expect they will do, and treating them accordingly. In such a case, our trust or distrust of other people is not exclusively a statement about our belief in their trustworthiness, but also (and in some cases even more so) a statement about our attitude towards others or towards particular groups. Here, distrust can differ from simple wariness, cautiousness, a particular skepticism, or a more general suspicion, and manifest in extreme forms of paranoia and fear. On the other hand, to trust regardless of evidence can turn into delusion and gullibility. Each of these different beliefs and attitudes has some practical consequences, and can support a view of society or about how we relate to others.

Our judgment of trust – of its basis, its function, and its value – depends on how we define its contours and therefore the assessment we make of the reasons why we refuse to trust. Distrust and lack of trust are nuanced in nature and, on the whole, require analysis as much as trust, since they relate to it in complex ways. Our moral and political judgement of whether and how much to trust depends on the assessment we make of what, in particular circumstances, it means not to trust. Patti Lenard (2008: 318–20) has shown, for instance, that we can distinguish a more stable and entrenched sense of distrust from a more ambivalent and reflective one, which in English she associates with the ordinary sense of "mistrust." She considers "distrust" to represent a general attitude of suspicion and cynicism, while "mistrust" is more akin to doubt and cautiousness. Although this is not the case across all the Romance and Germanic languages we mentioned at the beginning, lack of trust may depend on these different attitudes, which carry different consequences. Their application to politics, and particularly to democratic politics, is not a matter of indifference. While distrust may be justified in situations of entrenched dominion and asymmetrical power, it would seem to be ultimately destructive of the proper functioning of both horizontal and vertical relationships in politics. Mistrust, on the other hand, can play a salutary role as a way of regulating the relationship between different political powers, or between citizens and rulers. Understanding the more precise role and impact of different forms of distrust and lack of trust, and therefore to more precisely define the contours of trust, is of particular relevance in contemporary individualized (i.e., strongly individualist) and multinational or divided societies. In such societies, people and groups tend to distrust or mistrust others not just on grounds of prejudice or entrenched particularism, but also as a form of defence. These different motives are difficult to disentangle. One of the questions we must face is whether it is possible to develop strategies of trust that are as nuanced as its contours and conducive to creating social and political bonds, without jeopardizing the autonomy and independence of individuals and groups, or making them vulnerable to the abuse of power. Such strategies may be articulated at a more political level (cf. Weinstock 1999), though they need also to rest on the institutions of civil society. In the concluding section I will briefly sketch the way in which trust, as a social bond, can be fostered by such institutions.

THE PRINCIPLE OF TRUST IN CIVIL SOCIETY

In the previous section, I emphasized the complex nature of trust, and how its fostering may depend on contextual factors and the appropriateness of our attitudes and motivations in promoting social cohesion without undermining our autonomy and independence. I want to return now to the more general sense of trust and the ways in which this relates to the social order. Indeed, in different ways, both Locke and Hegel regarded trust as the very essence of the "bond of society," and therefore as carrying a distinctively normative sense. This is particularly striking in Hegel's analysis, where he suggests that it is in the social disposition of individuals, in their mutual knowledge of and reliance upon each other – in short, in their trust in each other – where the genuine ethical temper or the principle of civil society lies. He makes this argument explicit in his *Encyclopedia of the Social Sciences*, and furthers it in the section on civil society in the *Philosophy of Right*.

I think Hegel was broadly right in this regard. Nevertheless, as already hinted in the previous section, there is an acute paradox of trust in modern individualized and divided societies which we need to solve in order to balance trust and distrust in our social dealings (both between individuals and between groups, as well as between individuals and institutions). The paradox in question takes different forms, producing a number of tensions where the social bond and individuality (or particularity) seem to pull in different directions. It shows in the tension between individuality (autonomy) and sociality (dependence); between exchange relations and the gift economy; between possession and reciprocity; and between self-interest (not specifically selfishness) and solidarity.

The institutions of civil society are particularly apt to address these problems, though they also need to rely on politics, the state, and the more formal institutions at large. But, to remain within the realm of civil society, the reason why the associations and relations character-izing civil society can offer an important contribution to the partial solutions of the tensions listed above is because, in promoting the social bond and forms of social cohesion, they also promote, in con-nection with their intrinsic voluntary character, important forms and practices of autonomy and independence. The way this happens can perhaps be made clear by suggesting a general classification of the different kinds of civil society organizations on the basis of what they do, and, implicitly, on the basis of the kind of principles they uphold, and how the pursuit of such principles contributes to solving the problem of trust.

In short, civil society organizations (i.e., associations of a voluntary type) can be justified on three separate grounds, which, for brevity's sake, I shall define as three separate arguments involving three kinds of associations. They are: (1) The *autonomy* argument: "do-it-yourself" associations; (2) the *non-domination* argument: "prop-up" associa-tions; and (3) the *authenticity* argument: "listen-to-me" associations. We can present these three arguments in the following schematic way. The autonomy argument is based on the complexity thesis in modern society. It aims to develop the logic of personal independence through the pursuit of negative and positive forms of liberty in relation to the kind of "goods" involved in the activities that particular forms of voluntary associations pursue. The non-domination argument is based on the social functionality thesis. It aims to develop the logic of personal defence and control over outside power by providing opportunities for a political voice and self-determination, giving rise to associative forms as "sites of resistance" and "sites of involvement." Finally, the authenticity argument is based on the iron cage thesis. It aims to develop the logic of disinterested interest by allowing for the pursuit of shared purposes. What matters is checking and resisting the extraneous logic of bureaucratic, legal, and managerial systems.

By promoting, both ideally and institutionally, these three forms of voluntary associations and the related principles, it is possible – hopefully – to develop trust between individuals and groups within society while protecting their autonomy, independence, and conception of the self. In the language of social capital, this can be done by combining forms of *bonding*, *bridging*, and *linking* social capital (Castiglione 2008). It can also be done by paying particular attention to the way in which the promotion of the virtues of civil society, and the particular ways in which they in turn promote the social bond, can be reconciled with the virtues of *civic* society. The latter virtues have a crucial role in cementing political society, though they need to do this in a way that respects the more basic social bond upon which political society ultimately rests. The mutual support between the political and social bond is the central issue for multinational and divided societies. A politics of trust that promotes the principles and virtues of different forms of associations in civil society is essential to keeping them together, without subsuming one into the other.

REFERENCES

Baier, Annette. 1994. *Moral Prejudices*. Cambridge, MA: Harvard University Press.

Castiglione, Dario. 2008. "Social Capital between Community and Society." In *The Handbook of Social Capital*, edited by D. Castiglione, J.W. Van Deth, and G. Wolleb, 555–67. Oxford: Oxford University Press.

Elster, Jon. 2007. *Explaining Social Behaviour*. Cambridge: Cambridge University Press.

Hardin, Russell. 2002. *Trust and Trustworthiness*. New York: Russell Sage Foundation.

Hegel, G.W.F. 1991. *Elements of the Philosophy of Right*. Edited by A.W. Wood. Cambridge: Cambridge University Press.

– 1992. *The Encyclopaedia of The Philosophical Sciences in Outline*. Edited by E. Behler. London: Continuum.

Hollis, Martin. 1999. *Trust within Reason*. Cambridge: Cambridge University Press.

Lenard, Patti T. 2008. "Trust Your Compatriots, but Count Your Change: The Roles of Trust, Mistrust and Distrust in Democracy." *Political Studies* 56: 312–32.

Locke, John. 1967. *Two Treatises of Government*. Edited by P. Laslett. Cambridge: Cambridge University Press.

Pettit, Philip. 1995. "The Cunning of Trust." *Philosophy and Public Affairs* 24, no. 3: 202–25.

Portes, A. 1998. "Social Capital: Its Origins and Applications in Modern Sociology." *Annual Review of Sociology* 24: 1–24.

Uslaner, Eric. 2002. *The Moral Foundations of Trust*. Cambridge: Cambridge University Press.

Weinstock, Daniel. 1999. "Building Trust in Divided Societies." *The Journal of Political Philosophy* 7, no. 3: 287–307.

Williamson, Oliver. 1996. *The Mechanisms of Governance*. Oxford: Oxford University Press.

2

Democracy, Trust, and National Identity

Geneviève Nootens

Interest in trust is not new in the social sciences. Over the past two decades, and especially in the United States, many researchers have tackled the issue, in part because of concerns about a presumed decline in trust among citizens of democratic regimes and the ensuing interest in what might help revive such trust (see, e.g., Putnam 1993, 2000; Fukuyama 1995). From a different theoretical and normative framework, Will Kymlicka and Keith Banting (2006) have recently tried to determine whether multicultural policies impact upon the trust and solidarity that are presumed to be central to the successful functioning of the welfare state. Indeed, some (e.g., Barry 2001) have advanced the idea that multiculturalism actually undermines the conditions required for achieving a coalition in favour of a broad socio-economic equality. Yet, Kymlicka and Banting have demonstrated that blaming multiculturalism for the decline of the welfare state is ill-founded: while it may be the case that interpersonal trust is more difficult to achieve in ethnically diverse societies, they find no empirical evidence suggesting that there is a direct relationship between interpersonal trust and the basic functioning of the welfare state.

Three broad types of approaches dominate the literature on trust. They diverge according to whether they stress: the dispositions of individual actors and the conditions that lead them to trust other actors (e.g., Hardin 2002); the social organization as a whole and the relations between the system and specific social nodes (e.g., Barber 1983); and trust as a contingent, negotiated property of social relations (e.g., Tilly 2005). My aim here is not to discuss each of these approaches in terms of their usefulness and/or their flaws.[1] Rather,

I want to propose some guidelines for answering two basic questions pertaining to the dynamics of trust and distrust in plurinational democracies. Can trust be reduced to a fundamentally *interpersonal* phenomenon that would be a necessary condition for democratic politics to flourish? And how can we account for the complex mechanisms that pertain and relate to trust in societies forged by political histories, processes, and institutions marked by significant conflicts between nations? Let me stress that *unconditional* trust is not necessarily a good within democratic regimes: democracy requires qualified – or moderate – trust, since total integration of trust networks into public politics would deprive citizens of the means of providing *contingent* consent (Tilly 2005). And within plurinational societies, unqualified trust can actually threaten the ability of minority nations to negotiate fairer political arrangements, or, in extreme cases, their very existence. Yet trust seems necessary to reduce social complexity. It is displayed in the course of complex social relations, depending upon social perceptions, representations, and discourses as well as on party systems, relations among elites, and institutional mechanisms regulating relations among nations (GRSP 2010).

Hence, I will focus here on the links between trust relationships and public politics. Charles Tilly has shown that the democratization of political regimes depends, among other things, on the (partial) integration of the networks that embody trust relationships between individuals and groups into public politics,[2] such as when ethnic or regional leaders are co-opted by the central state or when people agree to trust the state with a part of their savings. He also has stressed that trust is not a precondition of democratic politics, but, rather, a significant part of democratization processes.[3] Trust is first and foremost a relationship – motivated, completed, or resulting from certain attitudes – that is recognizable by some social practices. It consists of participants placing valued outcomes (resources and enterprises) at risk in the face of others' malfeasance, mistakes, or failures (Tilly 2005: 12).

My aim in this chapter is thus to contribute to refining the possible answers to the two questions raised earlier. I will do so by building upon the critical analysis of an argument according to which democratic politics requires a kind of interpersonal trust grounded in a common national identity that, in the conditions of modern societies, substitutes for face-to-face relationships. There are at least two versions of this thesis. The "strong" version (defended by David Miller) relates it to the conditions of republican citizenship. The "thin" version is not associated with republicanism but nonetheless links democratic politics with a shared national identity (one can find this second type of thesis in some of Kymlicka's work, for example). The issue here is not, of course, that such a thesis defends the normative value of national belonging. Arguing for plurinational democracy requires that one recognizes national pluralism, meaning that minority nations possess a constituent power of their own. Instead, the problem lies in the rather incongruous way democratic politics and the sources of trust are related to each other in this type of thesis. Hence, I tackle the issue in a quite different manner than, for instance, Daniel Weinstock (1999), who argues that unity is on morally valid grounds when it is supported by trust, which does not presuppose sharing a national identity, values, or a conception of social justice. Trust is, indeed, an asymmetrical moral relation.

But what interest is there in analyzing the thesis that democratic politics depends on a very specific type of interpersonal trust? First, a critical analysis of this thesis allows us to specify a number of (provisional) statements about the nature of the trust that is crucial to democratic regimes. Second, it also allows us to stress important features of democracy and democratic politics themselves. Finally, despite the incongruity of the vision of trust that is conveyed by this thesis, it nonetheless tries to explain the indisputable significance of national belonging, and of the self-determination claims that generally go along with representations of a people as a nation. Approaches focusing on interests often struggle to incorporate such a significance within their theories: self-determination cannot be justified solely on the grounds of reciprocal interests, despite what some (e.g., Robert Goodin) have argued. One must first explain what makes some interests appropriate or relevant; and one must also be able to account for what makes groups significant for issues of democratic governance (Nootens 2009 and 2010). In other words, arguments like Miller's contain a twofold normative thesis – about claims to self-determination and about the nation as a source of such claims – which analyses of contemporary politics must be able to explain. This is certainly the case in plurinational societies, of course, but it is the case on the global scale as well. One of the fundamental stakes for democratic theory at these two levels is to be able to explain how to relate the two main types of social relations, the scope of which determines the borders of democracy: namely, political relations of solidarity *and* power relations (MacDonald 2003: 174).

In the first section of the paper, I will briefly recall the thesis that democratic politics requires a type of interpersonal trust that is grounded in a shared national identity that substitutes for face-to-face relationships. I will emphasize the "strong" version of this thesis. In this version, plurinational democracies are portrayed as a second-best option, and the possibility that transnational democratic spaces may develop is negated. The second section focuses on the problems conveyed by Miller's argument, four of which seem particularly important given my focus here: (1) Miller underestimates the role that institutions and social practices play in the interweaving of trust and public politics; (2) he implies that the polarization of nationality claims could be explained by mere interpersonal distrust; (3) he proposes a static and consensual conception of democratic processes that disregards the processes of mobilization and contention that are actually central to the democratization of political regimes; (4) he overlooks the significance of socialization processes in the building of national identities. In the third section, I address the issue of those democratic spaces, actual or potential, that are (wrongly) excluded *a priori* by the liberal nationalist thesis. I suggest that we should instead insist on the way that power relationships and solidarity relationships interweave in the socio-historical processes that have led to the democratization of some regimes. Such a move, I argue, allows us to shed new light on the issues of trust, public politics, and democracy. When public politics is at stake, trust cannot be reduced to an interpersonal phenomenon that would act as a kind of logical or chronological precondition for democratic politics. It is a much more complex mechanism, one that the liberal nationalist liberal thesis cannot allow us to appreciate properly.

IDENTITY, TRUST, SOLIDARITY

Liberal nationalists like Miller assume that the trust required by democratic politics builds upon a shared national identity and allegiance. Such an identity sustains trust, allowing for solidarity and cooperation between co-nationals. Therefore, the possibility of developing social and political solidarity outside the boundaries of the nation-state (both in plurinational societies and on the global scale) is severely constrained, given the absence of a shared national identity beyond the nation-state.

Miller supports a republican conception of citizenship that emphasizes the idea of the active citizen "who takes part along with others in shaping the future direction of his or her society through political debate" (1999: 62). This conception shares the liberal commitment to equal rights and obligations; but it further requires that citizens be willing "to take active steps to defend the rights of other members of the political community, and more generally to promote its common interests," and that they play an active role "in both the formal and informal arenas of politics" (62–3). Such a conception of citizenship is demanding, both from the point of view of motivation (citizens must be sufficiently motivated to carry out the tasks that citizenship involves) and from the point of view of responsibility (they must always try to promote the common good) (64–5). This requires having a long-term view of common interests, recognizing when trade-offs are to be made, and being willing to set aside personal interests and ideals "in the interests of achieving a democratic consensus" (65).

Miller argues that in advanced societies it is common nationality that has served to generate the trust and loyalty required by citizenship. Modern social conditions make it impossible to gather face to face in order to make laws. Thus, "something else must generate the trust and loyalty that citizenship requires. Common nationality has served this purpose in the advanced societies" (Miller 1999: 68). Indeed, this is why philosophers can endorse nationalism: it fulfils a valuable function by sustaining solidarity in vast, anonymous states (Miller 1993: 9). Only then can the conditions of mutual trust and certainty combine to make responsible citizenship possible. In other words, the quest for democracy and social justice presupposes national communities in which mutual trust stems from a shared identity. Miller argues that we cannot find states whose members lack such common identity but which are nonetheless democratic: "Genuinely multinational states have either been held together by force, as was the old Soviet Union, or else have been empires which allowed a substantial degree of self-determination to their constituent parts. Neither of these possibilities makes for flourishing citizenship on the republican model" (1999: 68). Let me stress that Miller allows for the possibility that some circumstances may make it impossible to appeal to a shared national identity as a basis for citizenship. For instance, this is the case in states whose members see themselves as belonging to rival nationalities. In such circumstances, if state bound-aries cannot be redrawn, a political structure must be established that will allow the different communities to live in comparative harmony – for example, a form of consociational democracy: "this may be unavoidable, but it has to be regarded as a second best by anyone who aspires to republican citizenship" (70).[4] The core ethical claim of Miller's argument is that one's sense of national identity allows us to mark out the universe of persons to whom special duties are owed because we feel bound to them "as sharing in a certain way of life, expressed in the public culture. The content of my obligations stems immediately from that culture" (Miller 1993: 14). Nationality thus comprises three inter-related propositions: it may properly be part of someone's identity that they belong to this or that national grouping; nations are ethical communities, and we have different, more extensive duties towards our co-nationals than towards human beings as such; and the people who form a national community in a particular ter-ritory have a strong claim to political self-determination. The three propositions are closely related. A common identity can support both the idea of the nation as an ethical community and the claim to self-determination; and "the fact that the community in question is either actually or potentially self-determining strengthens its claims on us both as a source of identity and as a source of obligation" (6).[5] The ethical argument thus establishes a specific theory of political obliga-tions that I will not discuss in detail here.

Miller does not deny that we have duties towards human beings as such (see, e.g., his 1993: 5). However, the functional role played by nationality in establishing the trust necessary for supporting democ-racy and social justice is a significant hindrance to any justification of some non-nation-state framework for realizing democracy and social justice. I have already pointed out that from Miller's perspec-tive, plurinational democracies are merely second-best options. Miller also uses his thesis about the sources of trust to sustain his critique of cosmopolitan citizenship. Among other things, he argues that at the international level, constituencies would be artificial bodies whose members have no reason to expect that they will be called upon to make future decisions together, are not involved in relations of reci-procity, and are not bound by communal ties or relationships of mutual trust (1999: 77). Transnational activism is not citizenship in any recognizable sense: the activist neither identifies politically with a determinate community nor stands in relations of reciprocity with them; she is not committed to seeking grounds of agreement with a group of fellow citizens; and she is not involved in a democratic debate with different ideas and points of view (Miller 2002: 90).

It is interesting to note that Kymlicka once expressed similar skepticism about the possibility that transnational institutions could become more democratic "in any meaningful sense" (1999: 119). This is why we can argue that this skepticism flows from a thin version of the liberal nationalist thesis – it is thin to the extent that Kymlicka does not defend a republican argument and does not (or at least not straightaway) consider plurinational democracies to be second-best options. He stresses that democracy is a system of collective deliberation and legitimation, in which decisions resulting from deliberation are legitimate insofar as they reflect the considered will and common good of the people as a whole (1999: 119). Democratic deliberation and legitimation require some degree of commonality amongst citizens, since deliberation is only feasible if participants understand and trust one another, and "there is a good reason to think that such mutual understanding and trust require some underlying commonalities" (119). As to the issue of the sort of shared identity that is required to sustain democracy, he concludes that "there are good reasons to think that ... 'national' linguistic/territorial political communities – whether they are unilingual nation sates or linguistically distinct subunits in multinational states – are the primary forum for democratic participation in the modern world" (120). Indeed, the average citizen only feels comfortable debating political issues in their own language, and national communities "are the most important forum for assessing the legitimacy of other levels of government" (121–2). There is "no meaningful forum of democratic deliberation and collective will-formation above the level of the nation-state" (124). Let me stress that Kymlicka does not deny that we need strong international institutions that transcend national and linguistic borders in order to deal with pressing issues. In fact, he later expressed doubts about the assumption that identity plays a paramount role in the capacity of citizens to cooperate with one another (Kymlicka 2003). However, I must point out how paradoxical it is to have one of the most famous tenants of the multinational state paradigm defending an argument very close to the one defended by some liberal nationalists concerning the relationship of democracy to trust. Such an argument may actually turn his objections to trans-state democratization against the very paradigm of the multinational state he defends.

DEMOCRACY, POWER, AND SOLIDARITY

Let us return to Miller's thesis. It portrays the trust involved in democratic politics as a strictly interpersonal phenomenon: I trust X, Y, and Z because they belong to my own national community, and this is why we stand together and feel responsible for one another, why I agree to value the common good more than my own interests, and so on. This common identity *replaces* the face-to-face gathering of citizens in the law-making process; national belonging is a substitute for such a gathering in establishing trust among citizens. It is not clear whether it fulfils this function because it allows one to assume that citizens have the very same interests, or because it would somehow allow one to understand the cognitive states and motivations of one's co-nationals; but I believe this possible difference does not have a significant impact upon my argument.

From my perspective, this thesis about trust works separately from the ethical argument – that is, the one according to which the content of my obligations arises immediately from the public culture that expresses a way of life. The question is thus whether people trust and act in a responsible manner *because* they belong to the same nation. I think that although it may be the case in some circumstances, we cannot make a generalizable thesis out of this. A very simple example will illustrate what I have in mind. Taxes play an important role in the redistribution of wealth; such a redistribution is usually seen as embodying a sense of solidarity among citizens. Of course, many of us worry about the fate of our fellow citizens, and we agree to participate in a collective attempt to improve the lives of the most underprivileged and to equalize opportunities. However, if the government were to rely solely on this sense of solidarity to collect enough revenue for such efforts, I am quite certain there would not be much money available to fund them.

This very brief example sheds light on the main problems with Miller's argument. First, it does not explain the significance of the mechanisms and institutions that formalize our obligations, control free riding, and dissuade failure to discharge duties. Institutions and social practices play a major part in reinforcing the mutual relationship between trust and public politics, particularly by limiting free riding, by sustaining an impersonal form of reciprocity, and by socializing individuals so that they comply with norms involving unconditional cooperation (Føllesdal 2001: 315).

Next, when analyzing democratic politics, it is simplistic to assume that a mere interpersonal *mistrust* based on cognitive assessments of how much someone can be trusted because of their nationality may lead straightforwardly to radicalization and polarization. Other factors are involved: the commitment or the disengagement of elites, the coalitions (or lack thereof) among groups, the ideas conveyed by the media, and special features of particular party systems. An analysis including these components, especially when applied to specific cases like the one of Belgium, certainly is much more instructive than simply reducing polarized nationality claims to individual mistrust or distrust.

The third problem facing this thesis lies with the static and consensual vision of democratic processes it conveys. Let us consider a very brief example here as well. Could a worker in nineteenth-century Manchester trust her employer or members of the political elite to make decisions in accordance with the common good *because* they belonged to the same nation? The answer is quite obvious. Miller's argument disregards the processes of mobilization and contention that are core to the democratization of political regimes, thereby conveying a view of democracy that does not fit with how it actually works. For as Tilly has demonstrated: "almost all of the crucial democracy-promoting mechanisms involve popular contention – politically constituted actors making public, collective claims on other actors, including agents of government – as correlates, causes, and effects" (2007: 78).[6]

Think of the mobilization for religious rights and parliamentary reform in nineteenth-century Britain, of the French Revolution, of women's struggle for voting rights, of the long struggle against racial segregation in the United States, and of the struggle against apartheid in South Africa. Ordinary people and segregated categories had to mobilize and contend in order to access the rights of citizenship, to get a secure and protected voice in public politics, and to have redistributive justice mechanisms. Their more powerful and wealthier co-nationals did not grant them these rights just because they belong to the same nation – nor do they hesitate, nowadays, to resist claims for a fairer redistribution of wealth. Indeed, as Bermeo and Tilly have shown, elite withdrawal figures importantly in historical cases of democracy's reversal (Bermeo 2003; Tilly 2005). Moreover, while it is true that contention may build on solidarity ties between members of some communities (based on social networks at a local level), national identity does not necessarily prevail, and nations are surely not homogenous groups. Other identities and solidarities can divide and polarize individuals and groups within a state; let us think, for example, of the civil rights movement. Of course, we must neither disregard nor forget the mobilizing potential of national belonging – the nineteenth and twentieth centuries have taught us a great deal in this respect – but we surely must take a broader view of the mechanisms and processes that provide for social solidarity and democratic politics.

It may be the case that when some forms of solidarity are institutionalized, and when institutions socialize people with a view to supporting the attitudes necessary for a significant redistribution, people will more readily compromise and think about the common good (which they may of course sometimes also do spontaneously). However, even then, national "solidarity" depends on a rather fragile balance, on temporary trade-offs, the content of which can evolve in accordance with changes in power relationships. The transformations of the welfare state in recent decades testify to this, especially since globalization makes it easier for powerful actors (like some economic agents) to evade solidarity and redistribution schemes by restricting the number of issues that can be debated and voiced in public-policy making. Institutions crystallize provisional social compromises, which in turn help to stabilize practices and expectations. However, this does not happen merely because people share national belonging.

The fourth problem rests with national identity itself. Identities embody social relationships, and, once again, it is because Miller's thesis overlooks political processes that are core to such relationships that its soundness is undermined. Identification with a nation largely depends upon socialization processes that play a significant part in the development of the sense of a shared past and the feeling of a shared destiny.[7] These processes have been documented in detail, and there is no point in spending more time on them here.

STATES, BORDERS, NATIONAL COMMUNITIES

Because of its flaws, the liberal nationalist thesis on trust and national identity does not allow us to appropriately tackle the issue of the democratization mechanisms and processes in plurinational societies or at the global level. The issue of trust among citizens, of the borders of democratic polities, and of the trust dynamics between communities cannot be dealt with in a static and univocal way using one specific instance of social "cooperation" – namely, the welfare state – as the model in the light of which all empirical democratization processes are to be assessed. This type of argument pays insufficient attention to the way in which power and solidarity relations combine in the historical and social processes that drove the consolidation of the modern state. It greatly underestimates the part played by institutions and popular contention in the democratization of the Western states.[8] It neglects the significance of power relationships; it idealizes the national community; and it is cut off from democratization processes, hence preventing the normative argument from having a strong grasp on empirical processes in the current context. For example, the spatial rescaling of functional systems has major consequences on the way that self-determination (self-governance) is exercised, and a static, consensualist vision of democracy gives us little grip on such a reality.[9]

Let us consider, for example, global power relations and the challenge that they pose to democratic theorists. It is true that definitions of democratization processes usually focus on interactions between groups of people presenting collective public claims, on the one hand, and the government of a state, on the other (see, e.g., Tilly 2007: 59.) According to Tilly (2007), democratization is a dynamic process whereby the political relations between the state and its citizens becomes broader, more equal, more protected, and more constraining. The fundamental processes are those that integrate trust networks into public politics (such as when people rely on government agencies for vital services); those that better insulate public politics from the major categorical inequalities (for example, by eliminating state controls supporting unequal relations between social categories); and those that decrease the autonomy of power centres that are important with respect to public politics (for example, by eliminating political intermediaries that used to be independent). Democratization thus means that "the bulk of a government's subject population acquires roughly equal rights to participate in public politics, a process that in turn establishes binding, protected, relatively equal claims on a government's agents, activities and resources. In a related process, categorical inequality declines in those areas of social life that either constitute or immediately support participation in public policies" (Tilly 2004: 15).

If we pursue this line of reasoning, the global level lacks a government or regime, strictly speaking. (Obviously, there is also no single national identity that we could count on to ensure that all would endorse the responsibilities of republican-type citizenship – a dimension of the argument I set aside because it does not speak to the democratization processes I am focusing on here.) Hence, there may be no point in looking for democratization processes in the "international society." Although I do not intend to develop this point thoroughly here, I want to suggest that we should wonder whether there actually are, at regional, continental, and global levels, counterparts to state governmental functions and agents, especially when looking at certain institutions and regimes (e.g., the IMF or WTO). Moreover, the significance of interdependency – of individuals, peoples, and states – coupled with the fact that such interdependency can be framed as a scheme of social cooperation from which there is no realistic exit option, seems to support the idea that the current international society actually is a type of polity. It surely is not unreasonable – although it is debatable – to understand the claims made by persons, associations, and groups internationally and transnationally as being very similar to those which drove the democratization of the liberal states from the eighteenth century on.

Actually, if we consider how domains of contention, their characteristic relationships, and the challenges they manifest are defined, it is quite clear that they apply to levels of governance and government other than the nation-state. For example, on the global scale, there are different legal categories defining the rights and obligations of different segments of the population in the interdependent global structure. Sassen points out that

> today we see the formation of several cross-border regimes that unbundle some of the universalisms contained in liberal democracies and move towards specifying classes of people; for instance, we are seeing the formation of specialized cross-border regimes that grant protections to some class of people (such as the regime for the cross-border movement of professionals that is part of the WTO and regional trade agreements) and withdraw protections from other classes of people (undocumented migrants, who have lost many protections over the last decade and are now often constituted as semi-criminal subjects). (2006: 36)

I think we can hypothesize that the most crucial thing lacking at the global level for democratization processes to unfold is not a shared national identity supporting interpersonal trust, but rather a capacity for some public agents to alter the existing distribution of non-state resources, activities, and interpersonal relations – that is, to enforce political decisions (see Tilly 2007). Indeed, such a capacity seems crucial if we hope to increase popular control over public politics. Tilly stresses that democracy requires the state to have the capacity "to supervise democratic decision making and put its results into practice" (2007: 15), even if capacity and democracy must be kept distinct (a high-capacity state may not be democratic, and vice versa). However, a low capacity does not mean that there is no political power held by autonomous centres. It is interesting to stress that "where low governmental capacity and little protected consultation prevail, political life goes on in fragmented tyranny: with multiple coercive forces, small-scale despots, and competitors for larger-scale power, but no effective central government" (McAdam, Tarrow, and Tilly 2001: 266). "Fragmented tyranny" seems to quite accurately describe today's international society, indeed.

What about plurinational societies? Miller's version of the liberal nationalist thesis explicitly makes such societies second-best options, and I have suggested that Kymlicka's argument against trans-state democratization could be used against the paradigm of the plurinational state. However, if the arguments I have developed in this chapter are correct, we cannot simply seal the fate of plurinational democracies by saying that they are devoid of a shared national identity – which would unfortunately lead to the following options for anyone concerned with responsible, united citizenship. Either these democracies are to be broken down into as many states as they contain nations, or we are to defend a normative thesis about the value of an overarching identity to which other non-state identities and allegiances would necessarily have to be subordinated. From my point of view, the recognition of national pluralism requires acknowledging that nations have a constitutive power of their own, and thus should participate as equal partners in setting the terms of cooperation. Of course, this also depends on some political mechanisms and processes: struggles for recognition, the assertion and defence of the ideal of self-determination (the "oldest political good," as Tully [1995] says), and the will and capacity to engage in substantive dialogue with others. From this perspective, while plurinational democracies are quite imperfect, they are interesting examples of the challenges faced when searching for fairer terms of coexistence and cooperation in a democratic regime.

As in all societies, the question of trust between governments and citizens depends on how (and the degree to which) public politics encompasses, and supports, relations whereby stakeholders choose to entrust precious resources to those who govern (and their agents). It also depends more broadly on the citizens' capacity to be agents of public politics. On the specific issue of the relationships between majority and minority nations, this is affected by the crystallization (or not) of the subordination of minority nations in institutions, historiographical representations, and so forth.

Therefore, when we are talking about democratic politics, what is at work is something much more complex than interpersonal trust. It is not that interpersonal trust is not valuable. I think that Weinstock (1999) is right to point out that trust among individuals can ground unity in a society where members do not necessarily share values, an identity, or a conception of justice. A society in which people completely distrust each other is surely not desirable (such an Orwellian prospect is indeed rather frightening). However, the liberal nationalist thesis is not really helpful in understanding what sustains the processes that democratize political regimes. It underestimates the part played by institutions and popular contention and, more significantly, it seems to obfuscate the issue of the power relationships that are key to public politics and to the relationships between regimes, subjects/citizens, and elite groups. Yet, if we are to gain a better understanding of trust as an integral part of public politics, this is precisely what we must understand and analyze.

NOTES

1 For such a discussion, see Tilly (2005).

2 Trust *networks* "build controls over malfeasance and safeguards against consequences of mistakes and failures" in the management of such resources (Tilly 2005: 13).

3 A number of other scholars have also examined the relationship between trust and democracy as a political regime, and the higher requirements that democratic regimes have to meet in this respect. (For example, see Levi 1997 and Warren 1999).

4 However, Miller is silent about the fact that the citizens of undemocratic states may share a common identity.

5 Note that the latter way of expressing the relationship between common identity and self-rule actually reverses Miller's initial proposal: it is now the fact that the community is self-determining that gives it a claim on people.

6 However, contention yields net movement toward democratization only under special conditions (McAdam, Tarrow, and Tilly 2001: 272).

7 Once again, I do not mean to say that national identities and allegiances are not politically or normatively significant.

8 I would propose, at least as a hypothesis to be tested, that institutional design plays a significant role in the processes that drive trust and distrust among citizens. Consider, for instance, how difficult it is to establish a constitutional court in plurinational societies that could be seen as a fair and final arbitrator by all parties to a dispute.

9 As Tilly and Goodin (2006) rightly state, "context matters," and we must be able to explain it adequately.

REFERENCES

Barber, Benjamin. 1983. *The Logic and Limits of Trust*. New Brunswick, NJ: Rutgers University Press.

Barry, Brian. 2001. *Culture and Equality*. Cambridge, MA: Harvard University Press.

Bermeo, Nancy. 2003. *Ordinary People in Extraordinary Times: The Citizenry and the Breakdown of Democracy*. Princeton: Princeton University Press.

Føllesdal, Andreas. 2001. "Union Citizenship: Unpacking the Beast of Burden." *Law and Philosophy* 20, no. 3: 313–43.

Fukuyama, Francis. 1995. *Trust: The Social Virtues and the Creation of Prosperity*. New York: Free Press.

Hardin, Russell. 2002. *Trust and Trustworthiness*. New York: Russell Sage Foundation.

Kymlicka, Will. 1999. "Citizenship in an Era of Globalization: Commentary on Held." In *Democracy's Edges*, edited by I. Shapiro and C. Hacker-Cordon, 112–26. Cambridge: Cambridge University Press.

Kymlicka, Will, and Keith Banting, eds. 2006. *Multiculturalism and the Welfare State: Recognition and Redistribution in Contemporary Democracy*. Oxford: Oxford University Press.

Levi, Margaret. 1997. *Consent, Dissent, and Patriotism*. Cambridge: Cambridge University Press.

MacDonald, Terry. 2003. "Boundaries beyond Borders: Delineating Democratic 'Peoples' in a Globalizing World." *Democratization* 10, no. 3: 173–94.

McAdam, Doug, Sidney Tarrow, and Charles Tilly. 2001. *Dynamics of Contention*. Cambridge: Cambridge University Press.

Miller, David. 1993. "In Defence of Nationality." *Journal of Applied Philosophy* 10, no. 1: 3–16.

– 1999. "Bounded Citizenship." In *Cosmopolitan Citizenship*, edited by K. Hutchings and R. Danreuther, 60–80. New York: St Martin's Press.

– 2002. "The Left, the Nation State and European Citizenship." In *Global Citizenship. A Critical Reader*, edited by N. Dower and J. Williams, 84–91. Edinburgh: Edinburgh University Press.

Nootens, Geneviève. 2009. "Democracy and Legitimacy in Plurinational Societies." *Contemporary Political Theory* 8, no. 3: 276–94.

– 2010. "Nations, Sovereignty, and Democratic Legitimacy: On the Boundaries of Political Communities." In *After the Nation? Critical Reflections on Post-Nationalism*, edited by K. Breen and S. O'Neill, 196–213. New York: Palgrave Macmillan.

Putnam, Robert D. 1993. *Making Democracy Work: Civic Traditions in Modern Italy*. Princeton: Princeton University Press.

– 2000. *Bowling Alone: The Collapse and Revival of American Community*. New York: Simon and Schuster.

Sassen, Saskia. 2006. *Territory, Authority, Rights: From Medieval to Global Assemblages*. Princeton: Princeton University Press.

Tilly, Charles. 2004. *Contention and Democracy in Europe, 1650–2000*. Cambridge: Cambridge University Press.

– 2005. *Trust and Rule*. Cambridge: Cambridge University Press.

– 2007. *Democracy*. Cambridge: Cambridge University Press.

Tilly, Charles, and Robert E. Goodin. 2006. "It Depends." In *The Oxford Handbook of Contextual Political Analysis*, edited by Robert E. Goodin and Charles Tilly, 3–31. Oxford: Oxford University Press.

Tully, James. 1995. *Strange Multiplicity: Constitutionalism in an Age of Diversity*. Cambridge: Cambridge University Press.

Warren, Mark E., ed. 1999. *Democracy and Trust*. Cambridge: Cambridge University Press.

Weinstock, Daniel. 1999. "Building Trust in Divided Societies." *The Journal of Political Philosophy* 7, no. 3: 287–307.

3

Trust:
The Key to the Progressive's Dilemma between Solidarity and Diversity?

David Robichaud

Many social science researchers have come to the same conclusion: heterogeneous populaces marked by strong diversity have greater difficulty maintaining efficient social, economic, and political institutions. Some do not hesitate to see this as a dilemma for progressive forces. Is the loss of our welfare state and political and social institutions really the price that must be paid to tolerate, protect, and promote ethno-cultural diversity within the populace? The following pages are indirectly devoted to this question. I will analyze the dynamic of trust and distrust at work in multinational democracies but also in most cases marked by ethno-cultural heterogeneity, and I will suggest an avenue for combining the protection of diversity with popular support for social and democratic institutions. Placing trust at the heart of this tension helps avoid the progressive's dilemma between diversity and solidarity. If we want to save solidarity and maintain diversity, we have to gain a better understanding of why trust is more difficult to establish between different people and try to take appropriate actions at that level. This is especially important in multinational democracies which, in addition to having ethno-cultural heterogeneity that results from (more or less recent) immigration, define themselves as having a heterogeneous populace due to the presence of many nations sharing the same institutions. In multinational democracies, tension exists at the very heart of the concept insofar as the presence of individuals belonging to different nations presents an obstacle to stable, efficient democratic and social institutions.

We have known for some time that ethnic and cultural "fractioning" in a region is associated with slower economic growth and lower salaries (Easterly and Levine 1997). We also now realize that the impact is not limited to economic institutions. Comparative analyses show that states, cities, and regions with heterogeneous populations suffer from less stable, less efficient governments (La Porta et al. 1999; Mauro 1995), and less effective public policies (Alesina, Baqir, and Easterly 1999). Cities and metropolitan areas with strong ethnic heterogeneity do not invest as much in social and public policy or in productive collective goods (ibid.). It has also been found that members of heterogeneous communities participate to a lesser degree in social activities, especially when such activities involve direct inter-ethnic interactions (Alesina and La Ferrara 2000). Members of ethnic minorities are also less likely to exercise their right to vote in national elections (Sandovici and Listhaug 2006).

I will focus my attention on the risk to the redistributive institutions of the welfare state posed by reduced solidarity. A recent comparative study conducted in Europe and the United States on redistributive policies identified marked differences between the two in terms of their generosity. After having controlled for a number of potential explanatory variables, the authors concluded that more than half the differences could be explained by racial fractionalization in the United States (Alesina and Glaeser 2004). This finding is supported by numerous studies identifying a correlation between unfavourable inter-ethnic relations, or negative opinions of underprivileged people belonging to ethnic communities, and weak redistributive policies.

We could conclude that we have a special interest in the welfare of those who are similar to us, a preference for members of our own community – that is, solidarity limited to the members of our moral community. We should not overlook this hypothesis, defended by a number of opponents of the welfare state. The history of humanity has unfolded mainly in homogeneous, egalitarian communities, and we can imagine how cooperation emerged as a dominant strategy given repeated interactions, and how strong reciprocity developed among those who were ethnically similar to one another (Bowles and Gintis 2004; Dubreuil 2010; Axelrod 1984). While it is not a moral *justification* for the expression of feelings or tendencies favouring members of our group, this evolutionary aspect provides a credible *interpretation* of the phenomenon. I will try to provide support for certain suggestions that the rejection of redistributive institutions in heterogeneous communities can be explained by an absence of trust, a constituent part of solidarity (Barry 1989) – rather than by the absence of solidarity, understood as a moral sentiment that cannot be acted upon.

The difficulty of maintaining trusting relationships in multinational democracies and communities that are generally characterized by ethno-cultural heterogeneity seems to explain the relative inefficiency of their institutions. Some authors who have analyzed the hypothesis that there is a link between diversity and distrust have come to the conclusion that there are indeed lower levels of trust and loyalty between people who do not share the same ethnic origins (Glaeser et al. 2000). There even seems to be a tendency to consider as less trustworthy anyone who is different from us in terms of age, place of residence, gender, and so on (Johansson-Stenman 2008; DeBruine 2002). Trust is often understood as being a social lubricant essential for the smooth functioning of social institutions, or as a condition predisposing people to social solidarity (Barry 1989: 171). The hypothesis that we need to look to trust to explain these difficulties is supported by many studies in experimental economics confirming that greater distrust persists among people with different identities. This hypothesis is also supported by sociological research in which it has been observed that generalized trust expressed by individuals living in areas with ethno-cultural and socio-economic heterogeneity is weaker than that expressed in more homogeneous areas (Alesina and La Ferrara 2002).[1] What is found in microeconomics or economics and experimental psychology coincides with what has been found in macroeconomics and sociology.

For anyone who wishes to save the welfare state while maintaining diversity, it seems to be critically important both to understand the dynamics of distrust involved and to identify ways of channelling them appropriately. Looking at various studies on inter-individual trust, I will try to shed light on the dynamics of distrust that arise in heterogeneous societies by describing two phenomena that often go together to create a vicious circle conducive to the emergence and maintenance of inter-individual distrust.

My hypothesis is that distrust occurs at two levels. The first is that of the collective reputations of groups and communities. We cultivate beliefs concerning certain communities and the individuals who compose them, and we sometimes behave as if those generalizations, prejudices, and other beliefs apply to all members of those communities. A community's reputation then influences the extent to which one trusts its members. This seems particularly true for groups living side by side, as is often the case for nations in multinational democracies. In such situations, inter-group contact seems to amplify the tension rather than alleviate it as the contact hypothesis predicts (Forbes 1997). The second level where trust seems more difficult to establish in heterogeneous contexts is that of direct, face-to-face interactions between two individuals belonging to separate communities. We seem to have greater difficulty interacting directly with people who are different from us, and we project this inter-individual uneasiness onto the level of community relations. My intuition is that greater distrust of individuals who belong to communities other than ours develops at these two levels. Unfortunately, it seems that the story does not end there. In effect, it seems that an unhealthy dynamic emerges, strengthening trust within some communities, but also reinforcing distrust between communities. We need to break the dynamic of distrust that emerges and escalates in certain circumstances. It is thus possible that it is not necessarily our refusal to integrate different individuals within *our moral community* and our circle of solidarity that poses the problem, but our distrust of them.[2]

In this chapter, I will outline a few elements that help us reflect on the troubling tension between solidarity and diversity – in plurinational democracies specifically, but in areas marked by heterogeneity more generally. For this, I will begin by distinguishing between two dimensions of "trust" found in the literature and in individuals' discourse on the question: expectations and pure trust. This will allow us to gain a better understanding of the problem and thereby suggest better possible solutions. Next, I will look at the question of the distrust dynamic, properly speaking, which seems to be at work in communities with ethno-cultural heterogeneity. Distrust seems to be generated at the level of the collective ideas that we form about other groups, but also, obviously, at the level of day-to-day individual relationships. These two sources of distrust may enter into a dynamic and strengthen each other in some contexts. I will thus analyze, on the one hand, how collective ideas can lead to the emergence of feelings of distrust towards members of a group; and, on the other hand, how distrust can emerge in individual interactions. Finally, I will discuss three types of dynamics that may develop in relation to these two sources of distrust, making distrust very difficult to reduce in heterogeneous communities.

TWO DIMENSIONS OF TRUST

The works on inter-individual trust are a good place to start. Three hypotheses have been proposed to explain the lower degree of inter-individual trust observed in heterogeneous communities. The first sees the presence of multicultural policies as the reason for a lower degree of trust. Kymlicka and Banting (2006) have brilliantly shown that no positive correlation exists between the problems of institutional inefficiency described above and the presence of *multicultural policies*. The problem thus does not seem to be at the level of policies for "managing" diversity. A second hypothesis has been that what suffers from diversity is trust in *institutions*. The fact that a populace does not identify with given institutions or with those who run them might explain lower levels of trust. However, the level of trust in institutions does not seem to be lower in heterogeneous communities (Alesina and La Ferrera 2002; Soroka, Johnston, and Banting 2004). The third hypothesis is that living in an ethno-culturally heterogeneous environment poses a problem to the establishment of trusting relationships between individuals, and causes disengagement in social institutions.

The literature on the nature of trust is rich and diverse, and no definition can be considered authoritative. However, both informally and academically, it seems possible to identify two dimensions of trusting relationships. The first considers trust more as an *expectation* with respect to an object or a person, as a form of managing risks and probabilities. When we say that we trust our dog not to bite people, our car to start in the dead of winter, Federer to beat Nadal, or strangers not to trip us, we are expressing expectations in relation to objects of "trust." We have expectations either about their capacity to act in the predicted manner or about external incentives motivating them to do so. We shall distinguish this form of trust, which can almost be considered a misuse of language, from *pure trust*, that does not assess the capacity of, or the incentives for, an agent to behave in a certain way. Rather, this latter form assesses our faith in their disposition to behave in a desired manner *despite* the absence of external incentives to motivate them to behave in that way.

We can say that we do not trust others insofar as we expect them not to behave in the expected way. Either we know or believe that they lack the capacity, or we know or believe that they lack the motivation or habit. However, we may also not trust others because we feel or are persuaded that they are not trustworthy. These two forms of distrust are interdependent. In order for a trust-based interaction to take place, pure trust will have to be even stronger if expectations are negative. We have to examine these two types of trust in order to fully understand the relevance of our approach to improving the situation and to avoid the dilemma between solidarity and diversity. I will first describe how we form our expectations about the behaviour of individuals who belong to communities different from our own. These expectations are determined by our beliefs concerning the probability that the members of a group will behave in an undesirable way. Next, I will look at potential explanations that could help us better understand the difficulties of trust-based interactions between individuals who belong to separate ethno-cultural communities. On the one hand, negative representations of communities are difficult to correct; on the other hand, we are unable (or we find it more difficult) to identify signs that reveal our counterpart's disposition to behave in a desirable way.

Distrust: From the Collective to the Individual and from the Individual to the Collective

FROM THE COMMUNITY TO THE INDIVIDUAL

Do we believe that members of communities other than our own are more likely to behave in an undesirable or problematic manner? Given equal anticipated advantage, do we believe that the members of some communities are less trustworthy? Whether or not our belief can be verified does not matter very much. The simple fact that we expect another person to behave improperly will make us more inclined to avoid interacting with them. Since the risk of being cheated is subjectively considered to be greater, a rational justification exists to prefer interactions with people who comply with the relevant standards of cooperation. Our beliefs concerning the disposition, motivations, habits, and knowledge of community members together form our judgment on the desirability of placing ourselves in a vulnerable position with respect to them.

In this case, distrust concerns two types of undesirable behaviour. We can be wary of *taxpayers* who contribute less than their fair share, and free riders: those who work under the table, submit false tax returns, *choose* not to work, and so on. We may also be suspicious of *recipients* who take more than their fair share (behave as *parasites*): those who commit fraud, receive benefits but do not seek employment, do not do what is necessary to make themselves employable, and the like (Gauthier 1986). In both cases, some people believe that certain categories of individuals, especially individuals belonging to certain ethno-cultural groups, are more likely to *under-contribute* to or to *overuse* the state's social programs.

In states that offer social protection, we regularly find that some people believe that certain communities are not as *deserving* as others. Identifying a community as "abusing the system" can have a radical effect on the willingness of members of other communities to continue funding public programs and universal social policies. Martin Gilens (1999) and Ed Glaeser (2005) describe the American situation in which members of the "black community" have been identified as "undeserving poor people." This stereotype has made it possible for opponents of the welfare state to mobilize a large proportion of the population against social programs perceived to disproportionately benefit undeserving black people.

We should also mention that our beliefs about others do not concern trustworthiness alone. We also have beliefs about our counterpart's dispositions concerning our own trustworthiness. We can be persuaded of the fact that a person is perfectly trustworthy, but believe that this person does not like us and will not behave as expected because of certain beliefs about us. Prejudices and beliefs that create antagonistic relationships between two communities are thus doubly problematic. They can make us suspicious of individuals belonging to communities other than ours, and they can lead us to anticipate that certain individuals will be warier of us than they are of members of their own community (Habyarimana et al. 2009; Foddy and Yamagishi 2009). To re-establish trusting relationships, it is thus not sufficient for the members of one community to adopt a positive perception of the members of the other community. They also have to be convinced that positive ideas about their own community have been re-established in the neighbouring community.

Beliefs and prejudices we have formed about the dispositions of members of certain communities can thus influence our own disposition to trust some of those people. Even if the beliefs only slightly alter our disposition to trust an individual who belongs to a community different from our own, this may be sufficient for us to favour interactions with members of our own group. We tend to prefer members of our own group when choosing whom to interact with even when our group has a reputation for being relatively untrustworthy or associated with a prejudice to that effect (Foddy and Yamagishi 2009). We may thus base our disposition to trust on known elements such as a characteristic that the group members are supposed to share or possess more often than members of other groups. The collective reputation of a community could influence our judgment about the individuals who compose it.

FROM THE INDIVIDUAL TO THE COMMUNITY: FIVE HYPOTHESES

Perhaps the problem is instead that it is difficult to establish trusting inter-personal relationships with individuals who are different from us. Do we have greater difficulty understanding individuals belonging to other ethno-cultural communities? In a number of studies on trust, it is observed that some people have a kind of "aversion to heterogeneity" (Alesina and La Ferrara 2002). Individuals tend to prefer members of their own group even when that group has a negative reputation and they have the possibility of interacting with an individual who belongs to a group with a positive reputation (Foddy and Yamagishi 2009). We will try to deconstruct this aversion in order to identify how diversity can pose a problem for establishing trusting relationships. Our working hypothesis will be that there are components of this difference that are more relevant than others and that it is not "difference" *per se* that explains our stronger distrust towards certain "different" individuals. We will suggest five hypotheses for understanding the phenomenon of aversion to heterogeneity.

(a) The first hypothesis that could explain the fact that there is less trust between agents is that *communication is impossible or difficult*. The level of cooperation in non-cooperative games, often associated with the level of trust, increases radically when agents have the possibility of communicating, especially when they communicate face to face (Ostrom 2003; Ben-Ner and Putterman 2009). Even in situations where they can only discuss things that are irrelevant to the game – not what strategies to adopt or their disposition to behave in a certain way – the findings still show a higher level of cooperation. The very great majority of studies on this topic point in the same direction: communication makes it possible to establish trusting relationships which in turn facilitate cooperation. Improving communication and increasing possibilities for communication and interactions could thus be means of improving the overall level of trust.

We know that trading information about the strategy to be adopted and exchanging promises are not the only things that change cooperation. However, we do not know exactly what, in communication, influences cooperative behaviour. We will thus move onto other hypotheses that will narrow the analysis.

(b) The second hypothesis is that knowledge of the reputation of the other person is important (Ostrom 2003). Knowing individuals' reputations and their history of interactions allows us to extrapolate and predict their behaviours in comparable situations. Indeed, there are examples of behaviours that are based on this type of information.

We will go over this quickly because, while this explanation is quite relevant in situations of repeated interactions and in contexts where we know the reputation of individuals we have not personally interacted with in the past, it is much less pertinent in cases of one-time, irregular, or infrequent interactions between individuals. Note simply that an individual's reputation, which we know through direct interactions or via other individuals who have interacted with them, will spread all the more easily if there are inter-community exchanges. The reputations of the least reliable or most untrustworthy individuals can be conveyed through the media, by word of mouth, and so on, and the efficient transmission of this information is increased, once again, by the possibility of many frequent interactions among individual members of different communities.

(c) The third hypothesis concerns *knowledge of the relevant norms* in the interaction. By simply observing other people, even if they are complete strangers, we obtain much information. In laboratory experiments on cooperation and trust, trust levels have been found to increase radically if the individuals are allowed to see each other, communicate, and interact in person. Fukuyama defines trust as "the expectation that arises within a community of regular, honest, and cooperative behaviour, based on commonly shared norms, on the part of other members of the community" (1995: 26). This idea can be interpreted in two ways. First, observing someone comply with very simple norms, such as those related to politeness and proper interactions, makes it possible to predict that the person will behave appropriately in other contexts. The fact that the individual *knows* certain norms, and that they correctly interpret the situation as being conducive to compliance with a specific norm, is used as a basis for forming the belief that they know other norms that will prove relevant in other contexts. Without knowing their motivation for complying with these norms, we can at least conclude that they have knowledge of them. Next, we can postulate that if they comply with those rules, they will comply with other ones that apply to them. In effect, we postulate that the other person has a certain moral personality, and even if we are wrong to do so – as has been shown by the situationist critique (Flanagan 1991; Doris 2002) – we nonetheless use this idea to predict the behaviour of other people. Under the first interpretation, we presuppose knowledge of pertinent norms in possible interactions based on trust; in the second, we presuppose that there are motives for complying with the norms in possible interactions. In both cases, knowledge of relevant social norms makes it more likely that there will be trusting relationships leading to cooperation (Habyarimana et al. 2009).

Now, there is nothing *necessary*, morally or otherwise, about the content of relevant norms in a specific context. Rules about lining up to wait, driving on the right side of the road (in Canada), placing the knife to the right of the plate, shaking an acquaintance's hand, returning a smile, and so forth are not superior to any other norm in terms of regulating such social behaviours. However, without passing moral judgment on those who do not know these rules, it may be entirely justifiable to hesitate when determining whether to interact with them. This is because it is possible that the interaction will not be successful, given that the agents do not interpret the situation in the same way, do not identify the same norms to be applied in a given situation, or are not disposed to comply with them.

(d) The fourth hypothesis concerns the many *signals and signs* that are conveyed on both sides during an interaction and reveal each individual's dispositions, emotional state, and motives for complying with norms or conventions (Oullier and Basso 2010; Gambetta and Hamill 2005; Darwin 2001; Frank 1988). We are astonishingly efficient at identifying lies and other traps laid by individuals, even when they are perfect strangers. Signals such as dilated blood vessels in the face, trembling, accelerated breathing, damp hands, and shifty eyes are indications that we have learned to recognize in order to get the most out of social interactions. When this is added to information coming from the type of clothing that a person wears, the newspaper they read, their way of greeting others, and other such details, we develop an idea of whom we are dealing with and their state of mind.

On the basis of this minimal information, we can determine whether the person is trustworthy; our conclusion will be uncertain, but more efficient than if we relied simply on random choices. Body language seems to be decipherable in an unconscious manner. It is a relic of our evolution and there is relatively broad consensus that there are universal signs shared by all of humanity. The same emotions seem to give rise to similar unconscious physiological reactions from one culture and "race" to the next (Darwin 2001; Ekman 2007).

Nonetheless, we should clarify two points. First, the fact that specialists in the field identify the same signals among individuals with different ethnic origins does not entail that we read the signals with the same degree of efficiency on faces that are not familiar to us. Even if we are only slightly less skilful in identifying and interpreting these signals beyond the borders of our ethnic community, we will have a partial explanation for distrust and the greater difficulties that come from cooperating with individuals belonging to ethnic communities different from our own. Second, even if the signals associated with emotions are universal, each culture has specific norms concerning the desirability of feeling certain emotions in general and in specific contexts. Being jealous of the success of a friend, angry about having lost a race, or envious of a relative's talent, to name a few examples, are emotions that are not considered acceptable in my culture, and so, even though unconscious signals may be associated with them, we use strategies to dissimulate our emotions (Ekman 2007). The latter point reintroduces the question of norms specific to each culture, and if we are not aware of those norms, it makes it more difficult to exercise our formidable talent for reading the emotional dispositions of others. If we interpret the behaviour of an individual as *abnormal* or *weird*, we will be less inclined to trust that person.

(e) The fifth and last hypothesis is that people who are members of the same group have greater expectations of cooperating in the future and of being able to punish counterparts who behave in an undesirable way. When this expectation is reciprocal, an ability to predict with greater confidence the outcomes of future interactions reduces the incentives for either party to act in an untrustworthy manner. If we expect mutual benefits to flow from future interactions, it is irrational to discourage our counterpart by acting in an opportunistic way (Axelrod 1984). In such situations, depriving a collaborator of possible advantageous interactions is a form of *passive punishment*. However, we can also think of active punishments in which direct costs are imposed on the agent who behaves inappropriately. The possibility of having a positive or negative influence on the utility an individual anticipates from an interaction increases desirable behaviour (Ostrom, Walker, and Gardner 1992). The more power we have to reward or punish an individual, the easier it will be to trust him or her. If interactions between members of different ethnic communities are scarce, our expectations of future interactions and our punitive power will be reduced, and it will be more difficult to have trust. What is important here is not the *assurance* that there will be future interactions, but knowledge of the simple *possibility* that such interactions may occur.

Experiments have shown that when it is made more difficult or costly for the parties to a cooperative endeavour to punish misbehavers, levels of trust and cooperation are lower. In contrast, when agents know that they are going to interact again with their counterpart, even when their respective identities are not revealed, more trustworthy behaviour is observed. This may have the effect of favouring individuals who are members of our own community over those who belong to other communities (Shermer 2008).

THREE DYNAMICS OF DISTRUST

Trust thus seems to be based on various elements, some of them occurring directly between individuals, and others shared by a community involving knowledge and beliefs about individuals. Distrust therefore seems to be created at the collective level, which makes interactions between individuals more difficult, but also at the individual level, which makes the creation and maintenance of negative prejudices all the more easy. Consequently, a troubling dynamic of distrust may entrench itself such that collective prejudices are supported by our own individual difficulties in identifying the trustworthiness of counterparts who belong to ethno-cultural communities different from our own. In fact, three dynamics are at work.

There is no doubt that collective prejudices influence our disposition to trust individuals who are members of given groups. We can be very skeptical about the credibility of some beliefs, though it only takes a small amount of doubt to influence our behaviour. If we can choose between individuals with whom we will interact, the slightest unfavourable belief about one of them will make us prefer to interact with the other. This little difference in the trust we place in members of different communities can have a significant impact if we do not interact regularly with members of the community we are prejudiced against, since we prefer the *safer* option of intra-community interactions. The barely greater trust in members of our own community means that we will interact infrequently with members of other communities. We will thus not have the encounters that could break down stereotypes or prove prejudices wrong. Inversely, we will accrue positive experiences of interactions with members of our own community. This absence of interactions between members of different communities contributes to the emergence and maintenance of beliefs that corrode inter-community trust and thus undermine the maintenance of social institutions shared by the populace as a whole. The less frequent the exchanges, the more difficult it will be to correct false beliefs and negative prejudices. This is one dynamic of distrust, but things get worse if we have reason to think that trust is also harder to establish in direct interactions between individuals.

If some of the hypotheses about why it is difficult to establish direct trusting relationships between two individuals prove correct, the greater difficulty of obtaining information about another person's disposition to behave in a desired manner can in turn be more conducive to interacting with people similar to us. If individuals belonging to different ethno-cultural communities are more *opaque* with each other regarding their intentions, this can discourage certain inter-community interactions. Once again, a slight difference in our capacity to *read* another person can justify opting for intra-community interactions when possible. The problem is also dynamic, in that the fewer inter-community interactions there are, the less the agents' opaqueness will be reduced. This dynamic is thus different from the first: the slight difference in our capacity to read others will motivate us to prefer interactions with individuals who resemble us, thereby decreasing the chances of improving our ability to read individuals belonging to other communities.

Finally, as mentioned above, we can identify a third dynamic of distrust at work in inter-community relations. If it is true that our greater distrust of individuals from other communities flows from two sources – one "macro," in which our beliefs about a community determine our disposition to trust its members, and the other "micro," in which we have more difficulty reading the dispositions of individuals different from us – then it is plausible that these two sources of distrust interact and support each other. Our prejudice against a given community could be supported by the fact that our direct interactions with members of that community are indeed more difficult. It could also cut the other way: we could explain our more difficult direct interactions with certain individuals by citing our prejudice against their community. The problem thus seems to be dynamic at another level: beliefs suggesting that members of a given group are untrustworthy are supported (or at least not refuted) in direct interactions between individuals belonging to separate communities.

These dynamics flow from different sources, though all make trusting relationships more difficult outside of identity borders. Alesina and La Ferrara (2002) have identified two points of equilibrium in trusting relationships. There is a positive equilibrium in which trust gives rise to successful interactions that in turn confirm that we were right to trust, and a negative equilibrium in which distrust prevents or sabotages interactions, which confirms that we were right to distrust. What we have to note is that distrust of a community does not have to be very extensive for interactions with their members to be very scarce. If we have even only slightly more trust in members of our own community, whether this is influenced by a belief or by greater facility in reading the dispositions of others, it will translate into more frequent interactions with members of our community. Moreover, if we interact only rarely with individuals who belong to different ethnocultural communities, it is very possible that successful interactions with them will not manage to persuade us that prejudices against them are false. A process called *confirmation bias* describes a cognitive phenomenon in which individuals place disproportionate importance on specific events that *confirm* their beliefs and fail to place equivalent importance on one-time events or general information that contradict them. This cognitive process makes it very difficult to attack shared, established beliefs when there are few interactions to produce counterexamples. In order to eliminate prejudices and false beliefs, it is important that individuals regularly come face to face with facts that refute them.

This vision is consistent with David Miller's observation: "Cultural differences do create barriers to trust – there is no question about that – but given the right pattern of interaction these barriers can be overcome" (2004: 29). Miller suggests attacking group alienation and segregation, both of which undermine widespread trust. Without interactions between groups, trust will not extend beyond group borders, owing to the dynamics identified above. Unfortunately, it is quite likely that it is a lack of widespread trust that motivates groups to avoid inter-community interactions. It is thus critical that we better understand the dynamics of distrust at work, in order to take action to reverse them and achieve the positive equilibrium of inter-group trust that is vital to the social state.

CONCLUSION

Obviously, the goal has not been to definitively demonstrate the existence and origins of a distrustful dynamic effectively at work in multinational democracies and heterogeneous communities; rather, it has been to propose several hypotheses supported by recent research findings. Work on the topic is still in its infancy and does not make it possible to draw definitive conclusions about the nature of the problem of distrust facing multinational democracies and heterogeneous communities. We are only beginning to understand the causes of trust, and questions about the tension between trust and difference have not given rise to much empirical research. Note also that most of the studies on the topic have focused on the American context, in which diversity is defined mainly as racial heterogeneity. The findings of future research on the topic, some of which is now underway in multinational democracies such as Belgium, Canada, and India, will greatly increase our understanding of the phenomenon and make it possible to more accurately identify avenues of action for improving the situation. These avenues have to be found quickly because, while we may not know exactly what is at work, there are strong research findings that identify tension between institutional effectiveness and solidarity, on the one hand, and the heterogeneity of the populace, on the other. As mentioned at the beginning, the very vitality of democratic and social institutions is threatened by this tension in multinational democracies.

The purpose of the hypothesis developed here is to encourage future research in order to obtain relevant data to refute or confirm it. We must improve our understanding of the situation in order to increase our chances of saving the social policies and redistributive institutions that have been adopted by many multinational democracies and states with heterogeneous populaces. This is all the more urgent when we see that a number of researchers believe that progressive forces are facing a dilemma between promoting socio-economic justice or supporting cultural justice and diversity. If there is confirmation of our hypothesis that diversity does not itself corrode solidarity but that trust can be more difficult to establish beyond ethno-cultural borders, then progressive forces will be facing a complex problem without facing a tragic dilemma between solidarity and diversity. Indeed, if our hypothesis is confirmed, the problem is not related to the composition of the populace. Instead, it is linked to the distrust that can be created between nations or communities. If this is in fact the problem, actions that promote certain inter-community interactions fostering trust will help guarantee the vitality and efficiency of institutions in plurinational democracies. The challenge remains formidable, but the progressive dilemma can be avoided.

It is evident that progressive forces must improve their understanding of the situation and the nature of the problem in order to suggest promising avenues for future action. Without a thorough comprehension of the problem, any normative proposal is condemned to be ineffective or even counterproductive. For example, David Miller's hypothesis is that we need a *shared identity* in order to eliminate the tension between solidarity and diversity; ours is that we need to get to know one another beyond identity borders (Robichaud 2012). These two hypotheses justify very different actions. According to Miller, building a shared identity may help members of every community to integrate into an inclusive national culture, leading to an increased level of solidarity and trust. However, if we have reason to believe that what we need is not to share a minimal national identity but to have better mutual understanding between groups, Miller's proposal could create new problems without solving anything. The difficulty is that in Miller's theory the causal link seems to be inversed. It seems that increasing inter-community social relationships is more likely to lead to the emergence of a shared identity and not the opposite. If Miller is right that integration improves trusting relationships (and we think that he is right on this point), and if we are correct that creating a shared national identity *will follow* and is not a necessary condition for such integration, then we have to find ways to promote such integration. We must therefore try to identify ways of improving relationships between individuals of different nations and different ethno-cultural communities, and try to eliminate the segregation of these communities that creates challenges for trusting relationships and makes it difficult to maintain a feeling of solidarity. One way of attacking segregation could be to promote inter-community exchanges and to soften identity-based separation. This could be done through a special institutional configuration, sharing a public language common to all individuals subject to the same redistributive institutions and other initiatives, that facilitates, encourages, and *imposes* inter-community exchanges. Facilitating exchanges will help to eliminate prejudices and stereotypes, establish healthier collective ideas, and, over time, create a positive history of interactions. Subsequently, the same dynamics will continue to operate, but they will not increase distrust – instead, they will lead towards a positive equilibrium of trust between individuals belonging to different nations and ethnic groups.

NOTES

Some of the research on which this text is based has been presented at conferences. I would like to thank my friends at the Centre de recherche interdisciplinaire sur la citoyenneté et les minorités (CIRCEM) and the Groupe de recherche sur les sociétés multinationales (GRSP), as well as Christine Straehle, Benoît Dubreuil, and Patrick Turmel for their informed comments and recommendations.

1 It is important to note that individuals were not questioned about how much trust they have in members of other ethno-cultural communities or social classes. They were questioned only about their general trust in members of the community.

2 Obviously, it would also be misguided to suggest that the only threat hanging over the welfare state is that which is posed by diversity with respect to solidarity. The political culture of a state and a conservative ideology are obviously factors that can directly motivate individuals to challenge social policies. However, there is reason to doubt that ideological positioning explains disengagement in the welfare state or that it could suffice to rally the majority against the welfare state. Various authors have convincingly argued that the rejection of the progressive agenda in the United States has been motivated more by greater distrust in institutions (Hetherington 2005) or fellow citizens (Gilens 1999) than by a more conservative political realignment. Note in passing that the purpose of my argument is not to provide a moral justification for the welfare state, but to shed light on a phenomenon that indirectly but perniciously places it in danger.

REFERENCES

Alesina, Alberto, Reza Baqir, and William Easterly. 1999. "Public Goods and Ethnic Divisions." *Quarterly Journal of Economics*: 1243–84.

Alesina, Alberto, and Edward L. Glaeser. 2004. *Fighting Poverty in the US and Europe: A World of Difference*. Oxford: Oxford University Press.

Alesina, Alberto, and Eliana La Ferrara. 2000. "Participation in Heterogeneous Communities." *The Quarterly Journal of Economics* 115, no. 3: 847–904.

– 2002. "Who Trusts Others?" *Journal of Public Economics* 85: 207–34.

Axelrod, Robert. 1984. *The Evolution of Cooperation*. New York: Basic Books.

Barry, Brian. 1989. *Democracy, Power, and Justice: Essays in Political Philosophy*. Oxford: Oxford University Press.

Ben-Ner, Avner, and Louis Putterman. 2009. "Trust, Communication and Contracts: An Experiment." *Journal of Economic Behavior and Organization* 70, no. 1–2: 106–21.

Bowles, Samuel, and Herbert Gintis. 2004. "The Evolution of Strong Reciprocity: Cooperation in Heterogeneous Populations." *Theoretical Population Biology* 65, no. 1: 17–28.

Brosnan, Sarah F. 2008. "Fairness and Other-Regarding Preferences in Nonhuman Primates." In *Moral Markets: The Critical Role of Values in the Economy*, edited by Paul J. Zak, 77–105. Princeton: Princeton University Press.

Camerer, Colin F. 2003. *Behavioral Game Theory: Experiments in Strategic Interaction*. New York: Russell Sage Foundation.

Darwin, Charles. 2001. *L'expression des émotions chez l'homme et les animaux*. Paris: Rivages.

DeBruine, Lisa M. 2002. "Facial Resemblance Enhances Trust." *Proceedings: Biological Science* 269, no. 1498: 1307–12.

Doci, Edward L. 1971. "Effects of Externally Mediated Rewards on Intrinsic Motivation." *Journal of Personality and Social Psychology* 18, no. 1: 105–15.

Doris, John M. 2002. *Lack of Character: Personality and Moral Behaviour*. Cambridge: Cambridge University Press.

Dubreuil, Benoît. 2010. *Human Evolution and the Origins of Hierarchies: The State of Nature*. Cambridge: Cambridge University Press.

Easterly, William, and Ross Levine. 1997. "Africa's Growth Tragedy: Policies and Ethnic Divisions." *Quarterly Journal of Economics* 112, no. 4: 1203–50.

Ekman, Paul. 2007. *Emotions Revealed*. New York: St Martin's Griffin.

Flanagan, Owen. 1991. *Varieties of Moral Personality: Ethics and Psychological Realism*. Cambridge, MA: Harvard University Press.

Foddy, Margaret, and Toshio Yamagishi. 2009. "Group-Based Trust." In *Whom Can We Trust? How Groups, Networks, and Institutions Make Trust Possible*, edited by Karen S. Cook, Margaret Levi, and Russell Hardin, 17–41. New York: Russell Sage Foundation.

Forbes, Hugh Donald. 1997. *Ethnic Conflict: Commerce, Culture, and the Contact Hypothesis*. New Haven: Yale University Press.

Frank, Robert H. 1988. *Passion within Reason: The Strategic Role of the Emotions*. New York: W.W. Norton.

Fukuyama, Francis. 1995. *Trust: The Social Virtues and the Creation of Prosperity*. New York: Free Press.

Gambetta, Diego, and Heather Hamill. 2005. *Streetwise: How Taxi Drivers Establish Their Customers' Trustworthiness*. Volume 10 of the Russell Sage Foundation series on trust. New York: Russell Sage Foundation.

Gauthier, David. 1986. *Morals by Agreement*. Oxford: Oxford University Press.

Glaeser, Edward L. 2005. "The Political Economy of Hatred." *The Quarterly Journal of Economics* 120, no. 1: 45–86.

Glaeser, Edward L., David I. Laibson, José A. Scheinkman, and Christine L. Soutter. 2000. "Measuring Trust." *The Quarterly Journal of Economics* 115, no. 3: 811–46.

Gneezy, Uri, and Aldo Rustichini. 2000. "A Fine Is a Price." *The Journal of Legal Studies* 29, no. 1: 1–17.

Habyarimana, James, Macartan Humphreys, Daniel N. Posner, and Jeremy M. Weinstein. 2009. "Coethnicity and Trust." In *Whom Can We Trust? How Groups, Networks, and Institutions Make Trust Possible*, edited by Margaret Levi, Karen S. Cook, and Russell Hardin, 42–64. New York: Russell Sage Foundation.

Henrich, Joseph P. 2004. *Foundations of Human Sociality: Economic Experiments and Ethnographic Evidence from Fifteen Small-Scale Societies*. Oxford: Oxford University Press.

Hetherington, Marc J. 2005. *Why Trust Matters: Declining Political Trust and the Demise of American Liberalism*. Princeton: Princeton University Press.

Johansson-Stenman, Olof. 2008. "Who Are the Trustworthy, We Think?" *Journal of Economic Behavior and Organization* 68: 456–65.

Kymlicka, Will, and Keith G. Banting. Eds. 2006. *Multiculturalism and the Welfare State: Recognition and Redistribution in Contemporary Democracies*. Oxford: Oxford University Press.

LaPorta, Rafael, Florencio Lopez-de-Silanes, Andrei Shleifer, and Robert Vishny. 1999. "The Quality of Government." *Journal of Law, Economics and Organization* 15, no. 1: 222–79.

Marschall, Melissa J., and Dietlind Stolle. 2004. "Race and the City: Neighbourhood Context and the Development of Generalized Trust." *Political Behavior* 26, no. 2: 125–53.

Mauro, Paulo. 1995. "Corruption and Growth." *Quarterly Journal of Economics* 110, no. 3: 681–712.

Miller, David. 2000. *Citizenship and National Identity*. Cambridge: Polity Press.

– 2004. "Social Justice in Multicultural Societies." In *Cultural Diversity Versus Economic Solidarity*, edited by Philippe Van Parijs, 13–31. Brussels: De Boeck.

Ostrom, Elinor, James Walker, and Roy Gardner. 1992. "Covenants with and without a Sword: Self-Governance Is Possible." *American Political Science Review* 86, no. 2: 404–17.

Oullier, Olivier, and Frédéric Basso. 2010. "Embodied Economics: How Bodily Information Shapes the Social Coordination Dynamics of Decision-Making." *Philosophical Transactions of the Royal Society B: Biological Sciences* 365, no. 1538: 291–301.

Robichaud, David. 2012. "La langue au service de l'état providence." In *Penser les institutions*, edited by D. Anctil, D. Robichaud, and P. Turmel. Québec: Presses de l'Université Laval, 79–103.

Sandovici, Maria, and Ola Listhaug. 2006. "Ethnic Minorities and Political Participation." Paper presented at the Annual Meeting of the American Political Science Association, Philadelphia, 31 August – 3 September 2006. http://citation.allacademic.com/meta/p_mla_apa_research_citation/1/5/3/2/1/pages153219/p153219-1.php.

Shermer, Michael. 2009. *Mind Of The Market: Compassionate Apes, Competitive Humans, and Other Tales from Evolutionary Economics*. New York: Holt.

4

Democratic Institutions and Representative Trust

Patti Tamara Lenard

Democracies are governed by a complex set of institutions, all of which play distinct roles in securing the efficiency and effectiveness of democratic politics. Among the roles these institutions play is an essential representative role: whatever else they do, institutions in democracies necessarily represent at least some citizens to some extent. As I shall suggest in this chapter, trust is an essential element of representation in the modern democratic state. If trust is at the foundation of representation, and if representation is a part of all democratic institutions, then we can see that trust is central to democratic politics. Moreover, when trust in democratic institutions is declared, as it so often is of late, to have declined precipitously, we can attribute this decline to the breakdown of what I term *representative trust* – that is, the trust that is at the heart of the representation that democratic institutions offer.

I shall begin by describing the way in which trust underpins effective representation in general. Then, I shall distinguish among five broad sets of democratic institutions according to the representative function they play, as well as according to the source of trust that underpins their capacity to carry out effective representation. In particular, I shall distinguish among these institutions using five criteria: (a) who is represented; (b) what is represented; (c) the source of trust; (d) what counts as betrayed trust; and, finally, (e) the mechanisms for responding to betrayed trust. The purpose of the chapter is analytic, with the intention of responding to the widespread claims that democratic institutions are no longer adequately representative. In order to decipher the truth of these accusations, and to understand how to remedy their representative capacities, we first need a better understanding of the ways in which democratic institutions are representative and what it means to say that they have failed to fulfill their representative responsibilities. In particular, because the declines in trust are so often attributed to the failure of democratic institutions to be representative, it is important that such an analysis be conducted through the lens of trust.

REPRESENTATION AND TRUST
IN MODERN DEMOCRACIES

Modern democracies rely on representation: typically, we think of individual representatives as elected with the purpose of representing the views of multiple citizens. Through their representatives, the preferences, interests, and values of individual citizens are said to find expression, and thus representation serves an important inclusive role in democratic politics (Plotke 1997). Historically, of course, the notion that representation is an essential element of democracy, rather than a dilution of democracy, is a recent one: Jean-Jacques Rousseau famously declared that no man can be represented in politics by any person other than himself. However, by the time John Stuart Mill articulated the details and structure of modern representative democracy in the late 1800s, it was accepted as a matter of course that representation served to make democracy in large communities manageable. So long as representation was carried out honestly, it served effectively to underpin modern democratic politics, and in particular to ensure that the diversity of views held by the citizenry finds a voice in central political institutions (Mill 1991 [1862]).

In order to ensure that the diversity of views is in fact represented in central political institutions, we need to *trust* that representatives are able to play this role. The conviction that trust is an essential element of the representative role is typically traced back to Edmund Burke, who distinguished between two ways of understanding representatives: as delegates and as trustees. Whereas delegates act only according to the expressed wishes of a constituency (for example, as electors in the American electoral college), trustees are permitted to act more flexibly and to assess a variety of considerations in speaking on behalf of a constituency. Representatives as trustees are taken to be individuals who will act in the best interests of their constituents, and who will use their considered judgment (along with extensive consultation) to understand those interests. In principle, the source of the trust that is extended to representatives stems (at least for Burke) from the coincidence of interests that supposedly extends throughout a territorial constituency, from the superior judgment skills that representatives possess, and from the willingness of representatives to seek their constituents' input with respect to their preferences and interests (Burke 1774; Eulau et al. 1959). In practice, the source of trust in modern democratic politics is more ambiguous, and is often attributed to the charisma or attractiveness of candidates running for office. In part, the difficulties of evaluating the competence of candidates explain the shift towards relying on intuition rather than evidence of trustworthiness.

In order to make better sense of what we mean when we say that representatives are evaluated for their trustworthiness, let me insert here a few words about the notion of trust itself. As many scholars have noted, trusting is inherently a risky activity: in extending trust to others, one makes oneself vulnerable to the actions of others, and, in doing so, risks being betrayed and disappointed by their actions (Baier 1994). The risks associated with extending trust seem greater when we are not intimately familiar with those to whom we are extending trust, that is, when we are distanced from the evidence that we ordinarily use to make judgments with respect to the trustworthiness of others, as is the case in large-scale social and political relations. Trust is often thought of in something like probabilistic terms: in trusting, we are making a judgment about the likelihood of our being disappointed by others, and when we judge that likelihood to be low, we extend trust to them. To make this judgment, we evaluate the evidence that others are likely to respond well to the trust we place in them; to some extent, then, trust is cognitive. Yet this probabilistic interpretation, favored by rational choice theorists (Hardin 2006), fails to capture in full how the term is conventionally used and how the concept is conventionally experienced. When extending trust or not, many people think of themselves as doing so on the basis of extensive knowledge of others, such as when we trust those who are closest to us with the things we care about the most. This trust is not experienced as extended after a probability calculation; rather it is extended *because* doing so is inherent to the relationship itself. To be friends, for example, partly means to extend trust. Alternatively, trust is extended on emotional, or psychological, or affective, or intuitive grounds.[1]

This is not to deny that our intuition can guide us poorly, or that it is often built on stereotypes and prejudices that might be better broken down in some way (for example, we might hope that trust isn't extended based on the perception that only whites are trustworthy). Yet, when we extend trust within the wider social and political world in which we operate, trust is felt to be extended intuitively or because "that's how we do things around here."[2] It is probably accurate to say that the trust we extend, or not, to our representatives is based in part on an evaluation of evidence to which we have access (past activities, stated platforms, and so on), and in part on the affective or emotional cues that guide us in extending our trust "intuitively."

TRUST AND REPRESENTATIVE INSTITUTIONS

This basic understanding of the source of trust in representatives continues to underpin contemporary accounts of representation, but the recent surge in theorizing on the nature of democratic representation suggests that it offers an inadequate account in contemporary democratic political environments. Among the central concerns of theorists of representation is the ongoing sense that the makeup of democratic institutions appears to be fundamentally unrepresentative of the population: across most Western democratic nations, representatives are generally male, white, and wealthy. In response, we have witnessed a surge in discussions of the value of "descriptive representation," the proposal that representation is best when representatives descriptively mirror those they represent. On this view, women should represent women, visible minorities should represent visible minorities, and so on. For those who defend descriptive representation, the experiences that are shared between represented and representative are significant, and give the representative unique insight into the preferences and values of those whom they represent. For those who reject this view, it treats "groups" as homogeneous entities whose preferences are determined entirely by their status as group members.[3] While this disagreement hinges on the *source* of trust – whether trust is extended as a result of shared experience, or whether it can be based on something broader – no one is suggesting that the fundamental understanding of representation, as based on trust, is suspect. I join these theorists in believing that this basic structure of trust and representation, while fundamentally sound, requires reconsideration.

In this chapter, I observe that while democratic institutions are vast and varied, they all play a fundamental representative function. Yet, they differ by what they represent, whom they represent, and the source of the trust that underpins the representation they offer. There are at least five major institutions in democratic polities, all of which have representative roles. These are: institutions of basic governance, political parties, the judiciary, civil society organizations, and national symbols. Let me begin by describing each of them in terms of who and what is being represented, and then the source of trust in each of them.

Institutions of Basic Governance

By institutions of basic governance, I mean those institutions to which we elect representatives, and in which representatives produce the laws that govern our lives – that is, the legislative and executive branches of governance. Although the executive and the legislative branches play distinct roles in democratic politics, they are both institutions in which representatives are elected by a voting populace. As a result, the individuals who are elected, and the institutions taken as a whole, are meant to represent all citizens. When Stephen Harper was elected to a majority Conservative government in the 2011 Canadian federal election, he told his cheering supporters that although they had elected him, his job was to represent the interests of all Canadians, even those who had not voted for him. In acting as our representatives – indeed, it is only in the executive and legislative arenas that the representation of citizens is done specifically by individuals who are formally termed *representatives* – citizens are represented along multiple dimensions. Our elected representatives are charged with working in our best interests, with acting more generally according to the values and norms we can be said to share, and with choosing policies that are in line with our preferences. Although in highly polarized elections, and even in elections more generally, "losers" tend to doubt the sincerity of winners who claim to offer comprehensive rather than partial representation, the fact remains that broadly understood those elected to sit in our legislative and executive institutions are at least nominally thought to be acting on our collective behalf (Anderson et al. 2005).

It is easy to confuse the trust that constituents might have in individual representatives with the trust that they can be said to have in the institutions more generally. In my view, it is incoherent to claim that individuals trust institutions – institutions themselves are inert, and they are trustworthy only to the extent that the individuals who operate these institutions are themselves trustworthy. Yet, it is a mistake to therefore claim that institutions do not have an essential connection to the trust that citizens extend to those who act on their behalves. The relationship between institutions and trust can be described as follows: well-designed institutions can generate the conditions under which trust can flourish in general. As a result, large-scale communities design institutions that can serve to mitigate the risk associated with extending trust, and therefore to make these relations more likely to extend and reciprocate. Institutions that require both the transparency and accountability of government play precisely this role (I will say more about these institutions, below).[4] In general, we can say that the source of trust in democratic institutions stems from the perception that the rules that govern their decision-making procedures are inclusive and therefore fair.[5] The trust that we place in representatives themselves is, as I indicated earlier, more complicated, and turns on a combination of publicly available evidence of representative trustworthiness and an affective response to potential representatives.

Political Parties

Political parties are organizations that attempt to collect individuals who share a platform or ideology, in order to participate in governance (by winning elections) with a view to creating policy that reflects that specific platform or ideology. All genuinely democratic political communities are characterized by competing parties, which offer their platforms to the electorate for their consideration. Once elected to office, they are then charged with doing what they can to implement policies that find support within their constituencies. Unlike the government more generally, political parties do not purport to represent citizens in general, at least not until they are elected, but rather purport to represent citizens who subscribe to a specific platform. However, it is not for self-interested purposes that they do so, but rather because they believe that this platform is good for the political community in general. When Republicans (if we are to take them at their word) defend corporate tax cuts as a solution to unemployment, they do so with the sincere belief that the former causes the latter, and moreover that this is the best way to resolve a dilemma that faces the community as a whole. They are not advocating that only Republican supporters are entitled to jobs; rather they are offering policy proposals that they believe to be in the collective best interest. The reason this matters is that political parties aim to run governments that, in theory at least, are aimed at governing on behalf of all citizens. The trust that can be placed in them, especially by those who do not support their platforms, hinges on the belief that, in spite of disagreement about *what* is in the best interest of the community, everyone's objective is in fact to aim at that best interest.

Within political parties, however, when candidates are vying to be the representative from a given constituency, trust in candidates stems from their capacity to articulate the party platform and from the perception that they will be zealous defenders of this platform if elected (as a candidate and then in government). In addition to distinguishing between the representation that candidates offer when they are members of the government and the representation they offer when they are competing to be the party's representatives in elections, we can distinguish, as with the legislative and the executive more generally, between the trust in the candidates (who in this case are perceived as able to articulate and defend the party platform) and the trust in the system that dictates how candidates are chosen. As with executive and legislative institutions, political parties can have structures that do or do not induce trust in party members; the mechanisms for candidate selection can be closed, breeding suspicion of corruption and cronyism, or they can be open and transparent in ways that produce trust among those with strongly divergent views on who to select as candidate.

The Judiciary

The judiciary plays an essential role in protecting democratic governance. Although courts play multiple roles in political communities (for example, penalizing criminals and adjudicating civil disputes), to the extent that the judiciary is charged with ensuring that the rights of citizens are protected, they have a particularly *representative* role in democratic politics. In principle, their goal is to protect the "right" instantiation of a constitution or set of human rights, which can be at risk of violation as a result of legislatively (i.e., democratically) determined legislation. Courts often work, in other words, to protect the rights of minorities, which are sometimes at risk of being eroded by majorities with legislative power. On the one hand, then, they can be described as representing "everyone" – they protect the set of rights that we have agreed are essential to our community. On the other hand, they are often derided for the ways in which they appear to thwart democratic decision-making. When, for example, a judge in Boston in the early 1970s declared that local schools would be forcibly desegregated via 'a complicated system of busing students from one neighborhood to another, opponents protested that the court had overstepped its boundaries, failing to represent the interests of the majority and to protect its rights. The court, they said, was not acting fairly and therefore did not deserve their trust. In general, then, the judiciary derives its legitimacy from the perception that it is implementing "our" rules fairly and carefully.

Civil Society Organizations

Multiple organizations form part of civil society, including interest groups, non-governmental groups, unions, and so on, and they all play a similar role in democratic politics. They serve to raise awareness of issues that are, or are at least perceived to be, of interest to the larger democratic community, and to try to persuade political actors that decisions should be made in their favor. The difference between interest groups and non-governmental organizations is often described in terms of interests and values: whereas interest groups lobby to have the interests of certain segments of the population taken into account (the car industry, the elderly, and so on), non-governmental organizations are typically described as protecting values that the community ought to share (environmental organizations, poverty fighting organizations, and so on). Historically, unions may have been described in terms of the collective values they protect; more recently, they have become described in terms that make them seem more like interest groups. What these and other civil society organizations share is that they are inevitably interpreted as offering partial representation to a specific constituency. Civil society organizations often emerge in response to the perception that state representatives are doing an inadequate job (either maliciously, or for lack of information) at protecting the interests of certain segments of the population (Cohen 1999; Chambers and Kopstein 2001). These organizations thus emerge to resist the power of the state, or to offer a countervailing political force that can lobby on behalf of citizens. Typically, they are trusted to the extent that they are effective lobbyists on behalf of that constituency.

National Symbols

Nations are defined by symbols, including flags, monuments, holidays, and so on (see for example Wingo 2003). They are meant to represent the community as a whole, and they serve to represent values and norms that define a community. Americans, for example, take the bald eagle to represent their nation's strength, and Canadians take the beaver to represent their nation's economic foundations in natural resources. Not all symbols are taken to represent values, of course. Some are simply preferences or loves that co-nationals share: Canadians sometimes describe their national sport as hockey,[6] and Brits are characterized by a commitment to tea at four in the afternoon. These features – preferences, values, and norms shared by co-nationals – are sometimes collective described as a nation's "public culture."[7] In principle, the symbols that compose a nation's public culture define or represent the nation as a whole, even if not all Canadians love hockey and not all Brits drink tea. In the ideal, these symbols are innocuous and inclusive, in the sense that while they do genuinely describe or define national values and preferences, they do not translate into a foundation for the xenophobic, violent, nationalist movements that haunted mid-twentieth-century Europe. In practice, as I shall describe in the next section, these symbols are often interpreted in exclusionary ways and require modification to shed this perception.

It may seem odd to consider the source of "trust" in these symbols. Above, I noted the same thing about institutions – that it may seem odd to say that individuals trust institutions, responding with the suggestion that in fact "trusting institutions" is a kind of shorthand for trusting the individuals who operate institutions that are themselves perceived to be fairly designed. The institutions are fair, and the operators are trusted to operate them effectively. Here, though, it probably makes more sense to describe symbols in terms of the support they receive, or the extent to which they are genuinely adopted as national symbols. Insofar as some citizens feel excluded from the representation these symbols offer (Aboriginal Canadians may feel that they are not represented by a large set of Canadian national symbols, for example), distrust is likely to exist among citizens – that is, between those who do and those who do not interpret the symbols as nationally representative.

BETRAYED TRUST AND RESPONSES
TO BETRAYED TRUST

Above, I have delineated the multitude of ways in which citizens are represented in democratic politics. The list I offered is undoubtedly not comprehensive, but its purpose was to illustrate that representation occurs throughout democratic politics, at multiple levels, and therefore that democratic politics is imbued with the trust that is essential for effective representation. I turn next to exploring when these institutions fail in their representative role, and therefore when they can be said to have betrayed the trust placed in them.

I also observed that trust is inherently risky. Extending trust requires opening oneself up to betrayed or disappointed trust; when trust is betrayed or disappointed repeatedly, distrust can emerge. In environments where the climate of trust is strong – where, in general, citizens extend trust to one another and to the political actors that govern their lives – trust can be disappointed more than once before it gives way to distrust. The breach of trust, in other words, does not automatically translate into distrust; only repeated breaches of trust do so. The reasons for this are complex, but mainly turn on the fact that a climate characterized by generalized trust, in which disappointed trust is rare, is resilient to disappointed trust for a time.[8] The resilience of trust is suggested by political communities in which political actors are accused of corruption, or self-interest, in which trust prevails nevertheless. Recently, of course, we have been treated to some evidence that trust is declining across Western democratic polities (Alford 2001; Van de Walle, Van Roosbroek, and Geert 2008; Hetherington 2008). Although the evidence should be treated carefully since what it purports to show is ambiguous, I believe there is good reason to believe that its source can be traced in part to the failure of adequate representation across some, if not all, of the five dimensions of democratic politics listed above. Since representation is based largely on trust, when representation fails, trust will inevitably decline.

In political life, betrayed trust can take a number of forms, and here I am concerned with failures in the trust that is central to the representative relationship. Rather than discuss the institutions I list above in distinct paragraphs, I will consider the several ways in which representatives can fail to fulfill the trust placed in them, and describe which among the institutions can fail in that way: via exclusion, via apparently self-interested decision-making, and via unjustified compromise.

The dominant way in which the representative relationship can fail to live up to the trust that is central to it is via exclusion. Recall that above I described representation in modern democracies as fundamentally about inclusion: the size of political communities in the modern era is such that politics is effectively impossible without representation, which serves as a way to ensure that the voices of the many are heard in relatively smaller decision-making environments. So long as voices are heard, the representation is effective, and the trust that is key to the representative relationship is respected. One observation to make here is that the inclusion that representation offers is not necessarily contingent on trying to make sure that all those who are represented have their preferences met or their interests served. Instead, the inclusion that representation offers has more to do with the perception that voices are genuinely heard, and that deliberation with respect to the best policy does not systematically exclude the views of some segments of the population.[9] The reason for making this observation is not only the obvious one that, in a heterogeneous community, it will be impossible to choose policies that satisfy everyone. It is also to observe that, in a community where representation functions effectively (i.e., when the trust that is central to it is respected in an ongoing manner), citizens will not even expect that all policies will be those that they prefer. A spirit of reciprocity can persist so long as inclusivity persists in the form of adequate representation.

With the exception of civil society organizations and political parties, exclusion is the most likely source of the violation of representative trust. Indeed, it is plausible to suppose that the widespread reports of declining trust in legislative and executive branches of government across Western democracies is linked to the perception that these institutions are producing decisions that exclude consideration of the views of the governed. When citizens believe that political actors are out of touch, or that they are acting selfishly, they are suggesting that representative trust is being violated. Similarly, when I cited the historical case of Boston school desegregation above, the complaint made against the judge who ordered the extreme measures was that he had inadequately considered the views of those who were likely to be affected by his decisions. To the extent that these are, or are perceived to be, violations of representative trust, they are violations that are the result of exclusion.[10]

Similarly, national symbols can be exclusive and therefore not perceived to be adequately representative. As a result, in some cases, they find insufficient support among a population to be genuinely representative. National symbols can come to be perceived as exclusionary in at least two different ways. One way is when a majority of the population adopts a symbol that is deliberately exclusionary: the commitment of the American South to the Confederate flag is one such example. A second way is historical: a symbol might be adopted by a community and be inclusive at a particular moment in history, but over time become exclusionary due to demographic or ideological shifts. The shift to permitting the uniform requirements of the Royal Canadian Mounted Police (RCMP) to be modified, so that Sikhs could join without having to don the traditional Stetson, was motivated by a desire to avoid the perception that the RCMP, a Canadian national institution, had become exclusive. The decisions to appoint women (and then immigrant women) to the position of Canada's governor general were made in part to illustrate that a significant ceremonial position in Canada was not the exclusive preserve of white men – that is, to ensure that the population continued to think of the position as representative of all Canadians.

Exclusion is not the only way in which trust can be betrayed in political life. The perception that decisions made by representatives are not in the interests of those who have placed their trust in them is a second significant way that representative trust can be violated. This is particularly a danger for those who operate in legislative and executive institutions, where decisions can often be made in ways (or decisions can be communicated in ways) that are perceived as failing to meet the interests or preferences of citizens at large. The trust violation here is distinct from the violation at the heart of exclusion: exclusion violates trust by explicitly or implicitly ignoring the views of some people during decision-making processes, but it does not necessarily require the perception that these decisions are intentionally designed to deny the interests and preferences of the electorate. On the other hand, the trust that is violated here is the trust that decisions will be made with the good-faith aim of meeting the interests of the electorate, and at least the appearance is that this care often has not been taken. Political representatives in the United States, for instance, were recently punished for appearing to ignore the interests of citizens at large by deciding to prop up certain key companies and industries, which had been guilty of the corruption and fraud that played a key role in the economic collapse; here, the trust that citizens felt had been violated was the trust that the government makes decisions in the best interest of citizens rather than corporate giants.

Finally, representative trust can be violated when compromises are perceived to be unjustifiably made. This form of trust violation is likeliest in the cases of civil society organizations, which are typically thought of as zealous defenders of a set of values, or protectors of a specific set of interests. When these organizations are perceived to compromise – in particular, when they are taken to be settling for "less" than what they've asked for or are entitled to – trust may be violated. It is worth pointing out, additionally, since this volume is centrally concerned with trust in multicultural and multiethnic political communities, that the violation of trust in the face of unjustified compromise is a significant risk in divided societies, where political parties are perceived to represent the interests of one specific group rather than the political community as a whole. In these cases, representatives are often given only a short leash to negotiate, and movements towards compromise with "enemies" are heavily scrutinized for signs of weakness and selling out. Indeed, representatives in divided societies may be treated more like delegates than trustees – as having a mandate that they are entrusted to promote, rather than the opportunity to exercise judgment according to their perception of the best interests of those they represent.[11]

MECHANISMS FOR REMEDYING BETRAYED TRUST

Trust itself cannot be repaired directly. As I suggested above, trust is part cognitive, in the sense that extending trust is partly a matter of weighing known risks for and against extending trust; and it is partly psychological, with the result that whether or not trust will be extended depends on a set of factors unique to the one extending the trust – factors that may be impossible to predict or control. Thus, in suggesting mechanisms with which to respond when trust is betrayed, it is important to realize that what we are in fact doing is attempting to create (or recreate) the *conditions* under which trust is likely to be extended. Recall that trust requires accepting a certain vulnerability to the actions of others; when trust has been betrayed, people feel poorly served by having accepted that vulnerability. In very general terms, then, remedying betrayed trust will require eliminating a considerable degree of the vulnerability that accompanies trusting acts, so that potential trusters can act "as if" they trust others. The reason for calling this phenomenon "as-if" trust is clear enough: if the vulnerability associated with extending and rewarding trust is eliminated entirely, we are no longer dealing in the realm of trust. Rather, these institutions are meant to create an environment in which limited cooperation, largely absent trust, can transpire. Once this as-if trust is rewarded enough, trust itself may grow in its place.

Typically, three different categories of policies are charged, in democracies, with protecting an environment in which trust is extended on a regular basis. These are transparency policies, accountability policies, and minority rights protection policies. Policies that demand transparency require that government officials make their decision-making public, or that they be open to demands for access to information, and so on (O'Neill 2002). The purpose of these policies is to give the citizenry the sense that they are not being fooled; the citizenry has access to the same information as political actors have, so they can evaluate whether decisions are being made properly. Accountability policies are those that hold decision-makers to account – regular elections are the most common of accountability policies (Rosanvallon 2008). In parliamentary democracies, question period is also an opportunity to hold the government to account. And finally, minority protection policies are those that protect the minority from having their rights violated simply because the majority might prefer to implement policies with that consequence. Knowing that their rights are protected permits minorities to extend trust to political actors.

The policies described above are meant to prevent the erosion of trust relations, and when they fail, one way to attempt to rebuild trust is to re-secure their successful implementation. Elections are certainly the most effective way to rebuild trust that has been betrayed by our elected representatives or party representatives. We can say more, however, about responding to betrayed trust with respect to the other institutions I delineated above. In the legal environment, the opportunities for appeal, and to reverse decisions, enables betrayed trust to be remedied to some extent.[12] When American courts began reversing decades-long discriminatory legislation enacted against African Americans, one thing they were doing was creating opportunities for African Americans to extend trust to political actors in the United States. Civil society organizations, whose supporters believe that their representatives have compromised, can remedy betrayed trust via attempts to justify compromises, and by further attempts at displaying aggressive lobbying on behalf of their supporters. Modification of national symbols to signal inclusivity can shift the public response to, and support for, these symbols.

CONCLUSIONS

The purpose of this chapter, as I said at the outset, was to delineate the ways in which democratic institutions rely on representation and, since representation is fundamentally about trust, to illustrate the myriad ways in which trust is implicated in modern representative democracies. The decline of trust in modern democracies can, in large part, be attributed to the failure of political actors across a range of domains to fulfill the representative trust that has been placed in them. The account I offered is by no means exhaustive, and others may have distinct ways of categorizing the political actors that play important roles in our politics. But the intention was to indicate that representation is not carried out merely by our elected representatives; it is a mistake to limit our analysis of representation and representative trust to that domain alone. Understanding the function of trust in each of these domains enables us to better understand, as I hope to have shown, the ways that trust can break down – as a result of exclusion, of appearances of self-interested decision-making, or of unjustified compromise – and therefore the ways that trust can be remedied once it has done so. Creating the conditions under which trust can be rebuilt is, to some degree, institution specific, and the purpose of the brief analysis in this chapter is to offer some insight on the institution-specific trust-remedying strategies that can be pursued in the event of the breakdown of representative trust.

NOTES

1 These terms are all deployed in the literature on trust, and although they have slightly distinct meanings, they are all intended to convey the non-cognitive aspect of extending trust.

2 In *Trust, Democracy, and Multicultural Challenges* (2012), I assess what it means to trust people as a matter of course in political communities, and attribute it in large part to a shared public culture which provides cues that insiders take as evidence of trustworthiness in others.

3 For discussions of the merits and demerits of descriptive representation, see Mansbridge (1999) and Dovi (2002).

4 Though, as Onora O'Neill has observed, too much transparency can be bad for trust, by signaling to those who are subject to additional transparency that they are not worthy of trust (see O'Neill 2002).

5 The meaning of "fair" is evidently ambiguous. For now, I am taking the term to be a synonym for "inclusive."

6 Several years ago, when tomatoes across the United States were said to be at risk for carrying toxins, a local Cambridge, MA, sandwich shop posted a sign about its tomatoes: "You can eat our tomatoes safely. They are Canadian and they love hockey." The humour rests on the widespread view that hockey is genuinely Canada's national sport.

7 For more discussion of "public culture," see Festenstein (2009), Miller (1995), and Lenard (2007).

8 For discussion of the ways in which trust is evidence resistant, see Weinstock (1999). See also more generally Gambetta (1988).

9 For a discussion of the importance of inclusion in deliberation, see Pearse (2008).

10 To be fair, another likely explanation for the strength of the anti-busing movement in Boston was the prevalent racism that made white Americans fear contact with African Americans.

11 The challenge of politics in severely divided societies, in which trust is conspicuously absent, is described well in O'Kelly (2006).

12 For a more extensive discussion of the judiciary and trust, see Ely (1980).

REFERENCES

Alford, John R. 2001. "We're All in This Together: The Decline of Trust in Government, 1958–1996." In *What Is It about Government That Americans Dislike?*, edited by John R. Hibbing and Elizabeth Theiss-Morse, 28–46. Cambridge: Cambridge University Press.

Anderson, Christopher J., André Blais, Shaun Bowler, Todd Donovan, and Ola Listhaug. 2005. *Losers' Consent: Elections and Democratic Legitimacy*. Oxford: Oxford University Press.

Baier, Annette. 1994. *Moral Prejudices: Essays on Ethics*. Cambridge, MA: Harvard University Press.

Burke, Edmund. 1774. "Speech to the Electors of Bristol." *Online Library of Liberty*. Accessed 22 August 2011. http://oll.libertyfund.org/title/659/20392.

Chambers, Simone, and Jeffrey Kopstein. 2001. "Bad Civil Society." *Political Theory* 29, no. 6: 837–65.

Cohen, Jean. 1999. "Trust, Voluntary Association and Workable Democracy: The Contemporary American Discourse of Civil Society." In *Democracy and Trust*, edited by Mark Warren, 208–48. Cambridge: Cambridge University Press.

Dovi, Suzanne. 2002. "Preferable Descriptive Representatives: Will Just Any Woman, Black, or Latino Do?" *American Political Science Review* 94, no. 4: 729–43.

Ely, John Hart. 1980. *Democracy and Distrust: A Theory of Judicial Review*. Cambridge, MA: Harvard University Press.

Eulau, Heinz, John C. Wahlke, William Buchanan, and Leroy C. Ferguson. 1959. "The Role of the Representative: Some Empirical Observations on the Theory of Edmund Burke." *American Political Science Review*, 53, no. 3: 742–56.

Festenstein, Matthew. 2009. "National Identity, Political Trust and the Public Realm." *Critical Review of International Social and Political Philosophy* 12, no. 2: 279–96.

Gambetta, Diego. 1988. "Can We Trust Trust?" In *Trust: Making and Breaking Cooperative Relationships*, edited by Diego Gambetta, 213–37. Oxford: Basil Blackwell.

Hardin, Russell. 2006. "The Street-Level Epistemology of Trust." In *Organizational Trust: A Reader*, edited by Roderick Moreland Kramer, 21–47. Oxford: Oxford University Press.

Hetherington, Mark J. 2005. *Why Trust Matters: Declining Political Trust and the Demise of American Liberalism*. Princeton: Princeton University Press.

Jones, Karen. 1996. "Trust as an Affective Attitude." *Ethics* 107, no. 1: 4–25.

Lenard, Patti Tamara. 2007. "Shared Public Culture: A Reliable Source of Trust." *Contemporary Political Theory*: 6, no. 4: 385–404.

– 2012. *Trust, Democracy, and Multicultural Challenges*. University Park: Pennsylvania State University Press.

Mansbridge, Jane. 1999. "Should Blacks Represent Blacks and Women Represent Women? A Contingent 'Yes.'" *The Journal of Politics* 61, no. 3: 628–57.

Mill, John Stuart. 1991 [1862]. *Considerations on Representative Government*. In *On Liberty and Other Essays*, edited by John Gray, 205–469. Oxford: Oxford University Press.

Miller, David. 1995. *On Nationality*. Oxford: Oxford University Press.

O'Kelly, Ciaran. 2006. "Public Institutions, Overlapping Consensus and Trust." *Critical Review of International Social and Political Philosophy* 9, no. 4: 559–72.

O'Neill, Onora. 2002. *Autonomy and Trust in Bioethics*. Cambridge: Cambridge University Press.

Pearse, Hilary. 2008. "Institutional Design and Citizen Deliberation." In *Designing Deliberative Democracy*, edited by Mark E. Warren and Hilary Pearse, 70–84. Cambridge: Cambridge University Press.

Plotke, David. 1997. "Representation Is Democracy." *Constellations* 4, no. 1: 19–34.

Rosanvallon, Pierre. 2008. *Counter-Democracy: Politics in an Age of Distrust*. Cambridge: Cambridge University Press.

Van de Walle, Steven, Steven Van Roosbroek, and Geert Bouckaert. 2008. "Trust in the Public Sector: Is There Any Evidence for a Long-Term Decline?" *International Review of Administrative Sciences* 74, no. 1: 47–64.

Weinstock, Daniel. 1999. "Building Trust in Divided Societies." *Journal of Political Philosophy* 7, no. 3: 287–307.

Wingo, Ajume H. 2003. *Veil Politics in Liberal Democratic States*. Cambridge: Cambridge University Press.

5

Vigilance, Trust, and "Fine Risks" in the Minefield of Multinational Democracies

Dimitrios Karmis and Darren O'Toole

In recent years, some authors have argued that generalized distrust is a problem for democracy, while various forms of mistrust – especially vigilance – are central to democracy and can be compatible with trust (e.g., Rosanvallon 2006; Lenard 2008). In what sense is vigilance key to multinational democracy? In what form is it reconcilable with trust? To what extent is it context dependent? These questions concerning the relationship between vigilance, democracy, and trust are becoming increasingly important in light of two major contemporary phenomena.

First, as Pierre Rosanvallon writes, we are experiencing the "rise of the *society of [mistrust]*" (2008: 9),[1] which brings into greater relief "the variety of democratic *experiences*" long overlooked by historians and political theorists largely preoccupied by the "electoral representative" dimension of democracy (5). This neglected dimension, inseparable from the "history of real democracies" (3), is what Rosanvallon calls "counter-democracy," not understood as the opposite of democracy, "but rather [as] a form of democracy that reinforces the usual electoral democracy as a kind of buttress, a democracy of indirect powers disseminated throughout society – in other words, a durable democracy of [mistrust], which complements episodic democracy of the usual electoral-representative system" (8).[2] This democratic form of political mistrust (which one could briefly define as society's responses to failures, incomplete achievements, and distortions of representative electoral democracy) is strengthened by the fact that, owing to scientific, macro-economic, and sociological factors, we are now experiencing a structurally marked "erosion of trust in contemporary society" (9), which is fertile ground for both mistrust and distrust. Counter-democracy is expressed and organized mainly through three modes (i.e., "counter-powers"): "oversight, forms of prevention and testing of judgement" (8). Yet – and this is where this chapter's introductory questions seem unavoidable – vigilance proves to be the primary component of oversight (33–41) and the central pillar of counter-democracy.

Second, as the work of the Groupe de recherche sur les sociétés plurinationales (GRSP) has emphasized, we have witnessed "a new and distinctive type of political association that is coming into prominence at the dawn of the twenty-first century – 'multinational democracy'" (Tully 2001: 1). In every case, this new type of democracy has largely resulted from struggles for recognition by one or more minority nations facing a majority nation that clings – in a more or less authoritarian manner – to the (single) nation-state model. The constitutive struggles have left lasting marks on numerous aspects of multinational democracy, of which two seem particularly important in this context. First, on the level of collective memory, constituting nations – especially minority nations – have generally been marked by traumatic events, which have generated strong distrust that can easily resurface, especially during periods of major political tensions. Second, on the level of culture and political institutions, both national political communities and the multination are marked by counter-democracy. In effect, in the multinational context, the people's political mistrust of electoral-representative democracy goes hand in hand with the minority nations' political mistrust of the majority nation, leading to the establishment of various "counter-powers," often through consociational or federal arrangements.[3] In other words, studying the relationship between vigilance and trust is key to understanding multinational democracies.

In his influential book entitled *Republicanism: A Theory of Freedom and Government* (1997), Philip Pettit has been one of the few authors to confront head-on the issue of reconciling vigilance with trust in the same structure of civility. He even makes this reconciliation a necessary condition of what he defines as the republican ideal *par excellence*, namely, freedom as non-domination. While his work does not focus specifically on multinational democracies, Pettit argues that the ideal of freedom as non-domination favours and strengthens "the tradition of defending minority or indigenous rights," a tradition that he – like many before him – bundles into the excessively vague epithet "multiculturalist," though he admits the term is imperfect (144).[4] Pettit believes that "freedom as non-domination is a pluralist ideal" (146), and that this pluralism includes the plurality of nations within a single state. We will return to this.

In the spirit of the republican tradition, Pettit emphasizes the need for vigilance as "the price of liberty," namely "eternal vigilance," especially "in relation to those who hold power within the state" (250). Now, while acknowledging that there are reasons that can lead us to think that such vigilance "may seem to fit uncomfortably with a dispensation of trust" (263), Pettit devotes a large part of a chapter to showing that "vigilance does not necessarily require a refusal of reliance, or an attitude of diffidence in reliance" (ibid.). To what extent does Pettit's thinking offer a way of reconciling vigilance and trust that is appropriate for multinational democracies? In this chapter, we will argue that while Pettit develops relevant conceptual distinctions and rightly insists on the importance of vigilance for freedom, his analysis underestimates the depth of the tension between vigilance and trust, especially in the context of multinational democracies.

Using the example of Canada to emphasize these points,[5] we divide the chapter into three parts. First, we situate Pettit's attempt to reconcile vigilance and trust in the framework of his general search for a structure of civility appropriate for a modern republic. Second, we argue that the historical dynamic of distrust that tends to prevail in multinational democracies considerably undermines Pettit's argument that constant vigilance involves only "expressive distrust" – different from "felt distrust" – and that expressive distrust is therefore compatible with trust. Third, we contend that one of the principal mechanisms that Pettit counts on to contribute to trusting relationships in contexts of constant vigilance – the mechanism he calls the "intangible hand" – could, on the contrary, result in greater distrust (both expressive *and* felt) among members of a minority nation. We will use the Durham Report and René Lévesque's "fine risks" (*beaux risques*) as examples that illustrate two types of counterproductive uses of the intangible hand.

NEO-REPUBLICANISM, FREEDOM AS NON-DOMINATION, AND THE STRUCTURE OF CIVILITY

As Jean-Fabien Spitz notes, in political philosophy since the 1980s, mainly around the work of Pettit and Quentin Skinner, we have seen the development of "an original current that claims to be republican and to open a third way between Rawlsian-inspired liberalism and communitarian criticism" (2001: 7; our translation). This current is often referred to as "neo-republican" because it seeks to extirpate the republican ideal of freedom as non-domination from the less desirable aspects of premodern republicanism.[6] Spitz points out that neo-republicans criticize contemporary liberalism for overlooking "certain 'hidden' forms of domination and inequality," thereby "favouring a rise in communitarianism and disaffection for democratic regimes" (ibid.). From a neo-republican perspective, the ideal of freedom as non-domination, unlike the liberal conception of negative freedom, makes it possible to highlight and combat the less obvious forms of domination and inequality that often affect members of minorities and marginalized groups. This is what leads Pettit to assert that "freedom as non-domination is a pluralist ideal" (146), and to try to "show that multicultural concerns can be supported by an appeal to that ideal" (144). But what is freedom as non-domination? And in what way does it require a structure of civility reconciling trust and vigilance?

Pettit devotes the first chapters of his book to redefining the republican ideal from a neo-republican perspective. In his view, the republican ideal is neither positive freedom as self-control, as some claim, nor negative freedom as non-interference. It is instead "the conception of freedom as non-domination which requires that no one is able to interfere on an arbitrary basis – at their pleasure – in the choices of the free person" (271). Unlike the liberal conception of negative freedom as non-interference, which tends to prevail in contemporary democracies, republicanism sees the *capacity* to interfere *arbitrarily*, rather than interference as such, as what leads to domination and loss of freedom. Domination "may occur without actual interference: it requires only the capacity for interference." Conversely, "interference may occur without any domination: if the interference is not arbitrary then it will not dominate" (272). This is to say that "freedom as non-domination requires that a person not be exposed to the possibility of interference on an arbitrary basis" (146), in the sense of being "controlled by the *arbitrium* – the will or judgment – of the interferer" (272). This ideal is pluralistic in that it is especially "dynamic." Citizens' interests and ideas can never be determined in a definitive manner:

As people interact, and organize, and affirm certain identities – say, identities as women or workers or members of an indigenous population – they are always liable to see what had been unquestioned, barely visible patterns in their relations with certain others as indices of a dominating relationship ... the notion of arbitrary power, ultimately the notion of domination, is developmental; so too is the complementary ideal of freedom as non-domination. The requirements of such freedom ... are subject to constant reinterpretation and review as new interests and ideas emerge and materialize in the society. (146–7)

In Pettit's terms, the ideal of freedom as non-domination is thus an "open-ended ideal" that facilitates the articulation of "diverse grievances," an ideal whose substance transforms through interpretation and re-interpretation "in the progressively changing and clarifying perspectives of a living society" (147).

In the middle of his book, Pettit concentrates on explaining the relevance of this ideal of freedom and the possibility of building "a modern image of republican institutions on that basis" (129). He then argues that these institutions cannot function without a supporting structure of civility reconciling trust and vigilance. According to Pettit, "if the state is to be able to find a place in the hearts of the people, and if the laws of the state are to be truly effective, those laws will have to work in synergy with norms that are established, or that come to be established, in the realm of civil society" (242). We should note that the interdependency of institutions and laws, on the one hand, and social norms embodied in civility or civic virtues,[7] on the other hand, is a constitutive feature of the republican tradition that has spread to other traditions of thought in recent decades, particularly among many liberal authors. As Will Kymlicka and Wayne Norman noted in the mid-1990s, "it has become clear that procedural-institutional mechanisms to balance self-interest are not enough, and that some level of civic virtue and public-spiritedness is required" (1994: 359).[8] As we wrote in the introduction, Pettit's position stands out because he explicitly argues that the "eternal vigilance" characteristic of the republican tradition, especially "in relation to those who hold power within the state" (250), "does not necessarily require a refusal of reliance, or an attitude of diffidence in reliance" (263). More precisely, Pettit imagines a structure of republican civility in which vigilance and trust are both widespread and in harmony. Thus, while acknowledging that "constant" (or "eternal") vigilance is imperative for maintaining freedom as non-domination, Pettit nonetheless asserts the importance of having personal trust, of trusting the persons in power instead of just the institutions – or else republicans "would be denying that the very tranquility and boldness that are traditionally associated with republican liberty is ever properly available" (ibid.). Put differently, republicans "would be saying that the price on which republican liberty is available, eternal vigilance, is a price which ensures that that very liberty loses much of its value" (ibid.). In the remainder of this chapter, we contend that although Pettit is right to insist on the importance of vigilance for freedom, his analysis underestimates the tension between vigilance and trust, especially in the case of multinational democracies.

REPUBLICAN VIGILANCE AND THE DISTINCTION BETWEEN FELT DISTRUST AND EXPRESSIVE DISTRUST

What is republican vigilance? According to Pettit, it is "the virtue of remaining alert, especially in dealing with powerful authorities, to the possibility that others may be behaving in a corrupt, sectional fashion" (263). In other words, it is a virtue of watchfulness based on the established wisdom that "power particularly needs to be watched, because power is essentially corrupting" (250). How can this vigilance be reconciled with maintaining personal trust in leaders? Pettit answers this question by establishing a twofold distinction that he sees as the key to his argument.

First, Pettit distinguishes between *having trust in someone* and *expressing trust in someone*, between *felt* and *expressed* forms of trust: "to trust someone in the sense of having trust in them involves confidently assuming reliance upon them. But whether or not I have such trust, I may or may not choose to express trust" (263). Second, considering that what applies to trust also applies to distrust, Pettit establishes a similar distinction between *distrusting someone* and *expressing distrust for someone*, between *felt* and *expressed* forms of distrust. According to him, there is "no tension" between personal trust and "the emphasis on maintaining eternal vigilance" (264). The lack of tension is explained by the fact that here Pettit understands republican vigilance as a form of expressive distrust:

The republican recommendation is that, whatever confidence people feel in the authorities, they will have all the more reason to feel such confidence – to enjoy such personal trust – if they always insist on the authorities going through the required hoops in order to prove themselves virtuous. To be vigilant in this sense will not be to feel an attitude of distrust towards the authorities – or at least not necessarily – but to maintain a demanding pattern of expectations in their regard. (264)

This means that republican vigilance involves setting up various institutional checks and constraints: "this may be the only way of guarding against arbitrary will and coping with corruptibility" (265). How can we ensure that authorities do not interpret expressive distrust toward them as felt distrust? Pettit maintains that "it is ... possible for people to make it clear to the authorities that they are espousing this *dual posture* ... They can go through the established routines of expressive distrust *and* show in other less established ways that actually they feel considerable personal trust in the authorities" (ibid.; emphasis added). In the end, people must more or less express something like this: "we are watching you closely because history shows that power very often corrupts, but we nonetheless have trust in you."

To what extent is such emphasis on vigilance relevant? First, we should point out that the distinction between *expressive trust/distrust* and *felt trust/distrust* is relevant from a heuristic point of view. As we will see, it is how Pettit uses it that is more problematic.[9] Second, Pettit's emphasis on vigilance seems to have interesting potential in terms of analyzing the dynamics of trust, distrust, and mistrust in multinational democracies. For example, multinational federal democracies may be analyzed as a mechanism of institutional vigilance for territorialized minority nations.[10] Pettit recognizes from the beginning that "a republic in which there are different groupings and different interests needs a politics of difference" (248). Moreover, vigilance can be conceived of as a necessary precondition for "partial forms of civility" (249). These forms of civility are associated with specific groups but they serve the shared ideal of freedom as non-domination – that is, they can pave the way to "contestation" when minority nations face institutions they regard "as alien impositions" (241). In Canada, this brings to mind the adoption of the Constitution Act, 1982 without Québec's consent, and the later claims and challenges that led to the Meech Lake and Charlottetown constitutional discussions.

That being said, we have to point out a major limitation on Pettit's analysis of vigilance. By separating the felt and expressive dimensions in a very rigid way, and seeking at all costs to make vigilance as expressive distrust the key to a harmonious structure of civility, Pettit seems to underestimate the inherent tension between trust and vigilance. We agree with Pettit that such a tension has the potential to be creative and compatible with civility. Nonetheless, we maintain that it has to be conceived of in a significantly more contextual way, and that we must consider the possibility of failures and the need for strategies to maintain or re-establish a balance between trust and vigilance. As Onora O'Neill notes, "since trust has to be placed without guarantees, it is inevitably sometimes misplaced: others let us down and we let others down. When this happens, trust and relationships based on trust are both damaged" (2002: 6–7). By somehow taking it for granted that vigilance must be associated with the *expressive distrust/felt trust* formula (conceived as universally possible and optimal), Pettit misjudges the importance and value of citizens' judgment in context.

This criticism often plays out in multinational democracies. Indeed, as we mentioned in the introduction, in such democratic minefields, the historical dynamics of strong (expressive *and* felt) distrust that tend to prevail between a majority nation and one or more minority nations calls for something other than Pettit's formula – at least in periods of seriously eroded trust. In Canada, for instance, during the period following 1982, it seemed that the general rule of expressive distrust had to first yield to the practical wisdom of the political actors. In such a context, there is every reason to believe that it is often the opposite formula that will be optimal for those who hope to build or rebuild trust: expressing trust while maintaining prudent, discreet vigilance, knowing that the background context is one of distrust. On the one hand, in such a case, trust is what has been seriously weakened, and it will be all the more difficult to build or rebuild it since there will be recalcitrant people – and even very determined opponents – in every camp. On the other hand, distrust is then a well-known reality and so does not need to be expressed. Of course, mistrust, in the form of vigilance, remains necessary. However, its expression may be limited to flexible procedural mechanisms; otherwise we run the risk of fanning the already strong flames of distrust.[11] Based on examples drawn from the history of Québec-Canada relations, Pettit's views on the "intangible hand" also need considerable revisions in order to provide a credible account for trust enhancement in multinational democracies.

THE RISKS OF THE "INTANGIBLE HAND"

In order to fully grasp the logic of the mechanism of the intangible hand in Pettit's *Republicanism*, it is important to understand how the author connects civility to trust. According to Pettit, "republican laws need the support of republican norms" – what he calls "civility" – and he wonders "what the republican state can do in order to facilitate the appearance and operation of the required civility" (251). In Pettit's view, civility will not flourish under "heavy-handed patterns of control" (254), or what he terms the "iron hand" mechanism. He instead prefers the mechanism of the intangible hand based on the premise that "people care about the regard of others" (ibid.). Pettit explains that "the intangible hand helps to nurture a pattern of behaviour by holding out the prospect that its manifestation will earn the good opinion of others and/or the failure to manifest it will earn the bad" (ibid.). In this way, "civility carries an inbuilt reward, and the lack of civility an inbuilt penalty" (ibid.).

How is civility connected to trust? For Pettit, "itemizing the need for widespread civility" and "indicating what the state can do to promote such civility" is "arguing in effect for a civil society where suitable forms of trust are exercised and rewarded" (261). One *initial variant* of the intangible hand may be a mechanism of social control that spreads civility and thereby develops different forms of trust. A *second variant* of the intangible hand is that "overtures of personal trust" can unleash the intangible hand mechanism (267–8). In this last section, we will see that when these two variants of the intangible hand mechanism operate in the context of asymmetrical power relations between a majority nation and a minority nation or nations characteristic of multinational democracies like Canada, there is a high risk that they will prove inefficient, if not completely counterproductive. As an illustration of the first variant, we will see that the Durham Report applied the intangible hand's logic to the project of assimilating French Canadians. As an illustration of the second variant, we will see that René Lévesque's "fine risks" were overtures of trust that failed to effectively activate the mechanism of the intangible hand, and, because of that failure, actually deepened the minority nation's distrust of the majority.

The Role of the Intangible Hand in the Assimilation Dynamic

As we have seen, according to Pettit, one of the state's tasks is "to establish the salient legitimacy of its laws" (252), and by extension to generate "a considerable measure of belief and respect" (241). Moreover, internalizing certain values involves "identifying with the groups whose interests are associated with those values" (257). In the Canadian federation, this means that both provincial governments and the central government have to establish the legitimacy of their laws and to make use of the intangible hand to generate trust. Fostering "a considerable measure of belief and respect," as well as developing an identity shared by the minorities and the majority, is a particularly challenging task for the central government of such a large and diversified country. Here one can easily think of the postwar efforts to foster a sense of shared Canadian national identity by making central institutions more "prestigious": the CBC, the National Film Board, national museums and art galleries, the delegation of Royal prerogatives to the governor general, a Canadian-born governor general, a Canadian national anthem (as opposed to "God Save the Queen"), the maple leaf flag, Canada Day (formerly Confederation Day), the repatriation and renaming of the Constitution, and so on. However, in Canada, the idea of using the intangible hand and infusing "national" institutions with enough symbolic capital to establish the legitimacy of the regime and create from scratch a shared national identity is an old one that predates the federal regime. It is clearly found in the thought of Lord Durham, whose 1839 report is arguably the founding text of this discursive chain.[12]

It is well known that Durham recommended that the Canadiens be assimilated.[13] Initially, he seemed to entertain the possibility of overcoming their resistance "in the most violent manner" (2004: 154). In effect, he believed that the "experience of the two Unions in the British Isles," namely the forced annexation of Scotland and Ireland, "may teach us how effectually the strong arm of a popular legislature would compel the obedience of the refractory population" (159). Durham explicitly evoked, then, what Pettit calls "the discipline of the iron hand," a "discipline associated with the deployment of centralized state sanctions and with the monitoring required for the application of those sanctions" (255). However, Durham acknowledged that the proximity of the United States made recourse to any such authoritarian methods virtually impossible: "The maintenance of an absolute form of government on any part of the North American Continent, can never continue for any long time, without exciting a general feeling in the United States against a power of which the existence is secured by means so odious to the people" (2004: 152). Due to the geopolitical realities of North America, Durham concluded that the "only power that can be effectual at once in coercing the present disaffection, and hereafter obliterating the nationality of French Canadians, is that of a numerical majority of a loyal and English population" (154). To achieve this result, Durham advocated the union of Upper and Lower Canada: "the union of the two legitimate Provinces would not only give a clear English majority, but one which would be increased every year by the influence of English emigration" (159). The first mechanism that Durham suggested to overcome the Canadiens' resistance was thus a policy of massive English immigration.

At first glance, when Durham wrote of "subjecting the Province [of Lower Canada] to the vigorous rule of an English majority" (2004: 159), it strikes the reader as a rather crass application of the tyranny of the majority. However, he noted that it had not at all been through the "iron fist" of state coercion that the English-speaking population, once it formed the majority in the state of Louisiana, managed to overcome the resistance of the French-speaking population:

> On the single fact, that in the constitution of Louisiana it is specified that the public acts of the State shall be "in the language in which the constitution of the United States is written," it has been inferred that the federal Government in the most violent manner swept away the use of the French language and laws, and subjected the French population to some peculiar disabilities which deprived them, in fact, of an equal voice in the government of their State. Nothing can be more contrary to the fact. (154)

While Durham advised that the "alteration of the character of the Province ought to be immediately entered on, and firmly," he added that this should be "cautiously followed up" (151). Like Pettit, who suggests that "the state must be very careful not to introduce heavy-handed patterns of control" and rather promote the intangible hand (254), Durham suggested a gentler measure to achieve the objective of assimilating the French-speaking population. According to him, "The influence of perfectly equal and popular institutions in *effacing distinctions of race without disorder or oppression*, and with little more than the ordinary animosities of party in a free country, is memorably exemplified in the history of the state of Louisiana, the laws and population of which were French at the time of its cession to the American Union" (2004: 154; emphasis added).

In order to follow Durham's thought, we need to take into account the fact that he was basing his arguments on the premise that, within any population, there always exists a fringe whose ambition coincides with their natural talent. Durham explicitly referred to Adam Smith as the source of this premise (162). According to Smith, "Nature, when she formed man for society, endowed him with an original desire to please, and an original aversion to offend his brethren ... She rendered their approbation most flattering and most agreeable to him for its own sake; and their disapprobation most mortifying and most offensive" (1976a: 116). This need for approbation generates competition for recognition and honour. In *The Wealth of Nations*, Smith wrote:

> Men desire to have some share in the management of public affairs chiefly on account of the importance which it gives them. Upon the power which the greater part of the leading men, the natural aristocracy of every country, have of preserving or defending their respective importance, depends the stability and duration of every system of free government. In the attacks which those leading men are continually making upon the importance of one another, and in the defence of their own, consists the whole play of domestic faction and ambition. The leading men of America, like those of all other countries, desire to preserve their own importance. (1976b: 622)

As we have seen, according to Pettit, the intangible hand involves "the gentle, sustained sort of pressure exercised under the desire of regard" (225). Similarly, Smith specifically refers to the intangible hand as a means of channeling the ambition of influential people and of thus ensuring a degree of social control. According to Smith, if the imperial parliament were to open its doors to representatives from among "leading men" in the Thirteen Colonies:

> a new method of acquiring importance, a new and more dazzling object of ambition would be presented to the leading men of each colony. Instead of piddling for the little prizes which are to be found in what may be called the paltry raffle of colony faction; they might then hope, from the presumption which men naturally have in their own ability and good fortune, to draw

some of the great prizes which sometimes come from the wheel
of the great state lottery of British polities. (1976b: 622–3)

In his *Report*, Lord Durham applied exactly the same logic to the
United States, but he substituted the federal Congress of the United
States for the imperial parliament, and Louisiana for Lower Canada.
In addition to numerical superiority, he suggested four other mechanisms that could channel influential people's need for recognition and
approbation, thereby achieving the objective of assimilation: economic
ascendancy, official bilingualism at the local level, official unilingualism at the national level, and a policy of attrition.

First, with respect to numerical superiority, Durham noted that
when Louisiana was annexed to the United States, the "French of
Louisiana, when they were formed into a state, in which they were
a majority, were incorporated into a great nation, of which they
constituted an extremely small part" (2004: 156). Following annexation, English speakers "crowded" into the state, and "year after
year their numbers have become greater, and it is now generally
supposed that they constitute the numerical majority" (ibid.). In
Canada, not only were the 150,000 English speakers in Lower
Canada and the 400,000 in Upper Canada sufficient to ensure
numerical superiority over the 450,000 French Canadians, but the
English majority would "be increased every year by the influence
of English emigration" (159).

Second, it goes without saying that the official language at the
central level was English. Third, with respect to the status of French
language at the local level, Durham remarked that, officially, it was
set out in the Constitution of Louisiana "that the public acts of the
State shall be in the language in which the constitution of the United
States is written." But in fact:

> Every provision was made in Louisiana for securing to both
> races a perfectly equal participation in all the benefits of the
> Government … In all cases in which convenience requires it, the
> different parties use their respective languages in the courts of
> justice, and in both branches of the legislature. In every judicial
> proceeding, all documents which pass between the parties are
> required to be in both languages, and the laws are published
> in both languages. (2004: 155)

Similarly, Durham acknowledged that in Lower Canada, "justice and policy alike require, that while the people continue to use the French language, their Government should take no such means to force the English language upon them as would, in fact, deprive the great mass of the community of the protection of the laws" (2004: 151). It is by recognizing the minority language at the local level that we avoid giving the impression of oppression and thus avoid hostile reactions and disorder. In other words, unilingualism at the central level would act as the first kind of intangible hand postulated by Pettit, namely, "the gentle, sustained sort of pressure exercised under the desire of regard" (225).

Fourth, Durham evoked economic ascendancy as a means to promote the gradual assimilation of French speakers. In Lower Canada, the "English language is gaining ground, as the language of the rich and of the employers of labour *naturally* will" (2004: 151; emphasis added). He wrote that, following the annexation of Louisiana by the United States, "the Americans long crowded into the State *in order to avail themselves of its great natural resources, and its unequalled commercial advantages*; there, as every where else on that continent, their energy and habits of business gradually drew the greater part of the commercial business of the country into their hands; and ... the English form the bulk of *the wealthier classes*" (155–6; emphasis added). He came back to this argument when he expressed certainty that "the French, when once placed, by the legitimate course of events and the working of natural causes, in a minority, would abandon their vain hopes of nationality" (159). According to Durham, "the advantages gained by the English were entirely the result, not of favour, but of their superiority in a perfectly free competition" (156). He insisted a number of times on the "hopeless" economic inferiority of the Canadiens (149). He even claimed that it was to "elevate them from that inferiority that I desire to give to the Canadians our English character," and that he desired "amalgamation still more for the sake of the humbler classes" (ibid.).

According to this logic of political economics, once these mechanisms are in place, we need only to allow the "natural" force of the need for recognition to play its role. Following Louisiana's annexation, the "eye of *every ambitious man* turned naturally to the great centre of federal affairs, and *the high prizes* of federal *ambition*" (Durham 2004: 156; emphasis added). This is where the importance of unilingualism at the level of central public institutions proves essential: "To speak only a language foreign to that of the United States, was consequently a disqualification for a candidate for the posts of either senator or representative; the French *qualified themselves* by learning English, or submitted to the superior advantages of their English competitors" (157; emphasis added).

Finally, time itself is a mechanism for assimilation. Durham recognized that a "considerable time must, of course, elapse before the change of a language can spread over a whole people" (2004: 151). We can see an analogy with the American policy against the Soviet Union in the 1980s: a *policy of attrition* in which superior economic productivity would gradually allow the West to outstrip the Eastern Bloc in the arms race and lead to either economic or military implosion.[14]

Thus, in contradiction with Pettit's aspirations for the "intangible hand," the Durham Report has left not only traces of expressive distrust, but also of a deeply felt distrust that remain clearly discernible in Québec's political discourse today. Marked by the inheritance of the Durham Report, the federal government's use of the intangible hand to make central institutions trustworthy in the eyes of Québec has stained the federal government's reputation there, and risks arousing strong distrust rather than engendering trust.[15] Does the unconditional overture of trust by the minority Québec nation, as a mechanism for unleashing the intangible hand, have a better chance of positively transforming the dynamic of Canada-Québec relations?

The Unconditional Overture of Trust: The "Fine Risks" of the Québec Nation

As mentioned earlier, Pettit advocates a structure of republican civility that reconciles vigilance, expressive distrust, and felt trust. However, he adds that this structure of civility has to leave room for unconditional overtures of trust,[16] otherwise the republican value of freedom could run the risk of looking "less attractive than we suggested" (267). Indeed, he writes: "much of what is best in life comes from overtures of personal trust, as when we initiate relationships of love and friendship by risking ourselves in such acts: by showing that we confidently put ourselves at the mercy of the other person" (ibid.). While such a way of formulating the issue initially seems to respond in part to the criticism we made above, the unconditional overtures of trust that

Pettit advocates as ways of generating trust seem problematic in the framework of multinational democracies. According to Pettit:

> Acts of personal trust can serve in certain contexts – particularly in contexts where the trustee is not entirely constrained by independent sanctions – to express either the message that the trustee is possessed of suitable virtue, or the message that if the trustee does not let down the trustor then they will be taken to have proved themselves suitably virtuous … The act of trust means that the trustee has something to win by proving reliable, something to lose by proving unreliable; it recruits the intangible hand in its own support. (269)

The unconditional overture of trust would thus involve a kind of "cunning of trust" (269). Here, the intangible hand mechanism places subtle pressure on the trusted person (or *trustee*) to comply both with the expectations of the one who has placed trust (or *trustor*), and the expectations of society in general by putting their reputation on the line. Expectations increase the cost of betrayal of trust, and constitute a subtle form of social control. A glance at the Canadian case seems, however, to bring out a major limitation of this mechanism: the risk to minority nations (as beneficiaries) that they will be manipulated by the majority nation (as trustee), due to the lack of a moral sanction within the general society controlled by the majority nation.

First, there are risks that come with unconditional overtures of trust as such. What an unconditional overture of trust requires is specifically that "we voluntarily and explicitly place ourselves *at the mercy of another*" (267), that "we confidently put ourselves *at the mercy of the other person*" (ibid.), or that we undertake "an act of putting [ourselves] *at the mercy of another*" (268; emphasis added). While Isaiah Berlin's definition of negative liberty involves the absence of interference, Pettit argues that it is possible to suffer domination without interference (21–4). As Spitz says, "the absence of effective interference in the exercise of will does not prevent from phenomena of domination and dependency that are just as real obstacles to authentic freedom" (2001: 8; our translation). In other words, the fact of being *at the mercy* of another party implies precisely that effective interference can arise in an arbitrary manner. While Pettit argues that vigilance and freedom as non-domination are "consistent" with personal trust (269), such an act of personal trust entails that we have to abandon a position of "constant" vigilance and freedom as non-domination, and accept in such cases the risk of taking a position of freedom as non-interference. In the end, Pettit abandons the classical republican position for liberalism's, since in this case trust rests on the hope that the other party will act in good faith and not abuse the possibility of interfering arbitrarily when it is effectively within their power to do so, owing to the fact that we are objectively vulnerable.

This vulnerability entails that we abandon not only constant vigilance, but also another fundamental component of counter-democracy which Montesquieu calls, in the context of political freedom, the "faculty to prevent" (qtd in Rosanvallon 2008: 121). According to Rosanvallon, historically, "All politics was thus organized around the idea of *prevention*" and prevention constitutes the original mode of action that structured the political field (2008: 127). Now, when he took what we term here René Lévesque's *first* "fine risk,"[17] the premier of Québec agreed to give up Québec's traditional demand for veto rights over any constitutional amendments, in exchange for an opting-out right with full financial compensation. This made it possible to join forces with seven other provinces and form a common front infamously known as the "Gang of Eight."[18] As Rosanvallon points out, "the people cannot remain free and in control unless they have a sort of 'reservoir of mistrust' in order to mount, if need be, effective opposition against government they themselves have consecrated" (122). The consecrated government was in this case from the Liberal Party of Canada, whose candidates had been elected to the federal parliament in seventy-four of Québec's seventy-five seats in the 1980 election. Following Trudeau's promise to "put their seats on the line" for constitutional reforms, we can question the astuteness of Lévesque's first "fine risk," at least from a republican perspective, since it surrendered the power to refuse, the faculty to prevent. Indeed, Lévesque immediately regretted it, as evidenced by the fact that he submitted a reference to the Québec Court of Appeal in the hopes of confirming Québec's historical claim to a conventional veto (*Re: Amendment to the Canadian Constitution*, 1982).

Second, Pettit's model implies that, for an unconditional overture of trust to unleash the "cunning of trust," there has to be what Russell Hardin calls "encapsulated interests" (2006: 18–20) between the majority and minority nations. We trust people because it is in *their* own interest not to go against *our* interests. In this respect,

Hardin has rightly insisted on the role of reputation as an encapsulated interest (24). As Pettit acknowledges, "the trustor will suffer the cost of the reliance ... But equally the trustee will suffer the loss of the trustor's good opinion" (269). While most of Pettit's examples are about overtures of personal trust at the level of civil society, Rosanvallon rightly points out that the aforementioned reputation is also "the reputation of a power." For this reason, "reputation thus became another of those *invisible institutions* upon which trust is ultimately based" (Rosanvallon 2008: 13). Notably, this is the case in federations, where overtures of trust occur between different federated states, as well as between federated states and the central state.

The result of what we have termed Lévesque's *first* "fine risk" was the imposition of the Constitution Act, 1982 with the consent of neither Québec's National Assembly nor the Québécois people. In other words, "the power to say no ... that informed the earliest conception of legitimate and viable social intervention in the political realm" (Rosanvallon 2008: 127) was seriously affected. Note that the Constitution Act, 1982 is in no way a piece of Canadian legislation, but simply Schedule B of an act of the imperial parliament in London, the Canada Act, 1982 (UK). Even though the act "was not initiated by Imperial *fiat*" (*Reference re: Secession of Quebec*, [1998] 2 SCR 217, para. 35), the Supreme Court of Canada nonetheless recognized "the refusal of the government of Quebec to join in its adoption" (para. 47). The Supreme Court of Canada even wrote "parenthetically" that "the 1982 amendments did not alter the basic division of powers in ss. 91 and 92 of the Constitution Act, 1867, which is the primary textual expression of the principle of federalism in our Constitution agreed upon at Confederation" (ibid.). Yet, in 1981, in *Reference re. Resolution to amend the Constitution,* the Court answered "yes" to the Québec government's question concerning the proposed amendment, which was: "would federal-provincial relationships or the powers, rights or privileges granted or secured by the Constitution of Canada to the provinces, their legislatures or governments be affected?" In any case, insofar as the Charter of Rights and Freedoms sets limits on the supremacy of Parliament, the 1982 amendments have nonetheless affected the *scope* of the powers set out in s. 92 of the Constitution Act, 1867. Moreover, provincial jurisdiction is not limited to those areas found under s. 92, but also notably include the powers in s. 93. In *Protestant School Board* (1984: para 36), the court recognized that the "Canada clause" in Charter s. 23

explicitly targets the "Québec clause" (ss. 72 and 73 of the Charter of the French Language): "It is therefore not surprising that *Bill 101* was very much in the minds of the framers of the Constitution when they enacted s. 23 of the *Charter*." Moreover, distrust was kindled not only by the fact that s. 23 was imposed on Québec without its consent, but also by its very content. In particular, that section opened the door to "bridge schools" (*écoles passerelles*)[19] and local bilingual-ism is still perceived as being a Trojan horse that will gradually under-mine the numerical superiority of French speakers within Québec. It is feared that with this loss will come a loss of control over "local" institutions, which French speakers consider to be *their national* institutions. In other words, in the eyes of many Québec nationalists (who are not necessarily secessionists), s. 23 makes it possible to implement policies recommended in the Durham Report, which then generates strong distrust of the Constitution itself.

What is more conventionally referred to as Premier René Lévesque's "fine risk," but which we term here his *second* "fine risk," began with his decision to accept Brian Mulroney's invitation to submit a list of constitutional amendments so that Québec's National Assembly would be able to sign the Constitution Act, 1982 "with honour and enthu-siasm." It was an unconditional overture of trust on the part of the government of Québec. Even if Québec was weakened, it nonethe-less agreed to trust in the Canadian constitution game. Obviously, the dynamics had changed somewhat following the elections on 2 December 1985, when the Parti Québécois (PQ) yielded power to the Liberal Party of Québec (PLQ) under the leadership of Robert Bourassa. While the PLQ is an umbrella party that runs the gamut from ardent Québec nationalists to staunch federalists, the stakes were the same, namely the weakening of the National Assembly's jurisdic-tion over language. However, the rhetoric of the "conditions" under which Québec would return to the fold of the Canadian constitution should not disguise the fact that Québec had very few coercive tools – power it could use – if its trust were betrayed again. In sum, Lévesque's second "fine risk," which Bourassa inherited, essentially remained part of the dynamic of an *unconditional* overture of trust.

The negotiation of these "conditions" eventually resulted in the 1987 Meech Lake Accord, which had the explicit objective of address-ing the exclusion of Québec from the agreement reached in 1982.[20] The five conditions set by the government of Québec and met by the accord arguably belong to what Tully (2006) calls "healthy distrust"

– something he considers necessary to maintain a veritable relationship of trust and which corresponds *grosso modo* to Pettit's vigilance. Both Tully and Pettit, then, express the need for vigilance and freedom as non-domination. However, this vigilance mostly concerned the *content* of constitutional amendments that would satisfy Québec, and very little the *process* leading to the adoption of such a constitution, precisely because Québec's negotiating position had been weakened to the point that it was unable to make any such *conditional* overture of trust. The result was that in 1990, when the process of ratifying the accord failed *in extremis*, Québec found itself back where it had been in 1982, except that it now had one more failure to address.[21] As such, this additional failure fuelled distrust towards the Canadian federation and the English-speaking majority, leading the sovereigntist movement to almost win the referendum of 1995. It has joined, along with the Durham Report and the Constitution Act, 1982, the list of traumatic events that have deepened the level of distrust. Such distrust not only resurfaces easily – especially in periods of exacerbated political tension – but it is all the more tenacious with the accumulation of negative experiences.

Thus, we see how in the minefield of a multinational democracy such as Canada, where asymmetrical power relationships work against minority nations, unconditional overtures of trust intended to promote the development of a trusting relationship between a majority nation and a minority nation can, on the contrary, add to the already long litany of complaints of historical injustices and thereby strengthen distrust. How can a gesture of trust be made towards a majority nation that does not seem to care much about its reputation in the eyes of the minority nation – which is, historically, more or less the way it goes? One thing is certain: constant vigilance has to be given priority (though not necessarily in the very expressive way conceived by Pettit), and Pettit's unconditional overtures of trust seem imprudent for anyone who wants to break the historical cycle of distrust. As Annette Baier writes, "when we trust we accept vulnerability to others" (1986: 132). This is why vigilance is all the more important in contexts of highly asymmetrical power relations.

CONCLUSION

Rosanvallon's idea that various forms of mistrust – especially vigilance – are central to democracy and can be compatible with trust is promising for understanding the dynamics of trust, distrust, and mistrust in multinational democracies. However, we have seen that despite several merits, Philip Pettit's attempt at reconciling vigilance and trust seems to underestimate the tension between trust and vigilance. By somehow taking it for granted that vigilance must be associated with the *expressive distrust/felt trust* formula (conceived as universally possible and optimal), Pettit neglects the contextual dimension of trust, the importance of situated citizens' judgment, the possibility of failures, and the need for strategies to maintain or re-establish a balance between trust and vigilance.

The historical dynamics of strong (expressive *and* felt) distrust that tend to prevail between a majority nation and one or more minority nations calls for something other than Pettit's formula, at least during periods of severe turbulence. In such contexts, there is every reason to believe that it is often the opposite formula that will be optimal for those who hope to build or rebuild trust: expressing trust while maintaining prudent and discreet vigilance, knowing that the background context is one of distrust. On the one hand, in such a case, trust is what has been seriously weakened, and it will be all the more difficult to build or rebuild it since there will be recalcitrant people – and even very determined opponents – in every camp. On the other hand, distrust is then a well-known reality and therefore does not need to be expressed. Of course, mistrust, in the form of vigilance, remains necessary. However, its expression may be limited to flexible procedural mechanisms; otherwise there is a serious risk of fanning the already strong flames of distrust. Based on examples drawn from the history of Québec-Canada relations, Pettit's views on the "intangible hand" also need considerable revisions in order to provide a credible account of trust enhancement in multinational democracies.

NOTES

1 Please note that we have modified the English translation of Rosanvallon's book: we translate "*défiance*" (Rosanvallon 2006: 16) as "mistrust" while both "*défiance*" and "*méfiance*" are translated as "distrust" (Rosanvallon 2008).

2 Rosanvallon notes that this counter-democracy has to be understood as "part of a larger system that also includes legal democratic institutions. It seeks to complement those institutions and extend their influence, to shore them up" (2008: 8).

3 It should be noted that this aspect is overlooked in Rosanvallon's book, in which the reflection on counter-democracy focuses mainly on the case of France.

4 All references to Pettit in this chapter will be to *Republicanism* (1997).

5 We argue that the case of the Canadian federation is relevant despite the fact that Canada is not formally a republic. In the same way that republicanism is a major tradition of critical thinking in the history of Canada (Harvey 2005; O'Toole 2010), Pettit's republican theory offers critical tools for thinking about the reconciliation of vigilance and trust in Canada. While Pettit seeks to promote freedom as non-domination in a society where republican values *already* reign, he nonetheless asks the question of what the state can do to foster civility when people do not "generally identify with ... institutions," or regard "them as alien impositions, for example, and [view] with disdain or distrust those who argued for their legitimacy and those who worked for their implementation" (241).

6 Pettit notes in particular that premodern republicanism reserved freedom as non-domination for "well-resourced males" (143) who belonged "to the mainstream culture of the societies in which they lived" (144).

7 While he uses the terms "civility" and "civic virtue" interchangeably, Pettit says he prefers "civility" (245).

8 This is what leads Stephen Macedo to speak of his liberalism as "civic liberalism" (2000: xi).

9 Rosanvallon makes a similar remark in a brief footnote (2006: 121).

10 On the concept of multinational federal democracies, see Karmis (2010).

11 It is important to note that, following Rosanvallon, we explicitly distinguish vigilance – an expression of mistrust – from the category of distrust. Pettit does not explicitly make this distinction and sometimes gives the impression that he makes vigilance an expression of distrust, and more precisely of expressive distrust. This apparent confusion may be the source of the problems associated with his *expressive distrust/felt trust* formula.

12 For the notion of "founder of discursivity," see Michel Foucault (1994). Following the rebellions in Upper and Lower Canada in 1837 and 1838, the imperial government appointed John George Lambton, Earl of Durham, as governor general of both colonies with a commission to investigate the causes of the rebellions. Lord Durham completed his report in 1839.

13 At the time, the term *Canadiens* applied only to French-speaking inhabitants of the former French colony known as "Canada." When the English settlers in Upper Canada began to identify themselves as "Canadians,"

they started referring to French speakers from the Lower Canada as "French Canadians."

14 The strategy of the US during the Cold War also involved a policy of *containment* – that is, preventing communism from spreading further. While this policy is not to be found in Durham's *Report*, it was essentially the policy of provincial governments in post-Confederation Canada.

15 The Union Act, 1840, modelled on the Union with Ireland Act, 1800 (39 & 40 Geo. 3 c. 67), followed the report. While the moderate Parti rouge members in Canada East managed to foil Durham's plans by forming an alliance with the Reformers in Canada West to obtain responsible government, the latter, under the influence of George Brown, nonetheless later became hostile towards the French and did not hesitate to raise the specter of "French Domination," a turn of phrase with a ring of the Norman Invasion of England that also refers to Durham's policies.

16 While Pettit uses the general term "overtures of trust," we think that adding the adjective "unconditional" provides a more accurate and precise representation of what he is doing.

17 The expression "fine risk" actually comes from the 1984 federal election campaign when Lévesque responded to an invitation by the head of the federal Progressive Conservative Party, Brian Mulroney, to suspend the Parti Québécois' sovereignist plans and to submit a list of conditions for supporting "with honour and enthusiasm" the Constitution Act, 1982, which had been adopted without Québec's consent. However, we feel that it also applies very well to the risk that Lévesque took when he prevented its adoption in the first place by joining forces with the premiers of seven other provinces, in 1980–81, against the Trudeau government's plan to repatriate the Constitution unilaterally. This is why we speak here of first *and* second "fine risks."

18 Lévesque was partly successful. Section 38(3) of the Constitution Act, 1982 provides for the right to dissent to constitutional amendments that concern provincial jurisdictions, while section 40 states that "Where an amendment is made under subsection 38(1) that transfers provincial legislative powers relating to education or other cultural matters from provincial legislatures to Parliament, Canada shall provide reasonable compensation to any province to which the amendment does not apply."

19 The expression "bridge schools" comes from the fact that s. 23(2) of the Canadian Charter of Rights and Freedoms stipulates that "Citizens of Canada of whom any child has received or is receiving primary or secondary school instruction in English or French in Canada, have the right to have all their children receive primary and secondary school instruction

in the same language." The problem is that it was not set out how long
a child had to have been educated in English in a private school before
his or her parents would be able to enrol all of their children in a public
English school.

20 Note that Québec's five conditions were: (1) recognition of Québec as
    a distinct society; (2) a veto over future constitutional amendments;
    (3) jurisdiction over immigration; (4) the obligation to appoint three
    judges trained in the civil law tradition to the Supreme Court of Canada;
    and (5) limits on federal spending power within provincial jurisdictions.

21 The failure gave rise to another, equally fruitless, round of constitutional
    negotiations terminating in the 1992 referendum on the Charlottetown
    Accord.

REFERENCES

Baier, Annette. 1994. *Moral Prejudices: Essays on Ethics.* Cambridge, MA:
    Harvard University Press.

Durham, John George Lambton. 2004. *Lord Durham's Report. An
    Abridgement of the Report on the Affairs of British North America by
    Lord Durham.* Edited by G.M. Craig. Montreal and Kingston: McGill-
    Queen's University Press.

Foucault, Michel. 2001 (1969). "Qu'est-ce qu'un auteur?" In *Dits et écrits
    I, 1954–1975,* 789–821. Paris: Gallimard.

Hardin, Russell. 2006. *Trust.* Cambridge: Polity Press.

Harvey, Louis-Georges. 2005. *Le printemps de l'Amérique française.
    Américanité, anticolonialisme et républicanisme dans le discours poli-
    tique québécois, 1805–1837.* Montréal: Boréal.

Karmis, Dimitrios. 2010. "'Togetherness' in Multinational Federal
    Democracies: Tocqueville, Proudhon and the Theoretical Gap in the
    Modern Federal Tradition." In *Federal Democracies,* edited by Michael
    Burgess and Alain-G. Gagnon, 46–63. London: Routledge.

Kymlicka, Will, and Wayne Norman. 1994. "Return of the Citizen: A
    Survey of Recent Work on Citizenship Theory." *Ethics* 104, no. 2:
    352–81.

Lenard, Patti Tamara. 2008. "Trust Your Compatriots, but Count Your
    Change: The Roles of Trust, Mistrust, and Distrust in Democracy."
    Political Studies 56: 312–32.

Macedo, Stephen. 2000. *Diversity and Distrust: Civic Education in a
    Multicultural Democracy.* Cambridge, MA: Harvard University Press.

Montesquieu, Charles Louis de Secondat, Baron de. 1979. *De l'esprit des
    Lois.* Volume 1. Paris: Flammarion.

O'Neill, Onora. 2002. *A Question of Trust*. Cambridge: Cambridge University Press.

O'Toole, Darren. 2010. "The Red River Resistance of 1869–1870: The Machiavellian Moment of the Métis of Manitoba." PhD thesis, University of Ottawa.

Pettit, Philip. 1997. *Republicanism: A Theory of Freedom and Government*. Oxford: Oxford University Press.

P.G. (Qué) v Quebec Association of Protestant School Boards. [1984] 2 RCS 66.

Re: Amendment to the Canadian Constitution. [1982] 2 SCR 791.

Re: Resolution to amend the Constitution. [1981] SCR 753.

Reference re: Secession of Quebec. [1998] 2 SCR 217.

Rosanvallon, Pierre. 2006. *La contre-démocratie: La politique à l'âge de la défiance*. Paris: Seuil.

– 2008. *Counter-Democracy: Politics in an Age of Distrust*. Cambridge: Cambridge University Press.

Smith, Adam. 1976a. *The Theory of Moral Sentiments*. Oxford: Oxford University Press.

– 1976b. *An Inquiry into the Nature and Causes of the Wealth of Nations*. Volume 2. Oxford: Oxford University Press.

Spitz, Jean-Fabien. 2001. "La philosophie politique républicaine aujourd'hui. Un état des lieux." *Politique et Sociétés* 20, no. 1: 7–23.

Tully, James. 2001. "Introduction." In *Multinational Democracies*, edited by Alain-G. Gagnon and James Tully, 1–33. Cambridge: Cambridge University Press.

– 2006. "Critical Distrust." Unpublished manuscript.

PART TWO

The Dynamics of Trust, Distrust, and Mistrust in Canada

6

The Conditional Nature of Trust in Canada's Multinational Constitutional Politics

Peter H. Russell

Thinking about Canada's constitutional politics in terms of trust, distrust, and mistrust is an entirely new venture for me – which I welcome. When I began I had no idea where this exercise might lead me, and it is still for me an ongoing inquiry. My approach will be rooted more in thinking about historical events than about political philosophy. When I began my career as a political scientist I did nothing but political philosophy. But gradually I moved to the more empirical side of the discipline, while always trying to keep in touch with developments in political theory. My reflections will fall mostly into the category that centres on institutions, politics, and constitutional developments.

INCOMPLETE CONQUESTS FORM THE ROOTS OF CANADA'S MULTINATIONAL NATURE

In several places I have written that Canada became a multinational society not by design but by stumbling into the consequences of two "incomplete conquests" (Russell 2000: 227; 2004: 9; 2017). The source of Canada's multinational nature is these incomplete conquests of already existing nations and their incorporation into the new state, Canada, many years ago. It is of fundamental importance to understand that this kind of diversity within a modern state is more deeply rooted and more latent with trust issues than the multicultural or multiethnic diversity characteristic of virtually all states in the world today.

The best known of the two incomplete conquests at the foundation of Canada relates to what did not happen after Great Britain established its rule over Québec in the eighteenth century. The British did not try to expel the Canadiens, as they had done just a few decades earlier to the Acadiens. Nor did they subject them to forced assimilation into an English-Protestant culture. Whether the British could have completed the conquest of the Québécois we do not know. In 1763, the Canadiens, without the support of France or New France's Indian allies, were militarily much weaker than the British. But, even so, the effort to complete the conquest would have been bloody and costly, and in the end might have failed – especially if the thirteen colonies to the south and the Iroquois Confederacy had withdrawn their support of Great Britain.

It was primarily for reasons of self-interest that the British did not try to complete the conquest of New France, thereby permitting a fundamental seed of Canadian multinationalism to be planted. There may have been a scintilla of a belief in the ideals of liberal pluralism behind the thinking that underlay this British imperial strategy. If there was, it was very faint. On the Canadiens' side, too, it was out of self-interest and not liberal ideals that they accepted British rule. They believed they could secure the vital interests of their society without continuing to resist the British.

The other incomplete conquest arose out of relations between European states and Amerindian nations. Through the first two centuries following contact, relations between European powers and these Indigenous North American nations were international in nature. Both France and Britain made alliances with Indian nations and confederations, and fought wars against Indian nations and confederacies. In these wars neither side prevailed.

After Britain's capture of Québec in 1759 and the surrender of Montreal in 1760, an alliance of Indian nations led by Pontiac, the Odawa chief, posed a serious challenge to British rule over the territory west of Montreal. Among the Delawares, Mississagas, Nipissings, Odawas, Ojibwa, Potawatomis, Shawnees, Wyandots, and other western nations there was much apprehension about the British taking over the forts that the French had built around the Great Lakes and in the Ohio Valley. The Indians feared that British possession of these forts, which the French used basically for trading purposes, would lead to a flood of settlers on their lands. These fears were fuelled by a movement, led by the Delaware prophet Neolin, urging Indians to return to their native roots and spurn the evils of European civilization. The Pontiac uprising began in May 1763. Within a few weeks every fort west of Detroit, except for Fort Pitt (formerly Fort Duquesne), was in Indian hands – most of them burnt to the ground (Anderson 2005).

In response, the imperial government in London advised King George III to include a commitment to Indian nations in the 1763 Royal Proclamation setting out the system of government for the North American territory ceded by France to Great Britain at the end of the Seven Years War. In this Proclamation, the British sovereign promised the Indian nations "with whom We are connected" that there would be no British settlements in "the Indian Territory" without the consent of the Indian nations. In 1764, Sir William Johnson, the British northern superintendent of Indian affairs, met approximately 2,000 chiefs representing twenty-four nations at Fort Niagara. Johnson's mandate was to persuade these Indigenous leaders to maintain relations with the British on the basis of the promise made in the Royal Proclamation. In a lengthy and elaborate ceremony, Johnson, on behalf of the British Crown, and the chiefs, on behalf of their nations, agreed to this arrangement for peaceful coexistence. This agreement is referred to nowadays as the Treaty of Niagara (Borrows 1997: 155).

It may seem a stretch to say that the agreement made at Niagara in 1764 marks an "incomplete conquest" by the British over the Amerindians. We do not know what would have happened if the Royal Proclamation had not been made and communicated to the Indians. Maybe the Indian nations would have consolidated their military dominance in the Great Lakes region and held back the tide of British settlement for quite some time. Nevertheless, it is likely that Britain would eventually have marshalled the military resources to prevail against the Indian nations. The Indians' military intelligence indicated that this was likely.

The Treaty of Niagara contains the seed of the other dimension of Canada's multinational nature. But, like the seed on the French-British side, it was based on calculations of mutual self-interest rather than a mutual acceptance of liberal pluralist ideals. The British would agree to share the Indian territories with Indian nations through treaties because it was a less costly way of facilitating western settlement than fighting wars with the Indians. And the Indian leadership thought it would be more prudent to permit British settlers on their lands according to the terms of negotiated treaties rather than trying to arrest the advance of European settlement by military force.

TRUST IN THE FOUNDATIONAL MOMENTS

In both cases – the Canadiens and the British, and the Indian nations and the British – there must have been a measure of trust for the two parties to establish lasting bonds with one another. But what kind of trust was it?

I find that Russell Hardin's concept of a trust based on "encapsulated interests" best captures the kind of trust that underlay the foundational moments binding Great Britain into ongoing political relations with the people of New France and the Indian nations. In both cases, each side had reason to trust the other because it saw that it was in the other's interest to stick to what seemed to be the key terms on which they agreed not to fight one another. In terms of Hardin's concept of "encapsulated interest trust," each side could say: "I believe you are trustworthy because I believe it is in your interest to take my interests seriously" (2006: 6).

The Canadiens sensed that the British believed it was in their interest to allow them to continue to be faithful Roman Catholics without being disqualified from participating in the colony's public affairs. If Great Britain had not made that crucial concession and kept to it, it faced the strong possibility that the Canadiens, who constituted nearly all of Québec's population, would not cooperate in the governance of the new regime and might turn to violent resistance. The 1774 Quebec Act went further than granting the Québécois religious freedom. It extended to the Canadiens the continuation of their system of civil law. Given the deep roots of the seigneurial system and the demographic dominance of the Canadiens, it would have been imprudent to have attempted to impose British land law, family law, and other aspects of civil law on the population. The British must surely have believed that because the Quebec Act secured the vital interests of their new French-speaking, Catholic subjects, they would cooperate in establishing a colonial regime. It was because of these encapsulated interests that both sides believed the other was to be trusted to comply with their initial understanding.

Encapsulated interests were also the basis of trust underlying the Treaty of Niagara. Leaders of the Indian nations had reason to believe that the British would stick to their undertaking in the Royal Proclamation of 1763 because if they didn't they would face a continuation of the costly Indian wars. And the British had reason to believe that by respecting the vital interest of the Indians in having the British respect their ownership and control of their traditional lands, they would be able to maintain peaceful relations with the Indian nations.

Trust based on encapsulated interests seems pretty close to what Jim Tully calls "groundless trust." These early political relationships between the British and both the French Canadians and the Indian nations were not based on a structure of shared values. The parties to these foundational arrangements were willing to lower their guard a little in order to see how well they could get along on the basis of their understanding of the commitments they had made to one another. Tully says that though the initial relationship might be based on groundless trust, the parties aim at an ongoing dialogue that will lead to shared norms and a deeper kind of trust. While I can see some evidence of this in the case of the British and French in Québec, I do not see any evidence of such an aim on the part of the British in their relations with Indian nations. The Indians certainly wanted to maintain an ongoing and evolving relationship of mutual support and friendship, whereas the British hoped the Treaty of Niagara and the Royal Proclamation would enable them to acquire land for settlement and economic development relatively cheaply. The British looked forward to the time when they had a clear military and demographic ascendancy over the Indians.

A condition underlying these early relationships was a rough equality of power between the parties. The mutual sense of an equality of power gives each side reason to believe that the other is likely to stick to the original agreement. Once that equality gives way, and one side becomes clearly much more powerful, the more powerful party is likely to abuse the trust of the weaker party, and the weaker side may lose any reason for trusting the stronger party. As Hardin puts it, "Large power differences undercut motivations to act on behalf of another" (2006: 152).

This is what happened to Britain's and Canada's relations with Indian nations in the nineteenth century. Fear that the same sort of thing might happen to the French Canadians became the reason that what Tully calls a tempered distrust came into play in French-English relations in Canada.

CONSTITUTIONAL CHANGE, DISTRUST, AND MISTRUST

From their foundational moments in the eighteenth century up to the present day, the relationships that give Canada its multinational character have undergone enormous constitutional change. The Canadiens have become a minority people in Canada but are the majority people in a province of the Canadian federation. The Aboriginal people have become embedded within a country in which they constitute just 3 per cent of the population and in which their nations continue to struggle for recognition and respect. The stories of how all this happened are long and complex. Here I will simply reflect on how feelings of trust, distrust, and mistrust have played out in these constitutional developments.

Relations with Indigenous Nations: A Story of Mistrust and Distrust

The story of relations between the Indigenous nations and the British Empire and its successor state, Canada, from the early nineteenth century until that late twentieth century, is one of broken promises on the part of first Britain and then Canada, and radical distrust on the part of the victims of this betrayal. The key explanation of this development is the dramatic shift in power – military and demographic – in favour of the European newcomers. Once the British and their colonists no longer needed the Indians as military or economic allies, and knew they could put them down with ease, they no longer had any interest in complying with the letter or spirit of the agreement into which they entered at Niagara and the treaties arising from that agreement.

By the mid-nineteenth century, British and Canadian settler policy, in both English and French Canada, was increasingly fuelled by racist attitudes. The latter half of the nineteenth century was the high water mark of racist Darwinism among European peoples. Europeans' belief in their own biological superiority and the superiority of their culture, justified, in their eyes, their imperial rule over non-white, non-European peoples. Aboriginal peoples in Canada, for over a century and a half, experienced the full force of those ignorant, disrespectful, and antagonistic attitudes, and the brutal policies they inspired.

The sad story of this imposition of a colonial relationship on Canada's Aboriginal peoples has been told many times, and most authoritatively in the first volume of the *Report of the Royal Commission on Aboriginal Peoples* (1996: 137). Here I will only record the principal developments.

Soon after the Treaty of Niagara, Sir William Johnson had written as follows to Thomas Gage, the British commander-in-chief in North America: "You may be assured that none of the Six Nations or Western Indians ever declared themselves *subjects*, or will ever consider themselves in that light, while they have any men or an open country to retire to. The very idea of subjugation would fill them with horror" (Stone 1865: 228). But British commanders and governors soon began to ignore Johnson's words and treat the Indian nations as totally subject to British sovereignty. As the frontier of British settlement moved west into what was to become Upper Canada and then Ontario, treaties were made with Indian nations. But while the Indians nations regarded these treaties as the basis for an ongoing, respectful basis for sharing land, the British regarded them as land "surrenders" that would confine native peoples to small reserves and open up most of their traditional lands and waters for European settlement and economic development in which the Indians would not share. The colonial legislature soon began to impose its will on the Indian nations. British colonial policy aimed at breaking up Indian nations and confining small communities of native people to reserves where they could be gradually "civilized." None of the Indian nations played any role in the creation of Canada in 1867. In Canada's founding constitution, the Constitution Act, 1867, the only reference to the nations indigenous to the Canadian territory is section 91 (24), which states that "Indians, and Lands reserved for the Indians" are subject to the exclusive jurisdiction of the Parliament of Canada.

After Confederation, the imperialist rule of the Canadian state over Indigenous peoples became even tougher. The Indian Act, passed by the federal parliament in 1876, built on the "civilizing" mission of colonial legislation a totalitarian administration of native peoples by the federal government. Under this act, governance of the fragmented Indian nations on reserves was subject to the direction of Ottawa bureaucrats. Every aspect of their lives on reserves was subject to outside authorities' control, including their mode of government, family relations, and the education of their children. The Canadian government continued to use treaties – in northern Ontario, across the prairies, in northeast British Columbia, and the Northwest Territories – as the means of acquiring land for non-Aboriginal settlers and industrial development. However, these Canadian treaties, like the British treaties that preceded them, aimed at confining Indians to tiny reserves, and contained legal language that differed from promises made orally at treaty negotiations. In effect these treaties allowed the federal government to do anything it wished on the vast, off-reserve traditional lands of the Indian nations. The treaties were exercises in state deception (Fumoleau 1973).

On the few occasions in the nineteenth century when Indian nations attempted to use Canadian courts to vindicate their treaty rights, they were treated ignorantly and with contempt by Canadian judges. In a case brought by the Sauteaux people of northern Ontario dealing with Treaty 3, Chancellor Boyd, one of Ontario's most senior judges, characterized the Indians as "heathens and barbarians" and denied that the treaties conferred any legal rights to Indians (Harring 1998: 137). In the twentieth century, when Indian nations began to hire capable lawyers to defend their rights in the courts, the Indian Act was amended, making it an offence for a Canadian lawyer to represent an Indian nation in the courts without the permission of the federal government.

A colonial relationship was also imposed on the other the two components of Canada's Aboriginal population – the Metis and the Inuit. There was a constitutional moment in 1869–70 when a trustful relationship might have been forged between Canada and the mixed European/Aboriginal population of the Red River settlement who had formed a national identity as the Metis. In response to indications that Canada was intending to make their area a new province, the Metis leader, Louis Riel, sent a delegation to Ottawa to negotiate the terms of the area's entry into Confederation. The negotiations resulted in the Manitoba Act of 1870 that included guarantees for the French language and Roman Catholic Schools. Ancillary arrangements provided 1.4 million acres of land for the Metis. But unfortunately Canada decided to distribute the land rights in the form of commercially exchangeable "scrip," which was quickly used by unscrupulous land agents and government officials as a medium for defrauding the Metis. Although the Metis regarded the Manitoba Act, supplemented by other promises, as having the status of a treaty, they soon discovered that neither Canada nor the new province of Manitoba, which quickly came under the control of an English-Protestant majority, would come close to fully honouring its terms. Canada showed that it would use force to have its way with the Metis when it sent 1,200 soldiers under

General Wolseley to Red River in the summer of 1870, forcing Riel to flee to the United States. Fifteen years later, the Metis who had moved further west rallied again under Riel to assert their rights. Again Canada used armed force to put them down. The Metis, who were not so much conquered as deceived, had lost any reason to trust Canada (Purich 1988).

Canada made no effort at all to gain the trust of the Inuit people. In 1880, Britain formally transferred to Canada sovereignty over the Inuit and all their lands and waters in Canada's Arctic north, without consulting or even informing the Inuit people. "Since there was no urgency to acquire large tracts of Arctic tundra for settlement, as was the case with Indian lands to the south, there was no need to establish rules of government or negotiate treaties with the Inuit" (Grant 2002: 25). In the 1920s Canada began to impose its rule on the Inuit by enforcing Canadian criminal law on its people. After World War II it used coercive means to relocate Inuit people from northern Québec to the high Arctic (Royal Commission on Aboriginal Peoples 1994). Canada gained control over the Inuit not through military conquest but surreptitiously through the incremental extension of its policing power over their territory. Missionaries and traders may have engendered some level of trust in Canada among the Inuit, but much of that trust was dissipated by the coercive and culturally insensitive means Canada used to consolidate its rule in the Arctic. The 1939 ruling of the Supreme Court of Canada that Eskimos (as Inuit were then called) are to be considered Indians under the exclusive jurisdiction of the federal parliament was hardly a trust-building event (*Supreme Court Reports* 1939, 104).

In the twentieth century, Canada became a prosperous and relatively progressive democratic state. But Aboriginal peoples, until well after World War II, were largely excluded from the benefits of this development. Most of them were confined to small pieces of marginal land. Their access to new labour markets and post-secondary education was extremely limited. They were not beneficiaries of new social programs sponsored by the federal or provincial welfare states. The historic Indian nations, the Metis, and the Inuit peoples were denied access for their communities to Canadian courts. Their individual members were denied access to the democratic franchise. In essence the people indigenous to the Canadian territory were treated as subjects rather than as citizens of the Canadian state. This was not a relationship that engendered trust. For the Aboriginal side of the relationship radical distrust was the only possibility. For Canadian settler society, their total estrangement from Aboriginal peoples must have engendered feelings of deep distrust towards these peoples so long as they maintained their strange ways.

Some Recovery of Conditions of Trust

After World War II, a change in relations with Aboriginal peoples became possible through the combination of two developments. In the aftermath of the war, racist imperialism was increasingly challenged internationally and within settler societies. The challenge was strong enough to give Indigenous peoples a hearing in Canada. And by this time enough Aboriginal people had become adept in the political techniques and skills of the dominant society to give voice to their concerns in the political space of that society.

The Canadian government now had interests that pointed in the direction of revising its Aboriginal policy. The poor living conditions of Aboriginal peoples and their exclusion from the benefits of full participation in the Canadian economy and welfare state were an international embarrassment to Canada in positioning itself as a progressive anti-colonial state. Moreover, given the remarkable growth trend in the Aboriginal population, it was also a serious domestic social problem. Aboriginal peoples continued to be concerned about the honouring of treaties, recognition of their historic societies, and securing access to traditional lands and waters. Added to these concerns, increasingly, was the interest of Aboriginal people in enjoying the benefits of formal education and participation in Canada's industrial economy. By the 1960s, Aboriginal people as individuals had been granted the right to vote in federal and provincial elections. They were now interested in obtaining access for their peoples as recognized societies or nations to Canada's constitutional politics.

These converging interests underlay the 1969 meeting between the Trudeau government and the National Indian Federation, a Canada-wide alliance of Indian associations (Weaver 1981). The meeting did not succeed in reaching an agreement. The federal government promised to terminate discriminatory Canadian policies that denied Aboriginal Canadians full access to the mainstream economy and social services. But, in return, the Indian leaders were asked to forget about their historic treaties, abandon their traditional societies, and become full, undifferentiated Canadian citizens. The

Indian representatives welcomed the end of discriminatory policies but were vigorously opposed to giving up their historic treaties and identities. Pierre Trudeau, Jean Chretien, and their political colleagues were disappointed that their new policy was rejected. They learned from this meeting that a deep reconsideration of Aboriginal policy was needed if it was to have Aboriginal support.

Following the 1969 meeting, federal political leaders and Aboriginal leaders began stumbling along a path towards a more consensual relationship. The Supreme Court of Canada led the way with a seminal decision in the 1973 *Calder* case, which essentially recovered and gave effect to the 1763 Royal Proclamation (*Supreme Court Reports* 1973). The court found that the Crown's recognition of Indigenous peoples' title to the lands they used and occupied when Britain claimed sovereignty applied to all of Canada, as did the Crown's commitment to permit settlement on such lands only through properly authorized treaties. This decision prompted the federal government, with the support of all parliamentary parties, to inaugurate a "Comprehensive Land Claims" policy. This policy created a process for making modern treaties with Aboriginal peoples who continued to live on their traditional lands but had never ceded land to Canada. A "Specific Claims" process was also introduced to deal with alleged failures of federal and provincial governments to honour their obligations under past treaties. Both processes were designed without consulting Aboriginal peoples and were seriously flawed. Nonetheless, they constituted a small, first step towards returning to a more consensual relationship with Indigenous peoples.

While these developments were occurring, the Indian nations, non-status Indians, the Metis, and the Inuit peoples were forming Canada-wide associations to represent their interests in Canadian public life. These organizations soon became engaged in the constitutional politics that were the principal preoccupation of Canadian politics in the 1970s. It is ironic that although it was Québec's constitutional discontents and aspirations that opened up the mega-constitutional debate in Canada, it is the Aboriginal peoples who, even though they were not yet admitted as formal participants in constitutional negotiations, in the end made the greater gains. The amendments to Canada's constitution made in 1982 as part of the process of "patriating" the Constitution included section 35, stating: "The existing aboriginal and treaty rights of the aboriginal peoples of Canada are hereby recognized and affirmed."[1] The Aboriginal peoples secured two further constitutional protections. Section 25 of the Canadian Charter of Rights and Freedoms, the most celebrated part of the patriation package, provided that nothing in the Charter could abrogate or derogate from the rights and freedoms of Aboriginal peoples recognized in the 1763 Royal Proclamation or established through historic or future treaties. A further section on constitutional conferences established the right of Aboriginal peoples to be included in constitutional conferences directly affecting their rights, and called for a conference within a year to further clarify their rights.

Of the four Canada-wide Aboriginal organizations, only the Metis National Council approved of the constitutional recognition of Aboriginal rights in the 1982 amendments. For the Indians and the Inuit there was still too much uncertainty about how their rights might be interpreted under these new constitutional provisions. In particular, they wanted explicit recognition that Canada recognized their "inherent right to self-government." After nearly two centuries of colonial subjugation they did not trust Canada to recognize their most fundamental collective right – the right of all peoples to self-determination. Between 1983 and 1987, four constitutional conferences with federal and provincial first ministers failed to garner provincial support to move forward with a constitutional amendment explicitly recognizing the Aboriginal peoples' inherent right to govern themselves. Aboriginal trust in the constitutional process was further shaken when, shortly after the failure of the fourth conference, on Aboriginal rights, the federal and provincial government moved ahead with a new package of constitutional reforms, the Meech Lake Accord, that ignored Aboriginal concerns.

The Aboriginal peoples made more progress in the courts than at the constitutional table. In 1990 the Supreme Court of Canada rendered two landmark decisions. In *R. v Sioui*, it rejected the disrespectful way in which courts in the past had settled disputes about the meaning of treaties. The court called for an approach that looks at all the historical records "to choose from among the various possible interpretations of common intention the one which best reconciles the interests of both parties at the time the treaty was signed" (*Supreme Court Reports* 1990: 1:1025). In *R. v Sparrow*, a unanimous court, in its first decision on what it means for Canada to recognize "existing aboriginal rights," said that "a generous, liberal interpretation of the words in the constitutional provision is demanded" (1075). The justices argued that such an approach was called for because in the past and over a great many years "the rights of Indians were often honoured in the breach."

In the 1990s, Aboriginal peoples began to have more success at the political level. Their Canada-wide associations were full participants in the constitutional negotiations that produced the Charlottetown Accord that contained a large section on Aboriginal rights, including recognition of the Aboriginal peoples' "inherent right to self-government within Canada." It should be noted that federal and provincial leaders' insistence on adding the words "within Canada" indicates their distrust of what Aboriginal peoples might try to do with their rights. Because of its rejection by a majority of voters in a 1992 referendum, the Charlottetown Accord did not become law. But negotiations of modern treaties with Aboriginal peoples soon moved beyond settling land issues to include self-government arrangements. Under this expanded treaty-making process, over a dozen Indian nations and all four of Canada's Inuit communities have made agreements with the federal government and, below the northern territories, the relevant provincial governments (Alcantara 2008).

The Mulroney government's appointment of the Royal Commission on Aboriginal Peoples (RCAP) in 1991 opened up another political path to a more trustful relationship. Four of RCAP's seven commissioners were Aboriginal leaders representing the four components of Canada's Aboriginal community – status Indians, non-status Indians, Metis, and Inuit. The other three commissioners were a provincial premier, a retired Supreme Court of Canada judge, and a senior Québec judge. RCAP had a broad mandate to review all aspects of past Aboriginal relations with Canada and make recommendations for a better relationship in the future. This Canadian Royal Commission was the first time in any settler country that a group of Indigenous and non-Indigenous leaders had fully researched together and reflected on the past, present, and future relationship between their peoples. The commission's final report in 1996 called for a restructuring of the relationship along nation-to-nation lines and expenditures on educational, health, social, and economic development programs that would narrow the gap between the living conditions of Aboriginal and non-Aboriginal Canadians. The report's findings and proposals stand as a benchmark for the changes needed to overcome the colonization of Aboriginal peoples. However, the commission failed to engage the interest of either the mainstream media or most of the 97 per cent of Canadians who have no Aboriginal background. As a result, governments have felt little public pressure to implement the commission's recommendations.

Two developments in the first decade of the twenty-first century have potential for lessening Aboriginal distrust of Canada. In 2008, in a moving ceremony in the House of Commons attended by Aboriginal leaders from all parts of Canada, Prime Minister Harper made an official apology for Canada's residential school policy – a policy which for nearly a century forcefully took Indian, Metis, and Inuit children from their families to be educated by Christian instructors at residential schools. A year after the apology, the federal government established a Truth and Reconciliation Commission that aims to engage Canadians in learning and acknowledging the hurtful and disrespectful practices that Canada inflicted on Aboriginal people.

This brief account shows some progress being made in moving away from the policies Aboriginal peoples were subjected to during the long period when British and Canadian policy was robustly imperial and racist. Has the reversal gone far enough to restore a modicum of trust?

At least it can be said that relations between Canada and Indigenous peoples today are not marked by pervasive, radical distrust. A significant number of Indigenous peoples have felt enough trust in the federal government to try its new programs for dealing with past violations of treaties and legal obligations, and for making agreements on land and self-government. The Inuit people, perhaps because they did not share the Indian nations' and the Metis' experience of broken promises and treaties, have been relatively more trustful and willing to use the modern treaty process – most notably in creating the self-governing territory of Nunavut in Canada's northeast Arctic. A few of the historic Indian nations – notably the Nisga'a and the James Bay Cree, some Yukon First Nations, and parts of the Dene nation in the Northwest Territories – have entered into inter-governmental agreements which they hope, and in that sense trust, will secure their vital economic and political interests (Alcantara 2008). But so far, many more have held back from entering into anything that could be regarded as a full and final agreement. Most First Nations are not desperate enough to make modern treaties with a federal government which insists that Aboriginal peoples "cease, release and surrender" their Aboriginal title over most of their traditional lands in return for being granted private ownership "in fee simple" of a small parcel of land close to their main settlement (Peniket 2006). Some Aboriginal communities have made informal, pragmatic agreements with federal and provincial governments to secure jurisdictional space and funding for services they wish to provide to their people (Papillon 2012).

For most First Nations and Metis communities, the Canadian government's policies for settling land and governance issues do not inspire trust. The land claims policies, instead of being aimed at establishing ongoing partnerships with Aboriginal peoples in stewarding lands and waters, seem primarily designed to clear the way for industrial resource development by extinguishing or confining Aboriginal title as much as possible. The self-government policy insists on treating Indigenous governments as a subordinate, sub-sovereign order of government that must be tailored to the federal government's administrative requirements. Absent from negotiations is any consideration of the federal and provincial governments' responsibility for the suffering and dispossession of Indigenous peoples under colonialist rule (Irlbacher-Fox 2009).

In recent years, several trust-building measures and activities have been developed that at least may protect Indigenous communities from further injustice. A number of Indigenous peoples who have agreed in principle to negotiate agreements on land and governance have tested the trustworthiness of federal and provincial governments by securing "interim agreements," in which governments commit during the many years that it will take to reach a "final" agreement to refrain from authorizing any development in the people's traditional country without their consent. In 2004, the Supreme Court of Canada rendered two decisions, in *Haida Nation* and *Taku River*, that recognized and enforced a duty of governments to endeavour to accommodate the interests of Indigenous peoples before authorizing developments on traditional lands to which an Aboriginal people claim title but have not yet made treaty with Canada (*Supreme Court Reports* 2004): 3:511, 3:550. The following year, in *Mikisew*, the Court applied the same principle to a First Nation's interests in off-reserve treaty lands (*Supreme Court Reports* 2005, 388).

Increasingly, Aboriginal peoples have not waited trustfully for Canadian authorities to treat them justly. Indigenous communities in many parts of Canada have resorted to occupations or blockades to block damaging encroachments on traditional or reserve lands. These "flashpoint events," which sometimes result in tragic deaths and usually in considerable public inconvenience, are often divisive and stressful for Indigenous peoples, and always create ill will towards Indigenous people in the non-Indigenous mainstream. Still, they tend to make governments more sensitive to Indigenous interests and the need to resolve long-standing grievances (Simpson and Ladner 2010).

The trust built in these situations is the "encapsulated interest" kind of trust rather than a trust built on sharing common values. The dialogue or conversation required to reach this deeper kind of trust has taken place only among relatively small numbers of people – for instance among the seven RCAP commissioners, and in interactions of Aboriginal and non-Aboriginal scholars. It has not and does not occur at the broad public level. This was clearly evident in the hostility of the mainstream media to the RCAP commissioners' understanding of the nation-to-nation relationship of Indigenous peoples with Canada. And it rarely, if ever, takes place at negotiating tables on land and governance issues where federal and provincial negotiators have no mandate to acknowledge past and continuing injustices.

The Canadiens, Québec, and Canada

The people of New France have never been betrayed by either Great Britain or its successor state Canada to the extent that the Indian nations have been betrayed. Consequently, radical distrust of *les Anglais* has never been as pervasive among French-speaking Canadians as it is among First Nations. Still, there is a continuing moderate distrust among French Canadians that the English-speaking majority might use its powers to destroy the distinct society to which many of them give their primary allegiance. This distrust has served the purpose of giving English-speaking Canadians an interest in tempering English Canadian nationalism and accommodating French Canadian aspirations in building and operating a federal polity. The key difference between these English-French relations and Canada-Aboriginal relations is that neither the English nor French in Canada accepted the Indian nations as partners in building a shared political community.

The Canadiens experienced the most direct threat to the survival of their distinct society when the British government decided to implement Lord Durham's recommendation that French Catholic Lower Canada and English Protestant Upper Canada be joined together in a single colony. The objective of this colonial restructuring was clearly to assimilate the Québécois into the emerging English-Canadian majority. The French majority in Canada East were able to resist this imperial stratagem and negotiate a federal union in which they would have a province, Québec, that could continue to serve as their homeland.

A certain amount of trust between French Canadians and English Canadians was necessary for successfully carrying out the negotiations that created the Canadian federal state in 1867. This trust, however, was not based on a shared understanding of the nature of the federal union created at Confederation. John A. Macdonald, George Brown, and Alexander Galt harboured very different visions of Canada's future from those of George-Étienne Cartier, Étienne-Pascal Taché, and A.-A. Dorion. The English Canadians looked forward to a highly centralized federation dominated by the English-speaking majority. The French Canadians hoped that the province of Québec would have all the powers needed to preserve and advance the distinct culture and interests of the Québécois. The English and French "fathers of confederation" certainly did not share a multinational vision of Canada (Waite 1962). Nor in the constitutional process was there any popular dialogue or conversation between French and English Canada (Russell 2003).

Despite the conflicting hopes and fears present at Canada's birth, the federation grew and prospered. The Québécois, the descendents of *les Canadiens*, were never great believers in the possibility that their interests could be secured in building a continental French-English Canada. The hanging of Louis Riel and the Manitoba schools crisis in the 1890s provided convincing evidence that the Québécois must secure their vital social and cultural interests in Québec (Silver 1982). The province of Québec was able to protect itself from the centralizing efforts of federal political leaders by getting unexpected support from the English law lords who controlled judicial interpretation of the Constitution through Canada's first seventy-five years. Also the Québec electorate used its leverage on federal politics strategically to produce governments in Ottawa either sympathetic to, or fearful of being hostile to, Québec interests. Below the surface of politics, the embers of distrust on the Québécois side remained warm and were occasionally inflamed, as in the conscription crises of both world wars. Any trust that existed between Canadian and Québec provincial leaders was definitely of the encapsulated interest kind.

In the 1960s the dynamics of Québec-Canada relations changed dramatically. Québec's provincial leaders moved from defending a traditional society and a respect for Québec's rights as defined in

Canada's founding constitution to pressing for a constitutional restructuring that would provide greater power for "the state of Québec."
This aggressive Québec nationalism provoked an aggressive Canadian
nationalist counterattack led by a Quebecer, Pierre Trudeau. The two
colliding nationalist forces opened up a struggle for constitutional
change that was soon joined by western Canada seeking protection
for its economic interests and the Aboriginal peoples seeking recognition and the right to self-determination. In 1976, the Parti Québécois,
led by René Lévesque, came to power in Québec promising to hold
a referendum in which Quebeckers could vote for an independent
Québec. In 1980, 60 per cent of Québec voters rejected a proposal
to negotiate a constitutional arrangement under which Québec would
be politically sovereign but in an economic association with Canada.

Two years later, the mega-constitutional struggle that was the primary focus of Canadian politics for a quarter of century produced its
first and only set of constitutional amendments. This was Pierre
Trudeau's "people's package," in which the most heralded parts were
patriation of the Canadian constitution (making it amendable in
Canada) and the Canadian Charter of Rights and Freedoms. These
constitutional changes were highly valued by Canadian nationalists,
but in no way did they respond to Quebecers whose nationalist aspirations had initiated the constitutional debate. Indeed, the amending
formula, adopted in the Constitution Act, 1982, actually treats Québec
simply like any other province, reducing Québec's power in the federation. "Many Quebeckers felt betrayed along the way when [Trudeau's]
solemn "I have understood you" of the pre-referendum was turned
into a reform that diminished the powers of the only government
controlled by Francophones" (Dufour 1990: 84). This sense of betrayal
was deepened by the political drama that played out in the constitutional negotiations, leaving Québec's premier René Lévesque suddenly
isolated after "the night of the long knives." The Supreme Court of
Canada's ruling in the 1982 *Quebec Veto Reference* that upheld the
exclusion of Québec from the constitutional process must surely have
confirmed fears that a Supreme Court dominated by English Canadian
justices could not be trusted to protect the Québécois' fundamental
interests (*Supreme Court Reports* 1982): 2:793.

Efforts to secure Québec's formal acceptance of the 1982 constitutional changes designed to meet Québec's concerns failed. That is
what the so-called Québec Round of constitutional negotiations based
on the Meech Lake Accord was all about. It demonstrated that a

majority of Canadians outside of Québec were not prepared to support constitutional recognition of Québec as "a distinct society" within Canada. The "Canada Round" of constitutional politics that followed saw the defeat, in the 1992 Canada-wide referendum, of the Charlottetown Accord, a potpourri of constitutional amendments aimed at responding to the constitutional concerns of all parts of the Canadian polity, including Québec and the Aboriginal peoples. Canadians learned from these constitutional failures that they are too divided in their fundamental understandings of the nature of Canada to act positively as a sovereign people.

After the defeat of the Charlottetown Accord, Québec turned to a unilateral process of constitutional change. The government of Québec in the 1995 Québec referendum sought a mandate from the Québec people for a sovereign Québec in an economic partnership with Canada. This second Québec referendum, unlike the first, came within a few thousand votes of producing a majority for the "yes" side. This is surely an indication of the extent to which French Quebecers' trust in Canada, as a political union in which they can secure their vital interests, had declined since 1980.

It is unlikely that constitutional events since 1995 have done much, if anything, to restore Québécois trust. In the 1998 *Quebec Separation Reference*, the Supreme Court of Canada balanced its denial of Québec's right to secede from Canada unilaterally with a finding that if a clear majority of Quebecers on a clear question vote in favour of secession, the rest of Canada has a duty to negotiate in good faith the terms of secession. This was followed by the federal parliament passing the Clarity Act and the Québec National Assembly passing the Québec Self-determination Act – each legislature claiming that it would be the arbiter of the legitimacy of any democratic effort by Quebecers to self-determine their future political status. The biggest trust casualty of these developments was the trust of the great majority of Canadians in their own capacity for resolving fundamental differences about the nature of Canada through formal, constitutional change.

MULTINATIONALISM AND TRUST IN PRESENT DAY CANADA

I agree with Alain Gagnon and James Tully (2001) that Canada, normatively speaking, should be regarded as a multinational society.

Congenial as this multinational understanding of Canada is to a majority of Quebecers and a majority of Aboriginal people, I do not think it is congenial to a majority of English-speaking Canadians. This is certainly the sense I get whenever I speak about Canada in multinational terms to English Canadian audiences. My multinational conception of Canada jars with their aspiration for a Canadian polity that is more strongly unified.

Despite this lack of coherence in Canadians' sense of national identity, the country remains governable and peaceable. The sense of trust between its national communities is limited and wary. Severe provocations of the "nations within" continue, as with the almost total exclusion of the Québécois from the celebrations opening the 2010 Winter Olympics, and the Harper government's branding of a possible federal coalition government depending on Bloc Québécois votes as being virtually treasonous. Similarly, the federal government's continued insistence on treating First Nations' governments as subordinate sub-sovereign nations, and its holding back for so long from endorsing the United Nations Declaration of the Rights of Indigenous Peoples, did nothing to strengthen trust in Canada among Aboriginal peoples. Nevertheless, Québécois and Indigenous leaders are reasonably confident that Canadian political leaders understand it is not in their interest to roll back or reverse gains in recognition made by the nations within, and that it may even be advantageous to allow more such gains to take place in the future.

This limited "encapsulated interest" kind of trust, as a foundation for a multinational society, falls far short of trust based on a body politic whose members share a common sense of citizenship. The liberal pluralism that played such a small role in Britain's disinclination to complete its North American conquests hundreds of years ago, and which is the philosophical foundation for a multinational society, today is embraced by a significant portion of Canada's intelligentsia, and many of its politically active citizens. This gives rise to my hope that over time, through many, many conversations, significant numbers of English, French, and Aboriginal Canadians will come to share a common understanding of Canada. Only if that happens will the kind of trust on which a multinational country can thrive be in place.

NOTE

1 Note that Canada's official documents at this time did not capitalize "aboriginal." Because the lower-case "aboriginal" is used as a racial

category, Aboriginal peoples prefer the upper case as it connotes a political not a racial category. Since the Royal Commission on Aboriginal Peoples, Aboriginal has been the accepted usage in most official documents and scholarly writing.

REFERENCES

Alcantara, Christopher. 2008. "Deal? Or No Deal? Explaining Comprehensive Land Claims Negotiation Outcomes in Canada." PhD thesis, University of Toronto.

Anderson, Fred. 2005. *The War That Made America: A Short History of the French and Indian War*. New York: Viking.

Borrows, John. 1997. "Wampum at Niagara: The Royal Proclamation, Canadian Legal History and Self-Government." In *Aboriginal and Treaty Rights in Canada*, edited by Michael Asch, 155–72. Vancouver: University of British Columbia Press.

Dufour, Christian. 1990. *A Canadian Challenge: Le defi Quebecois*. Lantzville, BC: Oolichan Books.

Fumoleau, René. 1973. *As Long as This Land Shall Last: A History of Treaty 8 and Treaty 11, 1870–1939*. Toronto: McClelland and Stewart.

Gagnon, Alain-G., and James Tully, eds. 2001. *Multinational Democracies*. Cambridge: Cambridge University Press.

Grant, Shelagh. 2002. *Arctic Justice: On Trial for Murder, Pond Inlet, 1923*. Montreal and Kingston: McGill-Queen's University Press.

Hardin, Russell. 2006. *Trust*. Cambridge: Polity Press.

Harring, Sidney L. 1998. *White Man's Law: Native People in Nineteenth-Century Canadian Jurisprudence*. Toronto: University of Toronto Press.

Irlbacher-Fox, Stephanie. 2009. *Finding Dahshaa: Self-Government, Social Suffering and Aboriginal Policy in Canada*. Vancouver: University of British Columbia Press.

Papillon, Martin. 2012. "Canadian Federalism and the Emerging Mosaic of Aboriginal Multilevel Governance." In *Canadian Federalism: Performance, Effectiveness and Legitimacy*, edited by Herman Bakvis and Grace Skogstad, 286–301. Toronto: Oxford University Press.

Peniket, Tony. 2006. *Reconciliation: First Nations Treaty Making in British Columbia*. Vancouver: Douglas and McIntyre.

Purich, Donald. 1988. *The Metis*. Toronto: James Lorimer.

Royal Commission on Aboriginal Peoples. 1994. *The High Arctic Relocation*. Ottawa: Canada Communications Group.

– 1996. *Report of Royal Commission on Aboriginal Peoples*. Volume 1. Ottawa: Canada Communications Group.

Russell, Peter H. 2000. "Canada – A Pioneer in the Management of
  Constitutional Politics in a Multi-national Society." In *The Politics of
  Constitutional Reform in North America: Coping with New Challenges*,
  edited by Rainer-Olaf Schultze and Roland Sturm, 227–34. Opladen,
  Leske & Budrich.
– 2003. *Constitutional Odyssey: Can Canadians Become a Sovereign
  People?* 3rd edition. Toronto: University of Toronto Press.
– 2004. "Can the Canadians Be a Sovereign People? The Question
  Revisited." In *Constitutional Politics in Canada and the United States*,
  edited by Stephen L. Newman, 9–34. Albany: State University of New
  York Press.
– 2017. *Canada's Odyssey: A Country Based on Incomplete Conquests*.
  Toronto: University of Toronto Press.
Silver, A.I. 1982. *The French Canadian Idea of Confederation, 1864–1900*.
  Toronto: University of Toronto Press.
Simpson, Leanne, and Kiera L. Ladner, eds. 2010. *This Is an Honour Song:
  Twenty Years since the Blockades*. Winnipeg: Arbeiter Ring Publishing.
Stone, William L. 1865. *The Life and Times of Sir William Johnson, Bart*.
  Albany: J. Munsell.
Waite, P.B. 1962. *The Life and Times of Confederation: Politics,
  Newspapers, and the Union of British North America*. Toronto:
  University of Toronto Press.
Weaver, Sally M. 1981. *Making Canadian Indian Policy: The Hidden
  Agenda, 1968–70*. Toronto: University of Toronto Press.

7

The Construction of Canada in Historical Perspective: Distrust as an Inherent Component of Constitutional Debates?

François Rocher

It would be impossible to discuss the trust/distrust dynamic in a multinational state such as Canada without taking a detour into how the representations of the shared political space have been established over time, or without a deep examination of the conditions that have presided over the dynamic's construction. Those conditions have taken many forms linked to specific readings of the federal regime that have been developed and transformed by the communities that are part of the dynamic, above all in accordance with the stakes those communities have considered important. Indeed, it is through shared political institutions that the norms and rules governing intercommunity relations are negotiated, the "purposes" of the political community are discussed, and the policies that embody them are defined and established. However, we cannot change these "purposes" unless we look back to the initial intentions and how they have been understood over time. This is why it is important to critically examine the different understandings that have gradually become entrenched, if only to understand the resulting political dynamic. It is a dynamic in which the vigilance on one side has been largely conditioned by reinterpretations on the other.

Three themes will be examined. First, we will look at a few conceptual clarifications concerning the notion of trust. We begin by adopting an approach that places the accent on the evaluative, constructed dimension of trust rather than on its moral aspects. Thus, trust is never given from the start. It develops in light of past experiences and expectations concerning what could happen in the future. Second, we will return to the understanding that political players had of the federal plan in the nineteenth and twentieth centuries. This requires looking at some of the arguments invoked at the time to justify earlier understandings to citizens, while taking into account the resistance to the plan that was expressed. We pay special attention to interpretations of the federal regime that appeared in the nascent historiography at the end of the nineteenth century, in writings by both historians and members of the political elite, which show that the national minority exhibited real feelings of distrust. This review will thus allow us to identify the foundations of the distrust and describe why it has continued. In the third part of the chapter, we return to the principal amendment made to the Canadian constitution in the early 1980s to show that, like the British North America Act of 1867, it has contributed to maintaining a dynamic powered by exacerbated vigilance with respect to shared political institutions.

OF TRUST, DISTRUST, AND INTERESTS

In its simplest sense, the notion of trust refers to a positive attitude toward another individual or group, since the person or group is presumed to act favourably toward us. Trusting means, in a way, being able to put oneself in the Other's hands. When we trust, we do not imagine that the Other could behave in a traitorous, fraudulent, or incompetent manner. Defined in this way, trust carries a great deal of emotional and moral weight. Trust cannot exist without its opposite, distrust – that is, the tendency to be wary or even suspicious of the Other. Jean-Marie Denquin notes that trust is both a "mysterious psychological state that ensures that both economic and political business runs smoothly" and that it is ambivalent (1997: 51–2; our translation). He points out that, for partisans of authority, it is a virtue expected of the humble and a requirement for governing people since it is a condition for command. In contrast, adversaries of authority insist on trust being an unnegotiable personal bond, which is thus archaic. Trust is thus an essential condition for the stability of a relationship and, *a fortiori*, a political regime. A person who trusts does not oppose and does not challenge the conditions for living together. Understood in this way, the notion of trust is ontologically apolitical because it excludes power relations, animosity, or even tension. We thus need to choose a definition of this notion that has broader analytical scope.

Russell Hardin has noted that there is a strong school of thought in the United States, Canada, and Great Britain testifying to the decline of trust in our societies: "Most of the voluminous literature on declining trust sees it as a major problem independently of any account of trustworthiness – but surely if there is a problem here it is with trustworthiness" (2006: 1). In reality, almost the entire analytic corpus on trust in social relations is based on an omnipresent confusion between the concept of "trust," which is a type of relationship, and that of "trustworthiness," which is a quality that a trusted person is presumed to have. What is the difference between these two concepts? Trust is born of a positive assessment of the trustworthiness of the Other. Trustworthiness refers to whether the Other's behaviour is predictable and fulfills expectations. When individuals have a high level of trustworthiness, it is certainly an advantage for a society and can help to increase the level of trust. However, a high level of trustworthiness is not necessarily the corollary of a high level of trust (and vice versa). Indeed, on the basis of past experience, one individual or community may be certain that the other will not behave in a way that protects the former's interests. The anticipated behaviour is thus predictable, thus trustworthy, but the assessment of the other person or group may be negative.

In a trusting relationship, the trustworthiness of the other person is taken into consideration, although this has no purpose unless the interests of the individual who grants such trustworthiness are respected. Despite the risks associated with such an approach, the chief interested party behaves in this way because they consider that their interests, and those of the other person, are consistent, and that, even if they might diverge for a short time, the other person would ensure that their shared interests are fostered.

Conceived of in this way, trust is the result of a calculation, an evaluation. It thus looks like a cognitive reality, not necessarily an emotion. The calculation is made in the framework of a lasting relationship tested by experience and based on knowledge of the Other, of their interests, and the general situation. Hardin uses the expression "the encapsulated interest account" to describe the situation when the interests of the trusting person coincide with those of the trusted people. According to him, "Distrust must have a similar logic. If we distrust you, that is because we think that your interests oppose our own and that you will not take our interests into account in your actions. In this view, trust and distrust are cognitive notions. They are in the family of terms that includes knowledge and belief" (2006: 17).

Thus, "*if trust is cognitive, then we do not choose to trust*. Rather, once we have relevant knowledge – of your moral commitments, your psychological or character disposition, or your encapsulation of our interests – that knowledge *constitutes* our degree of trust or distrust" (Hardin 2006: 17–18; emphasis added). Defined in this way, trust is not synonymous with social cohesion. It has no normative value since trust unwisely granted can have disastrous effects on society. Here, Hardin is in opposition to "social capital" thinkers such as Robert Putnam (2000) and Francis Fukuyama (1995), who conceive trust as an intrinsically positive value, and believe that a high level of trust automatically leads to enhanced social cohesion and collective action. In the political arena, cooperation is embodied in networks and institutions that establish the norms and rules that make such interaction possible, despite, and sometimes because of, this lack of trust.

The difficulty of taking into consideration the trust/distrust dynamic in multinational societies comes from the fact that all research on trust concerns the construction of the relationship of trust within "dyadic" interpersonal relationships.[1] So how can trust be measured when it involves groups of many individuals? Trust is a complex phenomenon that is built through accumulation of data by those concerned through a series of interactions spread out over time. It is the product of familiarity, a relationship of proximity, and a certain form of intimacy. The relationship of familiarity, owing to its cognitive requirements, cannot be simply transposed to the level of the individual's relationships with the state, which is a structure that is much too complex and polymorphous to lend itself to a relationship of familiarity.

Modernity is characterized by the plurality and complexity of what is at stake for individuals, organizations, and governments. This fact translated into an increase in the level of uncertainty in social relationships and a gradual loss of familiarity: "Most of us cannot sensibly claim to have the knowledge required for establishing the trustworthiness of government officials, agencies, or government generally. Therefore, we cannot trust them" (Hardin 2006: 160). In the same way, while it may be difficult to analyze the bond of trust between the individual and political institutions (and elite groups) because it is too complex, it is even more problematic to consider ties of trust between communities. However, it is less ambiguous to take into consideration the positions expressed and interests defended by political elites with respect to institutions and the role played by their counterparts within those institutions, as well as how this has been interpreted by observers of the political dynamic.

As mentioned, trust is a cognitive reality founded on knowledge and experience, the result of a calculation based on an assessment of one's interests and how they are perceived to be complementary and related to those of the other person with whom ties have been formed within an inter-dependent relationship. However, this reality is not simply cognitive. It also plays a role in the realm of politics, and can be measured in terms of the balance between majority and minority national groups. In a context where power relationships are asymmetrical, expectations of reciprocity with respect to trust also have to be asymmetrical. In other words, the most influential group does not have to trust its minority partners, because its interests are protected by the simple fact of exercising power. The majority group can use collaborative or partnership mechanisms, but it can just as well impose its will through legal norms or institutional control. It does not necessarily need to count on the trust of its minority interlocutors in order to govern. Trust facilitates relations and rules, but it is not a prior condition for them. The situation is different for minority groups. Political stability requires the establishment of a trusting relationship based on the group's conviction that the decisions taken will not be harmful to them. For a minority group to endorse proposed changes, it needs reasons, based on experience, that lead it to believe that its interests have been and will continue to be taken into account.

In these conditions, trust can be expressed strongly or moderately depending on the nature of the power relations between the actors. Since this dynamic also exists institutionally, the majority's capacity for action may be consistent with the interests expressed by the minority group such that, if strong trust exists, one party will not move without having first obtained the other's agreement. The majority group's capacity for action can be constrained by the possibility that the minority group could exercise a veto, flowing from agreements or enshrined in the Constitution, in cases where there is disagreement about the means for achieving the political regime's "purposes." It can be dissuaded by political action led by the minority group if the latter is opposed to alterations that would change the nature of the interdependent relationship. Finally, the majority group's capacity for action may not be hindered by the minority group, who would thus face the imposition of changes, against its will, that further reduce its power in the relationship, as tenuous as it may be.

In any case, for every relationship of trust, the normative aspect seems to be conditioned by the past, by the way that the parties' interests have been taken into consideration in the definition of the common good. Particularly in situations of moderate distrust, the common good mediates the future-oriented aspirations and interests of minority groups in ways that, under the guide of universal principles, express only the majority's ambitions and interests. Table 7.1 summarizes the various degrees of trust and distrust.

This dynamic is – despite the apparent redundancy of the term – dynamic, in the sense that it changes over time. It is influenced by the accumulation of experiences that are judged according to the measure of community aspirations. If we refer back to one of the definitions above, it changes both with respect to the political community (and a so-called difference-subsuming "national" community), and in accordance with the objectives it pursues. It is with regard to the parameters suggested above that we will try to show the nature of the trust/distrust dynamic in Canada.

CONFEDERATION: A HISTORY
OF MISUNDERSTANDING AND DISAPPOINTMENT

In this book, Peter H. Russell's contribution is explicitly inspired by Hardin's work concerning the role that trust/distrust played in relationships between French Canadians, Aboriginal peoples, and the British conquerors during the eighteenth-century conquest: "In both cases – the Canadiens and the British, and the Indian nations and the British – there must have been a measure of trust for the two parties to establish lasting bonds with one another. But what kind of trust was it?" (116). Further on, Russell explains that the trust displayed between Aboriginal peoples and the first European occupiers was not based on shared values, but on a community of interests, the harmonious pursuit of which was likely, in the best of cases, to result in dialogue and deeper relationships of trust. In other words, it depended on the partners' increased familiarity and proven reliability. According to Russell, this ascent towards a more "harmonious" form of trust did not occur in the case of Aboriginal peoples. While growing trust

Table 7.1
The trust/distrust dynamic in multinational contexts marked by asymmetry between communities

Type of trust	Power relationships	Institutional features	Cognitive dimension	Normative dimension
Considerable trust	Symmetrical	Double majority	Encapsulated interests	Trustworthiness, predictability and general interest
Moderate trust	Asymmetrical	Conventional/ constitutional veto	Diverging interests and shared "ends"	Dialogue, compromise and general interest
Moderate distrust	Asymmetrical	Political capacity to block	Diverging interests and disagreement on "ends"	Pressure, compromise and special interests
Radical distrust	Domination	Majority unilateralism	Opposing interests	Betrayal, dishonesty and special interests

may have been far from clear in the case of Aboriginal peoples, it seems to contrast with the case of French Canada when the latter began dialogue with the rest of Canada. Russell adds, however, essential elements concerning the importance given to the equality of the powers at the time, establishing a trusting relationship based on encapsulation of their reciprocal interests. As he explains, "the mutual sense of an equality of power gives each side reason to believe that the other is likely to stick to the original agreement" (117). However, we have to admit that "once that equality gives way, and one side becomes clearly much more powerful, the more powerful party is likely to abuse the trust of the weaker party, and the weaker side may lose any reason for trusting the stronger party. As Hardin puts it, "Large power differences undercut motivations to act on behalf of another" (ibid.).

Thus, the notion of trust is measured in terms of a "balance" principle, or reciprocal interests, but also by taking into account the degree of "power" of the stakeholders. In a way, this is historian Arthur I. Silver's (1997) argument when he considers that the relative balance of powers acted on the dynamic of trust between members of the political elite in French Canada (and Québec) and the rest of Canada. It was only after the balance of powers changed that members of French Canada's political elite rapidly shifted from moderate trust to moderate distrust in their relationships with the rest of Canada. Interestingly, Silver adds that in Canada, trust/distrust is also based on a specific reading of the protections granted by the 1867 confederative undertaking. As he explains, for some French Canadians at that time, who believed that French Canada and Lower Canada (later Québec) were one and the same thing, Confederation was not perceived as a threat, but rather as a necessary step towards establishing a state with a French-Catholic majority in British North America. Since the confederation plan was weighed in accordance with the degree of autonomy that it would give French Canadians – autonomy necessary for protecting its nation – there was no distrust on the part of the inhabitants of Lower Canada. This was because, for many of them, Confederation gave Lower Canada the powers of a quasi-independent state that above all ensured their survival. This idea resurfaces in the writings of certain historians belonging to the conservative nationalist movement of the early twentieth century, such as Lionel Groulx, who first approved of the union of North American colonies because it did not lead to the assimilation of French Canadians, and "contrary to the centralizing, assimilating spirit of the American constitution, the Canadian confederation recognizes and maintains the moral rights of various ethnic groups" (1914: 386; our translation).[2] Groulx was persuaded that "the new charter effectively made the Province of Québec an autonomous state. French Canadians would be masters in their own home; their legislature would govern all interests and would include all the components that ensure the life of a race" (398; our translation). Sir Thomas Chapais, historian and member of the Legislative Council of Québec, also displayed a degree of optimism regarding the Confederation plan. He was convinced that the 1867 federal union had given birth to the French-Canadian nation in the legal and territorial sense of the term. As he said in 1914:

And, above all in this part of the confederation that is specially the land of French-Canadian nationality, we cannot refuse to express gratitude [to the Fathers] for having brought out, from the chaos of diverging interests, and from the free-for-all of constitutional combinations, this little homeland, this province of Québec, which is so dear to us, and into which they breathed intense vitality! ... Yes, for what used to be called Lower Canada, their work is essential. It is good to have established the provincial government, the legislature that is absolutely ours, where we are the guardians of our deepest interests, the institution of which has finally brought us the objective towards which French-Canadian nationality has been travelling for a century, through so many perils and hazards. (1979 [1914]: 13–14; our translation)

These excerpts reveal a degree of moderate trust, insofar as the definition of the common political space was consistent with the aspirations or even the special interests of the groups concerned (in this case, the French Canadians).

However, this vision of the union was not unanimous. We can also find, in the writings of historians and political essayists, a counter-discourse that instead reveals radical distrust of the planned union and its purposes. Historically, this can be seen in the work of historians of the nationalist liberal school, such as Laurent-Olivier David (1840–1926), Arthur Buies (1840–1901), and Benjamin Sulte (1841–1923). Their distrust was inspired first by the feeling that there was a betrayal and dishonesty on the part of English Canadians, but also on the part of the clergy. For example, according to Sulte, "Upper Canada was brought into Confederation by the desire to reduce the French element to *quia*; the Catholic clergy of Lower Canada agreed to the pact in the hopes of expanding its influence" (1884: 147; our translation). Buies is just as critical:

The priests asked for only one thing: the Catholic religion, and they abandoned all the rest. Therefore, they joined with our conquerors, and pursued in concert with them the same work. They intervened in politics, and believed they were doing well by contributing to the maxims of theocracy; they saw only one thing in it: passive obedience; they recommended only one virtue: absolute loyalty to authority to the nation that had been persecuting us for 50 years. They renounced all national aspirations, and devoted themselves to a single goal, towards which they made the people work: the consolidation and empire of their order. (1864 [1978]: 40; our translation)

Politically, this radical distrust also existed among the liberals of Lower Canada, including in the writings of their main spokesperson, Antoine-Aimé Dorion. He deplored the fact that the union plan did not respect provincial autonomy. He also feared that the rights of the French-Canadian minority would not be protected and that their powers would not be maintained. Dorion raised the question in the House: "How can we hope that Lower Canada will be able to have great trust in the general government, which will have such immense power over the destiny of its section? Experience shows that majorities are always aggressive and prone to be tyrannical, and it cannot be otherwise in this case" (1865: 273; our translation). In fact, he argued that there was a possible imbalance of power in the union, an imbalance that could lead to relations of domination. There was thus radical distrust in the discourse of the planned federal union's opponents, but it failed to counter the discourse of the political elite which, like the clergy, praised the confederation plan to protect their interests. In order to rally supporters to their cause and persuade them of the advantages of a confederal union, they argued that their provincial autonomy in the union would be guaranteed. In fact, according to Silver, "There was agreement between Bleus and Rouges that the autonomy of a French-Canadian Lower Canada was the chief thing to be sought in any new constitution" (1997: 38). Such an objective could only be achieved if the federation coordinated the two orders of government and their actions, with each remaining sovereign in their respective areas of jurisdiction. By adopting this position, Lower Canada clashed with John A. Macdonald's plan for a legislative union as a condition for a strong state and central government that could prevent the disorder of civil war as seen in the American federation (Séguin 1997: 379). According to Silver, "the very heart and essence" of Lower Canada's pro-confederation position, as formulated and sold by the Bleus to the Lower Canadian electorate, stipulated that

> the Union of the Canadas was to be broken up, and the French Canadians were to take possession of a province of their own – a province with an enormous degree of autonomy. In fact, *separation* (from Upper Canada) and *independence* (of Quebec within its jurisdictions) were the main themes of Bleu propaganda. "As a distinct and separate nationality," said *La Minerve*, "we form a state within the state. We enjoy the full exercise of our rights and the formal recognition of our national independence." (1997: 41)

As Donald Creighton also notes:

> *La Minerve*, like the other *Bleu* or Conservative French-Canadian newspapers, quickly took up and firmly stuck to a more purist federal interpretation which stressed the autonomy of the local governments, though only – and this was an important limitation – in the social, cultural, and religious aspects of provincial life. "Confederation" declared *La Minerve*, early in the summer, "means a league of states that are independent of one another." French Canada, it predicted, would be "master in its own home with respect to everything concerning its social, civil and religious economy." (1964: 98)[3]

In light of these assertions, we could ask the following question: why did the Bleus not opt for pure and simple independence from Lower Canada? Part of the answer relates to military and economic reasons: the threat of annexation by the Americans and Québec's inability at the time to provide for its people in an appropriate manner. The heavy flow of French Canadians migrating to the United States was a clear indication of the province's economic vulnerability. According to the Bleus' argument, the union of the British North American colonies would create major improvements in defence and expand markets; thus it would foster economic development.[4]

For the Bleus, as already mentioned, the union was nonetheless not supposed to translate into a loss of autonomy for Lower Canada. It was in this spirit that Cartier, upon his return from London in the spring of 1867, rushed to say: "That is why I was careful to make sure that the federal government would receive only that amount of power which was strictly necessary to serve the general interests of the Confederation" (*L'Union des Cantons de l'Est*, 23 May 1867, cited by Silver 1997: 48). A little later, he argued that even the Imperial authorities were aware, at the time they were preparing and approving the British North America Act, that they were simply endorsing an agreement negotiated and concluded by the four colonies concerned. Silver holds that such statements support the view that Confederation was the product of a pact between the four original provinces, thereby reinforcing "the Quebec-centredness of French Canada's approach to Confederation, and the degree to which French Quebec's separateness and autonomy were central to French-Canadian acceptance of the new regime" (1997: 50).[5] We might think that, by insisting on these aspects, Cartier was establishing the ideas of trust and compromise by drawing attention to the fact that Confederation respected the interests of everyone, including the principle of provincial autonomy.

While provincial autonomy was a central issue, the Fathers of Confederation, although they were concerned about the fate of French-Catholic communities elsewhere in Canada, did not make this a serious structural component of the confederal project, since the concept underlying the project was not the establishment of a bilingual country. It was instead the establishment of a French-Catholic province in exchange for certain forms of protection for its Anglo-Protestant minority, within a union that would be essentially Anglo-Protestant.[6] Silver reminds us:

> Confederation was to be an association of national states, called provinces, united in a federal alliance (within the British Empire, of course). And in that alliance, the province of Quebec was to be the national state of the French Canadians. That province, as the French-Catholic province, might well be concerned to support French Catholics in other parts of the federation, but such support must never involve the acceptance of principles that would expose or endanger the autonomy of the French and Catholic character of Quebec itself. (1997: 61)

In reality, in 1867, French Canadians in Québec began to worry about the fate of French-Catholic minorities outside Québec given the way they were treated, first in New Brunswick, and then in Manitoba (with repercussions in federal parliamentary debates). This became a national issue that put strain on French-Catholic solidarity beyond the borders of Québec. Québec discovered that it had a mission to protect the French-Catholic communities in other provinces that was contrary to the principle of provincial autonomy with respect to education, and also contrary to Québec's own interests. Several events related to the status of French-Catholic communities outside Québec and the protection of their rights – combined with internal tension generated by the guarantees made to the province's Anglo-Protestant community – played a role in awakening the Québécois to their bonds with the Canadian and American French-Catholic diaspora, and changed their vision of Québec's role in the federation.

The government of New Brunswick's 1871 decision to stop funding the province's denominational schools was the first event that awoke the Québécois to the fact that there were French-Catholic communities outside Québec, such as, in this case, Acadians. A second more definitive event was related to Canada's westward expansion, particularly into Manitoba, where the Hudson's Bay Company's land was transferred to the Dominion at the time of Confederation and the Québécois discovered a French-Catholic Métis community.

The disputed trial and sentencing of Louis Riel were definitive turning points that saw Québec public opinion favour the Métis. Riel's hanging in 1885 was generally perceived as taking action not against a rebel, but against the standard-bearer of French Catholics in the west. The feeling of injustice was further exacerbated by later restrictions on French-Catholic education rights in Manitoba in 1890 and in the Northwest Territories in 1892. From then on, "the issue had become a French-Canadian national question because of the political atmosphere in 1889–90, in which the Manitoba school law had been passed at the same time as attacks were launched against the French language, and because of the unprecedented involvement of Quebec politics and opinion in the matter" (Silver 1997: 21).

A similar situation was also developing in French Ontario, a community that was Québec's geographical neighbour and closely associated with the Québec French-Canadian "nationality" from which it had come. Reflecting on the deterioration of the status of French Catholics in Ontario, beginning in 1885 the provincial government started converting unilingual French Catholic schools, which had been tolerated until then, into bilingual schools. Calls to abolish the separate school system in the province continued to intensify in the years that followed and led to the adoption of Regulation 17 in 1912 (Harvey 2000: 124). Thus, "all these changes in the position of the Acadians, Métis and Franco-Ontarians were followed much more closely by French Quebeckers after 1867 than they had been before. Confederation, by enabling the minorities to bring their cases to Ottawa, made them, in some sense, the affairs of the French Quebeckers" (Silver 1997: 23). In 1886, the election of the Mercier government in Québec, which would adopt much stronger positions in favour of autonomy and express the frustration of the Franco-Québécois, also contributed to deteriorating the general atmosphere with respect to French Catholic minority communities outside Québec.

This state of affairs led to conflict between Québec's desire for autonomy and its desire for solidarity with the French Catholics of the other provinces. With Henri Bourassa, it contributed to the emergence of the dualist conception of Canada and the different understandings of Québec and the federal government in this respect.[7] The debate around the rights of French Catholic minorities outside of Québec was symptomatic of the rising power of Anglo-Protestant Canadian nationalism over the course of the same period:

> Convinced that Canada could only survive if it had "national unity" and a single Canadianism, that only these could check the disruptive influence of Mercierism, many English Canadians began to press for measures of unification. And since the maintenance of the French language and of Catholic separate school systems seemed to encourage French-Canadian separateness and prevent the growth of a community of feeling among Canadians, these institutions became, more than ever, the objects of criticism. (Silver 1997: 185)

The rise of Anglo-Protestant nationalism was also the result of impatience with French Catholics – impatience that was quickly perceived in Québec as a threat, given Québec's weaker position within the federation. The combination of these conditions led to gradual but major changes in the Québécois view of the constitutional status of French Catholic communities outside of Québec. Silver paraphrases the new constitutional doctrine that began to take shape in the French Canadian press at the turn of the 1890s in the following way:

> In short, bilingualism – or biculturalism – was the very basis, the sine qua non, of Confederation. It was not just a question of the Manitoba Act, but of "a pact made in 1867 to guarantee equal rights to all in matters of education." Without such a guarantee, "it is certain that Confederation would never have been adopted." Aside from separate schools, it had been "the intention of the original federal pact to admit the official use of the two languages in each and every province of the confederation." (1997: 192)[8]

This conception was supported by the 1895 decision of the Privy Council in London authorizing the federal government to intervene directly to re-establish the separate school system in Manitoba (Brunet 1952: 15). In summary, the distrust that had appeared in 1867 among some opponents of Lower Canada's confederation plan was amplified by the treatment reserved for French Catholic communities outside Québec after 1890. Inversely, the moderate trust of members of the Lower Canadian conservative political elite and clergy in the confederation plan that promised a political space respectful of the general interest (the autonomy of provinces) shrank, owing to the asymmetrical power relations that were developing, and took the form of moderate distrust.

This makes it easier to understand Henri Bourassa's entrance into the picture with his theory of Confederation as the product of a pact between Canada's two founding peoples, and as the source of the provincial autonomy to protect the Québécois nationality. French-speaking minorities shared in that nationality and should, in principle, obtain equality at the level of Confederation. According to Bourassa, attacking minorities ran counter to the fundamental objectives of Confederation and also threatened provincial autonomy.

What kind of a summary of the trust/distrust dynamic can we now give with respect to this short historical overview? On the one hand, and not very surprisingly, we find that there was no unanimity concerning the 1867 confederation. For some, it was the result of a misunderstanding that, over time, produced veritable disappointment. The misunderstanding was related to the union's purpose and respect for provincial rights. The symmetrical power relationship needed for considerable trust never materialized. The complementarity of interests (the cognitive dimension) was also negated by decisions made by the central government, and by diverging French Catholic and Anglo-Protestant interpretations of the 1867 federal pact. Finally, it was the normative dimension (dialogue and compromise) that fed, at least for a time, the moderate feeling of trust among some French speakers in Lower Canada who had been enticed by the Bleus of George-Étienne Cartier on the promise of becoming full citizens of a French Catholic state within the new federation. However, this feeling transformed into moderate distrust when the federal government tried to implement this idea of compromise.

Indeed, disappointment stemmed from the implementation of the compromise. It came first from concessions demanded by and granted to the Québec Anglo-Protestant community. The concessions were obtained behind the French Catholic majority's back, and were denounced when they were made public. If we are to believe Silver, the emergence of disappointment followed the categorical refusal to grant the same concessions to French Catholic communities elsewhere in Canada.

The concessions granted to the Anglo-Protestant minority would probably have been seen with a more benevolent eye if they had been accompanied by analogous concessions for the French Catholic minorities of the other provinces. Or, to express it even more accurately: if the privileges granted to the French Catholic minorities had not been withdrawn one after another, after they had been legally guaranteed, as in Manitoba, or after they were tolerated for many years, as in Ontario and New Brunswick. The repeated process of dispossession made the lack of fairness to which their nationals were subjected in the other provinces even more odious in the eyes of French Catholics.

Since it could not have any influence on the destinies of minorities in other provinces, Québec was unable to persuade its provincial partners to reverse their policies. Moreover, it was unable to bring the federal government to use its power of disallowance to counter the actions taken against the French language and Catholic schools in the Canadian west. The Riel affair and many initiatives against the French Catholic minority outside of Québec helped to shift the attitudes of members of the political elite from moderate distrust, in the case of the most optimistic, to radical distrust. In the end, a look at the trust/distrust dynamic provides a better understanding of the origin of skepticism towards the federal political regime. The accumulation of negative experiences measured against the failure to take into consideration the aspirations of French-speaking communities; the imbalance in power relations between the federal government and the provinces; and the many disagreements about the shared purposes of the union all fuelled distrust that culminated in the events that led to repatriation of the 1982 constitution.

THE 1982 CONSTITUTION, OR THE FINALIZATION OF CANADA'S SOVEREIGNTY: TOWARDS RADICAL DISTRUST

Among the events that dramatically marked the nature of the relationships within the multinational space, none seem to have left as strong or telling a trace on the trust/distrust dynamic as the constitutional amendment episode of the early 1980s. In an analysis published shortly after repatriation, Donald V. Smiley noted that the 1982 constitutional reform was part of a more ambitious plan by the Liberal Party of Canada that had just returned to power in 1980. The plan's purpose was to promote Canada-wide unity and promote the federal government as the legitimate spokesperson for all Canadians: "These new directions had a coherence in the general assertion of the federal government that the power of the provinces, and the perceived disposition of Canadians to emphasize their provincial rather than national allegiances, 'has increased, is increasing, and ought to be diminished'" (Smiley 1983: 74). This approach was based on two premises that have left their mark on the normative dimension of trust in the federal context. The first is that "conflict rather than conciliation is the normal condition of federal-provincial relations," and that, in this context, any compromise is a last-resort solution. The second is that "the attachment of citizens to their respective provinces and to Canada are competing rather than complementary allegiances, and that steps must urgently be taken to strengthen national loyalties" (83).

Based on these two premises, Smiley concluded that the 1982 constitutional reform should be understood only as "an exercise in constitutional review and reform whose alleged objectives were to create more harmonious relations between Quebec and the wider Canadian community [but] has involved a betrayal of the Quebec electorate, a breach of fundamental constitutional convention, a recrudescence of Quebec nationalism, and an even more serious Quebec challenge than before to the legitimacy of the Canadian constitutional order" (1983: 78). The reason for this, according to Smiley, is that the 1980 referendum on Québec sovereignty was defeated using false claims, with Pierre Elliott Trudeau's speech at the Paul-Sauvé Centre on 5 May 1980 being a concise example. Trudeau's promise was equivalent to a breach of trust since the 1982 constitutional reform essentially took into account none of Québec's historical demands. This breach partly explains the subsequent breaking of the bond of trust between the Québec electorate and the federal Liberals.

However, history was probably not quite as one-sided as Smiley suggests. According to André Burelle, Pierre Elliott Trudeau's former advisor and speechwriter, in order to fully grasp the complexity of Trudeau's about-face, we have to keep in mind the many plans for constitutional reform that were tabled by the federalists over the two years preceding the [1980] referendum. We then have to understand that, while they were not clear and precise, Trudeau's referendum promises were strongly inspired by the proposals formulated in *A Time for Action*, the Pepin-Robarts Report, and Claude Ryan's Beige Paper: three "holy books" that Trudeau himself referred to in order to legitimize his post-referendum offers in the summer of 1980. Finally, we have to explain why, after Jean Chrétien had led intense summer negotiations with the provinces, the offers made in September 1980, which were consistent with the ideas that Trudeau had defended at the time of *Cité Libre*, were scrapped during the 1982 constitutional repatriation. (2005: 15; our translation)

This privileged witness rejects the betrayal hypothesis while recognizing that Trudeau's political and philosophical turnabout raises many questions. Central to the issue is Trudeau's famous promise, made at the Paul-Sauvé Centre on 14 May 1980,[9] just six days before the 1980 referendum vote. Before an enthusiastic crowd, Trudeau, acting on behalf of the government of Canada, his own behalf, and on behalf of Québec's Liberal members of Parliament in Ottawa, declared: "If the answer to the referendum question is N O, we have all said that this N O will be interpreted as a mandate to change the Constitution, to renew federalism ... We want change and we are willing to lay our seats in the House on the line to have change" (Burelle 2005: 60).[10] This promise was reiterated in the House of Commons on 21 May, the day after the referendum. Trudeau then called for a

new constitution [that] could include, if the people so wish, several provisions in our present organic laws, but, it will also have to contain new elements reflecting the most innovative proposals emerging from our consultations or from numerous analyses and considered opinions that have flowed in the last few years from the will to change of Canadians. I am referring, of course, to the many proposals made by the Canadian government since 1968, but also to the Pepin-Robarts report, to the policy papers issued by the governments of British Columbia, Ontario, Alberta and by almost every province but Quebec, to the constitutional proposals of the Liberal Party of Quebec [the Beige Paper by Ryan], many elements of which could orient the renewal of our constitution if they were ever put forward by the political authorities of that province.[11]

This solemn promise of constitutional reform, based on the principles in the references cited by Trudeau himself as well as in his prior writings and speeches, was not kept. In the Constitution Act, 1982, there is no trace of the idea that Canada is a multinational state and that Québec is in some way a distinct society.

Burelle's explanation of the breach of trust represented by the final version of the Constitution Act, 1982, in relation to what was implied by Trudeau's initial commitments, focuses on political, psychological, and philosophical dimensions. The author notes that Trudeau's first constitutional proposals, the day after the 1980 referendum, were indeed in line with the positions he had taken in the past. Among the factors that Burelle uses to explain Trudeau's change in direction in 1981, we find the following: the prime minister's aversion to what has been called the "Château consensus," perceived as an attempt by the provinces to arrogate more power at the expense of Canadians' rights; Trudeau's visceral individualism and anti-nationalism; the rise of pan-Canadian nationalism, which seemed to be replacing the old Loyalist nationalism of English Canada; the increased power of advisors from the Anglo-Canadian majority; the polarization of the political struggle led by Trudeau between the "people's package" (individual rights and freedoms), of which the federal government was portraying itself as the sole voice, and the "provinces' package," which was reduced to a petty provincial struggle for greater power; the need to raise language rights to the level of basic rights guaranteed by the Charter in order to neutralize certain provisions of the Charter of the French Language adopted in 1977 by the Québec Assemblée nationale; and the possibility of negotiating with a Québec premier who was coming out of a referendum defeat, giving the prime minister an irresistible strategic opportunity to pin the government of Québec against the ropes.

Even though Burelle resists the term "betrayal," his assessment is nonetheless severe. On the one hand, refounding Canada is awkward in multinational federations, as the prime minister preached when writing for *Cité Libre*. On the other hand, in an even more merciless manner, Burelle points out that Trudeau, "in September 1980,

renounced 'giving Canada a new, modern, functional federal constitution' inspired by proposals contained in *A Time for Action*, the Pepin-
Robarts Report, and Claude Ryan's Beige Paper, as promised in his
May 21, 1980 speech" (2005: 445; our translation). He withdrew
from the negotiating table his offer to recognize Québec as a distinct
society, which he had made public in an open letter to the people
of Québec on 11 July 1980. He also disregarded the constitutional
convention that had historically given Québec a veto with respect to
constitutional amendments. Smiley, in contrast with Burelle, does not
hesitate to speak of betrayal: "the pledges of constitutional reform
made to the Quebec electorate by the federal leaders have not been
honoured, and it is *not* too much to say that this electorate has been
betrayed" (1983: 76).

To this first breach of trust, a second was added during negotiations, with the rejection of the constitutional convention ensuring
that the powers of the Assemblée nationale could not be reduced
without its consent. Smiley tells us that the convention in question
was at the heart of the confederal pact of 1867, and that there would
have been no pact without it. Certain asymmetries in the Constitution
Act, 1867, particularly section 94 on the consolidation of property
legislation and civil law in the English-speaking provinces, did not
apply to Québec, and proved its special status within the Canadian
constitutional order. The abandonment of the Victoria Charter (1971),
following Québec's refusal to endorse it – despite the agreement of
the other provinces – is the most recent and clear example showing
that there was such a convention. In complete good faith, it should
have come into play and been sufficient in 1981–82 to prevent the
repatriation of the Constitution.

> In my view, the first-line protection of the rights of the franco-
> phone community of Quebec is and has been since Confederation
> among the powers of the Legislature and government of that
> province, and on this basis Canadian constitutional convention
> dictates that these powers should not be restricted without
> Quebec's assent. The historical record is clear that the Dominion
> of Canada emerged as a federal political community, albeit one
> with certain quasi-unitary features, only because the francophone
> leaders of Lower Canada would not have it otherwise, and
> several important terms of the BNA Act of 1867 gave explicit
> recognition to Quebec's particularity – most crucially, perhaps,

section 94, which envisaged a very different distribution of legislative powers between the Dominion and Quebec than the one
prevailing in the common-law provinces. (Smiley 1983: 77)

The 1982 constitutional reform was possible only on the condition
that this convention was rejected. By rejecting the convention, which
has now been institutionalized, there was a transfer of authority and
legitimacy from the provincial to the federal level with respect to
culture and language. In the end, the reform led to increased Québec
nationalism and stronger challenges to the legitimacy of the Canadian
constitutional order, by both sovereigntists and federalists in Québec.

In this context, it is not surprising that the 1982 constitution is seen
as profoundly illegitimate, in that it was created under false pretences
and without the agreement of the people on whose behalf the Canadian
political authorities were claiming to act. As Guy Laforest notes, the
authorities had neither asked for nor received such a mandate from
the people of Québec or the people of Canada. The constitution that
they negotiated and promulgated

has never been explicitly ratified by the Canadian or Québec
electorates ... At a time when popular sovereignty is rising more
or less everywhere in the world, it has to be observed that the
Canadian constitution suffers from a lack of legitimacy in this
respect. This remark applies everywhere in Canada, but with
even greater strength in Québec. (1992: 199; our translation)

With the repatriation of the Constitution in 1982, and especially
with the failure of the Meech Lake Accord in 1990, the principle of
dualism was thus scrapped, though it was at the heart of Québec's
understanding of Confederation. If the holders of moderate distrust
had believed in the capacity of the Canadian political regime to take
into account the fears expressed by Québec's political elite, they had
to go back to the drawing board. There is still a lot of work to be
done. In Québec, there are still those who express moderate distrust
and aspire to obtain constitutional guarantees. For example, the former
Québec Liberal Intergovernmental Affairs minister wrote that the
objective of the government he had been a part of was "to solidly
anchor Québec's specificity in the federal system and to enhance its
status as part of a relationship of mutual trust. Wanting Québec's
specificity to be enshrined in the Constitution is no mere caprice; it is

a necessity. Since the constitution of a country is a mirror, it is imperative for the people of Québec to be able to recognize themselves fully
in the Canadian constitution" (Pelletier 2010: 26; our translation).

This quest is somewhat reminiscent of the promises that George-
Étienne Cartier made at the time of Canada's founding. It was a
question of setting up a new political nationality based on a gamble,
fortified by a strong dose of faith in the possibility of the coexistence
of peoples with different cultures and religions (LaSelva 2002: 218).
The new political nationality gave way to the new Canadian nation,
which made individual rights absolute and fragmented collective
rights, thereby "indirectly rewriting the social and political contract
that had given birth to Canada and, even more fundamentally, overlooking the necessity for communities to act as instruments for trans-
mitting language and culture, which are, for every human being, a
form of social heritage before being an individual right" (Burelle 2005:
445; our translation). Given this observation, lucidity requires a dose
of pessimism that can be defined as optimism when it is oriented
toward using full information to address the problem.

CONCLUSION

Taken as a whole, these episodes were not only products of misunderstanding and sources of disappointment, but they caused feelings of
betrayal and powerlessness that have coloured French Canadian historiography in a specific way. When we add the Conquest to this mix-
ture, the feeling of betrayal takes on a melancholic hue tinged with
resentment. This is particularly evident among historians of the neo-
nationalist Montréal School of Canadian history such as Guy Frégault,
Michel Brunet, and, above all, Maurice Séguin. In Séguin's opinion, the
federal union only perpetuated and solidified English domination, for
when one speaks of "federalism," one also speaks of "restricted cultural
autonomy" and the impossibility for a minority nation to bloom fully
(to act on its own). Thus, according to him, "there is no possible equality between the MAJORITY NATIONALITY and the minority nationality in ANY true FEDERAL UNION" (1997: 178; capital letters in the
original, our translation). Michel Brunet also criticizes the federal
regime for ensuring inequality between the two peoples. From his point
of view, the French Canadians, who have been economically inferior
since the Conquest, did not join the federation as equal partners. As
the weaker minority, they were doomed to assimilation. If anything,

federalism accelerates such cultural assimilation because it imposes a pan-Canadian nationalism against which minority nations are power-less. In short, according to the Montréal School historians, the point of departure for French Canadians' inferiority was the British Conquest, but Confederation is what forever consecrated their inferior status. Thus, "let us repeat that there have never been equal rights or actual equality between the two nationalities: not in 1760, not in 1840, and not in 1867" (ibid.: 401; our translation).

This feeling of betrayal was to be taken up again among some contemporary authors following the 1982 constitutional reform (Laforest 1992; Seymour 2001; Brouillet 2005). When he looks at the way power relations have played out between Québec and the federal government, Peter H. Russell notes that "a certain amount of trust between French Canadians and English Canadians was necessary for successfully carrying out the negotiations that created the Canadian federal state in 1867" (129). The "certain amount of trust" that Russell refers to depends on the encapsulation of the parties' interests and the nature of the power relationship since the Conquest. The power relationship was certainly unequal, but not to the point of allowing the stronger central government to definitively thwart the weaker French Canadian or Québec government. Like wisdom, the trust that develops in such circumstances is not the simple expression of shared interests. In this case it also sprang from fear of the upheavals that were being experienced by neighbours to the south. Whether it was out of fear or interest, it was nonetheless insufficient to win substantial endorsement by French Canadians, who remained suspicious and managed to negotiate in such a way that the union of the British North American colonies – notwithstanding all the economic and political benefits that were anticipated, and despite the unitary objec-tives of John A. Macdonald – took the form of a federal state with the separation of powers clearly delimited.

The choice in 1867 was not simply an expression of the trust the two parties felt for each other, their interest in the new trade prospects that were opening up to them, or the alarmist reading they had of the continental political stakes. It was also – and this is the point that Russell does not emphasize enough – the expression of a power rela-tionship sufficiently challenged to justify a certain number of accom-modations in favour of the minority.

The first and second conscription crises, the 1980 referendum, Trudeau's promise of a constitutional reform that would be in line with Québec's aspirations, the "night of the long knives" in November 1981, the 1982 constitutional reform without Québec's consent, and the "tampering" with referendum rules by federalist forces in 1995 are all events that have fed into (and continue to feed) Québec's resentment and suspicion of the rest of Canada. The strong presence of the Bloc Québécois in Ottawa between 1993 and 2011 was a recent consequence of that distrust.

Owing to a mirror effect, the theory of Canada's binational nature encouraged English Canada to think of itself as a nation and to see the federal state as its national state. In fact, this tendency to fashion a unified Canadian nation was already present in the first days of Confederation through the very act of the union and the repressed desire to create a unitary state. The underlying components of that desire can be found in the very text of the Constitution Act, 1867, such as can be seen in section 94, which anticipates the standardization of civil law among the founding Anglo-Protestant provinces. This tendency was strengthened during each crisis, as well as through the development of public policies in provincial jurisdictions based on the centralization of tax resources in Ottawa as part of the design and implementation of the welfare state and/or Canadian identity.

Political crises related to Canada's participation in the First and Second World Wars polarized public opinion between French Canada (in Québec) and English Canada almost to the breaking point. They showed that, in such a power relation, victory belonged to the most powerful adversary. Recently, Québec nationalists have indeed tried to transform this unequal bilateral relationship into an equal relationship, with André Laurendeau advocating from a federalist perspective and René Lévesque from a sovereigntist perspective. Various reformers have promoted a distinct society, associated states, sovereignty-association, and other solutions, always on behalf of bilateral equality. According to Silver, in reference to Henri Bourassa's theory:

> Such a conception had little chance of general acceptance. Canada's parliamentary institutions and practices of responsible government were suited to majority decisions, as were the liberal ideals which prevailed among all mainstream political figures. What's more, biculturalism flew in the face of a strengthening conviction in English Canada that Canadians formed – or ought to form – a single people or nationality. (1997: 249)

It is to Trudeau's credit that he was able to recognize this conviction in English Canada and, through the 1982 constitutional reform, succeed in giving it a clear, lasting institutional expression. It was Québec's great tragedy that the reform threatened its identity and future, and that it failed to anticipate or react so as to escape its influence. With or without Québec's consent, the 1982 constitutional reforms secured the unifying and homogenizing face of Canada from that point on, and well into the future.

During crises between Québec and Canada prior to the 1980 reform, Québec still had enough political weight to stand up as a credible, unavoidable interlocutor when it came to matching Canadian power. The referendum failure in 1980 sounded the death knell for its special status. It marked the decline of Québec's negotiating power. It made possible the 1982 constitutional reform that turned Québec, *mutatis mutandis*, into a province like the others; and French Canadians, despite residual remainders of their former status, into a cultural minority alongside all the others within the multicultural community instituted by the Canadian Charter of Rights and Freedoms. This was one of the stated objectives of the 1982 constitutional reform. Later events – the Meech Lake and Charlottetown failures, the 1995 referendum, and the Clarity Act – were minor changes in a game where the determining moves had already been made in 1980 and 1982.

If we take a long-term view, despite their importance, all of these events – including those in 1980 and 1982 – were themselves little more than reflections of a strong trend in the changing power relations between Québec and Canada. The political scientist Réjean Pelletier has described this trend in his assessment, from Québec's point of view, of the Canadian experience. According to him,

one conclusion is clear: Québec's situation in the Canadian federation is gradually and constantly deteriorating for structural reasons … It is increasingly easy to overlook it [Québec], which was not always the case. The centre of gravity is no longer located in the two "central provinces" of Québec and Ontario. It has shifted to two other centres of gravity that exclude Québec. On the one hand, there is Ontario, which has significant demographic, economic, and political weight giving it great influence and, since Québec is getting left further behind in these areas, the divide between it and Ontario is growing. On the other hand, there is the Canadian west, especially Alberta and British Columbia, whose combined demographic weight will soon surpass that of Québec, already outpacing Québec economically, and will soon outstrip it politically. Québec will then move into third place, which will translate into a reduced minority position. The weaker a minority is, the less it is heard. (2008: 233; our translation)

Québec has definitely lost the position of strength that it managed to maintain from 1867 until the beginning of the 1980s. Moreover, the 1982 constitutional reform, through the Canadian Charter of Rights and Freedoms, changed the structure of the federal relationship. Priority is no longer given to people-to-people or even government-to-government relations, as under the Constitution Act, 1867, but rather to citizen-to-state relationships, with all levels of government taken as one. It is now from this angle that the trustworthiness of institutions has to be evaluated and trust has to be negotiated, even in Québec. At the same time, claims of the federated entities, beginning with those of Québec, are weakened if not delegitimized should they challenge the unity of the whole, owing to their fragmented nature. They are authorized only insofar as they are no longer a threat to the whole. This is how in 2006, motivated by a concern for appeasement twinned with an electoral calculation, the federal government was able to adopt a motion recognizing that the Québécois form a nation without that recognition having any impact on the definition of the Canadian nation as a whole. Even more recently, the quasi-disappearance of the Bloc Québécois from the House of Commons following the 2 May 2011 election (and confirmed by the 2015 general election) has not only marked the end of a period when Québec's status could still be considered an unavoidable stake, but has illustrated the province's marginalized (positive or negative, depending on the perspective) influence in Ottawa. Thus, *Globe and Mail* columnist Margaret Wente effectively summarized the dominant feeling beyond the borders of Québec when she wrote: "The Bloc, which squatted in Ottawa like a toad for 20 years, is gone. Mr. Harper has forged a new historic alliance between the west and Ontario, and he didn't need Québec to win. Quebeckers' mass infatuation with the NDP may not last longer than snow in April, but their ability to hold federal governments to ransom may be gone for good" (2011).

Peter Russell concludes his chapter by pointing out that Canada's multinational nature is far from being unanimously endorsed across the land. While we agree with Russell on this point, we nonetheless regret that he fails to include in his final analysis the deterioration of Québec's negotiating power within the federation. Russell prefers instead to conclude by vaguely putting his faith in good relations: "This gives rise to my hope that over time, through many, many conversations, significant numbers of English, French, and Aboriginal Canadians will come to share a common understanding of Canada" (132). This hope – and we have to wonder whether it is not somewhat ironic – does not bring us back into the realm of trust and power relationships, but into that of good faith. It is as if, in politics, good faith could compensate for the imbalance of power and interplay of interests. In this case, the Québécois and Aboriginal peoples are holding the short end of the stick, and will continue to do so for the foreseeable future.

NOTES

We would like to thank Jean-Claude Racine, whose contribution as a research assistant to the archival research, data gathering, and reflection greatly influenced this chapter.

1 By "dyadic relationships," we mean relationships between only two individual people.

2 Note that Groulx describes two readings of the federal regime. According to the first, the new political regime is associated with a quest for freedom, while his second reading is clearly more critical in this respect (Gagnon 1969: 35; Groulx 1918: 11, 239).

3 This is our translation of the passages from *La Minerve*.

4 Alfred Dubuc notes that the political elite was convinced that one of the things the union would make possible was an economic development policy focusing on Montréal's financial interests and those of the railway companies. The immediate economic advantages of the new union were numerous: it allowed each colony to break out of isolation, it created a greater force to counter the United States, it eased the weight of individual public debts, and it enhanced the whole structure's credit on international money markets (Dubuc 1969: 12).

5 Ramsay Cook argues that "the birth of provincial autonomy was accompanied by a constitutional theory that makes the history of Canada since Confederation more complicated. It is the pact theory, such that

Confederation was based on the provinces' agreement and cannot be amended without their consent. This theory, which is often attributed to Québec, was probably set out for the first time in Ontario, specifically in the statements by Olivier Mowat and in the editorials of the Toronto *Globe*" (1966: 35).

6 Note that this concern for protecting the rights of linguistic minorities and, moreover, the French Catholic minority, was raised in particular by Étienne-P. Taché during Canada's founding debates. However, this view was not predominant (Ajzenstat et al. 1999: 336–86). It would take some time for French speakers to take a broader interest in defending their interests both within Québec and in the rest of Canada.

7 Bourassa disagreed with Jules-Paul Tardivel, and described his vision of nationalism in the following way: "our own nationalism is Canadian nationalism based on the duality of the races and on specific traditions that this duality involves. We are working for the development of Canadian patriotism, which is in our eyes the best guarantee of the existence of the two races and the mutual respect they owe each other ... for us, the homeland is Canada as a whole, a federation of separate races and autonomous provinces. The nation we want to see develop is the Canadian nation composed of French-Canadians and English-Canadians, two components separated by language and religion, and by the legal provisions necessary to preserve their respective traditions, but united in a feeling of fellowship, with common attachment to the shared homeland" (Lamarre 1993: 74; our translation).

8 We also find this idea in the writings of Camille Roy. According to him, Confederation "places both the French and the English races on definitive equal footing in Canada" (1906: 13; our translation). He sees in the Constitution a means of guaranteeing the linguistic rights of French speakers. He thus pays tribute to the fact that "in 1867, the Canadian constitution of the Confederation decreed that the French language in Canada is, like the English language, an official language of the nation" (5; our translation).

9 In his book, Burelle gives 15 May as the date of this speech, but this is an error according to Radio Canada reports from the time.

10 The speech is online at https://www.collectionscanada.gc.ca/ primeministers/h4-4083-e.html.

11 Speech by the Honourable Pierre Elliott Trudeau, House of Commons Debates, 32nd Parliament, 1st Session: Volume 2, 21 May 1980, http:// parl.canadiana.ca/view/oop.debates_HOC3201_02/122?r=0&s=1.

REFERENCES

Ajzenstat, Janet, Paul Romney, Ian Gentles, and William Gairdner. 1999. *Canada's Founding Debates*. Toronto: Stoddart.

Brouillet, Eugénie. 2005. *La négation de la nation: L'identité culturelle québécoise et le fédéralisme canadien*. Québec: Éditions du Septentrion.

Brunet, Michel, Guy Frégault, and Maurice Trudel, eds. 1952. *Histoire du Canada par les textes*. Montréal: Fides.

Buies, Arthur. 1978. *Lettres sur le Canada: Étude sociale 1864–1867*. Montréal: Édition l'Étincelle.

Burelle, André. 2005. *Pierre Elliott Trudeau: L'intellectuel et le politique*. Montréal: Fides.

Chapais, Thomas. 1979 [1914]. "La naissance d'une nation." In *Anthologie de la littérature québécoise: Vaisseau d'or et croix du chemin*, volume 3, edited by Gilles Marcotte and François Hébert, 12–15. Montréal: Éditions La Presse.

Cook, Ramsay. 1967. *Canada and the French Canadian Question*. Toronto: Macmillan.

Creighton, Donald G. 1964. *The Road to Confederation: The Emergence of Canada, 1863–1867*. Toronto and London: Macmillan.

David, Laurent-Olivier. 1909. *Histoire du Canada depuis la confédération 1867–1887*. Montréal: Librairie Beauchemin.

Denquin, Jean-Marie. 1997. *Vocabulaire politique*. Paris: Presses Universitaires de France.

Dorion, Antoine-Aimé. 1952 [1865]. *Débats parlementaires sur la question de la Confédération des provinces de l'Amérique britannique du Nord*. In *Histoire du Canada par les textes*, edited by M. Brunet, G. Frégault and M. Trudel, 193–5. Montréal: Fides.

Dubuc, Alfred. 1966. "Une interprétation économique de la Constitution." *Socialisme 66*, no. 7. http://classiques.uqac.ca/contemporains/dubuc_alfred/interpr_eco_constitution/interpretation.html.

Fukuyama, Francis. 1995. *Trust: The Social Virtues and the Creation of Prosperity*. New York: Free Press.

Gagnon, Serge. 1969. "Historiographie canadienne ou les fondements de la conscience nationale." In *Guide d'histoire du Canada*, edited by André Beaulieu, Jean Hamelin, and Benoît Bernier, 1–59. Québec: Presses de l'Université Laval.

Groulx, Lionel. 1914. "La constitution fédérative de 1867: Origine, teneur, modifications, portée." *Revue canadienne* 14, no. 67: 385–98.

– 1918. *La Confédération canadienne: Ses origines*. Montréal: Le Devoir.

Hardin, Russell. 2006. *Trust*. Cambridge: Polity Press.

Harvey, Fernand. 2000. "Le français menacé. Le Canada français et la question linguistique." In *Le français au Québec: 400 ans d'histoire et de vie*, edited by Hélène Duval, Pierre Georgeault, and Michel Plourde, 193–209. Québec: Conseil de la Langue Française.

Laforest, Guy. 1992. *Trudeau et la fin d'un rêve canadien*. Québec: Éditions du Septentrion.

Lamarre, Jean. 1993. *Le devenir de la nation québécoise selon Maurice Séguin, Guy Frégault et Michel Brunet, 1944–1969*. Québec: Septentrion.

LaSelva, Samuel. 2002. "Federalism, Pluralism, and Constitutional Faith: Canada in Question." *Review of Constitutional Studies/Revue d'études constitutionnelles* 7, nos 1 and 2: 204–19.

Pelletier, Benoît. 2010. *Une certaine idée du Québec: Parcours d'un fédéraliste de la réflexion à l'action*. Québec: Presses de l'Université Laval.

Pelletier, Réjean. 2008. *Le Québec et le fédéralisme canadien: Un regard critique*. Québec: Presses de l'Université Laval.

Putnam, Robert. 2000. *Bowling Alone: The Collapse and Revival of American Community*. New York: Simon and Schuster.

Roy, Camille. 1906. *Études des anciens Canadiens: Nos raisons canadiennes de rester Français*. Québec: L'Action Catholique.

Séguin, Maurice. 1997. *Histoire de deux nationalismes au Canada*. Montréal: Guérin.

– 1999. *Les normes*. In *Les Normes de Maurice Séguin: Le théoricien du néo-nationalisme*, edited by Pierre Tousignant and Madeleine Dionne-Tousignant. Montréal: Guérin.

Seymour, Michel. 2001. *Le pari de la démesure: L'intransigeance canadienne face au Québec*. Montréal: Éditions de l'Hexagone.

Silver, Arthur Isaac. 1997. *The French-Canadian Idea of Confederation: 1864–1900*. Second edition with a new epilogue. Toronto: University of Toronto Press.

Smiley, Donald. 1983. "A Dangerous Deed: The Constitution Act, 1982." In *And No One Cheered: Federalism, Democracy and the Constitution Act*, edited by Keith Banting and Richard Simeon, 74–95. Agincourt: Methuen Publication.

Sulte, Benjamin. 1884. *Histoire des Canadiens-français 1608–1880: Origine, histoire, religion, guerres, découvertes, colonisation, coutumes, vie domestique, sociale et politique, développement, avenir*. Volume 18. Montréal: Société des Publications Historiques du Canada.

Weinstock. Daniel. 2008. "Dilemmes de la confiance." Presented at the GRSP workshop on trust and distrust in multinational democracies, UQAM, Montréal.

Wente, Margaret. 2011. "Here's Why Stephen Harper Really Won." *Globe and Mail*, 5 May.

8

The Delayed (and Qualified) Victory of the Meech Lake Accord: The Role of Constitutional Reform in Undermining and Restoring Intercommunal Trust

Jeremy Webber

The failure of the Meech Lake Accord in 1990 provoked a constitutional crisis, one of the manifestations of which was a crisis of confidence, experienced by many Quebecers, who doubted whether their vision of Canada – a vision that they believed had been fundamental to the founding of Canada – was shared by Canadians outside Québec. In the years following Meech, Canadian leaders responded with a series of initiatives, but many of those initiatives – particularly those designed to amend the Canadian constitution – themselves ended in debacle, compounding the damage. Further proposals for constitutional change seemed futile.

Still more troubling, the Canadian federation appeared to have lost cohesion. It was marked, so it seemed, by deep misunderstandings. The effort to welcome Québec into the Canadian constitution "with honour and enthusiasm" (in Prime Minister Brian Mulroney's words) had collapsed without hope of renewal. The nadir was reached in the Québec referendum of 1995, in which the secessionist project lost by less than 1 per cent of the vote, demonstrating the extent of disenchantment within Québec, but without establishing a clear way forward.

And yet, the initiatives that followed the collapse of the Meech Lake Accord did not completely fail. They did not result in constitutional amendments,[1] but, over time, the principles that underlay the accord came to be consolidated within Canadian political life to such an extent that one can plausibly claim that they now furnish the working assumptions of federal politics, accepted in practice by all sides, including the erstwhile opponents of Meech. The accord may have been defeated, but the defeat was (to adapt a phrase) pyrrhic. The approach to the Canadian federation reflected in Meech scored a belated victory.

But how effective a victory? Is it the kind of victory that can achieve what Meech was intended to do, namely reconcile Québec to the Constitution? Can it remedy the crisis in confidence that followed the defeat of Meech? This paper will start by reviewing the challenges posed by the patriation of the Canadian constitution in 1982, the tainted legitimacy of that project in Québec, and the abortive attempts in the Meech Lake and Charlottetown Accords to overcome that taint. It will then make the case that, despite the defeat of Meech, the principles underlying the accord (and indeed the bulk of the accord's specific proposals) now form part of the working assumptions of Canadian public life. It will describe how that victory occurred and the measures that embody it.

These measures have not taken the form of constitutional amendments. Does that matter? Many current discussions seem to treat constitutional reform as the entire object of the exercise. Until the Constitution is changed, nothing of importance will have changed, and the ideas that motivated Pierre Elliott Trudeau during the patriation process will continue to rule us from the grave. But this cannot be right. Constitutions are complex and dynamic, containing a multiplicity of strands even in their texts – certainly subject to a multiplicity of interpretations. They establish general frameworks for government that can be deployed to a plurality of ends. The lived Constitution, the Constitution as it operates at a particular time, is therefore richer, more complex, and more nuanced than might be suggested by the text alone, and certainly cannot be reduced to the intentions of one political actor, whose time in office ended more than thirty years ago. It is worth looking carefully, then, at the Constitution as it operates today, to see whether it conforms to the fears expressed as a result of patriation. As will become clear, I believe that it does not, and that its living reality is much closer to that projected in the Meech Lake Accord.

That alone does not end the inquiry, however. I accept that the challenges that resulted from patriation and its aftermath are well understood as matters of trust and distrust, where the principal damage caused by the failure of Meech had to do not just with the workings of government but with francophone Quebecers' sense of belonging within Canada – especially their confidence that Canada is willing to make room for a vigorous and dynamic French-speaking society, to see that society as a fundamental partner in Confederation, and to maintain constitutional arrangements that allow that society to flourish. When it comes to those questions, there is a real issue whether the lived constitution is as effective as formal changes to the constitutional text. This chapter therefore raises the relative roles of formality and informality, of expression and action, in the self-understanding of a country.

Their exploration is not merely an empirical exercise of weighing the relative force of text and practice. We, as constitutional analysts, are not mere observers. We play a role in interpreting the text and the lived constitution. We evaluate their adequacy and, in doing so, help to shape the public's sense of them. In the end, then, this essay is bound up with a set of normative issues: How *should* we conceive of the relative roles of expression and action? To which dimension should we give most credence? And, following from those questions, how should we evaluate the Canadian constitution post-Meech, specifically the adequacy of that constitution for Québec's place within Canada?

SOURCES OF CONSTITUTIONAL MALAISE

To understand Canada's predicament, it is useful to begin with patriation in 1982. The manner in which patriation occurred, and the constitutional measures put in place at that time, generated lingering dissatisfaction in Québec. The Meech Lake Accord attempted to respond to that dissatisfaction. Its failure produced the crisis in confidence that this paper examines (see Webber 1994; Burelle 2005: 56–89; Romanow, Whyte, and Leeson 1984; Russell 2004a).

Patriation was the culmination of a series of constitutional negotiations, proceeding in fits and starts, driven chiefly by the demands of successive Québec governments for provincial autonomy, especially in response to the centralization of the Canadian federation that had occurred during World War II. Those negotiations were given impetus by the Referendum on Sovereignty-Association, held by the Parti Québécois government in 1980. At a key point in that campaign,

Pierre Elliott Trudeau, then prime minister of Canada, promised that if the "No" side prevailed, he would seek to renew the Canadian federation (for an important record of these remarks, see Burelle 2005: 179–246). The "No" side did win, and Trudeau immediately began a process of constitutional reform.

That process produced the bundle of amendments that came to be known as the patriation package. The amendments did not address the traditional concerns of Québec. Apart from one provision strengthening provincial control over natural resources (prompted by the demands of Alberta and Saskatchewan), the package did not deal with federal and provincial powers at all. Instead, it put in place:

- A new constitutional amending formula, in which Québec would not have a veto over amendments but would have a right to opt out of certain amendments, receiving financial compensation for those in the fields of education and culture. It was this new amending formula that gave the package its name, for it meant that amendments could now be accomplished in Canada, without the intervention of the United Kingdom Parliament, thereby "patriating" the constitution.
- A new Canadian Charter of Rights and Freedoms which established a broad set of rights guarantees, including expanded protections for English and French throughout Canada and a provision that specifically overrode one aspect of Québec's Charter of the French Language. This latter provision expanded the class of children that had access to English-language public schools in Québec.
- The recognition of Aboriginal and treaty rights, together with an undertaking to hold further constitutional conferences to discuss those rights.

The constitutional package was adopted with the support of the federal government and nine of ten provincial governments, but over the objections of Québec. The fact that the amendments proceeded despite Québec's opposition caused considerable disquiet in Québec. It would have been very difficult to secure the support of the *indépendantiste* government for any arrangements acceptable to the federal government. Although the Parti Québécois government did participate in the negotiations in good faith, its vision of Canada was profoundly different from that of the Trudeau Liberals and, as a party ultimately committed to Québec's secession, it was not well placed to persuade others to make substantial changes to the Canadian federation (see Burelle 2005: 85–6; Webber 1994: 118–19). It is also true that the federal Liberals had very substantial electoral support in Québec and that Trudeau was personally very popular. But the government of Québec had long been seen, by Quebecers, to have a privileged role in protecting French Canadians' interests within the federation, for it was the only jurisdiction with a French-speaking majority. One expression of that role had been a right to veto constitutional amendments, a right that, while unwritten, was nevertheless acknowledged by many within Canadian politics, including by all major political actors in Québec.[2] The passage of such an extensive set of constitutional amendments, over the objections of the elected government of Québec, was bound to provoke unease even among those strongly committed to Canada.

"Unease" is probably the best way to describe the reservations held by a significant portion of Quebecers, including federalists. Most francophone Quebecers remained strongly committed to Canada, but they saw that commitment as being perfectly compatible with an attachment to Québec's distinctiveness. They wished to remain Canadian, indeed to participate more fully in the political life of Canada. They supported the strong role that Trudeau and others were playing on the Canadian stage. But they wanted that participation to be as French Canadians, maintaining a vigorous French-speaking society within North America. In that project, a vibrant Québec, able to defend its jurisdiction and serve as an expression of Québec's predominantly French-speaking society, even when currents in Ottawa ran against French Canadian interests, was fundamental. It was that role that patriation seemed to undermine.

Moreover, it was also clear that the principal actor in patriation, Trudeau, disagreed with the role itself. He saw the emphasis of francophone Quebecers on their province as parochial, always in danger of slipping into a narrow cultural nationalism. He therefore sought to use the Canadian Charter of Rights and Freedoms to affirm a unified Canadian citizenship, one in which individual rights, protected at the level of Canada as a whole, would shift Quebecers' allegiance from the province to the federal government (Russell 1983; Knopff and Morton 1985; Laforest 1992: 173–205). The most obvious manifestation of this strategy was the provision on minority language education rights in the Canadian Charter. It sought to limit the extent to which the Québec government could pursue educational policies designed to reinforce Québec's French character.

Quebecers' concerns were masked, to some extent, by the support of many Quebecers for elements of the package. Beginning in the early 1960s, during the "Quiet Revolution," Québec had become an emphatically liberal society. Support for the Charter on civil libertarian grounds was therefore strong in Québec, and it remains among the provinces with the strongest support. (CRIC 2002: 30–1; Nanos 2007: 51–2). Moreover, Quebecers were decidedly in favour of the Canadian government being their government too, not merely that of English Canadians, and therefore supported the increasingly bilingual character of the federal government. It was the negative dimension of Trudeau's program, the willingness to displace Québec as the champion of French Canada, that many Quebecers did not share.

There was also dissatisfaction with some of the terms of the patriation package, although this tended to be a specialist taste, advanced by political scientists and constitutional lawyers. The most obvious concern was with the lack of any measures dealing with the division of powers, especially the fact that no constraint had been imposed on the federal government's spending power, under which Ottawa had, since World War II, established programs within areas of provincial legislative jurisdiction. This had been the primary demand of Québec governments prior to patriation. The fact that the demand had not been addressed resurfaced quickly in patriation's aftermath.

There was also concern that patriation might have buttressed the role of federal institutions vis-à-vis the Québec government. This was the case in language rights, under which at least some of Québec's initiatives were now subject to review by the Supreme Court of Canada, whose judges were appointed by the federal government.[3] This was the most obvious and sensitive restriction imposed on Québec, but the Charter also limited the powers of all governments, federal and provincial, across a broad swath of areas, and therefore subjected Québec, alongside the other governments, to Supreme Court review in these areas. To the extent that review was confined to issues of human rights, there appeared to be substantial support among Quebecers. But amongst specialists, there was concern that this might lead, over time, to greater uniformity in Canadian law. This would be a risk especially if the Charter were interpreted broadly, so that many laws were held to raise Charter issues, and if the test for justifying Charter infringements were applied strictly, so that only the least restrictive measure would be upheld. If that happened, then the room for variation among provinces might be substantially reduced, as the Supreme Court imposed more and more restrictions on the scope for provincial legislation (Woehrling 1991: 153–4; Webber 1993: 213–15, 221–5; Brouillet 2005: 329–36).

It was those concerns that Canadian governments addressed in the Meech Lake Accord of 1987, led by a new Progressive Conservative government in Ottawa and a new Liberal government in Québec. That accord proposed the following set of constitutional amendments:[4]

- In its first and most important provision, it recognized "that Quebec constitutes within Canada a distinct society," directing the courts to take that into account when interpreting the constitution.
- It imposed limitations on the federal spending power, enabling provinces to opt out of new shared-cost programs in areas of exclusive provincial jurisdiction, with financial compensation, if the province carried on a program compatible with national objectives.
- It encouraged the negotiation of federal/provincial agreements in the shared field of immigration, giving these agreements greater force than exists currently for intergovernmental agreements.
- It provided a system for joint federal-provincial appointments to the Senate and the Supreme Court of Canada. Crucial elements of the Supreme Court would have been constitutionalized, including a guarantee that three judges of the court would be appointed from Québec.
- It also changed the formula for future constitutional amendments. It did not restore Québec's veto, but it extended the right of financial compensation for amendments that transferred authority to the federal government (making it easier for Québec to opt out), and extended the requirement of unanimity to more items, most controversially the creation of new provinces and certain elements of Senate reform (in effect allowing Québec – or any other province – to veto such amendments).
- Finally, it required that federal and provincial first ministers conferences be held to deal with constitutional questions not addressed in the accord and other matters of importance.

The Meech Lake Accord was initially embraced by all the federal and provincial governments in Canada. Those governments embarked on a process of ratification under the amending formula adopted in 1982. The story of the accord's unravelling is too complex to be told here (see Webber 1994: 134–62). Suffice it to say that it ultimately collapsed when two provinces, Newfoundland and Manitoba, failed to ratify within the period required.

The reasons for its defeat are many, and at least two – the opposition of Indigenous peoples and the lack of progress on Senate reform – had more to do with what was not in the accord than what was. Nevertheless, the defeat of the accord was taken very hard in Québec. It precipitated the crisis of confidence that is the subject of this paper, for this had been the "Québec Round" of constitutional negotiations, and the measures that were rejected spoke directly to Québec's long-standing constitutional concerns, especially the unease left as a result of patriation. They were moderate measures, causing no significant shifts in the responsibilities of Canadian governments; on the contrary, the provisions dealing with the division of powers tended to be oriented towards the future, implicitly accepting, for example, existing federal social programs in areas of provincial jurisdiction. And the principal provision criticized in the public debate on Meech, the distinct society clause, expressed what a broad consensus of francophone Quebecers took to be a premise of the Canadian federation – that Québec was a unique jurisdiction, with unique responsibilities given its significance for French Canadians, and that those responsibilities should be taken into account in the working of the Canadian constitution. The accord had been promoted by a newly elected federalist government in Québec. Its defeat was the defeat of the predominant federalist option, not (as in 1982) a sovereignist option. For many Quebecers, the repudiation of the accord was a repudiation of their place within Canada.

The failure of Meech was then followed by the bitter coda of the Charlottetown Accord (see Webber 1994: 162–75). Charlottetown retained the main features of Meech, but it introduced changes in wording which, though they did not materially change the effect of the provisions, did hedge them about with definitions and qualifications, significantly diminishing their symbolic force. Charlottetown dealt with dissatisfaction principally by including a long series of matters that had not been covered by Meech – Senate reform and Indigenous self-government chief among them. But in the end its compromises satisfied few. It was rejected by a national referendum. With that rejection, the constitutional process collapsed.

The concepts of trust and distrust capture well the nature of the disaffection remaining in the wake of Meech and Charlottetown, especially in Québec. But the distrust was of a particular kind. The concept of trust was deployed very effectively in the political science literature of the 1990s to describe the social bonds necessary for effective cooperation in democratic institutions, interactions governed by the rule of law, and honest and predictable state administration (see Putnam 1993). The essential idea was that these relations required a measure of confidence that other citizens would fulfil their obligations, operate within legal constraints, and respect ethical injunctions. These expectations were satisfied when individuals participated in a sufficiently dense pattern of interactions, in associations and other institutional settings, to establish a foundation for trust. Citizens did not need to know each other or like each other; the relevant trust was a "cool," impersonal expectation that others would, for the most part, observe ethical standards (Krygier 1997: 61–2). The analysis was buttressed by comparison between Western, democratic, relatively law-governed societies and the post-communist societies of central and eastern Europe, where generalized social trust had been undermined by decades of state surveillance, the discouragement of associational activity, utter dependence on the state, and endemic privilege and corruption.

The kind of social trust that was the focus of that literature has never been undermined in Canada. While there have been instances of misuse of state prerogatives (such as the sponsorship scandal under the Chrétien government, or the suspicions of wrongdoing by the Charest government in Québec, both of which have seriously weakened federalist parties), those cases have not caused public expectations of ethical conduct to collapse in a manner comparable to communist eastern Europe. On the contrary, the very vehemence of the public reaction reinforced those standards. Rather, the confidence in issue in Meech was specific to culturally divided societies: the expectation that the government of the country would adhere to principles taken to be fundamental to the minority. In Canada, the relevant principles did not concern outright oppression; no one expected that to occur in late twentieth-century Canada. Rather, they referred to the expectation that Canada would be a partnership of English and French, that Québec would retain its autonomy to govern its areas of jurisdiction in a manner responsive to its distinctive society, and that Québec would be able to take measures to sustain its vibrant, predominantly French-speaking society. It was the perception that those principles were threatened – indeed that they had been rejected with the rejection of Meech – that provoked the sudden erosion of trust within Québec.

To some extent, the lack of trust was mutual. To many citizens outside Québec, Trudeau's constitutional projects had defined Québec's: bilingualism, constitutionally entrenched rights, and active, emphatically bilingual federal institutions. They had accepted those, some people willingly, some grudgingly, and they were disconcerted by what were, to them, new and strident demands for autonomy and separate recognition, demands that Trudeau told them smacked of separatism. They too questioned the other partner's commitment to Confederation. And, outside this generalized anglophone funk, Indigenous peoples continued to chafe against the very idea of there being only two founding peoples, and the neglect of their most cherished interests.

THE BELATED VICTORY OF THE MEECH LAKE ACCORD

The deep sense of dissatisfaction and mutual distrust troubled many political actors: federalists within Québec, who hoped for a rapprochement, and Canadians outside Québec, distressed at the severity of the breakdown and the rise in support for secession. Following Charlottetown, constitutional reform seemed impossible. Attention therefore shifted to measures achievable without constitutional amendment. Over the next few years, a great many of the elements in Meech became part of the working assumptions of Canadian government, despite the lack of formal constitutional change.

When assessing this incremental and non-constitutional adoption of Meech's elements, it is important not to exaggerate the extent to which, in the first place, Meech had been rejected. Among political leaders, support for the accord had been and remained extensive (though not unanimous). Parliament and eight of ten provincial legislatures had ratified the accord. A ninth, Manitoba, would have done so given a few more days. The debate had been bruising for supporters of the accord: Meech had been fiercely attacked by its opponents, popular support outside Québec had plummeted, and commitment amongst political actors was often, by the end, prompted more by fear of the consequences of failure than by wholehearted acceptance.

Nevertheless, however battered, support among politicians was still widespread. Even among the public, opposition to Meech had very often been based on its omissions, rather than its inclusions (Webber 1994: 146–50).

It is also a mistake to associate the defeat of Meech with the triumph of a relentless individualism, one that could not countenance the idea that Canada was a multinational federation.[5] One of the main reasons for opposition to Meech had been a desire on the part of some Canadians for action on Indigenous self-government, a demand that was itself founded on a vision of a multinational Canada. And although Trudeau and his supporters pressed an individualistic and anti-multinational case, there were strong counterarguments. Even the patriation package had been qualified by these arguments. It is true that the Canadian Charter was committed to individual rights, emphasized freedom from the state rather than a more participatory democratic conception of freedom, enshrined first-generation civil liberties rather than second-generation economic and social rights, and treated the courts, not the legislatures, as the principal venue for the advancement of rights. But there were other strands as well. The Charter specifically recognized (in section 1) that rights could be qualified by other social objectives. The notwithstanding clause (section 33) allowed legislatures to override the courts' interpretation of some rights (although it is also true that many Canadians did not accept the rationale for the clause and, as a result, it became very difficult to use).[6] Even in the area of language rights, the patriation package did not simply enforce individual choice. It only explicitly changed one aspect of Bill 101 – the formula for access to minority-language schools – and even there, English schools were not opened up to anyone who wanted them. On the contrary, the new formula (the "Canada clause" as opposed to the "Québec clause") was one reportedly favoured by René Lévesque in the original framing of Bill 101 (Lévesque 1986: 389).[7] Indeed, this limited overriding of Bill 101 was of concern in Québec not so much because of its content but because it used a pan-Canadian instrument to change an important aspect of cultural policy in Québec, restricting the ability of Québec to set its own rules.

More broadly, the very focus on French and English emphasized Canada's duality in a way that recognized, implicitly, that the language of public institutions could not simply be a matter of individual choice; Canada was bilingual, so that English and French had a status quite different from German, Cantonese, Ukrainian, and Spanish (for example). It is true that the patriation package failed to recognize a distinctive role for Québec in expressing Canada's duality. This was an important defect, one that drove much of what followed. But it is also true that the treatment of language was not purely individualistic. And this aspect of the package coexisted with other dimensions of the constitution – older dimensions, still premised on cultural autonomy, including the federal division of powers itself. Finally, the patriation package explicitly recognized "aboriginal and treaty rights," affirming a dimension of Canada's national diversity that the Trudeau Liberals had, at one time, sought to eliminate in the name of individual rights (Constitution Act 1982, section 35; Weaver 1981). One should not exaggerate the communitarian dimensions of the patriation package – there is no doubt that the individualistic dimensions predominated – but the individualistic theme competed with other themes firmly rooted in Canada's diversity.

These various themes were not, however, reconciled either in the text of the Constitution or in the debate in English-speaking Canada. The latter in particular tended to draw on strands of political theory that had little to say about cultural or linguistic difference. One of the depressing aspects of the Meech debate had been the tendency to treat the accord as an unprincipled compromise, a concession to strident political demands, in contrast to the ostensibly principled position taken by the accord's opponents. But this was one feature that, in the wake of Meech, began rapidly to change. A number of theorists set out to express the principled foundation of the accord, exploring the relationship between culture and political engagement (Taylor 1992, 1993; Tully 1995; Kymlicka 1998; this is also the principal objective in Webber 1994). Those works have become extraordinarily important. Some of the primary treatments of cultural difference in political theory, setting the agenda internationally, were written by Canadian scholars stimulated by the constitutional debates (in addition to the works just cited, see Kymlicka 1989, 1995). It would be too much to say that these works transformed opinion on the accord, causing a kind of mass conversion; but they did shift the context of the debate, making it clear that there were principled arguments in favour of asymmetrical federalism, the recognition of Québec's distinctiveness, and Indigenous governance.

These arguments had, I believe, a material effect. It is difficult to chart their impact, but there is no doubt that what was once widely considered to be an unprincipled political compromise is now seen to be supported by a coherent, if still controversial, vision of the country. That said, the increasing tendency to accept the Meech principles, described below, was as much the result of the exigencies of Canadian politics as of a change of heart. Over time, it became clear to virtually all parties, including many who had been strongly opposed to Meech (such as leaders of the old Reform Party), that the country could only be governed by some accommodation between Quebecers and Canadians outside Québec, and, for that to occur, something like the Meech principles had to be respected.

I will explore the acceptance of those principles under categories drawn from the Meech Lake Accord. In the following section, I will assess the fact that the subsequent developments departed from Meech, notably through the use of mechanisms other than constitutional reform. I will therefore be using Meech as the implicit standard of evaluation throughout. That itself is controversial. Some commentators in Québec, at the time and since, have believed that the accord itself was insufficient, perhaps even deeply misconceived, and those opinions still shape some constitutional commentary (see, e.g., Seymour 2006). Nevertheless, it is remarkable the extent to which Meech has become the privileged point of comparison, even among many of those who opposed it at the time. It has been especially significant as the measure of constitutional misunderstanding between Quebecers and other Canadians. Meech Lake has become the standard against which progress (and regress) has come to be measured.

In this account, I will focus on the positive agenda that sought to address Québec's longstanding constitutional concerns, not what came to be known as "Plan B" – measures to regulate the consequences of failure, especially an attempt by Québec to secede (such as the federal Clarity Act;[8] see Russell 2004a: 241–7). Plan B was an important part of the story of the post-Meech years. It also had an impact on trust and distrust: by contemplating what might happen in the case of secession, it reinforced an antagonistic relationship between Québec and the rest of Canada, emphasizing conflict, not reconciliation. But the elements of Plan B would only be triggered by some future move towards secession. They did not address Canadian governance as a going concern. Here, I am concerned with the latter – with attempts to recast the day-to-day operation of Canadian federalism along the lines of the Meech Lake Accord.

Recognition of Québec as a Distinct Society

Had Meech Lake been adopted, the distinct society clause would have provided clear recognition of Québec's role in representing the French fact in Canada. That role had, for its principal advocates, both external and internal aspects. In its external aspect, it suggested that Québec should be considered a privileged voice for French Canadians. Not the only voice – Meech's advocates agreed that French-speaking Canadians should also be full players in federal politics – but a principal voice, which was a status reflected, for example, in Québec's traditional claim to a constitutional veto. This was complemented by the internal aspect. Québec was the only jurisdiction in Canada in which French was the predominant language of public interaction. It thus had a particular importance for French-speaking Canadians, for it was the one jurisdiction in which debates that occurred in French directly shaped policy-making. This meant that the clause had significance for more than just cultural matters in the narrow sense of the term. Québec was distinct because people governed themselves predominantly in French, participating in debates that, because they occurred in a different language, had substantial autonomy from debates in the rest of Canada. That autonomy affected the whole gamut of political questions (Webber 1994: 127–9, 200–15).

The recognition of Québec's distinctiveness in Meech was more than symbolic. It directed the courts to consider the clause when interpreting the Constitution. It did not change the terms in which rights or powers were expressed, but it changed the interpretive lens, so that Québec's distinctiveness would have shaped how those provisions were applied. This would have had a subtle but material effect, counteracting the view that governments should be neutral on questions of language and culture. For its advocates, then, the most obvious impact of the distinct society clause would have been on the courts' interpretation of the Canadian Charter of Rights and Freedoms, for the clause would have legitimized a distinctive, culturally based role for the government of Québec and would have countered any tendency to interpret the Charter as requiring uniformity in Canadian law.[9]

Despite the failure of Meech, there is a strong argument that the Charter has been interpreted in a manner that reflects the principles underlying the distinct society clause. First, the courts have resisted the temptation to interpret the Charter in ways that would produce an increasing homogenization of Canadian law. The courts did flirt with disaster by adopting a very broad interpretation of certain provisions in the Charter, especially freedom of expression (a right that was especially sensitive, given its relationship to language and culture). If they had then imposed a very demanding test to justify infringements of that freedom, their decisions might have significantly narrowed the room for provincial variation. But in fact, they have generally not done so. Instead, they have relaxed the test for limitations on rights when dealing with complex social policy, allowing the legislatures substantial leeway in pursuing their policies.[10]

Second, they have expressly accepted Canada's cultural diversity, and have acknowledged that that diversity must have an institutional dimension and not rely on individual choice alone. They have, for example, accepted that inherent in federalism is a principle of variation among provinces, and that the Charter's guarantee of equality should not be used to foreclose that diversity. They have even accepted that this principle can result in the different application of *federal* law from province to province (this was decided in a case dealing with the sentencing of young offenders, where facilities for young offenders vary from province to province; see *R. v S. (S.)* 1990: 291; see, also, *R. v Advance Cutting & Coring* 2001: par. 275–6; Kelly 2001). When addressing French-language education in Alberta, they emphasized the role of minority-language schools in sustaining communities. As a result, they built a dimension of community-control into the Charter's education guarantees (*Mahé* 1990). There has also been a vast expansion in the number of cases on Indigenous rights since their recognition in the Constitution Act, 1982, and these have clearly been premised on the recognition of Indigenous peoples as collectivities (Hogg 2006: par 28.8). And throughout all these decisions, the courts have made clear that the individual rights in the Charter do not override the recognition of cultural diversity in other branches of the Constitution – language rights, federalism, guarantees of publicly funded religious schools, Indigenous rights – although they have certainly reflected upon how culturally specific institutions might fit together with individual rights. In the early cases, the court tended to avoid even that consideration, treating instances of collective recognition as simple political compromises that could trump, but might still be in tension with, the rights in the Charter (see, e.g. *Société des Acadiens* 1986: 578). But over time the court has departed from this position, sought to explore the principled foundation for collective recognition, and invoked such principles in its decisions. In retrospect, then, the emphasis placed on individual rights in the Charter has not entrenched a hegemonic and uncontested individualism. On the contrary, it has engendered a process of collective reflection through which the courts and Canadians generally have had to balance, even if not always successfully, freedom, equality, and the institutional and cultural frameworks within which such values are necessarily pursued.[11]

Third, the courts have recognized Québec's distinctiveness and used it to shape their interpretation of the Charter. This was especially clear in the Supreme Court of Canada's decision in *Ford*. That case dealt with the requirement, in Québec's Bill 101, that only French be used on commercial signs. *Ford* was decided principally on Québec's Charter of Human Rights and Freedoms, not the Canadian Charter, because Québec had invoked the notwithstanding clause with respect to the Canadian Charter, although the court made clear that it would have used the same reasoning had the Charter applied. The court invalidated the sign law, but, interestingly, it did not hold that the language of signs should be left to individual choice, or that English and French must be treated equally. Instead, it decided that Québec was entitled to "take steps to assure that the '*visage linguistique*' of Québec would reflect the predominance of the French language," given the need to protect French against the demographic and economic pressure of English. It struck down the provision only on the basis that a complete ban on other languages went too far. It held that requiring the "marked predominance" of French would have been sufficient (*Ford v Quebec* 1998: par. 72–3).

The *Ford* decision was not well received in Québec. The Bourassa government revised the provisions and then invoked the notwithstanding clause to protect them, this time under both the Canadian and Québec Charters (Québec 1988). But the reason for that rejection was not that the government disagreed with the substance of the court's decision. Five years later, the Bourassa government amended the provisions to bring them into line with the decision and repealed the notwithstanding clauses, with very little opposition (Québec 1993; see, also, the position of Lucien Bouchard as premier of Québec, in Burelle 2005: 464). The problem was rather Quebecers' perennial concern with having the Assemblée nationale's decisions on language overruled by an institution that was federally appointed, with a majority from outside Québec. Once again, the problem was not the content of the decision, but that language policy in Québec was being determined by a body over which Quebecers had no control.

That problem is not one that Meech Lake would have fixed. Indeed, it was inherent in the very idea of a constitutionally entrenched charter of rights, enforced by the Supreme Court. In one sense, this problem was similar to concerns expressed in other parts of the country about the role of the courts under the Charter, second-guessing the decisions of democratically elected legislatures. Quebecers, like Canadians elsewhere, have been divided between support for individual rights and unease with the courts' overruling of democratic decisions. That unease has an added edge in Québec, however, especially when it comes to questions of language, because of the exclusively federal composition of the Supreme Court of Canada.[12]

The court has, then, interpreted the Canadian constitution in a manner consistent with the principles of the Meech Lake Accord. It has expressly recognized the distinctive linguistic concerns of Québec. It premised its decision in *Ford* upon that fact.[13] More generally, it has recognized that many features of the Canadian constitution are premised on the need to adapt public institutions to cultural and linguistic diversity, and has refused to interpret individual rights in a way that would undermine that adaptation. Although, in particular cases, one might quarrel with the ways in which the court has done this, its approach has been consistent with Meech. This consistency has, however, been achieved through the courts' exercise of their incremental, interpretive role. The succession of decisions did not provide – it could not provide – the prominent symbolic recognition that the distinct society clause would have accomplished. Even with respect to that recognition, however, some steps have been taken.

The first was the adoption by the House of Commons in 1995 (and by several provinces at about the same time) of a resolution recognizing Québec as a distinct society (Chrétien 1995b).[14] The effect of that resolution was very limited, as might be expected of an initiative by then-prime minister Jean Chrétien, one of the chief opponents of the distinct society clause. It was hedged about by definitions and limitations: by its terms it only applied to Parliament and the federal executive, not to the interpretation of the Constitution, and, as a mere resolution, it did not even bind them. Chrétien expressed his willingness to entrench it in the Constitution, but it was clear that that could not happen anytime soon.[15]

The federal resolution was followed, two years later, by a declaration adopted by the premiers of all provinces and territories except Québec: the "Framework for Discussion on Canadian Unity," known as the "Calgary Declaration." The declaration affirmed "the unique character of Quebec society, including its French speaking majority, its culture and its tradition of civil law," and recognized Québec's role "to protect and develop the unique character of Quebec society within Canada." It also stated a number of other principles, including the equal status of all provinces, and held that "if any future constitutional amendment confers powers on one province, these powers must be available to all provinces." The signatories suggested that these principles should "form the basis for a grass-roots discussion on constitutional renewal."[16] In November 1997, the House of Commons passed a resolution (proposed by the Reform Party and supported by the Liberal government) endorsing the process begun by the declaration.[17] However, the Calgary Declaration too was limited by many qualifications, the change in terminology (from "distinct" to "unique") muddied the waters, and, in any case, the refusal of the Parti Québécois government to participate meant that the process could only end in failure.[18]

A much more significant step took place nine years later, in November 2006. The Bloc Québécois had proposed a motion to recognize "that Quebeckers form a nation" (Québec's Assemblée nationale had adopted, unanimously, a similar resolution in 2003). Prime Minister Stephen Harper responded that his government would propose its own resolution, simply adding "within a united Canada" to the Bloc Québécois's wording.[19] The government's motion passed by a vote of 265 to 16, with even the Bloc Québécois voting in favour. The Bloc's own motion, without the reference to a united Canada, was defeated.[20]

This resolution was, like the previous attempts, purely symbolic. On its own, it had no legal effect. But it was remarkable for the degree of convergence it expressed. Its wording was not subjected to a host of qualifications and definitions. It adopted what had generally been considered stronger language to that of "distinct society" – stronger because the language of nationhood had often been used to argue for a single Québec nation, an exclusive pole for Quebecers' allegiance, separate from an English-Canadian nation – although, by 2006, many had argued that nationhood could be understood in a plural fashion, so that it made sense to speak of Quebecers being full members of both a Québec and a Canadian nation (see, for example, Webber

1994: 23–6). It was in this sense that the federalist parties supported
the resolution. Most importantly, the resolution had been embraced
by all the major federal parties, including former members of the
Reform Party (including Harper himself) who, in the mid 1990s, had
strongly resisted any special recognition of Québec, and the great
majority of Liberal MPs, who had, during the Trudeau years, deeply
distrusted the language of "distinct society" and vehemently rejected
that of "nation."[21] The government's motion closely tracked the terms
proposed by the Bloc Québécois, albeit adding the reference to a
united Canada. The resolution therefore represented a substantial
shift; perhaps not a complete change of heart (political calculation
certainly played its role), but significant nevertheless.

How then should one summarize the position today? There is no
doubt that formal recognition of Québec – as a nation, or as a distinct
society – has been disjoined from the question of legal effect.
Recognition has been achieved through resolutions of the House of
Commons and of some provincial legislatures, resolutions that have
no binding force. That caveat granted, however, there has been substantial coalescence around the terms of the recognition, uniting even
parties that formerly opposed those terms. The recognition is still often
qualified by the "equality of the provinces" (though this was not the
case in the 2006 resolution). But that language itself has been ambiguous; it has at times been used to oppose special treatment for Québec,
but what constitutes unequal treatment is itself a matter of debate,
especially given Québec's distinctiveness. We will return to that dimension below. Moreover, there is a strong argument that the Supreme
Court of Canada has internalized Meech Lake's approach to the interpretation of the Constitution, even without the accord. Many of the
fears about the homogenizing effect of the Canadian Charter have not
been realized, and the court has expressly interpreted the Constitution
in a manner that recognizes the distinctive character of Québec.

Division of Legislative Powers

Meech Lake did not make dramatic changes to the division of powers.
Instead, it limited what had long been Québec's chief concern: the
use of the federal spending power to encroach on existing areas of
provincial jurisdiction. It did so by giving provinces a right to opt out
of, and receive financial compensation for, new programs established
in areas of exclusive provincial jurisdiction, on condition that the

provinces exercising that right established their own programs that met "national objectives." The only other substantive provision on division of powers dealt with agreements to regulate the joint field of immigration. That provision empowered the provinces and Ottawa to enter into negotiations to determine their respective roles. Any agreement would have constitutional effect, changeable only with the consent of both the province concerned and the federal Parliament, although Ottawa would retain authority to set national standards and objectives for immigration (Webber 1994: 129–31).

Although the failure of Meech meant that provinces no longer have a constitutional right to opt out of new shared-cost programs, successive federal governments, Liberal and Conservative, have stated their intention to allow non-participating provinces to do so on terms equivalent to Meech. The Chrétien government stated this in the 1996 Speech from the Throne. The Harper government did so in its March 2007 budget document. In his reply to the Speech from the Throne in October 2007, Prime Minister Harper stated his intention to enshrine the Meech principles in legislation (this has not occurred, although, to be fair, that was a truncated Parliament, coming to an abrupt end with the election of 2008).[22] It seems clear that, for the foreseeable future, federal governments will feel bound to follow the Meech provisions.

Now, there has been one prominent instance in which the Chrétien government pursued an initiative that did clash with Québec's antipathy to the spending power: the Social Union Framework Agreement (SUFA), signed by Ottawa and all provinces (except Québec) in 1999.[23] That agreement sought to harmonize social programs across the country under federal leadership, establishing principles and procedures to improve coordination. It was rejected by the Québec government under Lucien Bouchard. It is difficult to see how the Bouchard government could have assented. If there has been one common theme in positions taken by successive Québec governments, it has been the maintenance of autonomy in areas of social policy. Québec has sometimes agreed to principles of portability and the like, but it will not restrain its ability to take new initiatives through a comprehensive structure like SUFA. Indeed, the very language of "union" is anathema, suggesting a singleness and unity that clashes with Québec governments' views of the differentiation at the heart of federalism. As Christian Dufour (2002: 10) has said, a federal structure implies not just shared jurisdictions, but separate jurisdictions.[24]

That said, even SUFA respected the Meech constraints on new
spending power programs. Although it did not speak of "opting out,"
it did allow room to establish different programs, with compensation,
as long as the agreed objectives were attained. Meech, too, would
have required that opting-out provinces establish programs that met
"national objectives." Moreover, SUFA would have gone beyond the
Meech provisions: it applied to programs in areas of joint federal/
provincial jurisdiction, not merely in exclusive provincial jurisdiction;
it applied to block-funded in addition to cost-shared programs; it
required consultation on direct grant programs; the Canada-wide
"objectives" were to be determined collaboratively (Meech had been
silent on how the "national objectives" were to be decided); and any
new programs would require the support of a majority of provinces.
It is said that Lucien Bouchard rejected SUFA because it did not retain
the opting-out provision in a previous provincial and territorial first
ministers' agreement, but under that provision, the right to opt out
would have been still wider – much wider than in Meech (Dufour
2002: 7–8; Richer 2007: 14–15). Those promoting SUFA overesti-
mated the potential for unifying social policy, but even when doing
so, they respected the Meech constraints. Nor have there been any
repercussions to Québec's rejection of SUFA.[25]

On the contrary, there have been, since Meech Lake, a series of
intergovernmental agreements under which Ottawa and the provinces
have substantially redefined their roles, expanding effective provincial
jurisdiction. The most extensive has occurred in the field of immigration, where Québec now has responsibility for the selection, reception,
and integration of immigrants under quotas established by the federal
government (those quotas are established after consultation with the
provinces, Québec having a guaranteed share) (Becklumb 2008; Seidle
2010; Banting 2012; see, also, the favourable evaluation in Burelle
1995: 137–9). There have also been a series of Labour Market
Development Agreements regulating manpower training. Different
forms of agreement exist, but under Québec's, Québec has sole responsibility for the delivery of training (with federal funding) (Klassen
1999: 40; Alboim and McIsaac 2007: 7–8). The Martin and Harper
governments have also acknowledged considerable provincial autonomy in the field of health care, even as they sought improvements in
health care delivery.[26]

These have not removed all irritants. As long as Ottawa remains
in these fields, coordination will be required, with the potential for

friction. And Ottawa is very likely to have a significant role in at least some of these fields as long as Canada survives: elements of social policy are now an important dimension of Canadian citizenship for many Canadians (as Meech Lake implicitly recognized, for the opt-out applied only to new programs); immigration has always been a concurrent power; and manpower training too involves overlap (because of Ottawa's responsibility for Employment Insurance). It is also true that without a formal constitutional amendment, all these agreements might one day be overturned (although, once provincial presence is established, it becomes much more difficult for Ottawa to reverse the situation: see Webber 1994: 286–7). That caveat aside, these agreements have certainly followed on the trajectory suggested in Meech.

It is sometimes said that these developments depart from Meech in that they have all been premised on a strict symmetry of treatment of provinces.[27] That, however, is not right. Some concessions have been made to parity of treatment (but of course Meech did so too: the rights to opt out of spending power programs and to request immigration agreements were available to all provinces). But there is no doubt that the outcomes have been asymmetrical, with Québec taking on larger responsibilities than other provinces. This is in part the result of the provinces' own choices, but it is hard to see how that fact in any way devalues the agreements for Québec. Surely when it comes to division of powers, what matters to Québec are the powers that it can exercise, not whether other provinces also have such powers. Moreover, it would be a mistake to conclude that the negotiations are scrupulously symmetrical. All actors know that Québec has interests that other provinces do not have and that this is certain to result in different outcomes. That expectation has itself shaped negotiations – including the negotiating position of the federal government – especially in the field of immigration, where the agreement with Québec would not be duplicated with other provinces.

In the end, then, the handling of federal and provincial powers appears fully consistent with Meech, subject to the caveat that this has occurred as a matter of governmental practice, not constitutional right.

The Senate and Supreme Court of Canada

Meech also briefly addressed the Senate and the Supreme Court of Canada. I will concentrate only on the latter. Senate reform was not one of Québec's principal issues; it was placed on the agenda by the western provinces, not Québec. However, Québec was very interested in the Supreme Court of Canada.

Meech's provisions on the court would have done two things. First, they would have made clear that the structure of the Supreme Court of Canada was entrenched in the Canadian constitution. The patriation package had left substantial ambiguity about the constitutional status of the Supreme Court. Section 41(d) of the Constitution Act, 1982 did specify that amendments to the Constitution of Canada dealing with "the composition of the Supreme Court of Canada" required the unanimous support of the Senate, House of Commons, and legislatures of each of the provinces, and section 42 subjected all other amendments regarding the court to the general branch of the amending formula. But the problem was that there were no provisions in either the Constitution Act, 1867 or the Constitution Act, 1982 that expressly regulated the court. The court's structure and method of appointment were contained within the Supreme Court Act – an ordinary statute of the federal Parliament adopted under section 101 of the Constitution Act, 1867. There was a significant argument, then, that Parliament could continue to change the court's composition simply by amending its statute; on this view, sections 41 and 42 would only begin to apply when the legislatures sought to introduce provisions dealing with the court into one of the Constitution Acts (Hogg 2006: paragraph 4.2(c); Hogg 1985: 63–5; Brun, Tremblay, and Brouillet 2008: 232–5). Meech Lake would have clarified this situation by expressly entrenching some aspects of the Supreme Court's structure in the Constitution Act, 1867. Québec's principal interest was the requirement that three of the court's nine judges be from Québec. Meech would have constitutionalized that requirement.

Second, Québec has long been concerned that the federal government appoints Supreme Court judges without any participation from the provinces – a situation especially problematic given that the Supreme Court is the final arbiter of the division of powers, the Charter's application to provincial law, and the interpretation of most areas of provincial law (Brun, Tremblay, and Brouillet 2008: 411–12; Brouillet 2005: 253–5, 330; Brouillet 2011: 286). Meech would have required federal and provincial concurrence in the appointment of Supreme Court judges.

Now, the failure of Meech meant that the first purpose (clarification of the Supreme Court's entrenchment in the Constitution) was not immediately fulfilled. In 2014, however, these provisions came before the Supreme Court when the Harper government sought to amend the Supreme Court Act to ensure the appointment of Mr Justice Marc Nadon. In that case, the court ruled that the composition and other essential features of the court – especially the provisions of the Supreme Court Act governing appointments from Québec – had been impliedly entrenched by sections 41 and 42 of the Constitution Act, 1982 *(Reference re Supreme Court Act* 2014). It held, in effect, that the relevant aspects of the Supreme Court's structure were already entrenched. As a result, the clarification provided by Meech is no longer required.

The same cannot be said of the provisions on appointment. Indeed, this is one element of Meech that has manifestly not become part of Canadian constitutional practice: appointments are made by the federal government alone. The government generally consults with a variety of actors, including provincial attorneys-general, prior to making an appointment, but this consultation is not standardized and its impact on the outcome is very difficult to gauge. It certainly does not amount to joint appointment. The lack of provincial involvement makes a difference. It especially affects the perceived legitimacy of the court when issues of language and culture are in issue, as we saw in Québec's response to the decision in *Ford* (the sign law case). This problem could be resolved. The Supreme Court Act could be amended to require provincial participation, or to put in place a non-partisan process in which both Ottawa and the provinces would have an equal role. The changes would not be constitutionally entrenched, but they would establish a clear benchmark, difficult to reverse. I suspect that this has not occurred because of the difficulty of providing for joint appointment without giving predominant weight to one of the two levels of government, and without creating the possibility of deadlock (which would itself undermine the legitimacy of the court, for there would be fewer than the required number of Québec judges for as long as the deadlock continued). Nevertheless, if the Supreme Court is to be seen as a genuinely impartial institution when language rights and the division of powers are in issue, then some revised appointment process has to be secured.

Changes to the Constitutional Amending Formula

Finally, Meech Lake would have changed the constitutional amending formula. It would not have restored Québec's veto, but it would have subjected more items to unanimous approval (which means, in effect, that Québec could veto such amendments), and it would have expanded the right to compensation when provinces opted out of amendments that detracted from provincial powers. Some combination of unanimity and the right to opt out had been treated as a substitute for the veto in all the negotiations leading up to and following patriation – a substitute that enabled the leaders to reconcile Québec's veto with some notion of the equality of the provinces. Indeed, René Lévesque himself had agreed to such a position prior to patriation (Webber 1994: 110–11; Burelle 2005: 64).

Now, one might think that the amending formula is something that certainly cannot be changed by informal means. Remarkably, there have been attempts to address even this issue. The approval of the federal Parliament is required for any amendment to the Canadian constitution. In 1996, as part of its package of responses to the 1995 referendum, the federal government undertook not to introduce certain amendments for approval unless there was support from each of five regions, with Québec considered as one of those regions.[28] This was referred to as the "regional veto." In effect, it extended Québec's right to prevent amendments. Not every amendment was covered. It applied to amendments that were not already subject to a right to veto or opt out. This is a small but potentially important subset of amendments. The central features of Senate reform and the creation of new provinces fall within it.

The regional veto was enshrined in an ordinary federal statute. Such a statute has limited effect. Even if it binds the government for the time being (and there is doubt even about this), it could be repealed by an ordinary majority in Parliament. It really amounts, then, to a formal declaration of self-restraint on the part of the federal Parliament.[29] It is nevertheless significant, for it would make it politically much more difficult for a government to proceed without the support of the five regions. In that respect, it goes some distance towards achieving the objectives of Meech.

THE STRENGTHS AND LIMITATIONS
OF INFORMAL CONSTITUTIONAL CHANGE

There is a strong case, then, that with the notable exception of provincial participation in appointments to the Supreme Court, the central features of Meech Lake have become the working assumptions of

Canadian governance, accepted by the leaders of all the federal political parties, including Meech's former enemies. Is that enough – *should* it be enough – to restore the confidence of Quebecers? How should we assess changes that occur without formal amendment?

The question is a real one. Many of us remember the old chestnut about the constitutions of the former Soviet Union: they were great on paper, but they bore no relation to the government of that society. There is a lot to be said for a regime in which constitutional norms are not just written on parchment but engrained in the day-to-day practices of officialdom, from the prime minister down to the police officers, welfare agents, and clerks in the régie de l'assurance automobile, who are (after all) the face of government to the vast majority of citizens.

In what ways, then, are the above measures constrained by the fact that they have not occurred through constitutional amendment? To begin, most obviously, informal changes benefit from no special legal protection. They may be respected now, but they might, at least in theory, be changed tomorrow, through nothing more than a shift in majority opinion – and of course, given Canada's demography, that majority can be a purely anglophone majority. If Quebecers' conception of the country were written into the Constitution, it would be placed beyond the power of a simple majority to change.

This advantage of constitutional reform is, I believe, complemented by three more. First, the very act of reducing constitutional principles to writing crystallizes them, creating a bulwark against their piecemeal erosion. Ottawa's intrusion into areas of provincial jurisdiction through the use of the spending power occurred gradually, through a series of individual measures, each of which looked very attractive to the majority of Canadians, including many Quebecers. They were difficult to resist (although the Québec government tried). But the result was a huge shift in the effective division of powers. In contrast, constitutional provisions create a line in the sand, one that can be defended more easily against encroachments.

Second, the text of the Constitution has an immense symbolic charge. The very prominence of a constitutional statement, its formality, its condensed expression, its presence in the foundational document of the political community, gives it a rhetorical impact that far outstrips a well-meaning scholar's interpretation of the working assumptions of Canadian governance or even a declaration of principles in a resolution of the House of Commons. That rhetorical impact helps to consolidate those principles, giving them instant authority in political argument (see Webber 1999).

Third, the very difficulty of amending the Constitution – the challenge of marshalling opinion across both federal and provincial legislatures, surmountable only by concerted effort over time – conveys that these are important principles, subscribed to by the quasi-unanimity of Canadian citizens (or at least by their governments). That contributes to the principles' rhetorical force. It can also increase the confidence of those depending on the principles: the principles are not simply an opinion expressed by a majority of MPs on one day in one legislature; they are the summation of opinion in the country.

These, then, are the advantages of constitutionalization: heightened protection against change; clarity; rhetorical prominence; and a special authority deriving from quasi-unanimous support. These advantages are not provided by the informal developments canvassed above, at least not to anything like the same extent. Does this matter? Should it undermine Quebecers' trust in Canadian structures of governance?

To answer those questions, it is worth focusing first on a line of criticism of the post-Meech developments that is somewhat separate from the question of form. I argued above that those developments demonstrate the increasing acceptance of the principles of the Meech Lake Accord – certainly not in the text of the Constitution, perhaps not in the inner reaches of the politicians' minds (although that appears to be true for some of them), but at least in political practice. Other commentators would vehemently disagree. The disagreement would focus on two things: (1) the supposed domination of a conception of individual rights inimical to Québec's concerns, a conception identified with Trudeau (see, e.g., Burelle 1995: 41–2; Dumont 1997: 47); and (2) the extent to which the recognition of Québec's distinctiveness has been qualified by a commitment to the equality of provinces, so that Québec is treated not as one of two equal partners, but one of ten (see, e.g., Dumont 1997: 47; Seymour 2006; Bock-Côté 2007: 12–13).[30]

It is common to treat Trudeau's position on individual rights as though it were written into the constitution of 1982. André Burelle (2005: 469), for example, refers to the need to open "les portes de la prison idéologique où M. Trudeau a enfermé le Québec aussi bien que le reste du Canada."[31] Burelle's work is generally wonderful and his constitutional prescriptions are very close to my own, but surely this is hyperbole. As I argued above, even patriation contained a variety of strands, many of which embraced the recognition of cultural difference, and the developments since patriation have, if anything, accentuated those strands. Indeed, if there is one group more disturbed by constitutional developments post-Meech than *politologues* in Québec, it is people devoted to Trudeau's position.[32] Moreover, it is remarkable how abstract many of the arguments for the impact of the Canadian Charter are, often concentrating entirely upon Trudeau's views (who clearly continues to torment people from the grave). They pay scant attention to the fact that the Charter has been interpreted in light of the Constitution's federal structure, and they tend to assume, rather than demonstrate, that individual rights now foreclose any serious respect for collectivities in political discourse (see, e.g., Caron, Laforest, and Vallières-Roland 2006: 162–3).

Moreover, one must not presume too great an opposition between the protection of individual rights and the concerns of Quebecers. Quebecers remain among the strongest supporters of the Charter (CRIC 2002: 30–1; Nanos 2007: 51–2).[33] They may have difficulty understanding how the Charter should work together with their other commitments, but in that they are far from alone. And of course Meech Lake itself would have retained the Charter, including its provisions dealing with language rights. It is a great mistake to assume that the Charter is, in itself, inimical to Quebecers. Indeed, I suspect that Quebecers' concerns with the Charter may often merge with criticisms of charters of rights generally. Citizens frequently support charters of rights because citizens believe deeply in a series of principles: freedom of expression, equality, etc. But under charters of rights, courts do not simply affirm general principles. They decide how those principles apply to highly specific cases where the considerations are, almost always, more complex and therefore more contestable. It is common, then, for citizens to support charters of rights in the abstract, but have real doubts about the way in which they override democratic decision-making in practice.[34]

The Charter's protection of individual rights is not an "ideological prison." It is in tension with cultural recognition, but that tension is deeply engrained within Québec (and Canadian) society. It is likely to be always with us, whether or not we emancipate ourselves from Trudeau's legacy. The "equality of the provinces," on the other hand, is more troubling. That formula was used, during the Meech debate, to oppose any recognition of Québec's distinctiveness and any move towards constitutional asymmetry.

All of the post-Meech developments have made some concessions to that formula. I have written against the formula, arguing that it confuses equality among institutional structures with equality among citizens (Webber 1994: 232–4). But it is worth noting that, even if one concedes the formula, its implications are very much open to debate. One can treat the provinces equally – by, for example, giving all provinces a right to opt out of new spending programs, as Meech would have done – and still end up with a substantial measure of asymmetry in practice (because only some provinces exercise that option). Moreover, if different provinces are situated differently – and, of course, one notable difference is that only Québec has a French-speaking majority – provinces can be treated differently in that respect without offending equality. The devolution of powers in different ways to different provinces (e.g., in the field of immigration) suggests that, to some degree, these differences in cultural positioning are being acknowledged. Although it would be better if we did not make a fetish out of the "equality of the provinces," its constraint should not be exaggerated.

In fact, many criticisms of the formula focus on the vision of the country that "equality of the provinces" propounds, not its practical effect. These criticisms often advance a binational idea of Canada, under which Canada should be an equal partnership of a French and an English Canada. There is no doubt that something like this notion has resonance in Québec, but it is, I believe, just as deficient as "equality of the provinces." First, it tends to use Québec as the model for the rest of Canada. There are very few Canadians outside Québec who think that their nation is "English Canada." Their sense of nationhood attaches to all of Canada. Second, the binational vision tends to treat English Canada as a single entity, without noteworthy internal differences, which should speak with a single voice. But although the commitment to provincial autonomy outside Québec is not expressed in the same way as it is in Québec, there is deep attachment to political communities at the provincial level, at least in many provinces. There is great resistance, then, to a vision of Canada that treats English Canada as a unity. Third, the binational vision has difficulty opening itself to other national components of the Canadian conversation, specifically those of Indigenous peoples. As many have noted, taking those contributions seriously requires a significant rethinking of all nationalisms, English-Canadian and Québécois (Laforest 1995: 1; Burelle 2005: 438–40).

Even for Quebecers, the binational vision has significant limits. Many Quebecers conceive of Québec using different imagery: as a distinct society; as an expression of French Canada; or, in Trudeau's vision, as a civic entity exercising legislative powers, but with no more claim to represent French Canada than Ottawa has. More importantly, however, the binational vision clashes with the sense of federal citizenship inherent in Quebecers' political engagement. Quebecers do not see themselves as relating to the rest of Canada as a single bloc; instead, they see themselves as participating in two levels of political community, Québec and Canada, where, even in the latter, they participate as individuals, with their own complex concerns and range of disagreements. Consider the Bloc Québécois. It is, in many ways, the clearest expression of the binational vision; it was created to represent all Quebecers, as a unit, vis-à-vis English Canada. But it was far from Quebecers' preferred option. It was the product of the pathology of Canadian politics, not its health – a response that many Quebecers believed had been forced upon them by Canadians' rejection of Meech. Recently, with the rise of the New Democratic Party in Québec and now again the Liberals, Quebecers have returned to their customarily plural approach to federal politics.

Indeed, the genius of Meech was that it imposed neither a binational nor an equality-of-the-provinces vision. Instead, it would have recognized what was undeniable – Québec's distinctness – and left it at that, without forcing our relations into a simplistic mould. It would have left the tensions in place, allowing us to work them out over time. The accord failed, and we have lived with the consequences ever since. But in the years since its failure, its wisdom has proven itself through practice. Hence the convergence described above.

One great benefit of informal as opposed to formal change is that it does not need to fasten upon a single definition of the country. The clarity, rhetorical force, and appearance of unanimity achieved through constitutional amendment have a sting in their tail. The formulas we use, such as "nation-to-nation," are far simpler than the reality. Writing a single vision into the Constitution, unless it is very carefully chosen, can do violence to the complexity of people's relationships to the country. Roderick Macdonald (1991: 292) has written a wonderful paper in which he discusses the "statute" and the "compact" theories of Confederation. He notes that there are things to be said in favour of both of them and concludes that they may be like the particle and the wave theories of light: both are necessary to capture the phenomenon, even if they remain in irreconcilable tension with one another. Jean Leclair has written that federalism contains inherent tensions, but that those tensions are apt, for they mirror the tensions that exist in Quebecers' relationship to their two countries, Québec and Canada. Alain Noël has argued that one should not confuse conflict with incoherence in intergovernmental relations; a relationship can be both conflictual and (fruitfully) coherent (2001: 1–7). Informal mechanisms, if they are working well, allow one to live with complexity, without forcing it into simplistic boxes.

But can informal mechanisms sustain the trust of national minorities, especially given the ambiguity and uncertainty that those mechanisms necessarily imply? This is a challenge, especially when one is faced with the task of rebuilding confidence after it has collapsed. Confidence is always a work in progress in the face of a society in which there are, always, people arguing strenuously for positions that one rejects. National minorities will be especially vulnerable to an erosion of confidence given that they cannot rely on numbers to impose their will. Well-drafted constitutional provisions can help sustain confidence. That is why it is regrettable that Meech Lake was rejected. But if formal mechanisms are beyond reach, what should one look for when assessing non-constitutional means?

First, it is too much to expect that there will be unanimity around one's most cherished vision, so that it is placed outside contestation.[35] An open society is too diverse for that. What matters is whether the balance of opinion is sufficient to keep the framework within an acceptable range, without erosion of the minority's position. That will, of course, be a challenging judgement call.

Second, it is acceptable that the framework be sustained by the exigencies of political practice; it need not be grounded in the deep convictions of the participants. It may well be, for example, that the principles of Meech have been accepted by its enemies more because of political necessity than personal conviction. But in a diverse society that will often be the case – or at least, the approaches followed in practice will always be a complex amalgam, born of the interaction of the different attitudes in society. The fact that practice has a normalizing effect that ultimately serves the interests of minorities should be comforting, not disturbing; it shows that the framework has stability that is, to some degree, independent of the vagaries of individual leadership. It is always better, of course, for that framework to be understood and embraced. One can then reinforce and learn from it, not unwittingly undermine it. For that reason, scholarly reflection on Canadian government is valuable. But the acceptance of the framework will always be less than unanimous.

Third, it is possible to create a framework that enables different visions of society to co-exist, without choosing among them. The visions may be profoundly different from one another. Indeed, constitutions are, in the end, more about establishing a framework for action than about stipulating specific visions (Webber 2000, 2015). One example is Meech's strategy of granting, to every province, the right to negotiate each government's role in immigration. Ostensibly, this treats all provinces the same. For that reason it has sometimes been criticized as a travesty of Québec's demands (e.g., Seymour 2006: 219–21). It is true that it would be better to have a frank acknowledgement of asymmetry, primarily because that would allow Ottawa to continue to fulfil roles for the rest of Canada that most Canadians outside Québec would prefer. But I have difficulty seeing how the concession to equal treatment in the immigration provision at all undermines Québec.[36] Québec still has the powers it sought. It can use them to serve the purposes that it, distinctively, wants to achieve. And in practice the devolution has not been symmetrical. At most, there has been a symmetrical *capacity* to devolve powers. Precisely because different provinces relate asymmetrically to the issue, the requests for devolution and the devolution granted have been different for different provinces.

It is a mistake to think that a constitution must settle conclusively all these questions of national vision. It may provide a framework in which different visions coexist. Indeed, to a certain extent it must do this or it will be a confining and illiberal constitution, for of course, within any society (including Québec) different constitutional visions contend. It is an empirical question whether, under an ambivalent framework, the scope for pursuing one's own vision is sufficient. The question is one of pragmatics: how can one *live* under that constitution?

To be clear, I am not advocating a merely individualistic and materialistic calculus of a constitution's benefits, like the *fédéralisme rentable* of Robert Bourassa. One may care deeply about the non-pecuniary dimensions of life – about the vigour of one's culture, the quality of democratic engagement, the extent to which popular debates shape public policy, the capacity to draw on resources developed in one's own language and culture, and the ability to collaborate with others whose views have been shaped within different languages and cultures.

These are the things I care most about (Webber 1994; 2011). But we should keep the focus on our capacity to attain them, not simply on whether they are written into the Constitution.

Another way to make this point is to focus on the object of our trust. That object should not be the constitutional text, nor even the subjective understandings held by our compatriots of another culture (although, I confess, I do hope for greater understanding), but rather our practical capacity for self-determination. Even this focus should be tempered by the stimulus of encounter with others. We don't want to be so solipsistic that we shun encounter; Canada is the country it is precisely because of this stimulus. This does mean acceptance of tension, of things being left unresolved. That in turn leaves open the possibility of a sudden loss of confidence. But the quality of leaving things unresolved has allowed the continuation of a relationship that has been, outside its crises, immensely fruitful.

Burelle quotes the response of the early Trudeau – the Trudeau who believed in true federalism – to the possibility that Canadians outside Québec might not grasp the value of a deeply pluralistic federation: "tant pis pour eux" (Burelle 2005: 436).[37] Burelle says that this response cannot be taken seriously, for Quebecers are a minority. But surely, on this, Trudeau is right. What matters is Quebecers' practical capacity for self-determination, not whether it is grasped by everyone in Canada. As long as that practical capacity exists, it really is "tant pis pour eux." One of Trudeau's great strengths – a strength to which Quebecers responded enthusiastically – was that he saw that self-determination was fundamentally about the actions one takes oneself, not about the recognition conferred by others.

Of course, even when one pursues that approach, one may find that the existing structures frustrate one's aspirations. Constitutional frameworks are not entirely neutral among aspirations. There may, then, be reason to change them. I am not arguing against constitutional reform. But I am arguing against the fetishization of the word – the tendency to assume that the constitutional text defines who we are as a country, or to try to make it do so. In *Madame Bovary*, Gustave Flaubert describes a scene in which Emma Bovary and her soon-to-be lover speak of their feelings, talking themselves into declaring their love. Flaubert (1971: 239) comments wryly on the spectacle, "D'ailleurs, la parole est un laminoir qui allonge toujours les sentiments."[38] There may be times when we need to adjust our constitutional arrangements, but we should be careful what we ask of them. Our attempts to speak always narrow a much wider reality, imposing order and simplicity. There is the real possibility of over-definition, as we translate something elusive and dynamic into the exactitude of a legislative definition. And in focusing only on the word, not on the lived constitution, we may talk ourselves into fore-closing what is most of value. What matters, in the end, is how we are able to live under constitutional arrangements, not what they say.

There may be wisdom, then, in the apparent decision of citizens in Québec to acquiesce in the view that constitutional reform is impos-sible, and to pursue, through non-constitutional means, the vigour of Québec's society. I regret, as do others, that Canadians did not coalesce around the constitutional recognition of Québec as a distinct society, but that does not mean that Québec is indistinct, nor that Québec is prevented from pursuing its distinctiveness, nor even that Québec's distinctiveness is excluded from the workings of Canadian govern-ment. Quite the contrary, as we have seen from the practice of Canadian politics over the last twenty-five years.

NOTES

1 This is not quite accurate: one limited dimension of the Charlottetown Accord – the bilingual character of New Brunswick, which only required the assent of the Senate, the House of Commons, and the New Brunswick legislature – was entrenched in the constitution (*Constitution Amendment, 1993a*). Since that time there have also been amendments changing the guarantees for confessional schools in Québec and Newfoundland, alter-ing the Terms of Union of Prince Edward Island, and changing the name of the province of Newfoundland (the latter were not, however, part of Meech and Charlottetown): *Constitution Amendment, 1997a*; *Constitution Amendment, 1997b*; *Constitution Amendment, 1993b*; *Constitution Amendment, 1998*; *Constitution Amendment, 2001*.

2 The obvious exception has been the federal Liberals, but even they paid it lip service. See, e.g., *House of Commons Debates*, 35th parl, 1st sess., no. 267 (29 November 1995) at 16972 (Jean Chrétien). One might well doubt the sincerity of such statements, given the Trudeau government's actions during patriation and its position in the Québec veto reference (*Reference re Objection by Quebec to a Resolution to Amend the Constitution* 1982), but the fact that the Liberals claimed to support the principle is itself indicative of its broad acceptance in Québec.

3 It is noteworthy that in a survey conducted by the Centre for Research
   and Information on Canada (CRIC 2002: 30), Québec respondents voiced
   the highest support for the Canadian Charter but among the lowest levels
   of satisfaction with the Supreme Court of Canada (although opinion
   within all provinces falls within a narrow range, suggesting the difference
   is not profound). For similar results, see Fletcher and Howe (2000: 8, 13).

4 For the text of the accord, see Peter W. Hogg (1988). For a discussion of
   the accord's contents, see Webber (1994: 127–33).

5 This is Burelle's essential argument, which does indeed align with
   Trudeau's reasons for opposing the accord. But, as I argue in the text,
   the public's reasons for rejecting Meech cannot be reduced to a one-nation
   vision of Canada. Burelle (2005: 462–4) acknowledges that the court's
   interpretation of the Canadian Charter did not conform to this vision.

6 In this regard, it is very important to distinguish between the use of section 1 and that of section 33. The latter has indeed become difficult to use,
   but the former is used constantly. Indeed, the principal argument for the
   existence of a dialogue between legislatures and courts over the interpretation of the Charter relies on the use of section 1 (Webber 2002: 77–8, 99).

7 The "Canada Clause" extended the right to English education to the children of citizens who had received their primary school instruction in
   English *in Canada*; the "Québec clause" extended the right to those who
   had received their elementary education in English *in Quebec*. Compare
   Constitution Act 1982, s. 23(1); *Charter of the French Language*, RSQ
   1977, c. C-11, s. 73.

8 *An Act to give effect to the requirement for clarity as set out in the opinion of the Supreme Court of Canada in the Quebec Secession Reference*,
   SC 2000, c 26.

9 There was also hope among many of the clause's advocates that it would
   shape the interpretation of the federal/provincial division of powers. That
   impact was much more difficult to gauge, and assessments of the clause
   almost always focus on its impact on the Charter. For a characteristic
   example, see *House of Commons Debates*, 35th parl, 1st sess., no. 267
   (29 November 1995) at 16978 (Lucien Bouchard).

10 See Webber (1993) and the early and influential cases, *R v Edwards Books
   and Art* 1986; *Irwin Toy* 1989; *Reference re sections 193 and 195.1(1)c
   of the Criminal Code (Man.)* 1990. The court's approach has not been
   flawless. In one of their most criticized decisions, *RJR-MacDonald* 1995,
   which concerned a federal statute, they lost sight of this principle of
   restraint, intruding into difficult policy judgments and ignoring the relative importance of the expression in issue. For a nuanced interpretation of

the Charter's effect that is very close to that advanced here, see Otis (1995–96: 276–8). Brouillet (2005: 335–6) acknowledges that the court has recognized this room for manoeuvre among provinces but falls back upon arguments about the universalist nature of rights and the courts' use of comparisons to maintain that the Charter tends to enforce uniformity. But the more the arguments focus on the general tendencies of rights discourse, the more they merge with general criticisms of constitutionally entrenched rights guarantees and the less they appear to be specifically about Québec.

11 Increasing attention by English-Canadian feminists to cultural diversity is one example. This, and other factors, caused divisions between Québec feminists and feminists from the rest of Canada during the Meech Lake debate. See, for example, Sheppard (2010: 46–51).

12 See, for example, Brouillet (2005: 253–65) and Woehrling (2006). Brouillet starts by criticizing the "activism" of the court in interpreting the constitution. Similar critiques are often made of the judicial interpretation of charters of rights. But Brouillet specifically suggests that the activist interpretation tends to promote the values of the majority, often at the expense of minorities (2005: 259). This is surely a simplistic reading. Her findings are more convincing when she rejects the idea of federally appointed Supreme Court judges (253–5, 330). Woehrling's arguments focus primarily on the disadvantages of universal rights charters. While he does not claim that they have a significant effect on the balance of powers within the federation, he does argue that federally appointed judges have tended to interpret the Constitution in a centralizing fashion.

13 See also *Reference re Secession of Quebec* 1998, paragraph 59, where the court outlines the relationship between federalism and Québec's ability to promote its language and culture.

14 *House of Commons Debates*, 35th parl, 1st sess., no. 275 (11 December 1995) at 17536–7. Ontario, New Brunswick, Nova Scotia, and Newfoundland had adopted resolutions recognizing Québec as a distinct society during the 1995 referendum campaign.

15 Chrétien immediately acknowledged as much. See *House of Commons Debates*, 35th parl, 1st sess., no. 267 (29 November 1995) at 16972 (Jean Chrétien).

16 Ted Glenn, "The Calgary Declaration," Legislative Research Service Backgrounder B-19 (24 April 1998), online: Ontario Legislative Library, http://www.ontla.on.ca/library/repository/mon/1000/10273337.htm. The Declaration was later approved by resolutions of the Northwest Territories and all provinces except Québec. Allan Gregg (2005: 50–9)

interprets Calgary as resulting from the premiers' realization "that their previous insistence on equal treatment for all provinces was a non-starter for Quebec, and that they must satisfy its demand for even greater autonomy."

17 *House of Commons Journals*, 36th parl, 1st sess., no. 37 (25 November 1997), 259.

18 Alain Dubuc's criticism of the Calgary Declaration was apt: "It is normal ... for Quebeckers to welcome this initiative with as much circumspection as the premiers put into formulating it" (quoted by Brien 1997: 2154). The fate of these initiatives shows that in order to elicit trust, one must be willing to extend it.

19 *House of Commons Debates*, 39th parl, 1st sess., no. 84 (22 November 2006), 5197 (Stephen Harper). For the motion itself, see *House of Commons Journals*, 39th parl, 1st sess., no. 86 (24 November 2006), 803. For the Bloc Québécois notice of motion, see: *House of Commons Order Paper and Notice Paper*, 39th parl, 1st sess., no. 84 (22 November 2006), 4. For the resolution of Québec's Assemblée nationale, 30 October 2003: http://www.saic.gouv.qc.ca/publications/resolutions/20031030.pdf.

20 *House of Commons Journals*, 39th parl, 1st sess., no. 87 (27 November 2006), 811–16. Fifteen Liberals and one Conservative opposed the government's resolution. Only the Bloc Québécois and Louise Thibault (independent from Rimouski-Neigette) supported the Bloc's resolution.

21 The Reform Party criticized even the 1995 resolution on distinct society as being part of "this 30-year old federal two step to appease Quebec separatists." *House of Commons Debates*, 35th parl, 1st sess., no. 267 (29 November 1995), 16962 (Preston Manning). Indeed, Manning proposed an amendment to limit it further, supported by his colleague in the Reform Party, Stephen Harper, and Reformers voted against the main motion.

22 Canada, *Speech from the Throne*, 27 February 1996, Privy Council Office: http://www.pco-bcp.gc.ca/index.asp?lang=eng&page=information&sub=publications&doc=sft-ddt/1996_e.htm; Canada, *Restoring Fiscal Balance for a Stronger Federation* (Budget 19 March 2007), 42, Department of Finance: http://www.budget.gc.ca/2007/pdf/bkfbsfe.pdf; Canada, *Speech from the Throne*, 16 October 2007, Privy Council Office online: http://www.pco-bcp.gc.ca/index.asp?lang=eng&page=information&sub=publications&doc=sft-ddt/2007-eng.htm. See also Stéphane Dion (1999: 98).

23 "A Framework to Improve the Social Union for Canadians: An Agreement between the Government of Canada and the Governments of the Provinces and Territories," signed in Ottawa, Ontario, 4 February 1999: http://www.socialunion.gc.ca/news/020499_e.html.

24 Alain Noël calls SUFA an instance of hegemonic cooperation, given federal dominance in the process (2000: 9–14).

25 In retrospect, Noël's (2000: 14–18) suggestion that Québec would be "marginalised" by SUFA seems exaggerated, although I agree that SUFA has not been a positive step towards recognizing asymmetrical federalism in Canada, and that it did not conceive of Canadian federalism as a partnership between Québec and the rest of Canada. The latter are Noël's principal claims.

26 They have at times been subjected to fierce criticism because of it. Courchesne (2008: 30) concludes that these measures combine de jure symmetry with de facto asymmetry. This has received some criticism (e.g., Gregg 2005: 50).

27 See, e.g., Gregg (2005: 53). Russell (2004b: 9–18) does not misrepresent Meech or Charlottetown as Gregg does, but he too says that the approach has been "religiously symmetrical – not offering deals to one province that are denied to others." For reasons given in the text, that is not quite right, and in any case it depends upon a notion of symmetry that concentrates on the right to negotiate, not the outcomes of negotiations.

28 *An Act Respecting Constitutional Amendments*, SC 1996, c 1.

29 In fact, although adopted by Parliament, the act only purports to bind ministers of the Crown, preventing them from proposing amendments unless the requisite consents have been obtained. See Canada (1996a: s. 1).

30 A number of works treat both of these concerns together, sometimes in combination with multiculturalism, as manifestations of an attempt to establish a one-nation vision of Canada. See, e.g., Laforest (1995), although he too recognizes the limitations of a binational vision (1).

31 Translation: to open "the doors of the ideological prison where Mr Trudeau imprisoned Quebec as well as the rest of Canada." See, also, Dumont (1997: 48).

32 See, for example, Gregg (2005). The title on the cover of that issue captures his article's spirit: "Quebec Is Gone!"

33 For this reason, it is a mistake to treat Lucien Bouchard's and others' acceptance of bilingualism in commercial signs, subject to French predominance, as a victory for Trudeau's position, as Burelle does (2005: 464). There is broad acceptance in Québec of a strong anglophone presence, and willingness to allow that community to have representation in popular interaction, as long as that does not occur in a manner that denies the predominance of French and that leads to an erosion of the French fact. The question is one of getting the balance right. See for example,

Quebecers' support for minority language education rights reported in CRIC (2002: 10).

34 I share those concerns. I have argued for statutory as opposed to constitutionally entrenched rights where the latter do not yet exist, and for judicial reticence in the interpretation of entrenched rights where they do exist (Webber 2000, 2006a, 2006b).

35 The assumption that there must be a shared vision, and dismay that it is not shared, is a common theme in criticisms of the constitutional debates. See e.g., Burelle (2005: 460–1, 467).

36 Seymour's position (2006: 218–21) is instructive. It appears to be concerned with differentiation as such, not with Québec's actual capacity to make autonomous decisions, for Seymour suggests that the extension of the same right to other provinces vitiates its value. In contrast, Burelle's proposals (2005: 467) are consistent with formal symmetry.

37 Translation: "too bad for them."

38 Translation: "Besides, words are a rolling mill that continually extends our sentiments."

REFERENCES

Alboim, Naomi, and Elizabeth McIsaac. 2007. "Making the Connections: Ottawa's Role in Immigrant Employment." *IRPP Choices* 13, no. 3: 1, 7–8.

Banting, Keith. 2012. "Canada." In *Immigrant Integration in Federal Countries*, edited by Christian Joppke and F. Leslie Seidle, 79–112. Montreal and Kingston: McGill-Queen's University Press.

Becklumb, Peggy. 2008. *Immigration: The Canada-Quebec Accord.* Parliamentary Information and Research Service. BP 252-E (revised in October 2008). Accessed 14 January 2018. http://www.parl.gc.ca/Content/LOP/ResearchPublications/bp252-e.pdf.

Bock-Coté, Mathieu. 2007. "Cahier de recherche: De la reconnaissance du Québec à celle des Québécois: Retour sur la reconnaissance de la nation par le gouvernement de Stephen Harper à l'automne 2006." *Institut de recherche sur le Québec*. Accessed 30 November 2011. http://irq.qc.ca/storage/etudes/IRQ-Etude_MBC_final_8.pdf.

Brien, Pierre. 1997. *House of Commons Debates.* 25 November, 36th parl., 1st sess., no. 37, 2154.

Brouillet, Eugénie. 2005. *La Négation de la Nation: L'identité culturelle québécoise et le fédéralisme canadien.* Sillery: Septentrion.

– 2011. "La légitimité fédérative du processus de nomination des juges à la Cour suprême du Canada." *Revue générale de droit* 41, no. 2: 279–93.

Brun, Henri, Guy Tremblay, and Eugénie Brouillet. 2008. *Droit constitu-tionnel*. 5th ed. Cowansville: Éditions Yvon Blais.

Burelle, André. 1995. *Le mal canadien: Essai de diagnostic et esquisse d'une thérapie*. Montréal: Fides.

– 2005. *Pierre Elliott Trudeau: L'intellectuel et le politique*. Montréal: Fides.

Caron, Jean-François, Guy Laforest, and Catherine Vallières-Roland. 2006. "Le déficit fédératif au Canada." In *Le fédéralisme canadien contemporain: Fondements, traditions, institutions*, edited by Alain-G. Gagnon, 148–83. Montréal: Presses de l'Université de Montréal.

Constitution Amendment, 1993a (New Brunswick), SI/93-54.

Constitution Amendment, 1993b (Prince Edward Island), SI/94-50.

Constitution Amendment, 1997a (Quebec), SI/97-141.

Constitution Amendment, 1997b (Newfoundland Act), SI/97-55.

Constitution Amendment, 1998 (Newfoundland Act), SI/98-25.

Constitution Amendment, 2001 (Newfoundland and Labrador), SI/2002-117.

Courchene, Thomas. 2008. "Reflections on the Federal Spending Power: Practices, Principles, Perspectives." IRPP *Working Paper Series* 1: 1–49.

CRIC (Centre for Research and Information on Canada). 2002. *The Charter: Dividing or Uniting Canadians? The* CRIC *Papers 5*. Montréal: CRIC.

Dion, Stéphane. 1999. *Straight Talk: Speeches and Writings on Canadian Unity*. Montreal and Kingston: McGill-Queen's University Press.

Dufour, Christian. 2002. "Rétablir le principe fédéral: La place du Québec dans l'union sociale canadienne." IRPP *Policy Matters/Enjeux Publics* IRPP 3, no. 1: 1–27.

Dumont, Fernand. 1997. *Raisons communes*. Montréal: Boréal.

Flaubert, Gustave. 1971. *Madame Bovary*. Paris: Garnier Frères.

Fletcher, Joseph F., and Paul Howe. 2000. "Canadian Attitudes Toward the Charter and the Courts in Comparative Perspective." IRPP *Choices/Choix* IRPP 6, no. 3: 4–29.

Ford v Québec (Attorney General). [1988] 2 SCR 712.

Gregg, Allan. 2005. "Quebec's Final Victory." *Walrus* 2, no. 1: 50–9.

Hogg, Peter W. 1985. *Constitutional Law of Canada*. 2nd ed. Toronto: Carswell.

– 1988. *Meech Lake Constitutional Accord Annotated*. Toronto: Carswell.

– 2006. *Constitutional Law of Canada*. 5th ed. Toronto: Carswell.

Irwin Toy Ltd. v Québec (Attorney General). [1989] 1 SCR 927.

Kelly, James B. 2001. "Reconciling Rights and Federalism during Review
    of the Charter of Rights and Freedoms: The Supreme Court of Canada
    and the Centralization Thesis, 1982 to 1999." *Canadian Journal of
    Political Science* 34, no. 2: 321–55.

Klassen, Thomas. 1999. "Job Market Training: The Social Union in
    Practice." *Policy Options/Options Politiques* 20, no. 10: 40.

Knopff, Rainer, and F.L. Morton. 1985. "Nation-Building and the
    Canadian Charter of Rights and Freedoms." In *Constitutionalism,
    Citizenship and Society in Canada*, edited by Alan Cairns and Cynthia
    Williams, 133–82. Toronto: University of Toronto Press.

Krygier, Martin. 1997. *Between Fear and Hope: Hybrid Thoughts on
    Public Values*. Sydney: ABC Books.

Kymlicka, Will. 1989. *Liberalism, Community, and Culture*. Oxford:
    Clarendon Press.

– 1995. *Multicultural Citizenship: A Liberal Theory of Minority Rights*.
    Oxford: Clarendon Press.

– 1998. *Finding Our Way: Rethinking Ethnocultural Relations in Canada*.
    Toronto: Oxford University Press.

Laforest, Guy. 1992. *Trudeau et la fin d'un rêve canadien*. Québec:
    Septentrion.

– 1995. *Trudeau and the End of a Canadian Dream*. Montréal and
    Kingston: McGill-Queen's University Press.

Lévesque, René. 1986. *Attendez que je me rappelle...* Montréal:
    Québec/Amérique.

Macdonald, Roderick A. 1991. "...Meech Lake to the Contrary Notwith-
    standing (Part I)." *Osgoode Hall Law Journal* 29, no. 2: 253–328.

Mahé v Alberta. [1990] 1 SCR 342.

Mulroney, Brian. 2007. *Memoirs*. Toronto: McClelland & Stewart.

Nanos, Nik. 2007. "Charter Values Don't Equal Canadian Values: Strong
    Support for Same-Sex and Property Rights." *IRPP Policy
    Options/Options Politiques IRPP* 28, no. 2: 50–5.

Noël, Alain. 2000. "Without Quebec: Collaborative Federalism with a
    Footnote?" *IRPP Policy Matters/Enjeux publics IRPP* 1, no. 2: 1–26.

– 2001. "Les prérogatives du pouvoir dans les relations intergouverne-
    mentales." *IRPP Policy Matters/Enjeux Publics IRPP* 2, no. 6: 1–28.

Otis, Ghislain. 1995-96. "La justice constitutionnelle au Canada à l'ap-
    proche de l'an 2000: Uniformisation ou construction plurielle du
    droit?" *Ottawa Law Review* 27: 261–79.

Putnam, Robert D. 1993. *Making Democracy Work: Civic Traditions in
    Modern Italy*. Princeton: Princeton University Press.

Québec. 1975. *Charte québécoise des droits et libertés de la personne.*
– 1977. *Charte de la langue française,* LQ.
– 1988. *Loi modifiant la Charte de la langue française.* LQ.
– 1993. *Loi modifiant la Charte de la langue française.* LQ.
R. *v Advance Cutting & Coring Ltd.* [2001] 3 SCR 209.
R *v Edwards Books and Art.* [1986] 2 SCR 713.
R. *v Kapp.* [2008] 2 SCR 483.
R. *v s. (S.).* [1990] 2 SCR 254.
RJR-MacDonald Inc. v Canada (Attorney General). [1995] 3 SCR 199.
*Reference re Objection by Quebec to a Resolution to amend the
    Constitution.* [1982] 2 SCR 793.
Reference re Secession of Quebec. [1998] 2 SCR 217.
Reference re sections 193 and 195.1(1)c of the Criminal Code (Man.).
    [1990] 1 SCR 1123.
Reference re Supreme Court Act, ss. 5 and 6. [2014] 1 SCR 433.
Richer, Karine. 2007. *The Federal Spending Power.* Parliamentary
    Information and Research Service. PRB 07-36E, 14–15. Accessed
    14 January 2018. https://lop.parl.ca/content/lop/ResearchPublications/
    prb0736-e.pdf.
Romanow, Roy, John Whyte, and Howard Leeson. 1984. *Canada ...
    Notwithstanding: The Making of the Constitution 1976–1982.* Toronto:
    Carswell/Methuen.
Russell, Peter H. 1983. "The Political Purposes of the Canadian Charter of
    Rights and Freedoms." *Canadian Bar Review* 61, no. 1: 30–54.
– 2004a. *Constitutional Odyssey: Can Canadians Become a Sovereign
    People?* 3rd ed. Toronto: University of Toronto Press.
– 2004b. "Can the Canadians Be a Sovereign People? The Question
    Revisited." In *Constitutional Politics in Canada and the United States,*
    edited by Stephen L. Newman, 9–34. Albany: State University of New
    York Press.
Russell, Peter H., Rainer Knopff, Thomas M.J. Bateman, and Janet L.
    Hiebert. 2008. *The Court and the Constitution: Leading Cases.*
    Toronto: Emond Montgomery.
Seidle, F. Leslie. 2010. "Intergovernmental Immigration Agreements and
    Public Accountability." *Policy Options/Options politiques* 31, no. 6:
    49–63.
Seymour, Michel. 2006. "La proie pour l'ombre: Les illusions d'une
    réforme." In *Le fédéralisme canadien contemporain: Fondements, tradi-
    tions, institutions,* edited by Alain-G. Gagnon, 211–36. Montréal:
    Presses de l'Université de Montréal.

Sheppard, Colleen. 2010. *Inclusive Equality: The Relational Dimensions of Systemic Discrimination in Canada*. Montreal and Kingston: McGill-Queen's University Press.

Société des Acadiens v Association of Parents. [1986] 1 SCR 549.

Taylor, Charles. 1992. *Multiculturalism and "The Politics of Recognition": An Essay*. Edited by Amy Gutmann. Princeton: Princeton University Press.

– 1993. *Reconciling the Solitudes: Essays on Canadian Federalism and Nationalism*. Edited by Guy Laforest. Montreal and Kingston: McGill-Queen's University Press.

Tully, James. 1995. *Strange Multiplicity: Constitutionalism in an Age of Diversity*. Cambridge: Cambridge University Press.

Weaver, Sally M. 1981. *Making Canadian Indian Policy: The Hidden Agenda 1968–70*. Toronto: University of Toronto Press.

Webber, Jeremy. 1993. "Tales of the Unexpected: Intended and Unintended Consequences of the Canadian Charter of Rights and Freedoms." *Canterbury Law Review* 5, no. 2: 207–34.

– 1994. *Reimagining Canada: Language, Culture, Community, and the Canadian Constitution*. Montreal and Kingston: McGill-Queen's University Press.

– 1999. "Constitutional Poetry: The Tension Between Symbolic and Functional Aims in Constitutional Reform." *Sydney Law Review* 21, no. 2: 260–77.

– 2000. "Constitutional Reticence." *Australian Journal of Legal Philosophy* 25, no. 2: 125–55.

– 2002. "Institutional Dialogue between Courts and Legislatures in the Definition of Fundamental Rights: Lessons from Canada (and Elsewhere)." In *Constitutional Justice, East and West: Democratic Legitimacy and Constitutional Courts in Post-Communist Europe in a Comparative Perspective*, edited by Wojciech Sadurski, 61–99. The Hague: Kluwer Law International.

– 2006a. "A Modest (but Robust) Defence of Statutory Bills of Rights." In *Human Rights Without a Bill of Rights: Institutional Performance and Reform in Australia*, edited by Tom Campbell, Jeffrey Goldsworthy, and Adrienne Stone, 263–88. Aldershot: Ashgate.

– 2006b. "Democratic Decision Making as the First Principle of Contemporary Constitutionalism." In *The Least Examined Branch: The Role of Legislatures in the Constitutional State*, edited by Richard W. Bauman and Tsvi Kahana, 411–30. New-York: Cambridge University Press.

– 2011. "Un nationalisme ni chauvin ni fermé." *Les cahiers de la Fondation Trudeau 3.*

– 2015. *The Constitution of Canada: A Contextual Analysis.* Oxford: Hart Publishing.

Woehrling, José. 1991. "Le principe d'égalité, le système fédéral canadien et le caractère distinct du Québec." In *Québec-Communauté française de Belgique: Autonomie et spécificité dans le cadre d'un système fédéral: Actes du Colloque tenu le 22 mars 1991,* edited by Pierre Patenaude, 119–68. Montréal: Éditions Wilson and Lafleur.

– 2006. "Les conséquences de l'application de la Charte canadienne des droits et libertés pour la vie politique et démocratique et l'équilibre du système federal." In *Le fédéralisme canadien contemporain: Fondements, traditions, institutions,* edited by Alain-G. Gagnon, 251–84. Montréal: Presses de l'Université de Montréal.

9

Federalism as Rejection of Nationalist Monisms

Jean Leclair

The nature of the master is much less important to me than the obedience.
Alexis de Tocqueville, *De la démocratie en Amérique*
(1840: Vol. 2, Book 4, Ch. 6)

Before pursuing any normative reflection on the twofold concept of trust/distrust, the question arises of the epistemological perspective adopted by the researcher when considering the role played and space occupied by the individual in the social and political world. For someone who conceives of the nation as constitutive of the individual, as a social totality logically and ontologically prior to the parties who compose it, federalism will be above all a means of managing the relationship between groups that are very often thought of as mutually exclusive. In contrast, for someone who sees social phenomena as flowing, at least in part, from the behaviour and actions of individuals, federalism allows for an accommodation of diversity that places as much emphasis on the interests of constituted groups as it does on the interests of the people who form them. This perspective also reveals the fragility of such social totalities, which do not always have all the concreteness we attribute to them.

The way that we see the trust/distrust concept thus depends on these epistemological stances, which are too often unexpressed. This is what I would like to examine. In the first part of this chapter, I thus hope to show how methodological nationalism contributes to cultivating a feeling of distrust by providing only a partial glimpse (although I am not saying an erroneous one) of Canada's federal dynamics. During this discussion, I will also try to show that for some proponents of methodological nationalism, the role of the social sciences and law is above all to preserve and protect the integrity of the nation as they define it. In the second part, I develop the idea that, for a number of people in Québec, and even in other provinces – in particular for a number of Indigenous peoples – federalism can guarantee a form of political morality that does not have the rubbery flabbiness that, in Québec, is too often considered a feature of any attempt to engage in federal thinking. Such a perspective is based on an epistemological stance in which the unquestionable socialization of individuals is recognized, while allowing them some reflexive autonomy. This reflexive capacity authorizes them to express a measure of healthy distrust of political proposals.

My thesis is the following: In Canada, federalism makes it possible for a citizen to refuse to be instrumentalized by nationalist programs, *all* of which have the common denominator of flattening the teeming complexity of the life of citizens. While, in the minds of theoreticians such as James Madison, federalism makes it possible to guarantee individual freedom by increasing the number of *political* communities, today, in a world dominated by *identity* claims, federalism can help loosen the clasps of the cultural straightjackets that some would like to impose on citizens. This perspective thus allows some dignity, and above all legitimacy, to be accorded to those who refuse to wear a specific cultural badge.

Authors who embrace methodological nationalism – whether Québécois, Anglo-Canadian or Indigenous – are often reduced to resorting to psychological analyses to explain Canada's failure. If I may be allowed to exaggerate, I would sum up their reasoning as follows: for Québec and Indigenous nationalists, whether explicitly stated or not, if one rejects the Québec or Indigenous national program it is because of – in decreasing order of politeness – a lack of information, a lack of patriotism, a lack of courage, a form of blindness or the confused mindset of the colonized, or, worst of all, unconditional love for the Rocky Mountains. In contrast, Quebecers who do not embrace Canadian nation-building are accused by Anglo-Canadian nationalists of misconstruing the concept of equality, lacking gratitude, or being paragons of egoism or narrow-mindedness. Given their methodological and thus normative point of view, all of these authors – some of whom are veteran researchers – cannot imagine that there could be a liberal-inspired form of federal morality that would allow a Quebecer, for example, to reject *both* totalizing nationalist proposals. They refuse to admit that there could be a position of principle other than "I subscribe to the Québec national program" or "I adhere to the Canadian national program." Any other attitude can only be "ambivalent" or "ambiguous." It cannot be principled.

However, if we accept the hypothesis proposed here, it is possible to understand why some people in Québec endorse the Canadian federal regime, or even like it, although they may feel a low level of trust towards their Anglo-Canadian fellow citizens. Their federal stance flows more from the distrust they have for the nationalist programs promoted by both *provincial and federal* political parties. In other words, their distrust is not singularly directed towards the Other as constructed by nationalist discourse, but also towards the Self as conceptualized and defined by this same discourse. In short, the federal perspective proposed here can be summarized by the Tocquevillian aphorism cited in the epigraph: from the point of view of the citizen, the nature of the master is much less important than obedience.[1]

METHODOLOGICAL NATIONALISM, OR SHRUNKEN REALITY

It goes without saying that a coherent apprehension of reality requires conscripting certain concepts. Without concepts, even if they are unexpressed, life would be terrifying. They make it possible to establish order in the flow of our perceptions. They also make science possible. Even if they do it unconsciously, all authors organize reality using abstract or semi-abstract entities. However, such conceptualizations, even in disciplines with descriptive vocations, always have epistemological consequences (Revel 2001: 63–4, 71–2) and, very often, normative implications (Leclair 2009a, 2013b).

Some anthropologists or sociologists, for example, hold that individuals, or rather an aggregate of individual decisions – which are often inconsistent and not premeditated – are at the origin of collective actions (methodological individualism). Hence, they will not examine reality using the same criteria as an anthropologist or sociologist who instead believes that individuals are above all products of socialization processes that they do not control (methodological holism). However, what belongs essentially to epistemology – the study of knowledge – can carry researchers, sometimes unknowingly, down the normative, if not the prescriptive, path. From methodological individualism, anthropologists can thus slide towards moral individualism if they say, for example, that members of Indigenous communities *must be* able to invoke the Canadian Charter of Rights and Freedoms against autonomous Indigenous governments. In contrast, from methodological holism, other anthropologists may move towards moral holism and say that since Indigenous peoples are the children of a cultural tradition that transcends them, they *should not be* allowed to invoke individual rights because to do so would threaten the very essence of "indigeneity."

These two methodological perspectives are certainly interesting, but the monism that characterizes them leads both to obscure part of reality. Consequently, it is important to point out their weaknesses since the conclusions that they allow, once mobilized by politicians or lawyers, can have important normative consequences. As Raymond Boudon points out concerning theoretical models for grasping the social and especially social change, "it is important not to interpret these models in a realistic way, not to give them a predictive power they do not have: the real is always bigger than the rational, especially when what are in question are particularly complex phenomena such as social phenomena" (1984: 238; our translation).

I would now like to examine the way in which the methodological nationalism employed by some Québec researchers leads them to judge Canadian federalism in a way that, from my point of view, only partially explains the present reality.[2] The researchers of whom I will speak are political and legal theorists who are, in other words, trained in disciplines with normative, if not prescriptive, vocations. Thus, unveiling their methodological perspective is even more fundamental if we want to put in perspective their "judgments" of federalism.[3]

The following paragraphs will be devoted to describing and criticizing the main characteristics of methodological nationalism. As we will now see, the first consists in postulating an isomorphism between society, nation, and state.

The Confusion between State, Nation, and Society

The prevalence of methodological nationalism is easy to explain.[4] My goal is not to say that it is not relevant, but simply to point out its inability to explain everything, and above all to elucidate the dynamics of a federal state. Why is it so prevalent? Because, since at least the beginning of the nineteenth century, in the circles of political authors, the nation-state has become *the* standard model of political organization in the modern world. It has come to be apprehended as the necessary, "natural" organizational principle of modernity. The nation-state has become, so to speak, the preferred cognitive lens within the social sciences.

To this "naturalization" of the nation-state has been added, in the minds of proponents of methodological nationalism, a confusion between the nation, the society, and the state they aim to describe and to analyze. As a result, society has not only come to be thought of as stopping at the borders of the state, but the nation is now presumed to shadow it down to the last millimetre. In short, the study of society is now often confused with the study of the nation-state. This methodological perspective has engendered, for example, a conception of social development such that it would be the result of factors that are purely endogenous to the national society. "External" factors are perceived as simply belonging to an "environment" to which the national society adapts. They are not considered as direct influences on social change. The only truly relevant explanations of change are the social phenomena arising within the nation's borders.

By presupposing the consubstantiality of nation, society, and state, methodological nationalism also encourages researchers to look only at the actions of national *governments* and political parties, overlooking the actions of other social actors (Skey 2009). Indeed, if the state is the nation's voice, it goes without saying that we should give priority to its actions. However, by doing so, we give far too much weight to the producers of official discourse and we too easily presume that political parties express the feelings of all citizens.[5] Furthermore, the erosion of trust and of the deference of voters to the provincial and federal political classes in no way supports an argument in favour of citizens blindly endorsing official discourses. Finally, the British-style parliamentary system, combined with a first-past-the-post electoral system and extremely strict party discipline, makes it very difficult to develop political platforms that are able to express in a nuanced manner the whole range of the electorate's political convictions (Nevitte 1996 and Leclair 2006b). However, not satisfied with having bound society, nation, and state tightly together, the followers of methodological nationalism sometimes postulate the existence of a nation that is ontologically transcendent and external to the individuals who claim to belong to it.

The Nation as a Subjective Entity

What is striking, when we examine "nationalist" research, is the presumption, often implicit, that the nation is "natural" and not artificial. In other words, its source would lie in an authority that transcends individuals and is prior and superior to them; its existence would flow from a quasi-natural historical process independent of individual wills. Methodological nationalism has ontological dimensions insofar as the nation would exist as a subjective entity with a materiality separate from those who comprise it. It would exist as an organic, integrated totality, as a thing to be taken for granted, as a construction that is already terminated.

In reality, the nation is the result of a social process of identity-building (Deloye 1996: 55). This building has been considered essential for solving the following political problem: How can we transfer to the state the loyalty that used to be felt for the family, local community, or religion? Such loyalty is necessary for the stability, not to mention the very survival, of the state. What then needs to be done so that, in the hierarchy of feelings and allegiances, primary belongings give way to state patriotism? In short, the nation is not a given. It was born of a political program designed to impose a core identity. This undertaking supposed the implementation of cultural homogenization policies so that, within the preserve of the state, the population could gather around the cultural and political flag woven and waved by the state. Primary allegiances with geographical scope extending beyond that of the nation-state have thus been depoliticized, that is, relegated to the private level. This explains why the *Canadiens français* eventually had to yield to the *Québécois*.

However, if we accept this political dimension of the national phenomenon, it is difficult to presume the ontological materiality of the nation or the permanence of any nationalist program: "By recognizing the essentially political dimension of the national construction, we affirm its own historicity. National character varies: it is not an essential factor for unifying a community except insofar as the state *tends* to retain the monopoly of its production. The nation thus loses all permanent dimensions. It cannot fight against time except through constant effort to build a unifying identity" (Deloye 1996: 58; our translation).

If we accept the historicity of national identity-building and the important role of political action in promoting and maintaining "national consciousness," then a question arises. In a federal state within which *two* orders of government, both of which are equally intent on forging the electors' consciousness, *legitimately* coexist, is it not plausible to suppose that the duality of nationalist discourses could have influenced the structuring of the national mindset(s)? If we accept, as nationalist authors hold implicitly or explicitly, that the flow of socialization carries individuals along *despite themselves*, why disqualify the mark left by federal institutions and discourses, and place value only on the role and impact of their Québec counterparts?[6] Why would the nearly 150-year presence of *two* orders of government not have left any marks in the political mindset of Quebecers? Why should it have *necessarily* brought Quebecers to distrust *everything* associated with a federal regime?

Could we not suggest the relatively banal hypothesis that the *strength* of the feeling of loyalty, or at least of deference, of Quebecers towards *both* orders of government varies depending on the time and the stakes? If this is the case, why constantly take the pulse of the Québec political community and immediately diagnose a malignant tumour when support for the nation-building program – whether Québec's or Ottawa's – is dropping? The answer is simple: for proponents of methodological nationalism, whether they are Quebecer or Anglo-Canadian, nationalist monism disqualifies (i.e., relegates to the private realm) any attachment that intellectually, emotionally, culturally, or geographically extends beyond[7] or falls beneath[8] the nation-state threshold. Our attention will now focus on this monism.

Methodological Nationalism: A Monist Conceptualization

Methodological nationalism supposes the existence of a crucial existential "centre" – the nation or rather the nation-state – and an "elsewhere" that has no political or cultural relevance. If the nation is One, it is because this is the price of state stability. As we have seen, the allegiance of citizens must recentre on the state while the individual's primary affiliations (family, work, religion, etc.) must be relegated to the private sphere. From this perspective, citizenship requires the citizen to give priority to fellow compatriots and to no one else. Monism is an imperative with which citizens *must* comply:

> Citizenship ... is much more than a legal principle; it also implies much more substantial elements from the psychological point of

view, and the consequence of this is that individuals will assign priority to their fellow nationals, in terms of the moral obligations that each has to the rest of humanity ... Today, still, this monistic conception of citizenship continues to exert an extremely powerful attraction in terms of the need for the members of a political association to have a unitary and indivisible feeling of identity. (Caron and Laforest 2009: 31)

Jean-François Caron and Guy Laforest devote a whole article to describing and denouncing the monist nature of the Canadian nation-building program promoted since the end of World War II (2009: 35). However, it is amusing to see that after having described with such accuracy some of the features of methodological nationalism, they in turn sink – all the way to their necks – into the very pitfall they criticize. Indeed, throughout the article, only federal claims are presented as unitary and never those of Québec. Yet, as I will try to show, their conception of the Québec nation is just as monist as that of their adversaries.

Methodological nationalism obscures the following reality: Canadian federalism is – and always has been – the place of confrontations between *two*[9] mutually exclusive nationalist programs. Caron and Laforest's primary objective is not so much to denounce the methodological nationalism characteristic of a certain line of Anglo-Canadian political thought, as to denounce the very legitimacy of Canadian nation-building. For nationalist authors, the purpose of the nation is to fence in political space to make the nation-state the *only* holder of power. A nation cannot endure the existence of a rival within its own territory. It follows logically that one of the nationalist programs *has to be* illegitimate.

Owing to this totalizing nationalist logic, when a follower of methodological nationalism ends up accepting that federalism can accommodate a dual allegiance, it is on the condition that the dual allegiance be defined in the following way: within the Canadian federal state, Quebecers have the right to be part of the Québec nation, as Anglo-Canadians have the right to be part of the Anglo-Canadian nation. The categorical imperative of nationalism prohibits one from simultaneously feeling part of both Québec *and* Canada. As we will now see, this single allegiance required by methodological nationalism goes hand in hand with a totalizing conception of "national culture."

A Totalizing Conception of National Culture

It is interesting to note the fascination nationalist authors have with
the source of political power rather than with its exercise. When you
read their work, it would seem that simply identifying the "right"
nation would suffice to resolve conflicts. Once identified, the nation
should have jurisdiction over everything, except for a few odds and
ends – here the conclusions of the *Allaire Report* (1991)[10] come to
mind. As I will try to explain, the totalizing definition given to the
concept of "culture" carries away, like a windstorm, nearly everything
under the sun, laying it in the nation's lap.

Since the process of identity-building involves cultural homogenization policies, it is not surprising to learn that we find "culture" at the
heart of nation-building. This vital centre must be totally occupied
by the state to avoid any erosion of the national bond. Those who,
in a spirit of conciliation, attempt to fill the centre not with substantial
content made of shared memories, but with so-called universal procedures and values, run a strong risk of being accused of spineless-
ness.[11] The proponents of methodological nationalism instead take
for granted that the totality of what makes a nation falls within the
scope of "national culture."[12]

Very often, such proponents merely assume the homogeneity of the
societies of which they speak and the unanimity reigning in their midst
concerning the very marrow of the national culture in question. I do
indeed say *societies*, for the Anglo-Canadian nation and identity also
go through the reification mill. Generally, Canada outside of Québec
is portrayed as a gigantic undifferentiated block, as if Newfoundlanders
– and their culture – could be substituted for Ontarians without the
analysis being affected.

This reciprocal dehumanization is not the ideal environment for
incubating a feeling of trust. This portrait of the Canadian nation as
a subjective entity of which Ottawa would be the voice also makes us
forget that, behind the "Ottawa abstraction," there are many Quebecers
who work within the federal government in various capacities, implement policies, administer laws, and, once their work day is over, go
home to watch *Hockey Night in Canada* with separatist friends.

All too often the nationalism of both parties and its cultural content
are represented as being "self-evident." However, this presumption is
based on an unverified premise, namely, that national audiences blindly
adopt the raw perspectives of political parties, that the people who

compose those audiences are unreflecting sponges who all soak up the same media, and, moreover, that the media merely parrot a singular dominant ideology. All of this is of course false.

Even though Québec nationalist authors are not entirely wrong, as part of the population quite likely thinks as they suppose (e.g., the 40 per cent of the Québec population that invariably cherishes the plan for true national independence), their presumption of the homogeneity of Québec society and its unanimity on the cultural question is certainly not supported by the facts.

It has to be acknowledged that most of these authors are not interested in how non-separatist citizens of Québec understand the national or cultural issue. They prefer their concepts to reality. Yet, as Michael Skey says, "we need to actually ask who takes their identity for granted, who is passionate and mobilised by a sense of nation identification and when ... who rejects such a framework ... and then try and understand broader general patterns in order to address the complex question of why" (2009: 337).

The reality of Quebecer and Anglo-Canadian identities is of course more complex than the portrait painted by these authors.[13] In both cases, identity is neither a substrate impervious to historical change nor a subjective entity without internal divisions. In both cases, culture lacks the geometrical contours that it is cast as having. In short, we must be careful not to present a rigid image of phenomena that are, on the contrary, ontologically malleable. Moreover, if there is one self-evident truth, it is the absence of unanimity concerning the Québec national program itself, regardless of the more general question of Québec identity. From independence, to sovereignty-association, to renewed federalism, to the form of autonomy promoted by the Action démocratique du Québec, not to mention the barometric nationalism of Lucien Bouchard,[14] the Québec national program is constantly being rebuilt and reimagined – which is, in passing, neither surprising nor "abnormal."[15] After all, conflict, much more than consensus, characterizes modern societies (see Montesquieu 1734: 64–5, chapter 10). In fact, the more or less caricatured portrayal of other peoples' identity or cultural reality fails to conceal the nationalist authors' conviction of the greater dignity of *their* national program.

The methodological nationalism of some authors even leads them to say that the only way to reconcile the various components within Québec society is through independence, *despite* dissent within the French-speaking Québec community about the contours of its collective identity.[16] In short, national aspirations *must* be achieved despite this uncertainty because the nation, in the end, is greater than us all and has to fulfill its destiny.

As I said above, grafted onto this presumption of unanimity and homogeneity is a totalizing definition of the concept of culture. This conception of culture is understood not only as a set of *facts*, but also as the product of a *moral* consensus on common values. Understood in this manner, culture entraps nearly all social, economic, or cultural phenomena. In the name of "Québec values,"[17] now associated with Québec's "culture," the state of Québec can legitimately claim, at least from the nationalist perspective, the exclusive right to intervene on behalf of the Québec nation, even with respect to issues that, at first sight, have little to do with what we would associate with culture. Think, for example, of the environment, the economy, and so on.[18]

This totalizing approach also has the strategic advantage of raising to the rank of "cultural" intervention legislative measures and political decisions that, if they emanated from English Canada, would instead be interpreted as showing a will to achieve much more "humdrum" ends like governmental or economic efficiency. In addition, from this perspective, all stakes are given an equal value. Everything is essential to the cultural survival of the nation. Regulating forestry and the environment acquires the existential aura of linguistic issues. Managing political claims then becomes impossible. Finally, if any issue, regardless of its nature, can be draped in the cloak of Québec culture, federal legislative interventions, including those authorized by the federal constitution of 1867, become not only illegitimate, but fatal to Québec's national culture.[19]

The primary defect of this totalizing conception is that, once again, it is based on a presumption of unanimity regarding the definition and content – allegedly unique and intangible – of Québec culture. Moreover, to repeat an argument that has already been advanced, if we accept, as methodological nationalism would have us do, that culture is the product of a socialization that transcends the individual, why should we conclude *a priori* that, in a federal state, the cultural influences affecting an individual stop or should *necessarily* stop at the borders of the Québec nation-state? Finally, on what empirical bases are Caron and Laforest able to peremptorily assert that the creation of Radio-Canada[20] and the Canada Council for the Arts is a manifestation of Canadian nationalism that undermines Québec identity while the establishment of state institutions such as

Télé-Québec, the Régie des rentes du Québec, and the Caisse de dépôt et de placement seems to them to be perfectly natural (2009: 35)? Of course, all of these institutions have the symbolic function of asserting the legitimacy of two mutually exclusive nationalist programs. Yet, do these institutions determine, in a mechanistic, immediate manner – one in terms of evil and the other in terms of good – what creates the luxuriant complexity of the culture of Québec's citizens today? This example shows the degree to which nationalist authors see reality only through the prism of the nation-state. For them, "culture" and "state power over culture" are one and the same thing. Québec culture stops where the nation-state is no longer able to intervene. Hidden behind this point of view is the idea that culture has to be produced by the state (and thus one single state) or else be controlled by it, since its primary function is to ensure that the state will last.

If we examine reality from a more nuanced point of view like that of a citizen, we can see things in a different way. Take support for the arts, a cultural issue *par excellence*. At first sight, some could think that such a sector should be the exclusive prerogative of the province of Québec. Yet, if the federal government were to withdraw from this sector, since it spends 32.4 per cent of its arts budget in Québec, while the province accounts for only 23.2 per cent of Canada's population, it is likely that Quebecers would lose something in the transaction (Colbert and Courchesne 2010). Some will oppose the argument that Canada has an obligation to honour Québec's cultural difference. They will claim that, should the federal government withdraw from the cultural field, it would then have to pay to the Québec state the same amount that it used to spend to promote the arts in the province. This may be true. However, federalism has another advantage: it increases the number of public funding agencies and thus frees artists from being confronted with a monopoly held by a single level of government (ibid.). In short, even with respect to cultural matters, there is something good about rivalry – on condition that we do not look at things from the sole point of view of the Québec state.

Such thinking, however, means accepting that citizens have some freedom when it comes to choosing what comprises their culture. It means recognizing that an authentic Quebecer can drink from the source of Québéco-Québécois heritage, as well as subscribe to French, English, Innu, or whatever culture he/she chooses. It means accepting that the relationships of Quebecers to foreign non-francophone culture are often appreciative rather than defiant.

I would add that, should we ever accept a totalizing definition of culture, we would have to, in all logic, accept that it also includes political culture. Now, if this is the case, we would have to conclude that federalism – in the same way as parliamentarianism, the rule of law, and the protection of rights and freedoms – is one of the elements that constitutes the culture that shapes us in spite of ourselves. Who has the authority to conclude otherwise? Who has the power to approve the cultural heritage that we are nonetheless told exists in our souls from the very moment of our birth? In sum, it seems to me that while nationalist authors may excel at writing a social history of the political that reveals the logic at work in political life, it would do them no harm to write a political history of the social that would this time reveal the imprint of the political on the social.

Of course, implicit in the above is always the following question: is it cultures or individuals that have to be protected? For nationalists and communitarians, the nation or community plays a *constitutive* role in personal identity. Absent a primordial attachment to a culture that is greater than themselves, individuals could not achieve full humanity. This perspective thus rejects the central idea of liberalism, according to which culture is essential, but only as a *means* for the development of the individual: "it is not the past, history, or the distinct culture of minority groups that have value, but their contribution to the dignity and freedom of each individual" (Audard 2009: 598; our translation).

As I conclude this section, I would like to point out two methodological dangers that threaten us all, and from which nationalist authors are not immune: hyperbolization of a single facet of reality and overdetermination of facts.

The hyperbolization of a facet of reality is a methodological reflex that leads researchers to transform an unquestionably true, though limited and circumscribed, statement (e.g., "some individuals are egotistical") into a universal statement ("all individuals are egotistical"). Thus, because it is true that power sometimes oppresses, some conclude that power always oppresses. The impact of the Canadian Charter of Rights and Freedoms on Québec society seems to me to be an object of such hyperbolization.

After having quoted a passage by André Burelle (1995: 64, cited in Caron and Laforest 2009: 38) stating that the Canadian Charter has allowed the federal parliament to circumvent the division of powers – which is a completely false assertion from a legal point of view[21] – Caron and Laforest take pains to demonstrate that the Charter shows the central government's desire to impose a monist view of Canadian identity. There is, to be sure, a portion of truth in this conclusion. For example, there is no doubt that the principle of equality stated in the Charter, even if it has not had the *legal* impact claimed by Burelle, has nonetheless, owing to its *symbolic* dimension, influenced the behaviour of political actors. Thus, on the basis of a mathematical conception of equality, some Anglo-Canadians have called for the provinces to be treated more uniformly. In contrast, pleading for a geometrical concept of equality (i.e., to each according to their merits and needs), Québec has demanded unique treatment, given certain differences between it and the other provinces. In short, political actors in both camps have used equality as a symbol to promote opposing political aims.

However, Caron and Laforest's conclusions go far beyond this observation. Noting the conclusions of an earlier study by Laforest, they conclude that Quebecers "are now estranged from the Charter and the Canadian political experience, feeling like aliens in their own country, in a form of 'internal exile'" (2009: 39). I hate parsnips, but does this mean that I refuse to eat all root vegetables? It may be true that Quebecers – though not all Quebecers – disagree with the language provisions in the Charter. They may also be against the strategic use of the concept of equality to counter their political goals. However, should we jump to the conclusion that there is a general loathing of the Canadian Charter by Quebecers? Survey information (Girard 2008: 64–5) and Québec court decisions since 1982[22] confirm the interest, even fascination, Quebecers have with this legal instrument. If we insist too much on the infringement of the "communitarian" concerns of Quebecers, we forget that, in their cultural heritage, one of the things we find, among others, is liberalism.[23]

This exaggeration of the impact of the Canadian Charter on the psyche of Quebecers leads me to point out the danger, when trying to identify such unobservable states as what is going on in the minds of citizens, of overdetermining a fact or event. What I mean by this is that we must remember that a given fact or event can lend itself to many different contradictory interpretations that we will not always be able to separate, since they can all be perfectly compatible with the data (Ogien 2002: 538–41). In short, since the "intent" or "will" of a citizen does not have the material consistency of a tennis ball, it is much more difficult to delimit its contours.

It is often repeated, for example, that the advent of the Charter dealt a significant blow to the collective, pluralist, and communitarian conceptions that underpinned Canadian federalism before 1982.[24] Moreover, according to some authors, the Canadian Charter would be incompatible with the communitarian values at the foundation of the Québec national program. There is quite certainly some truth in the first assertion, and most probably in the second, if we reduce Québec society to only those who share the totalizing nationalist stance. However, another interpretation could also explain the interest that all Canadians, including Quebecers, have in the Charter.

The reason that the Canadian political universe was dominated by collective, pluralist, and communitarian views before 1982 was perhaps that there was hitherto no constitutional text guaranteeing the protection of rights and freedoms that could thwart the will of Parliament.[25] Before the advent of the Canadian Charter, federal-provincial disputes occupied almost the entire constitutional field. Owing to circumstances, the "Constitution" in the broad sense of the term was thus the concern of governments, not of citizens. Through skilful recourse exploiting the division of powers, some people nonetheless succeeded in obtaining the equivalent of a right to freedom of expression and religion (Chevrette and Marx 1982: 712–21, 1274–368, 1410–15). However, these were at best indirect successes. That said, can we not advance the idea that the Charter, far from creating from scratch a form of liberal individualism that limited the communitarian conceptions of all, could simply have served to galvanize ideological convictions that were already present? The next section will be devoted to a typical characteristic of Québec methodological nationalism, namely, the 1867 constitution fetish.

The Fetish of the Written Constitution

I will begin by recalling that, since nationalist authors are more concerned with the source of political power than with its exercise, it follows that once the existence of the nation has been established, the extent of its power is generally presumed. It goes without saying that the nation-state has to control everything. There is thus no point in wasting precious time on justifying why such and such power has to belong to the nation since tourism, sports, care for the elderly, moose hunting, education, language, maple syrup production, and so on are all assumed to be part of the national cultural totality. Such an approach is strategically useful since it eliminates any possibility of error. In short, once the point of departure – the existence of the nation – has been established, the end point is already known.

In a federal state marked by a division of powers between a central government and federated entities, methodological nationalism naturally poses a problem. The solution for Québec nationalist authors is to (1) fetishize the strictly legal and more specifically the judicial dimension of federalism, thus reducing its political dimension – intergovernmental relations – to the status of an epiphenomenon; (2) sanctify the Judicial Committee of the Privy Council's interpretation of the division of powers, consequently denouncing any deviating interpretations that were given after 1949 when appeals to the Privy Council were abolished; (3) presume that the division of legislative powers is a zero-sum game; (4) ignore the *already-there* in favour of the *always-more*; and, finally, (5) disqualify collaboration by confusing the principle of exclusivity with that of non-subordination.

The federal constitution of 1867 is a law. It may be a fundamental law, but nonetheless it is a legal text. As such, it is normal for it to be interpreted by the courts so that it can be adapted to new realities. There is no doubt that we can debate the relevance and wisdom of decisions rendered by the Supreme Court. However, as I have shown elsewhere,[26] a careful analysis of positive law does not in any way support the conclusion of nationalist authors according to whom "the federal regime has taken a resolutely centralizing path of evolution, to the point that, in the name of the national interest, *all of Quebec's legislative powers* can be whittled down by the will of the federal parliament and the Supreme Court of Canada; and that [Quebecers must remember] that the ultimate result of such an evolution can consist in the *complete dissolution of Quebec cultural identity in Canadian identity*" (Brouillet 2005: 384; our translation, emphasis added).[27]

Aside from its inaccuracy from the point of view of positive law, such a conclusion is based on a totalizing conception of Québec culture,[28] which transforms any federal intervention into an attack on that indefinitely expandable, reconfigurable substrate. Such a conclusion also testifies to what Jean-François Gaudreault-Desbiens calls "judicial fetishism," understood as the epistemological attitude that consists in taking the pulse of a political regime such as federalism by relying solely on the *judicial* treatment it has received. Such an attitude ignores the whole periconstitutional world made up of inter-governmental relations and the agreements they generate, even though such agreements often have the effect of moderating and inflecting, to the satisfaction of all parties, the impact of judicial decisions (Gaudreault-Desbiens 2009: 301–30).[29]

Moreover, when we read texts such as those by Caron and Laforest, or Patrick Fafard, François Rocher, and Catherine Côté, we are struck by their account of federalism: their image is that of a regime in which the principle of exclusive jurisdictions should always suppose a clear, watertight demarcation between the responsibilities of the two orders of government. That a given matter could be governed by both orders of government seems to them to contradict the idea of federalism.[30]

In their survey measuring the intensity of Canadian feelings toward a "federal culture," Fafard, Rocher, and Côté come to the conclusion that it is very low. In order to support their findings, they invoke various arguments, including the fact that a majority of the Canadians questioned – including some Quebecers, though a proportionally smaller number – preferred collaboration between the two orders of government rather than a recognition of clearly divided powers between the provincial governments and the central government.[31] The sectors in which the respondents considered it appropriate for the two orders of government to collaborate were the following: negotiation of international agreements, environmental regulation, integration of immigrants, and promotion of the arts. The authors conclude: "If a federation is, following K.C. Wheare, characterized by a clear division of powers, Canadians are not particularly strong federalists. It would appear instead, that Canadians prefer their governments to co-operate" (Fafard, Rocher, and Côté 2010: 28).[32] Oddly enough, in light of Canadian constitutional law, there is absolutely no doubt that the last three sectors mentioned are fields of jurisdiction *not* entrusted exclusively to either order of government. The situation is less clear for the first area. Contemporary constitutional law thus makes possible the cooperation desired by citizens. The authors can most certainly deplore the fact that current positive law authorizes cooperation in cases where they would like to see a clear division of powers, but we have to wonder why the collaboration desired by citizens and permitted by the Constitution would be in contradiction with federal culture.

What yardstick did these authors use to measure the federal culture of Canadians, if not positive law? In fact, their federal ideal is a copy of the model developed by the Judicial Committee of the Privy Council in London, the ultimate arbiter of Canadian judicial disputes up until 1949, when appeals to that London institution were abolished.

The Privy Council always preferred the so-called watertight compartments interpretation, in accordance with which it tried to partition federal and provincial jurisdictions as much as possible. Its interpretation was based on the fact that the 1867 constitution explicitly states that the powers allocated to both levels of government are mutually exclusive. The Privy Council's approach, without surprise, rapidly became the mantra of Québec nationalists. However, the "watertight compartments" interpretation has proven difficult to maintain because of the advent of the welfare state, as well as the more tightly woven social, political, and economic threads of the modern federal state. The Supreme Court has thus adopted a definition of exclusivity which, by emphasizing the legislative purposes whose pursuit is authorized by the diverse heads of power, does not exclude legislative overlaps that were formerly difficult, if not impossible, to justify.

In order to grasp the significance of this approach, christened the "double aspect" doctrine, let us examine, for example, its impact on the field of environment regulation.[33] Since the 1867 federal constitution says nothing about this issue, the Supreme Court has concluded that both orders of government can intervene in this matter, but only in the exercise of their *exclusive* powers. According to the court, the nature of each and every federal and provincial field of jurisdiction allocated under the 1867 federal constitution determines the scope of the purposes that can be pursued by each level of government. Thus, the federal parliament, which has exclusive jurisdiction over criminal law, may sanction a polluting activity, but only if it harms human health or the environment – that is, purposes falling within the purview of criminal law. As for the provinces, they can regulate the pollution emitted by local enterprises, not because they have any jurisdiction over criminal law (which is exclusively federal, as just mentioned), but because the Constitution gives them the exclusive power to legislate over matters related to intra-provincial commerce and local industry. In short, in Canadian constitutional law, federal and provincial legislative powers, though mutually exclusive, are not barrels placed side by side, but rather are projectors, the beams of which can cross but are never allowed to be superimposed over each other. Autonomy and exclusivity thus do not prohibit both orders of government from regulating the very same thing.

From the above, it is clear that autonomy and exclusivity must not be confused with non-subordination. A province can be perfectly autonomous in exercising its powers, even if the federal government may regulate, in exercising its own powers, identical subject matters. If this happens, the province is not subordinate to the will of the central government. However, it is true that if a conflict arises between a valid provincial law and a valid federal law, the latter is considered paramount over the former. Such paramountcy could indeed endanger the principle of non-subordination. However, to guarantee the greatest possible latitude to provinces, the Supreme Court has resorted to a very restrictive definition of conflict that can be summarized as follows: there will be no conflict between a provincial law and a federal law unless the former says "yes" and the latter says "no." In accordance with this logic, the court, for example, has concluded that a provincial law that is more severe than a prohibitive federal law is not in conflict with it. Indeed, if more severe, it necessarily meets and exceeds the threshold set by the federal law. Coming back to our example, the central government can set minimum environmental standards that the provinces, in the exercise of their own powers, are authorized to exceed.

Nationalist political theorists rarely mention this fine-grained interpretation of exclusivity and paramountcy. For them, it could be said that reality is written in the text of the 1867 constitution as it was interpreted in 1949. The "double aspect" doctrine, if they are aware of it, is thus of little interest to them.

Naturally, we may prefer the Privy Council's interpretation to that of the Supreme Court, but it goes without saying that the chasm between the discourse of nationalist authors ("the Constitution is composed of watertight compartments") and the contemporary interpretation of the division of powers distorts their analysis and their evaluation of the Canadian federal regime. Indeed, based on the ideal type selected by these authors, any evaluation of federalism is necessarily negative. Thus, from my point of view, Fafard, Rocher, and Côté should have instead concluded that the intensity of federal culture among Canadians varies depending on whether it is assessed in accordance with the federal model now proposed by the courts, or the one proposed by the Privy Council during the 1940s. This is the only way that their readers would truly have been able to determine whether today's federal system meets the expectations of citizens.

Citizens' trust in the federal regime stands to be harmed if the latter is misrepresented to them. This is the case if the falsehood is driven into their heads that the Constitution guarantees a provincial autonomy so watertight that any federal intervention that encroaches on a provincial jurisdiction, even in the slightest fashion, is unconstitutional. As I have tried to show, the reality is infinitely more complex. We may lament it, but if we want to do scientific work and avoid accusations of political activism, a great deal of nuancing needs to be done.

Methodological nationalism also appeals to criteria for assessing the success or failure of Canadian federalism that emphasize only the issue of provincial autonomy. Although the texts of Caron and Laforest and Fafard, Rocher, and Côté both refer to the responsibility of federated entities in maintaining the federal alliance, they nonetheless measure federalism using only the yardstick of how much autonomy federated entities are recognized as having, without considering the responsibilities that such entities have in cultivating federal solidarity.

It is rather droll to see that Quebecers are portrayed by Fafard, Rocher, and Côté as the only true federalists, given their great desire for autonomy. For instance, to the question of whether Québec should have greater autonomy than the other provinces, 73 per cent of Quebecers answered "yes," while 61 per cent of Anglo-Canadians said "no." However, 53 per cent of Anglo-Canadians were in agreement that the federal government should continue to sign asymmetrical agreements with Québec regarding health care and immigration. Of course, 82 per cent of Quebecers were favourable to this idea. Yet, from these findings, the authors draw the conclusion that Anglo-Canadians have a relatively weak federal culture, since their refusal to recognize greater power for Québec demonstrates that they do not accept the consequences of diversity. Once again, the intensity of Anglo-Canadian federal culture may be weak, but I would have liked to know how Québec respondents would have answered the following questions: "Do you consider it just that Indigenous nations in Quebec be given special political status?" and "Would you accept that Indigenous nations in Quebec be given territorial rights that would not be held by non-Indigenous Quebecers?" If memory serves me well – and I know it does – the 2002 announcement of the agreement in principle between some Innu First Nations and the two orders of government – the Joint Approach – raised much more mud than enthusiasm in the Saguenay, an area that, according to the criteria of Fafard, Rocher, and Côté, should possess a highly developed federal culture, if not the most highly developed in Canada. In short, concluding that there is a federal culture in Québec based solely on the benefits that can accrue to Quebecers, and without ever going to the trouble of testing the intensity of the federal spirit when it makes an appeal to solidarity, seems methodologically dubious. Moreover, it is surprising to see that the federal culture of which nationalist authors speak does not appear to be based on a principle of justice. Such a principle generally refers to seeking mutual advantage in contexts where conflicting interests exist. As a way of measuring the intensity of federal culture in Québec, it would have been interesting to ask Quebecers whether their federal culture would be as intense if they were debtors rather than creditors in the equalization system (as in the current situation). Indeed, some of the eloquence employed in the service of asymmetry and difference should rub off on reflections relating to Québec's obligations to the rest of Canada.

To a certain degree, however, this methodological bias can be explained. Indeed, another characteristic of Québec methodological nationalism is that, from its perspective, the balance sheet of Canadian federalism has no column for assets. Only liabilities count. Any advantage obtained by the province is completely unimportant since, given conceptual "totalism," *by definition* any power attributed to the nation already belongs to it. It is thus normal for nationalist authors to ignore the autonomy that Canadian provinces are already recognized as having, an autonomy that would make many other federated entities jealous. The lack of interest in what is already there leads some authors to make assertions that are surprising to find in peer-reviewed journals.[34] Methodological nationalism also explains intellectual stances that simply measure the intensity of English Canada's federal spirit according to its willingness to give *additional* powers to Québec.

Finally, as we have seen above, the emphasis placed on the principle of autonomy, combined with misunderstanding the principle of exclusivity developed in positive law, disqualifies collaboration between the two orders of government in the eyes of nationalist authors. Yet, Canadian constitutional law makes many mechanisms available to governments so that they can collaborate in ways that are both efficient and compliant with constitutional legality (administrative inter-delegation, legislation by reference, conditional legislation, etc.). From the nationalist perspective, however, collaboration is associated with an abdication of power, or the manifestation of a consumerist rather than a civic relationship with the state; the sole end of collaboration is, in their opinion, the delivery of better services. Thus, such a relationship to the state is considered to be too instrumental to be able to replace the feeling of loyalty or patriotism that is required for a genuine federal culture.[35] I will return to the question of loyalty below. Here I will merely point out that unless we consider all stakes equally important, it is difficult to see why collaboration, in general, would have something mean-spirited about it. While autonomy sometimes requires refusing to collaborate, does this mean that all-out opposition should be taken as a position of principle? Of course, a purely consumerist relationship is a very weak hook on which to hang the existence of a state. However, is it right to argue that the only effect of successful collaboration is greater efficiency in the delivery of public services? Is not such collaboration an homage paid to the very concept that resides at the heart of federalism: the *feodus*, the alliance?

The Presumed Morality of National Partiality

As I have tried to show in the preceding pages, in Canada there are two – if not more, counting Indigenous aspirations – mutually exclusive nationalist programs. They are mutually exclusive because the very idea of the nation is ontologically associated with the One. A nation and the state that embodies it cannot, in all logic, admit any rivals.

As we have seen, this unity has been justified by the need to ensure the coherence and stability of the state around a citizen loyalty that would transcend any primary allegiance. However, nationalist authors also base the primacy of the nation on the following observation: most people feel intuitively bound to their compatriots by obligations and duties that are more numerous and stringent than those they feel towards people from other countries.[36] This intuitive preference would be at the origin of the *duty* that renders it incumbent on citizens to give preference to their compatriots, to whom they have special obligations which they do not have to others. Quebecers would thus be morally bound to give priority to the bond that ties them to their ethnic or cultural community.

This approach raises a number of difficulties. First, we need to prove that our intuitions are not themselves unjust. If, owing to the socialization to which I have been subjected, I am convinced that all Muslims are terrorists, doubt can be cast on my intuition. Second, why should that intuition be binding? Because of a shared history or shared culture? But what if I disapprove of part of that heritage (Weinstock 1999a: 536)? I may, for example, find my great-uncle's decision to volunteer for the war effort against the German invasion more morally acceptable than the decision of the majority of French Canadians, who resisted any form of engagement.[37] At most, we can say that I *may* prefer my ethnic cultural community, but not that I *must* do so. Third, if we *have to* follow our pre-reflective intuitions when they carry us towards our fellow countrymen, why should we not rely on them to establish distinctions within the national community? Why must the power of intuition stop at the nation's borders? What justifies recourse, within the nation, to liberal principles of impartiality? Are Quebecers intuitively impartial among themselves? Finally, do all of our intuitions guide us towards our compatriots? Do we not each have a range of affiliations that, depending on the circumstances, could take precedence over the interests of our fellow compatriots?

Finally, would a person socialized in a federal state *necessarily* experience a single feeling of allegiance? In my view, the question is worth asking. Moreover, if it were true, as communitarians argue, that cultural identification is essential to an individual's *moral* construction, I would still need to be convinced that, in a state such as Canada, my culture only produces a Québéco-Québécois perfume.

****

The methodological nationalism described in the preceding sections does not foster feelings of trust. Indeed, even if we adhere to a very tenuous definition of trust, like those suggested by Daniel Weinstock[38] or Jean-François Gaudreault-Desbiens,[39] which are essentially based on the conviction of a person or group that the Other will not knowingly attempt to harm them, we have to admit that methodological nationalism raises a problem. This is because it cultivates the idea that a political community has only one centre that, consequently, radically disqualifies any affiliation that extends beyond the nation's borders. Above all, it makes it possible to transform the Other into a disincarnated, monolithic subjective entity that is perceived as having the intention, in this case, of suffocating Québec's national identity.

This said, there is no doubt in my mind that the methodological nationalism perspective is embraced by many Quebecers – as well as Anglo-Canadians and members of Indigenous communities. The predominance of this way of seeing things is so great today that there is little chance of it fading away in the near future. Nonetheless, I remain strongly persuaded that methodological nationalism obscures reality so much that we have no choice but to challenge the dominant role it plays in the social sciences. Indeed, if it were true, as the nationalists argue, that the Québec nation is being shortchanged – and that it has been since 1760 – then we have to wonder why the national dream has still not become a reality, despite all the sovereigntists' efforts to "evangelize" the population about the necessity of sovereignty. In reality, the answer is simple. The society of Québec is not the same thing as the nation of Québec as they understand it. Introducing a little reflexivity into methodological nationalism would, however, be too upsetting for its proponents, since it would force them to break with their postulated isomorphy of nation, society, and state.

Nonetheless, it should be noted that some authors have toned down their conclusions. Thus, after having determined that there is very weak federal culture in Canada, Fafard, Rocher, and Côté add: "The majority of public servants we met with, as well as the respondents to our survey, and perhaps even Canadians themselves [including many Quebecers] may be articulating an inherent preference for a more integrated and/or competitive federation (as may also be the case for at least some citizens in the USA). In this model, citizens look to governments to act as checks on each other" (2010: 41).[40] The authors hasten to note, however, that, if this instrumental conception of citizenship continues, it could threaten Canada's very survival as a country.

I would now like to explore another avenue, which will not explain the behaviour of all Quebecers, but could, at least, give some dignity, until now refused, to those like me who see federalism as a liberating wedge that can be thrust between the nationalisms that confront one another in Canada.

OUTLINE OF A LIBERAL THEORY OF FEDERALISM

As a reminder, I shall repeat the thesis I am defending here. In Canada, federalism makes it possible for citizens, who so desire, to refuse to be instrumentalized by nationalist programs, *all* of which have the common denominator of flattening the teeming complexity of their lives; it can be used to undo the clasps of the cultural straightjackets that people are forced into. From this perspective, distrust is not directed only towards the Other as constructed by nationalist discourse, but also towards the Self as it is conceived by the same discourse. The conception of federalism proposed here certainly has a moral dimension, though it also has epistemological, political, ontological, anthropological, and methodological dimensions.

On the epistemological level, the federal stance is not only distinct from methodological nationalism, but also from its antithesis: "methodological cosmopolitanism" (Beck 2005). Indeed, rather than developing a radically different concept presupposing a national *before* and a postnational *after*,[41] following Daniel Chernilo's example (2006: 11–12), I find it more relevant to simply challenge the presuppositions of methodological nationalism and to suggest an approach based on an already existing political conceptualization. In this way, we avoid falling into the Manichean dichotomies at times generated by disciples of methodological cosmopolitanism: a static, culturally homogenous past versus a fluid present rich with colourful hybridity and shimmering complexity.[42] We also avoid the trap threatening cosmopolitans, namely that of lending to the "nation" (which they nonetheless challenge) a degree of ontological materiality that it has never had historically.

Epistemologically, the federalist perspective begins with the principle that all conceptualization is an approximation, and that the researcher's task is thus to propose a form of axiomatization that will do justice to the complexity of the real world. In other words, rejecting both nihilism and relativism, this stance recognizes the impossibility of developing a social theory on infallible principles. At a minimum, however, it supposes that researchers who claim to describe the real world focus on citizens' lives as they are lived, not as they should be lived.

On the moral and political level, federalism as it is described here is envisaged as a principle of freedom. While it is accurate to say that federalism focuses on the problem of the *source* of political power or "who can do what" – a problem that in multinationalism universes occupies all the political space – it is also concerned with the *exercise* of power. And, if I may be allowed to repeat myself, in a world dominated by *identity* claims, federalism may serve to counter the cultural confinement threatening citizens. Moreover, proponents of federalism prefer to place trust in political institutions – which in Canada are not problem-free – rather than in the presumed virtue of citizens or the political parties that represent them.

Federalism – like nationalism – is thus not a simple descriptive thesis. While accepting, for example, the importance of the socialization processes that structure human existence, it postulates that the individual *must* adopt a reflective attitude with respect to them, otherwise he/she will not be truly free.

On the ontological level, federalism, as opposed to nationalism, supposes that our humanity – at least to some degree – is independent from the social, and that the individual is thus able, through a conscience partly educated by reason, to put the social at a distance and even to contribute to its renewal.

The liberalism proposed here does not however encourage asocial or antisocial individualism, because it does not *deny* the influence of society's various powers. On the contrary, without a social framework, a person could not develop individuality. What this form of liberalism seeks to do is to *limit* this influence. What it rejects is the instrumentalization of the individual in the name of a transcendent authority – God or the Nation. The individual is not here conceptualized as an abstract atomized entity, but rather as a subject engaged in a constant process of individuation through which he/she (re)creates himself/herself *with* the support of others and not always in opposition to them.

Freedom becomes inconceivable if we deny individuals the capacity to modify their commitments, to distance themselves from their primordial affiliations. Solidarity is likewise unimaginable if we reject the individual's reflexive ability, since then we also reject their capacity to find public justifications for their affiliations, which is the only way to avoid violence and build bridges between oneself and others.

Epistemological and methodological consequences follow from all of this. First, nationalist authors should be a little more prudent when they conflate society, nation, and state. Second, we should not disqualify as displays of individualism all stances that do not aim at strengthening the powers of the nation-state.

Moreover, since, from this perspective, the state or party *doxa* ceases to be the final word on history, it follows that national culture and history are no longer sacred totalities, but components of the social world that the citizen can rightfully approach without genuflecting. This perspective does not require silencing the parts of one's past and culture that do not fit into the official mold. It also takes root in rejecting teleology. The 1760 Conquest did not set in motion anything definitive.

In short, contrary to theories requiring that citizens have a primordial attachment to a single community of fate, federalism is an avenue for those who reject such confinement. Although the latter do not deny the weight of what Fernand Braudel calls *l'histoire de longue durée* (long-term history), they judge themselves capable of making decisions on the basis of considerations that are not always nor entirely defined in national terms. Indeed, why would a decision based on a consideration other than concern for the nation be evidence of ambivalence about one's identity? What is the worth of this pejorative judgment if it is based on a scale that has only one unit of measurement: the unique, indivisible nation? Can we not see a perfectly reasonable liberal position in the repudiation of two nationalist programs judged equally unappealing given some of their aspects? In a position that rejects the "miniaturization of human beings" (Sen 2006: xiii) proposed by both programs? A refusal not resulting from a Pavlovian reflex of cowardice, but instead based on the reasoned decision of someone who, in light of liberal normative criteria, prefers conflict to the mirage of joyous solidarity? This is a position based on the idea that among the citizen's identity referents, whether they be geographical origin, sexual orientation, social class, profession, place of residence, marital status, and so on, Québec or Canadian nationalism is not always at the top of the list (Maclure 2000: 29; Leclair 2010a). Can there not be times and situations that justify mobilizing one referent rather than another?[43] Why should everything be melted down in the bottomless crucible of "national culture"?

Finally, it is true that the liberalism I am defending entails what I would call a "Socratic" attitude, that of Socrates in the *Apology*, one who refuses unconditional participation (Leclair 2013a). It is the attitude of one for whom moral integrity involves, above all, being in agreement with oneself, being consistent with oneself. Such agreement and consistency may require a reflective effort that can sometimes be painful. However, it teaches us that dialogue with the Other is only possible if, before anything else, one accepts the importance of engaging in discussion with oneself.

* * * *

Can the moral and methodological federalism proposed here be substituted for the trust needed for the survival of a federal state? Perhaps not. However, since it places the emphasis on federalism as a limit on power, it makes it possible to escape from the unquenchable thirst for recognition and neurotic fetishism of constitutional texts that have fuelled multinational federalism for nearly thirty years. These are two phenomena that have corroded the political climate, fed resentment, and thus undermined trust. Proponents of the moral federalism defended here do not expect the state to make them happy by raising the identity flag (with a maple leaf or a fleur de lys). If constitutional recognition of the cultural specificity of Québec were to occur someday, it would be a powerful symbol. Nonetheless, I am convinced that Anglo-Canadian nationalist authors would immediately say that Québec had been given too much, while their Quebecer counterparts would complain that it had not been given enough.

One last clarification is required. The justification for federalism advanced here is not a substitute for all the others that have already been suggested by persons more learned than I am. It is an addition to that fruitful legacy. If, as some promise, post-national states should someday be realized, then of course the proposal made here would become less pertinent. However, as the saying goes: "if 'ifs' and 'ands' were copper pans, there'd be no need for tinkers' hands." Quite frankly, I cannot see the day when the line of prophets wishing to enclose our lives in neat little boxes will ever be extinguished.

CONCLUSION

In conclusion, I would like to make clear that the moral federalism I have proposed is not synonymous with political disengagement or indifference. It simply authorizes citizens to understand federalism as a mechanism reminding political parties that social reality extends far beyond their reifications. This does not entail rejecting political platforms in their entirety. We can find a myriad of interesting proposals within them. However, we can oppose having our existence instrumentalized for the benefit of some national program. We can be irritated at being reminded of a moral duty *compelling* us to support the objectives of our closest fellow compatriots. We can refuse to think of nations as entities ontologically separate from those composing them. We can choose to see the "nation" unveiled for what it is: a political and narrative construction. We can reject the totalizing conceptions of culture being proposed to us. In short, we can adopt a moral stance that consists in refusing to subject our freedom to abstract entities that speak only through the mouths of political parties and their partisans.

NOTES

I would like to thank the Social Sciences and Humanities Research
Council of Canada for the financial support that made this study possible.
This is part of a more general research project on federalism as an avenue
for reconfiguring relationships between the Indigenous peoples of Canada
and Canadians in general. See Leclair (2006a, 2007, 2008, 2009a, 2009b,
2010a, 2012, 2013a). I would also like to thank Dimitrios Karmis for
reading and commenting on the manuscript of this text. Naturally, I take
sole responsibility for the ideas expressed here.

1   The point of view expressed in this chapter has much in common with
    ideas expressed by the following authors: Karmis and Maclure (2001);
    Schouls (2003); Karmis and Norman (2005); and Panagos (2008).

2   Since I have limited space and have elsewhere examined the aspects of
    conceptual totalism characteristic of the thought of some Indigenous
    authors (Leclair 2009a, 2013b), here I will concentrate on the method-
    ological nationalism of Québec authors.

3   My objective is to sketch a portrait of methodological nationalism as an
    ideal type. In order to illustrate some of its characteristics, I will some-
    times refer to the three following publications: Caron and Laforest (2009);
    Fafard, Rocher, and Côté (2010); and Brouillet (2005). I would however
    like to point out that the weaknesses of the methodological nationalism
    that I criticize in this chapter do not all appear in these publications! I
    could have chosen other authors or articles. I chose these ones partly
    because it was convenient (they are recent) and partly because they were
    written by political theorists who have been very influential in academia
    and elsewhere in recent years. As for the book by Eugénie Brouillet, it has
    now become required reading. I have also criticized it elsewhere on the
    basis of arguments similar to those I develop here (Leclair 2007, 2008).

4   The next pages were inspired by the works of the following authors:
    Wimmer and Schiller (2003), Beck (2005), Chernilo (2006), Skey (2009),
    Smith (2009), and Baron (2009).

5   The following passage from Caron and Laforest (2009: 30) provides a
    good illustration of this point: "After more than a decade of political
    polarization between nationalist voters – the vast majority of whom sup-
    ported the Bloc Québécois – and voters who favored a centralizing feder-
    alism – the vast majority of whom supported the Liberal Party of Canada
    – the election of a Conservative government came as good news to many."
    Supposing that the platforms of the political parties mentioned do in fact
    correspond to this description – independence/centralization – it would be
    an error to conclude that the vast majority of voters shared this

antagonistic vision. It seems to me that the authors are assuming what they should instead be proving.

6 Concerning the impact of the institutional context on actors' choices, the panorama sketched by Lecours (2002) is very interesting.

7 In the case of Québec or Indigenous nationalists.

8 In the case of Anglo-Canadian nationalists.

9 Or even more so, if we keep Indigenous claims in mind.

10 This report, quickly forgotten, was handed down by the constitutional reform committee of the Liberal Party of Québec. It recommended massive transfers of legislative powers from the federal to the provincial governments, leaving the former with jurisdiction over national defense, tariffs, the postal system, currency, equalization payments, and the federal debt.

11 Connolly (2000: 192): "To cling to the logic of the nation while shucking off its religious, ethnic, gender and sensual core is to present yourself to its virulent defenders as an unreliable and weak advocate of the centre you purport to support."

12 See my criticism of Eugénie Brouillet's book in Leclair (2007).

13 For an interesting study of the varying intensity of nationalist feeling in English Canada, see Raney (2009).

14 A national liberation program that consists in metaphorically dipping your political finger in divinatory saliva and, once the direction of the national and international winds have been checked, setting a date – and if possible an hour – when it will be possible to obtain (in a state of jubilation, of course) 50 per cent plus one of the votes.

15 For example, Lamonde (2000: 63) argues that, on the eve of the British Conquest, the identity of the Canadiens was already "bivalent."

16 For instance, sociologist Jacques Beauchemin (2002: 23–4; our translation) says:

> I am aware, moreover, that the Francophone community of Québec is itself just as divided concerning its self-representation as it is with respect to the political objectives it should pursue. It is thus for convenience that I postulate its relative unity. Indeed, I am not seeking so much to show the homogeneity of the group as to show, more generally, the fact that there is expressed in it, and beyond the divisions within it, a feeling of belonging to a community. In this context, the Québec national question reveals itself in all of its complexity. The challenge that Québec society has to meet is to compose anew the political community around a reconciled political subject that could then adopt a blueprint for a society in which the various components of today's Québec would be part. The consent of Québec society to the nationalist

aspiration of a majority of francophones thus finds its relevance in the need to establish new foundations for the Québec political community so that social stakes can be debated without the discussion always being hindered by the persistence of the national issue.

17 Politicians are especially partial to this new argument. The nearly defunct Bloc Québécois used to portray itself as the champion of Québec values. See the Bloc Québécois document (2010: 6; our translation), where it is asserted that the Bloc is "the worthy representative and spokesperson for Quebec values."

18 While acknowledging that it is based on a particularly demanding communitarian perspective ("*thick* communitarianism"), Caron and Laforest (2009: 43) cite the following definition of the word "culture" in the English version of the 1956 *Report of the Royal Commission of Inquiry on Constitutional Problems* (the Tremblay Report):

> Even before Man has become aware of himself, of his presence in the world, of his destinies and his responsibilities, there intervenes the influence of the environment, both of family and of society, which presides over the first awakening of his personality, the putting into motion of his development; which supplies him with his first instruments of culture, the foundation on which he will later build his personal formation and the spirit in which he will pursue it. This culture, special to a given environment, is by definition the nation's informing principle. *It is the national culture: the totality of the rational and spiritual values forming the collective patrimony of a determined human group; modes of life, morals, customs, traditions, language, laws, etc.* (emphasis added)

19 For example, in the following excerpt, Caron and Laforest (2009: 48) seem to argue that all federal laws could be injurious to Québec culture, including those enacted pursuant to the federal constitution of 1867. They say that simply recognizing the multinational character of the state would not allow Canada to extricate itself from a nation-state logic because "despite this recognition, the laws [could] continue to be enacted as if there were only one people who should be submitted to the same equal treatment ... It could be the case that a federal legislation might go against the cultural values of a minority nation." However, what federal laws are we talking about here? Those whose adoption is authorized by the Constitution, or those that allow for the implementation of the federal spending power in areas under provincial jurisdiction?

20 These authors criticize in particular Radio-Canada's obligation to broadcast "Canadian content." Given that federal cultural institutions recognize and support Canadian linguistic dualism, I would like it to be proven once

and for all how the obligation to meet the requirements of "Canadian content" has eroded Québec identity. There is something Pavlovian about the repetitive invocation of this argument which has become irritating.

21 Jean-François Gaudreault-Desbiens (2003), an undisputed expert on constitutional questions, has demonstrated that, on the contrary, the Supreme Court has been sensitive to the federal component in its interpretation of the Charter.

22 A search performed on the site run by CanLII, a non-profit organization managed by the Canadian Federation of Law Societies mandated to offer free online access to Canadian law, shows that the Canadian Charter has been invoked in 8,185 Québec decisions as of 14 December 2017. Moreover, this statistic does not include the significant number of cases dealt with orally in the Court of Québec (Criminal and Penal Division) that also include Charter-based arguments.

23 Lamonde (2000) provides an eloquent overview of the complexity and depth of the intellectual exchange of ideas that has been going on in Québec since the British Conquest of 1760. We not only see a "nationalist" discourse emerge, but the incorporation of that discourse as part of a proliferation of ideas that includes liberalism.

24 Caron and Laforest (2009: 34) write: "As has been observed many times before, the Charter has the effect of focusing definitions of political life on how individuals relate to the state and weakening the collective, pluralistic and communitarian notions that underlie the older tradition of federalism."

25 For reasons that would be too long to explain, the Québec Charter does not have, in positive law, the same status as the Canadian Charter. However, I would like to emphasize that this in no way reduces the essential role it plays in Québec law.

26 Leclair (2007, 2008). Let me say in passing that I do not hold that it would be impossible for the Supreme Court to interpret the Constitution in a way that would clearly limit provincial autonomy. I am simply saying that this is not always the case and that I do not think it will happen anytime soon. This does not mean that we do not need to defend, with conviction, the provinces' point of view when circumstances require it. For example, see Leclair (2010b) and Karazivan and Gaudreault-Desbiens (2010).

27 If only they were talking of the power of the *provinces* and not just that of the province of Québec. Indeed, any interpretation of the Constitution that would diminish Québec's powers would immediately apply to all of the provinces. Despite what some wish to believe, Québec is not the only province that is touchy about the integrity of its powers.

28 According to Eugénie Brouillet, for example, the nation is the principal
    means by which people find fulfillment (2005: 71). She notes that a nation
    is a "specific historical community, more or less institutionally complete,
    occupying a given territory and with members who share a common cul-
    ture" (64; our translation). From this perspective, a people can have only
    one shared culture. She then says that culture (and cultural identity more
    specifically "encompasses all elements of human activity, whether they are
    social, religious, linguistic, political or economic" (ibid., 289; see also 65,
    143–4, 155, 237).

29 Concerning inter-governmental agreements in the federal context, see
    Poirier (2004, 2005).

30 They seem, however, to consider the environment to be an exception, rec-
    ognizing that it is not a matter that officially pertains to any specific order
    of government.

31 Caron and Laforest (2009: 28): "Rather than prefer a clear demarcation
    of what each order of government does (important, among other things,
    to maximize accountability) ... Canadians appear to prefer a sharing of
    power and responsibility."

32 Although their thesis is that a federal culture among Canadians is weak,
    the authors acknowledge that this preference for collaboration could also
    be interpreted as reflecting "what some might describe as the essence of
    federalism" (Caron and Laforest 2009: 30).

33 For a more complete account of this issue, see Leclair (1996, 2003,
    2005).

34 Caron and Laforest (2009: 48): "Despite minimal recognition, Canada
    still has much in common with the nation-states (France, Greece, Japan)
    that continue to espouse a traditional conception of the state as unitary
    and monist."

35 Caron and Laforest (2009: 39–40): "we argue that a culture of federalism
    implies a particular conception of citizenship that is much more complex
    than a thin conception of citizen as client or consumer of government ser-
    vices. Rather, a political culture of federalism implies ... a complex hori-
    zontal and vertical dimension of citizenship that links citizens to the state
    and to each other and is supported by a reservoir of loyalty and patriotism
    that gives legitimacy to the state."

36 This section was inspired by Weinstock's excellent article (1999a).

37 My great-uncle died on 5 March 1945 at the age of twenty-three when his
    Halifax bomber exploded.

38 Weinstock (2001: 84, 86; our translation): "In contrast with cohesion, and
    the high level of cooperation that cohesion makes possible, trust supposes

simply that members of various groups do not perceive the people who are members of other groups as threats to the interests that distinguish them as members of specific groups ... to encourage the perception that the interests that individuals have as members of distinct groups will most probably be better served inside rather than outside of the federation." See, also, Weinstock (1999b: 293).

39 Gaudreault-Desbiens (2009: 325): "the belief that the Other will not wilfully do anything to harm us."

40 Caron and Laforest (2009: 49) concede at least this: "We do acknowledge however that accommodation of national minorities can compromise the political unity and stability of the states affected by this type of ethnocultural diversity."

41 The advent of the postnational world, as many have underlined, may perhaps have been reported a little prematurely.

42 These dichotomies are criticized by Wimmer and Schiller (2003: 596) and Skey (2009: 39–40).

43 For a good example of what Canadian federalism offered as possibilities for the gay rights movement, in contrast with the obstacles that the same kind of regime set up in the United States, read Smith (2009: 844–6).

REFERENCES

Allaire, Jean. 1991. *Un Québec libre de ses choix: Rapport du Comité constitutionnel du Parti libéral du Québec*. 25ᵉ Congrès des membres.

Audard, Catherine. 2009. *Qu'est-ce que le libéralisme? Éthique, politique, société*. Paris: Gallimard.

Baron, Ilan Zvi. 2009. "The Problem of Dual Loyalty." *Canadian Journal of Political Science/Revue canadienne de science politique* 42, no. 4: 1025–44.

Beauchemin, Jacques. 2002. "Le poids de la mémoire franco-québécoise dans un Québec pluraliste." *Globe* 5, no. 2: 21–55.

Beck, Ulrich. 2005. "The Cosmopolitan State: Redefining Power in the Global Age." *International Journal of Politics* 18, no. 3–4: 143–59.

Bloc Québécois. 2010. *Plan d'action 2010*.

Boudon, Raymond. 1984. *La place du désordre: Critique des théories du changement social*. Paris: PUF.

Brouillet, Eugénie. 2005. *La négation de la nation: L'identité culturelle québécoise et le fédéralisme canadien*. Québec: Septentrion.

Burelle, André. 1995. *Le mal canadien: Essai de diagnostic et esquisse de thérapie*. Montréal: Fides.

Caron, Jean-François, and Guy Laforest. 2009. "Canada and Multinational Federalism: From the Spirit of 1982 to Stephen Harper's Open Federalism." *Nationalism and Ethnic Politics* 15, no. 1: 27–55.

Chernilo, Daniel. 2006. "Social Theory's Methodological Nationalism: Myth and Reality." *European Journal of Social Theory* 9, no. 1: 5–22.

Chevrette, François, and Herbert Marx. 1982. *Droit constitutionnel: Notes et jurisprudence.* Montréal: PUM.

Colbert, François, and André Courchesne. 2010. "Centraliser le soutien aux arts à Québec: Une bonne idée?" Étude réalisée pour *L'idée fédérale*—Réseau québécois de réflexion sur le fédéralisme. http://ideefederale.ca/wp/wp-content/uploads/2010/03/ifculture_web.pdf.

Connolly, William. 2000. "The Liberal Image of the Nation." In *Political Theory and the Rights of Indigenous Peoples*, edited by Duncan Ivison, Paul Patton, and Will Sanders, 183–98. Cambridge: Cambridge University Press.

Deloye, Yves. 1996. *Sociologie historique du politique.* Paris: Éditions La Découverte.

Fafard, Patrick, François Rocher, and Catherine Côté. 2010. "The Presence (or Lack Thereof) of a Federal Culture in Canada: The Views of Canadians." *Regional and Federal Studies* 20, no. 1: 19–43.

Gaudreault-Desbiens, Jean-François. 2009. "The Fetishism of Formal Law and the Fate of Constitutional Patriotism in Communities of Confort." In *The Ties That Bind: Accommodating Diversity in Canada and the European Union*, edited by John Erik Fossum, Johanne Poirier, and Paul Magnette, 301–30. Bruxelles: P.I.E. Peter Lang.

– 2003. "La *Charte canadienne des droits et libertés* et le fédéralisme: Quelques remarques sur les vingt premières années d'une relation ambiguë." *Revue du barreau* (numéro spécial), 271–310.

Girard, Magali. 2008. "Résumé de résultats de sondages portant sur la perception des Québécois relativement aux accommodements raisonnables, à l'immigration, aux communautés culturelles et à l'identité canadienne-française." Memorandum presented to the Commission de consultation sur les pratiques d'accommodement reliées aux différences culturelles. http://www.accommodements.qc.ca/documentation/rapports/rapport-6-girard-magali.pdf.

Karazivan, Noura, and Jean-François Gaudreault-Desbiens. 2010. "On Polyphony and Paradoxes in the Regulation of Securities within the Canadian Federation." *Canadian Business Law Journal* 49, no. 1: 1–39.

Karmis, Dimitrios, and Jocelyn Maclure. 2001. "Two Escape Routes from the Paradigm of Monistic Authenticity: Post-Imperialist and Federal Perspectives on Plural and Complex Identities." *Ethnic and Racial Studies* 24, no. 3: 361–85.

Karmis, Dimitrios, and Wayne Norman. 2005. "The Revival of Federalism in Normative Political Theory." In *Theories of Federalism*, edited by Dimitrios Karmis and Wayne Norman, 1–22. New York: Palgrave Macmillan.

Lamonde, Yvan. 2000. *Histoire sociale des idées au Québec, 1760–1896.* Volume 1. Montréal: Fides.

Leclair, Jean. 1996. "Aperçu des virtualités de la compétence fédérale en matière de droit criminel dans le contexte de la protection de l'environnement." *Revue générale de droit* 27, no. 2: 137–71. http://ssrn.com/abstract=1769012.

– 2003. "The Supreme Court's Understanding of Federalism: Efficiency at the Expense of Diversity." *Queen's Law Journal* 28, no. 2: 411–53. http://ssrn.com/abstract=1720061.

– 2005. "The Elusive Quest for the Quintessential 'National Interest.'" *The University of British Columbia Law Review* 38, no. 2: 355–74.

– 2006a. "Federal Constitutionalism and Aboriginal Difference." *Queen's Law Journal* 31, no. 2: 521-35.

– 2006b. "Jane Austen and the Council of the Federation." *Constitutional Forum Constitutionnel* 15, no. 2: 51–61.

– 2007. "Vers une pensée politique fédérale: la répudiation du mythe de la différence québécoise 'radicale.'" In *Reconquérir le Canada: Un nouveau projet pour la nation québécoise*, edited by André Pratte, 39–84. Montréal: Éditions Voix parallèles.

– 2008. "Forging a True Federal Spirit – Refuting the Myth of Quebec's 'Radical Difference.'" In *Reconquering Canada: Quebec Federalists Speak Up for Change*, edited by André Pratte, 29–74. Toronto: Douglas & MacIntyre.

– 2009a. "Les périls du totalisme conceptuel en droit et en sciences sociale." *Lex Electronica* 14, no. 1. http://ssrn.com/abstract=1749523.

– 2009b. "Le droit et le sacré ou la recherche d'un point d'appui absolu." In *Le droit, la religion et le "raisonnable": Le fait religieux entre monisme étatique et pluralisme juridique*, edited by Jean-François Gaudreault-Desbiens, 476–90. Montréal: Éditions Thémis.

– 2010a. "'Vive le Québec libre!' Liberté(s) et fédéralisme." *Revue québécoise de droit constitutionnel* 3. http://www.aqdc.org/volumes/pdf/Jean_Leclair.pdf.

– 2010b. "'Please, Draw Me a Field of Jurisdiction': Regulating Securities, Securing Federalism." *Supreme Court Law Review* (2ᵉ série) 51: 555–601.

– 2013a. "Federalism, Socrates and Ulysses." *Review of Constitutional Studies* 18, no. 1: 18.

– 2013b. "Le fédéralisme: un terreau fertile pour gérer un monde incertain." In *Fédéralisme et gouvernance autochtone/Federalism and Aboriginal Governance*, edited by Ghislain Otis and Martin Papillon, 29–50. Québec: Presses de l'Université Laval.

Lecours, André. 2002. "L'approche néo-institutionnaliste en science politique: Unité ou diversité?" *Politique et Sociétés* 21, no. 3: 3–19.

Maclure, Jocelyn. 2000. *Récits identitaires: Le Québec à l'épreuve du pluralisme*. Montréal: Québec Amérique.

Montesquieu, Charles Secondat. 1866 [1734]. *Considérations sur les causes de la grandeur des Romains et de leur décadence*. Paris: Imprimerie et librairie classiques de Jules Delalain et fils.

Nevitte, Neil. 1996. *The Decline of Deference: Canadian Value Change in Cross-National Perspective*. Toronto: University of Toronto Press.

Ogien, Ruwen. "Philosophie des sciences sociales." In *Épistémologie des sciences sociales*, edited by Jean-Michel Berthelot, 521–75. Paris: PUF.

Panagos, Dimitri. 2008. "Aboriginality, Existing Aboriginal Rights and State Accommodation in Canada." PhD thesis, Queen's University. http://www.collectionscanada.gc.ca/obj/s4/f2/dsk3/OKQ/TC-OKQ-1310.pdf.

Poirier, Johanne. 2004. "Intergovernmental Agreements in Canada: At the Crossroads Between Law and Politics." In *Canada: The State of the Federation 2002: Reconsidering the Institutions of the Canadian Federalism*, edited by J. Peter Meekison, Hamish Telford and Harvey Lazar, 425–62. Montréal: McGill-Queen's University Press.

– 2005. "Les ententes intergouvernementales et la gouvernance fédérale: aux confins du droit et du non-droit." In *Le fédéralisme dans tous ses états: Gouvernance, identité et méthodologie/The States and Moods of Federalism: Governance, Identity and Methodology*, edited by Jean-François Gaudreault-Desbiens and Fabien Gélinas, 441–74. Montreal/Bruxelles: Yvon Blais/Bruylant.

Raney, Tracey. 2009. "As Canadian as Possible … Under What Circumstances? Public Opinion on National Identity in Canada Outside Quebec." *Journal of Canadian Studies/Revue d'Études Canadiennes* 43, no. 3: 5–29.

Revel, Jacques. 2001. "Les sciences historiques." In *Épistémologie des sciences sociales*, edited by Jean-Michel Berthelot, 21–76. Paris: PUF.

Schouls, Tim. 2003. *Shifting Boundaries: Aboriginal Identity, Pluralist Theory, and the Politics of Self-Government*. Vancouver: University of British Columbia Press.

Sen, Amartya. 2007. *Identité et Violence*. Paris: Odile Jacob.

Skey, Michael. 2009. "The National in Everyday Life: A Critical Engagement with Michael Billig's Thesis of *Banal Nationalism*." *The Sociological Review* 57, no 2: 331–46 .

Smith, Miriam. 2009. "Diversity and Canadian Political Development: Presidential Address to the Canadian Political Science Association, Ottawa, May 27, 2009." *Canadian Journal of Political Science/Revue canadienne de science politique* 42, no. 4: 831–54.

Tocqueville, Alexis de. 1962 [1840]. *De la démocratie en Amérique*. Volume 2. Paris: Gallimard.

Weinstock, Daniel. 1999a. "National Partiality: Confronting the Intuitions." *Monist* 82, no. 3: 516–41.

– 1999b. "Building Trust in Divided Societies." *The Journal of Political Philosophy* 7, no. 3: 287–307.

– 2001. "Vers une théorie normative du fédéralisme." *Revue internationale des sciences sociales* 167, no. 1: 79–87.

Wimmer, Andreas, and Nina Glick Schiller. 2003. "Methodological Nationalism, the Social Sciences, and the Study of Migration: An Essay in Historical Epistemology." *International Migration Review* 37, no. 3: 576–610.

10

Linguistic Groups and Civil Society: Trust, Cooperation, and Accommodation in Canadian Voluntary Associations

Alexandre Pelletier and Richard Simeon

There is now a great deal of interest in multinational democracies (Gagnon and Tully 2001). The question of multinational civil societies has, however, been left on the sidelines within this literature (Pelletier and Morden 2012). The publication of *Language Matters* (Cameron and Simeon 2009) provides a welcome foray into the world of voluntary associations in Canada. Updating research by Vincent Lemieux and John Meisel (1972), this work has allowed us to take a fresh look at the way in which voluntary associations (such as trade associations, professional associations, or environmental organizations) cope with the presence of the two languages, in terms of both communication and representation. It is a useful body of work for engaging in an exploration of the dynamics linking trust, accommodation, and cooperation in a context other than that of formal political institutions.

Two questions guided this research. First, how do voluntary associations accommodate the presence of two linguistic groups in Canada? Second, how does trust contribute to these dynamics? The present chapter argues that trust is a prior condition for cooperation and, above all, for the mutual accommodation of linguistic groups in Canadian voluntary associations. In a multinational society, relationships between groups are based on four main states of equilibrium: substantive trust, instrumental trust, assurance-based trust, and the absence of trust. Substantive trust is the equilibrium best able to combine cooperation and accommodation efficiently. Of course, mutual cooperation cannot be simply reduced to a matter of trust.

The political and social context and the nature of broader social networks also influence these relationships. However, mutual trust is a necessary, though certainly insufficient, condition for cooperation between groups.

This chapter examines relationships of trust and cooperation between francophones and anglophones in Canadian voluntary associations, and to do so, it uses the case studies in Lemieux and Meisel (1972) and Cameron and Simeon (2009).[1] The first section highlights two limitations of the theories on trust and cooperation, to which this chapter responds. It identifies and establishes the relationship between the concepts of trust and cooperation. The second section describes the state of relationships between francophones and anglophones within voluntary associations in Canada. The third uses the notion of trust to explain the dynamics observed. Finally, the last section discusses the four states of equilibrium observed in the second and third sections, and thus contributes to our understanding of trust in multinational contexts.

TRUST AND COOPERATION

Trust is a complex phenomenon that includes several types and dimensions.[2] The inter-group, institutional, and procedural dimensions, which we focus on here, are at the heart of the relationships between francophones and anglophones in voluntary associations in Canada. However, the existing definitions have two main limitations.

Generally, no conceptual distinction is made between trust and cooperation, which means that scholars often employ cooperation as a synonym for trust. However, *rather than being one and the same phenomenon, trust is one of the conditions necessary for cooperation* (Axelrod 1984; Gambetta 2000; Smets, Wels, and van Loon 1999). We argue that much can be gained, from a theoretical point of view, by treating trust as an independent variable and cooperation as a dependent variable.

Trust is often defined based on its function – that is, the role that it plays. According to Annette Baier, trust is necessary when an agent needs help in creating something, achieving a goal, or taking care of a good that they value highly (Baier 1986: 236). Trust means that agents yield part of their actual or potential power and control over a certain good to other autonomous agents, who have the potential to disappoint them (Sztompka 1999: 26–7). Trust is necessary because, since the other actors are autonomous, they have the potential to behave in ways that are against the interests of the association.

Cooperation requires trust because it necessitates a positive interpretation of the Other's intentions. Trust is required because of the limits of "our capacity ever to achieve a full knowledge of others, their motives, and their responses to endogenous as well as exogenous changes" (Gambetta 2000: 218). Trust is *retrospective* in the sense that it is made possible by a history of previous (positive) interactions (Axelrod 1984). It is also *predictive*. Since both endogenous and exogenous changes in cooperation situations can occur and are unpredictable, the Other's possible behaviour has to be anticipated on the basis of an assessment of their intentions, dispositions, motives, and qualities.

Because prediction is always incomplete, trust involves accepting or tolerating a certain degree of vulnerability. It requires living "as if" we knew the intentions and possible behaviour of the Other. As Guido Möllering puts it, trust requires "suspension," which is a "mechanism that brackets out uncertainty and ignorance, thus making interpretive knowledge momentarily 'certain' and enabling the leap of favourable (or unfavourable) expectation" (2001: 414). In other words, trust does not require the absence of uncertainty, which is proper to "mutual guarantees," but the presence of some uncertainty or risk that is judged acceptable (Yamagishi and Yamagishi 1994: 160).

This brings us to the second limitation that has been identified in the literature. Trust and cooperation are often presented as dichotomous variables that can be reduced to the dyads of trust/distrust or cooperation/conflict. However, we argue that *we need to deconstruct the concepts of trust and cooperation and treat them as ordinal variables*. In this chapter, we show that more (or less) substantive trust makes more (or less) meaningful cooperation possible. In the case of relationships between linguistic groups, we will see that cooperation may or may not be combined with accommodation and representation. In other words, like trust, cooperation may be more or less substantial.

Piotr Sztompka identifies six dimensions affecting the degree and depth of mutual commitment: the value of the object in one's eyes, the scope of the consequences of the action, the duration of the commitment, the possibility of being able to withdraw from the relationship, the risk associated with a breach of trust, and the presence or absence of guarantees (1999: 29). The need for certainty concerning these six dimensions is what has to be suspended, at least partly. Thus, the greater the mutual trust, the fewer guarantees needed, the more and longer the actors are able to cooperate toward purposes that have great value, and the better they can tolerate the possibility of a breach of trust.

Trust affects the model and associative structure adopted by linguistic groups in their relationships.[3] Indeed, every association articulates each of the previous six dimensions differently. For example, the scope of the consequences and the risks associated with a breach of trust is much more substantial when the groups share power than when they share only resources and information (Lemieux 1972: 42). The same is true when cooperation is limited to periodic contacts rather than collaboration agreements or participation in shared decision-making bodies. Finally, the very value of the object is different, depending on whether it concerns political, utilitarian, or simply social (networking) objectives (see Lemieux 1998).

We argue that the nature of trust indicates whether cooperation will be more functional or more sporadic, combined with some accommodation measures or marked by full recognition and mutual representation. Our study identifies four main states of equilibrium. *Substantive trust* happens when trust concerns the other group itself. It opens the way for internal accommodation of groups, recognition, and, thus, power-sharing. *Instrumental trust* is when trust is based on "encapsulated interests," which is the interdependence of a set of actors for the achievement of some goals. It opens the way for a more functional cooperation, one that tends to set aside questions of representation and focuses on the sharing of resources. *Assurance-based trust* is when trust is based on institutions and contract-like guarantee measures that regulate the relationship between actors. It allows for a more sporadic cooperation from the outside, often limited to specific objectives. Finally, the *absence of trust* simply prevents cooperation.

ACCOMMODATION OF LINGUISTIC DUALITY IN CANADA: TAKING STOCK

How do voluntary associations cope with Canada's linguistic duality? The work by Meisel and Lemieux (1972) and the update by Cameron and Simeon (2009) provide an interesting historical perspective on the issue. The contrast between the two periods is striking. While the first was generally conflict-ridden and marked by debates about the representation of linguistic groups, the second was marked by stability that suggests a degree of normalization and the institutionalization of inter-group relations.

First, the voluntary associations studied in these two books made progress concerning their public relations (websites, publications, services). Bilingualism is now the norm, whereas in the 1970s it generally posed a problem (Cameron and Simeon 2009: 176). However, when it comes to internal communications, English still clearly dominates (appendix 1). Simultaneous translation is sometimes offered at annual general meetings, although board and other executive meetings – in short, where power is exercised – still take place mainly in English. In Simeon's terms, there is "asymmetrical bilingualism" in associations, and the burden of accommodation rests on the francophones rather than on the whole association (Simeon 2009: 118). In such cases, the cost of mastering a second language, and even the simple fact of having to express complex ideas in a second language, is not negligible (Laponce 1987: 11–15). As Simeon says, we do not know how many French speakers decide not to participate in pan-Canadian bodies owing to language issues (Simeon 2009: 118).

Second, concerning *representation*, the equality of provincial associations is the most common principle for selecting board members (appendix 2). There is, in fact, no special representation for francophones, either at annual general meetings or on ad hoc committees. Moreover, no association has a board of directors that faithfully represents the proportion of francophones in Canada, and even less the idea of a multinational Canada. The representation of ethnocultural minorities, rather than linguistic dualism, seems to be more of a concern for the associations today (Cameron and Simeon 2009: 176). There has also been, over time, a chronic under-participation of francophone members at annual general assemblies and in associative decision-making bodies. Francophones participate, intervene, and assume positions within these associations in fewer numbers, even when the activities take place in Québec.

Third, concerning the associative structures, we find two main models. There are those structures in which groups cooperate mainly from the *inside* (within the association), and then those in which they cooperate from the *outside* (through two separate associations). When the cooperation occurs from within, the sharing of positions, resources, and power is done either *impartially* or by *taking into account* linguistic differences. When groups cooperate from the outside, linguistic differences are recognized de facto, yet the interactions do not generally involve *representation* within shared institutions. In Canada, the two main linguistic groups generally work though distinct, autonomous associations. According to William D. Coleman, there is in Québec a "system of independent associations at the provincial level that functions in parallel with federal systems"; a "system of interest intermediation that is close to the type of system that we find in a sovereign nation-state" (Coleman 1995: 52; see also Laforest and Philips 2001). The great degree of autonomy of the groups, acquired through the creation of distinct associations, tends to reduce the need for trust, as well as the very possibility of such trust, because of less frequent contact. Interestingly, most of these separate organizations were created following notable conflicts, not following mutually negotiated accommodations and settlements.

In conclusion, we can see that the linguistic issue has generally been dealt with in Canadian voluntary associations from the perspective of *communications* rather than *representation*. In the past, though, some associations *did* adopt power sharing and *representative* measures for linguistic groups. Today, however, it is only through communication that linguistic issues are dealt with. How can this situation be explained?

TRUST AND DISTRUST
WITHIN VOLUNTARY ASSOCIATIONS

Context, Intersubjective Dynamics, Shared Objectives, and Cooperation

Canadian voluntary associations sometimes experience substantial and irreconcilable conflicts between francophones and anglophones. These conflicts revolve around issues such as the goals pursued by each group, the nature of the association, and the ideology of the members.

Cooperation is sometimes unlikely or impossible, with or without inter-group trust. Pascale Dufour (2006), who studies the evolution of anti-globalization protest movements, shows for instance that the different articulations of the "national project" and the "reaction to the process of globalization" explains anglophones' rejection of free trade and francophones' support of free trade in the 1990s (see also Bashevkin 1991; Vickers 2000). Anglophones were generally attached to the idea of *one* pan-Canadian association and often feared a division within the movement if representative measures were to be adopted for francophones. Cooperation was impossible.

At the heart of these disagreements are different normative visions of Canada, the political community, and the role of federal and provincial institutions (Jenson 1993). For example, deep disagreements about the constitutional responsibility of the federal government in the areas of education and municipalities explain conflicts within the Canadian Union of Students and the Fédération canadienne des municipalités (Meisel and Lemieux 1972). Yet, when normative visions appear less central to the actors, shared objectives may re-emerge. For example, Dufour shows that since protests against the FTAA are no longer related to the pan-Canadian national program, pan-Canadian coalitions and the formation of alliances between francophones and anglophones have arisen despite separate associative networks (2006: 336).

Beyond trust, the groups have to have a minimum set of shared interests to foster cooperation. In other words, the benefits drawn from the cooperation have to be superior to the costs associated with mutual accommodation (Meisel and Lemieux 1972: 291). However, the very perception of these "costs" is subjective and refers more broadly to the identity of the groups and the associated power dynamics. According to Jean Laponce (1996: 77), "when [English-Canadians] communicate, they dominate ... [It makes them] mentally ill-equipped to find administrative and political solutions that would reassure and appease the minority languages over which they keep trespassing without noticing them." The majority/minority dynamic thus affects the perspective that groups have of this calculation, in particular their sensitivity to the intentions of the Other. Consequently, the expectations of, and commitment to, the relationship differ, often feeding mutual distrust. For example, the majority group generally tends to be satisfied with relationships based on number (communication in the language of the majority), or accommodation based on bilingualism; whereas the minority group would like to see representative measures included (such as power sharing or even, sometimes, veto power). According to Karen Cook, Russell Hardin, and Margaret Levi, trust is especially sensitive to dynamics of power asymmetries: "those in powerful positions are generally less focused on the details of the relationship and less attentive to their own behaviours that might be perceived as inhibiting the development of a trusting relationship with 'subordinates'" (2005: 43).

Group identities are also closely linked to what is taking place in the political sphere. The period studied by Meisel and Lemieux (1950–1970) was marked by two tendencies. At first, there was rapprochement between francophones and anglophones, resulting from the edification of the Canadian policy community, economic integration, and the sincere intentions of most pan-Canadian associations to accommodate linguistic and "ethnic" duality. Then there were splits between anglophone and francophone associations because of their inability to achieve satisfactory accommodation.

To this was added a second series of breakdowns: those of the French Canadian associative networks themselves. Faced with secularization and the establishment of a Québec civil society during the Quiet Revolution (Turgeon 1999), French Canadian associations gradually lost the foundation that made it possible for them to transcend provincial borders. The failure of the Estates General of French Canada may have been a turning point with respect to the interest that members of Québec civil society took in the (French) Canadian political sphere.

This rupture within French Canada also had an important consequence. It reconfigured the foundations on which the groups met within national associations; it was no longer a question of cooperation between two pan-Canadian groups, but rather between one pan-Canadian group and a Québec association. From then on, it became "difficult if not impossible to structure [an association's] national board on binational rather than provincial lines" (Simeon 2009: 119).

Trust is also shaped by the groups' relative positions within the political space (Horowitz 1985: 143–7). Following Sim B. Sitikin and Nancy L. Roth (1993: 371), mutual distrust is stronger when it involves the perception of conflicting values: "the threat of future violations of expectations arises because the person is ... seen as a cultural outsider – as one who 'doesn't think like us' and may, therefore, do the 'unthinkable.'" The judgment that accompanies trust, shaping prediction and suspension, is informed by perceptions and memory, along with the dominant discourse and counter-discourse (Wright and Ehmert 2010: 116–17). The intensity of the conflicts observed by Meisel and Lemieux can be explained in part by the context of the Quiet Revolution. It charged the debates of the time with a political and emotional content that has long since faded.

Finally, conditions surrounding the associations themselves may improve contact between groups. Today, the severe inequality that used to exist between francophones and anglophones has been reduced. From a symbolic point of view, the Official Languages Act and a better representation of francophones in the public service have changed the domestic space in which groups cooperate (Simeon and Cameron 2009: 181).

Trust and the Accommodation Dynamic

This brings us to the question of trust more directly, which is necessary for cooperation as well as to the dynamics of communication and representation in the Canadian voluntary sector. At the level of communications, distrust comes mainly from the minority group and is largely asymmetrical. Distrust is related to the *intentions* and the *trustworthiness* of the Other, the majority group. For example, francophones fear that the language issue might not be as important to anglophones as it is to them. They thus feel that they have to remain vigilant if they want to maintain bilingualism within their organization. In return, francophones feel like, and are often perceived as, *demandeurs* seeking a privilege. Fear results from the fact that the groups often have very different ideas about the purposes of the accommodation: francophones see bilingualism as a question of minimum respect, while anglophones see it as a series of additional constraints and costs (Simeon 2009: 118).

Distrust also concerns the process and, more specifically, the extent to which the other group is *fair* and *just*. In fact, the failure to respect bilingualism often generates distrust about the attention paid by the anglophone to the interests and positions of francophones. In other words, *distrust* may transform a conflict over communication (bilingualism) into one concerning representation (power sharing). These relations may acquire a more symmetrical nature when there is a clear, mutual commitment between the groups, even if it is sometimes only symbolic.

At the level of representation, offsetting dynamics of power asymmetries requires an increase in interdependency through, for example, the creation of a power-sharing structure. Both trust and distrust flow from the feeling that the other group will (or will not) take the interests of the other into account; that both groups will (or will not) see their union as just that, a union, rather than a means for each group to pursue its own interests. The development of trust may sometimes lead to more formal recognition, as was the case within the Canadian Council on Social Development. Within the council, an ad hoc committee became a veritable tool for francophone representation. Moreover, permeating "various activities and organizational choices was a recognition of cultural and linguistic issues and a clear tendency to see both French and cultural differences as of particular relevance to Quebec members" (Jenson and Laforest 2009: 124). However, when this representational binationalism became communicational bilingualism (often ad hoc), francophones felt growing discomfort. It led, among other things, to the creation of the Conseil Québécois de développement social.

The Canada Junior Chamber of Commerce experienced a similar fate when the adoption of binational structures was undermined in the 1950s and 1960s by competing perceptions. The main problem was related to the expectations of the two groups: the francophones wanted separate associations that would be linked by a liaison committee, while the anglophones wanted a common association in which both nations would be recognized. According to the francophone members, the anglophones tended to underestimate the language barrier: "they did not understand that the differences go hand in hand with cultural differences, and that those cannot be reduced by the translation process" (Meisel and Lemieux 1972: 136).

Distrust also affects the very potential for accommodation, mainly because of a fear of anticipated results (prediction). For example, the reform of the Canadian Federation of Students along binational lines was hindered by a debate about the limits and scope of that model regarding decisions on bylaws and rules. While the francophone associations proposed submitting all votes to a double majority system, the anglophone associations were opposed to the idea. Some suggested limiting issues submitted to a double-majority vote as much as possible, by making a list of those issues, or by restricting those votes to narrow cultural questions or questions concerning institutions specific to French Canada (for example, language and education). Although distrust encouraged the imposition of such limitations, some did prefer a solution based on "mutual trust": for the students of the University of Toronto, no issues should be considered as *a priori* fundamental, rather the choice should be left to the actors if a substantial conflict were to arise (Meisel and Lemieux 1972: 94). That proposal was, however, unsuccessful. As we can see, a fear of unpredictable outcomes encourages actors to imagine solutions that limit the other group's realm of action. In other words, in a condition of distrust, groups seek to limit the other group's ability to disappoint or its capacity to go against the first group's interests. The proposal made by students in Toronto expressed some mutual trust, since they hoped to temporarily "suspend" the inability to predict the behaviour of the other group.

The inability to predict the behaviour of the other group, as well as the long-term consequences of the new structures, concerns aspects as different as the loss of institutional control, the division of the movement, the administrative confusion, the increase in conflict, and the return to asymmetry. These fears were sufficient to block discussions about accommodation within the Canada Junior Chamber of Commerce and the Conseil canadien de coopération.

Yet, the adoption of rigid structures that make better predictions possible and reduce the number of elements to be "suspended" has a perverse effect: such structures make it difficult to adapt to change. The 1935 agreement, which created the Fédération des scouts catholiques de la province de Québec, quickly became limiting when the association tried to adopt a *pan*-Canadian French-language mission. The breach of trust occurred when the anglophones refused to revise the agreement and the francophones decided to "take things in hand and organize the group in violation of the agreement" (Meisel and Lemieux 1972: 53).

Dynamics of distrust have two potential consequences. First, in relations between groups, distrust of the Other's intentions may lead to fear of the process (whether it will be fair and just), and, finally, to fear of the results of potential accommodations. Second, with respect to accommodation, the distrust of the Other's intentions, or of the process, or of the result, may inhibit the groups' flexibility and openness to accommodation requests. In other words, trust and distrust affects first the very potential for cooperation and, eventually and above all, the depth of the cooperation through accommodations and power-sharing measures.

Cooperation without Accommodation

The weak performance of the associations studied regarding accommodation can be partly explained by dynamics of distrust. This does not mean that there will be no cooperation between the two groups, but that they find it much easier to cooperate when they form separate associations. According to Grace Skogstad, the paradigm used by farm associations in Canada makes it possible to overcome cultural divisions and build bridges between the two linguistic communities. This success is the result of a model based on the respect for bilingualism and shared material interests (Skogstad 2009: 72). Similar *modus vivendi* have been formed in other associations, such as the Heart and Stroke Foundation of Canada and the Conseil canadien de la coopération.

What factors make cooperation possible? Trust between groups is generally forged in three manners. First, sharing common interests is not sufficient. One group's interest has to depend on the achievement of the other group's interest for the associations to be inclined to cooperate. For example, Skogstad (2009) points out that, owing to the important role of Québec farms in Canadian agriculture, any credible organization wishing to speak on behalf of the sector must necessarily involve Québec in its ranks. Simeon shows that in the world of heart disease associations, only Ontario would have the means to operate independently, which thus creates an incentive to cooperate (2009: 112). Moreover, the advantage of pooling resources, and the fact that Québec is a stronghold of research on heart diseases, encourages cooperation between linguistic groups (109).

Second, our case studies highlight the idea that to be successful, relationships among leaders have to be "pragmatic" and "depoliticized." By eliminating conflictual issues from the discussion, particularly those concerning recognition, and by adopting a strictly pragmatic approach (exchange of information, sharing of expertise), groups generally find it much easier to cooperate. For example, relations between the Union des municipalités du Québec and the Canadian Federation of Mayors and Municipalities have been influenced in a positive way by a change in approach within the latter, which now concentrates on sector-specific issues and service delivery (low politics) rather than on political and constitutional issues (high politics) (Stevenson and Gilbert 2009: 88). According to William Coleman and Tim Mau (2009: 50), the cohesion of business associations is also due to their pragmatic approach, which places the accent on class ties rather than on identity issues.

Third, the personal commitment of the leadership is also central. According to Cameron and Simeon, in several cases, linguistic conflicts were resolved "only when strong, committed leaders emerged to take the matters in hand" (2009: 180). The recognition of the importance of bilingualism – not only as a national value but also as promoting the legitimacy of the association – as well as the more pragmatic approach taken by (non-nationalist) Québec leaders count for a lot in cases where cooperation was successful (ibid.). The inter-*group* dynamic is thus defused by building inter-*personal* trust. This played a crucial role, for example, in improving relationships within the Canadian Federation of Mayors and Municipalities (Stevenson and Gilbert 2009: 80–1). Such trust remains, however, contingent on the presence of certain individuals within the associations, as well as on the agreement of the members, especially francophone group members, to function on the terms desired by the other group.

Consequently, trust between linguistic groups is generally built by depoliticizing relationships and reinforcing complementary, pragmatic interests. To borrow the expression used by John Dryzek (2005), linguistic groups tend to pursue "analgesic" strategies rather than "agonistic" ones in their shared relationships. Quarantining controversial elements, such as demands for formal recognition or power sharing, simplifies cooperation by reducing the number of things that have to be bracketed (suspended) and subjected to prediction. However, it makes this form of cooperation less sensitive to accommodation requests and makes cooperation dependent on its own success.

There are four states of equilibrium between trust, cooperation, and accommodation. We will now describe each of them in detail.

FROM SUBSTANTIVE TRUST TO THE ABSENCE OF TRUST

Substantive Trust

Substantive trust involves the most demanding form of commitment, since it requires mutual obligations and deep solidarity. Under this form, trust is toward the Other, who is the subject of the trust. According to Daniel Weinstock (1999: 293), "trust requires that the person being trusted act because of how she stands to me rather than of how she stands to that which I am entrusting to her." Trust concerns the other group, rather than the situation or the institutional context, and it is not a form of strategic trust, but something closer to an "affective" trust, to use an expression by Daniel J. MacAllister (1995).

Based on shared attachment, it involves reciprocal concerns and care (Rousseau et al. 1998: 399). We have seen, for example, that such trust developed within the Canadian Council on Social Development, while it was insufficient within the Canadian Federation of Students. What are the consequences of this form of trust?

Substantive trust involves the feeling that the parties will not act in an egotistical manner, that they will not exploit the Other's vulnerabilities, that they will take the Other's interests into account, and that they will work in good faith and fairly (McKnight and Chervany 1996). Such trust "thus strengthens the will of the groups to support each other and to *expand* the spectrum of resources pooled" (Rousseau et al. 1998: 399). The solidity of such a relationship, forged over time, tends to be better able to resist conflicts about objectives and power (Sitkin and Roth 1993: 372).

Given that trust does not concern the object, but rather the subjects of trust, it can lead to the sharing of power particularly through measures of coordination and representation. Faith in the Other "as an agent with his or her own interests" makes it possible to be open to the unpredictable, especially concerning the Other's future behaviour within the association.

Instrumental Trust

Instrumental or strategic trust corresponds to Russell Hardin's idea of encapsulated interests. In this case, when one party trusts another, it is because it is convinced that it is in the latter's interest to take the former's interest to heart (Cook, Hardin, and Levi 2001: 5). Under this form, trust moves from the Other to the object, and from a shared attachment to the very interdependence of interests (Sheppard and Sherman 1998: 423–6). By contributing to the interests of both parties, as well as to their future interests, the actors have incentives to avoid contravening the conditions of their union, to avoid acting in a manner that would not be trustworthy. According to Robert Putnam, this form of trust and reciprocity consists in "short-term altruism for long-term self-interest" (1993: 173). This trust is strategic. First, it makes it possible to achieve an end. It is based on the predictability of the Other (reputation, history of cooperation), and the Other's reliability, competency, and transparency. In Canada, we have observed this dynamic especially in farm, heart disease research, and municipal associations.

Instrumental trust has consequences for the type of cooperation that may exist. Such trust is generally based on the strict delimitation of the objects included in the relationship. The nature and extent of the relationship are circumscribed, through arrangements or contractual obligations (Baier 1986: 251). Such a situation has been observed in the Boy Scouts of Canada, the Canadian Amateur Hockey Association, and the Canadian Student Association, within which there is the specific desire to leave only "material achievements" to the pan-Canadian association, while provincial associations manage educational, and thus cultural, activities (Meisel and Lemieux 1972: 74).

By eliminating certain elements from the conversation, particularly those concerning representation, it becomes easier for the actors to *predict* the intentions of the Other and to *suspend* areas of uncertainty (which are, by definition, much smaller). Hence, "the problem of divided societies is [often] solved by *avoiding* rather than by *allowing* genuine democratic deliberation" (Noël 2006: 420). However, there is reason to believe that these ties are contingent on the successful achievement of common objectives and that the relationship is at risk if there is breach of trust (Rousseau et al. 1998: 400). Speaking about farming communities, Skogstad (2009: 71) explains: "built on self-interest and the respect and trust that have accumulated over decades, these ties are not sentimental ... They persist because – and to the extent that – they work." Although this trust can lead to long-term commitments, it is maintained precisely because it can end at any time without serious consequences for the actors (Baldassari and Diani 2007: 743). Consequently, this instrumental trust would come under strain if groups were to design new institutions of power sharing or accommodation. They would create commitments that would, over the long term, be incompatible with instrumental trust. This brings us to the paradoxical role of institutions within inter-group relations.

A Paradoxical Role for Institutions

Generally, institutions have offered a relatively efficient means of limiting distrust and allowing trust. In a context of power asymmetries, institutional guarantees can protect against the use of institutions by one group in favour of its own group. Such guarantees can also ensure that rules and agreements will be applied fairly (Weinstock 1999: 296). Representative institutions provide a guarantee to group members that they will have the chance to achieve their objectives and interact on equal terms with the other group. Institutions thus have the capacity to encourage the development of mutual trust, whether strategic or substantive (Rousseau et al. 1998: 400–1).

Inversely, institutional controls can also undermine trust, especially when formal mechanisms tend to needlessly entrench and formalize responses to inter-group conflict. As we have seen, this occurred in the Boy Scouts of Canada. Moreover, when faith is placed in institutions, rather than in the subject or the object of the relationship, there are fewer opportunities for creating inter-group trust (Zucher 1986; Rousseau et al. 1998: 400).

Institutional trust has many implications when it comes to cooperation, especially regarding the potential for mutual accommodation. In general, the implications of institutional recognition or accommodations are highly unpredictable. Recognition and accommodation measures have "interpretative flexibility," the potential to lead to a wide variety of consequences and to support a wide range of meanings. They also have "litigation potential," the creation of new spaces and opportunities able to generate other unexpected consequences (Manfredi 2004: 37). The actors thus have a lot to gain from reducing the ambiguity of these measures of recognition, which can be a source of unexpected outcomes.

When actors are unable to "suspend," institutions come to the rescue. They help to reduce uncertainty concerning future relations (prediction) and thus make it possible to live comfortably despite reciprocal distrust. Like a contract, formal arrangements reduce the actors' realm of action and set strict limits. All this is done to reduce the uncertainty linked to the future of the Other's behaviour. While it is difficult to separate it from power relations within an association, it should be noted that this dynamic affects both groups at the same time. The debate surrounding the implementation of the double majority in the Canadian Union of Students is a good example of this.

Assurance-Based Trust

Institutions often make cooperation possible when there is no trust (Hardin and Cook 2001). In this case, cooperation is no longer based on substantive or instrumental trust, but on the presence of structural guarantees offered by institutions, such as contracts, regulations, legal recourse, and strict procedures (Yamagishi and Yamagishi 1994). Institutions make it possible to have a feeling of security, not *with* the

Other, but *against* the Other (McKnight and Chervany 2001: 44). It is thus the most radical response to distrust. As in a contract, actors try to limit grey areas of uncertainty as much as possible by setting up rigid processes as well as limiting the scope of mutual interactions (Manfredi 2004). In other words, actors try to circumscribe the intentions of the Other and to codify the processes and potential outcomes of cooperation.

The failure of numerous internal negotiations (e.g., in the Canadian Junior Chamber of Commerce, the World University Service of Canada, and the Conseil Canadien de Coopération) reveals how difficult intercultural dialogue is. The ethics of dialogue proposed by some scholars of multiculturalism (e.g., Tully 1995; Taylor 1994; Maclure 2006) – which involves a posture of openness, the presumption of equal dignity, and the tolerance of unfinished conversations, deadlocks, and reasonable disagreements among groups – seems to require a significant amount of mutual trust. Often this trust is absent. It is trust that makes the ethics of dialogue possible, rather than the other way around. Roderick M. Kramer and Peter J. Carnevale (2008) show that trust supports negotiations and provides openings for accommodation demands to be made and agreed to.

Finally, the last point of equilibrium, which we mention only in passing, is the *absence of trust*. In this case, cooperation is nonexistent and characterized by the ideas that "good fences make good neighbours."

Table 10.1 summarizes these four states of equilibrium. We can see that the deeper and more substantial cooperation is, the more critical are apprehensions of the Other's future behaviour, and the more important mutual guarantees become. The first form of trust opens the way for representation and proves to be more resilient despite differences concerning the object of cooperation. The second quarantines identity issues, the nature of the subjects, to focus on the object of cooperation. Moreover, this form of trust is conditional on the participation of leaders and the presence of encapsulated interests. The third form of trust redirects trust outside of the relationship, insists instead on guarantees, and generally favours "containment" measures (i.e., limiting the other's realm of action). The containment measures are, in turn, obstacles to inter-group trust. Consequently, if a conflict erupts outside of established guarantees, the weak inter-group trust resurfaces and may thus undermines any resolution process.

Table 10.1
Four main states of equilibrium: nature and limits of trust, cooperation, and institutions

State of equilibrium	Nature of trust	Type of cooperation	Roles and limits of institutions
Substantive trust	– The Other is the subject of trust – Trust is affective, based on the formation of a common attachment – Trust allows exposing resources and powers to unforeseen developments	– Internal accommodation, sharing of power – Limits on majority's institutional control through representation of linguistic groups – Resistant to conflict, which tend to be seen as contextual rather than fundamental	– Rectify power asymmetries in communications (bilingualism), coordination (committees), and representation (sharing of power)
Instrumental trust	– Interdependency is the object of the trust – Trust is strategic, based on long-term interests – Trust is possible by circumscribing the objects concerned by the relationship	– Cooperation on the inside or from the outside – Quarantining of identity issues: bilingual communication without group representation (sharing of resources rather than powers) – Insistence on functional inter-dependency (encapsulated interests) – Contingent on the success of the cooperation itself.	– Rectify asymmetries in communication and coordination – Can encourage the development of substantive trust – Limit the objects concerned by trust and limit the unpredictability of recognition norms (flexibility, potential for conflict) – Institutional inflexibility can undermine trust by entrenching and formalizing responses to conflict
Assurance-based trust	– Institutions and guarantees are the objects of trust – Feeling of security against the other	– Cooperation from the outside and in an ad hoc manner – Goal-oriented cooperation within specific limits	– Limit uncertainty concerning intentions, processes, and outcomes, through contract-like agreements and interactions – Limit or prevent dialogue
Absence of trust	– None or very limited	– None	– Ensures the autonomy of actors

CONCLUSION

The exploration of trust and distrust dynamics in voluntary associations in Canada remains in its infancy. However, four observations can be made. First, trust and cooperation have to be distinguished analytically and deconstructed according to their intensity and scope. We have shown that trust can be substantive, instrumental, or essentially institutional (assurance-based), and that cooperation can be deep (combined with accommodation or measures of power sharing), instrumental or pragmatic (limited to specific goals and generally ad hoc). We have also shown that distrust is sometimes about the intentions of the Other, the decision process, or the potential outcomes of accommodation measures. Our typology helps understand the relationships between groups within Canadian voluntary associations.

Second, this chapter has highlighted the ambiguity of institutional trust. Obviously, when two groups in an association are uneven in size, institutional accommodations are unavoidable. Such measures provide minority groups with some form of recognition and institutional guarantees, and thus make possible the emergence of inter-group trust. However, we found that the very nature of these institutions results from pre-existing inter-group trust. If there is no substantive trust, groups tend to make such institutions ever more rigid in order to limit their mutual realm of action as a means of compensating for their lack of trust.

Third, examining trust and cooperation as two separate entities makes it possible to understand certain institutional choices. For example, containment measures aim, like a contract, to limit uncertainty as much as possible in intergroup relations. Containment measures emerge out of distrust of the Other's intentions, the decision process, or the possible behaviour of the other groups within actual or new institutions. Consequently, distrust is detrimental, not only to recognition, but also to the flexibility needed by institutions for groups to possibly renegotiate the parameters of their association.

One strategy we saw involved limiting the depth of dialogue between associations, either by adopting a pragmatic-instrumental approach or by cooperating from the outside in an ad hoc manner. Paradoxically, recent approaches to recognition favour an agonistic, flexible, non-goal-oriented approach to inter-cultural dialogue (Tully 2004). In reality, the actors do not pursue such a demanding ethics. They are instead naturally inclined to favour an "analgesic," non-flexible, and goal-oriented approach in their own relationships. Our findings thus question the extent to which this demanding ethics of inter-cultural dialogue is at all attainable.

Fourth, this chapter sheds light on the bidirectional, though asymmetrical, nature of trust relationships. Trust not only has to be oriented from the minority group to the majority group, but also has to be shared by all of the groups. In effect, the majority's distrust of the minority, and its future uses or abuses of mutual institutions, explain why it is so difficult for majorities to recognize and accommodate minorities. Paradoxically, the trust that would be needed from the majority to recognize the minority is often only achieved if the conditions that perpetuate power asymmetries are maintained; in other words, if recognition does not take place.

The study of voluntary associations makes it possible to understand the dynamics specific to multinational states from a new perspective, outside of classical frameworks of inter-governmental relations, constitutional recognition, and the division of powers. Given that the issues are not framed in the language of rights and justice, and that the groups are not restricted within the pan-Canadian framework (it is easy for them to secede), it is possible to observe a greater variety of responses to the question of inter-group arrangements. More specifically, it is possible to isolate trust as a central variable within these relationships.

Table 10.2
Communication and bilingualism

	Canadian Chamber of Commerce	Canadian Federation of Agriculture	Canadian Federation of Mayors and Municipalities	Heart and Stroke Foundation of Canada	Canadian Council on Social Development	World University Service of Canada	Amnesty International Canada
Outside communication (publications, web site)	Yes (publications generally accessible)	Yes	Yes	Yes	Yes	Yes	Yes (in their relations with the other language chapter)
Activities/services	Yes	N/A	Sometimes	N/A	Yes	Yes	No
Annual general meeting	Yes	Yes (simultaneous translation)	Sometimes	No	N/A	No	No
Board meetings	No	Yes (simultaneous translation)	Sometimes	No	No	No	No
Other executive meetings (committee meetings)	No	Yes	N/A	No	No	N/A	No

Source: Table by the authors, drawn from conclusions of case studies in Cameron and Simeon, *Language Matters*, 2009.

Table 10.3
Representation (power sharing)

	Canadian Chamber of Commerce	Canadian Federation of Agriculture	Canadian Federation of Mayors and Municipalities	Heart and Stroke Foundation of Canada	Canadian Council on Social Develop.	World University Service of Canada	Amnesty International Canada
1 Cooperation on the inside (cooperation within the association)	No.	No	No	No	No	No	No
2 Other accommodation structures (committees, reserved seats, etc.)	No	No	No	No	No (although there was a French-language committee in the past)	No (although there was a French-language committee in the past)	AIC and AIQ both have international representation rights
3 Type of structure	Mixed confederal (provincial chambers and individual members)	Federal (representation according to the size of the farming community in each province)	Unitary (cities are members)	Federal (provincial representation, decentralized structure)	Unitary	Unitary	Separate

Table 10.3
Representation (power sharing) (continued)

4 Cooperation on the outside (cooperation within separate associations)	Yes	Yes	Yes	Yes	No	No	Yes
5 Type of structure	Chambre de commerce du Québec	Union des producteurs agricoles du Québec	Union des municipalités du Québec	Fondation des maladies du Coeur du Québec	Conseil Québécois de dévelop. social (ended operations in 1994)	Entraide universitaire mondiale du Québec (ended operations in the early 1970s)	Amnesty International Québec
6 Nature of the ties between the Québec and pan-Canadian associations	Collaboration (studies and publication), ad hoc coordination	Participation (annual general assembly, regional conferences, directors' meetings)	Ad hoc collaboration	Participation as a province	Collaboration (in 1994)	N/A	Coordination

Source: Table by the authors, drawn from conclusions of case studies in Cameron and Simeon, *Language Matters* (2009).

NOTES

The authors would like to thank François Rocher and Dimitrios Karmis, along with Vincent Lemieux, John Meisel, David Cameron, André Lecours, Alain-G. Gagnon, Guy Laforest, Marie-Joëlle Zahar, and Patti Lenard for their valuable comments and suggestions on earlier versions of this text.

1 This chapter is based on the case studies in Meisel and Lemieux (1972) and Cameron and Simeon (2009). They include the following groups: Scouts catholiques du Canada/Boy Scouts of Canada, the Union générale des étudiants du Québec/the Canadian Union of Students, the Fédération des jeunes chambres du Canada français/Canada Junior Chamber of Commerce, the Association des médecins de langue française du Canada/Canadian Medical Association, the Chambre de commerce de la province du Québec/Canadian Chamber of Commerce, the Union des municipalités du Québec/Canadian Federation of Mayors and Municipalities, the Conseil canadien de la coopération, the Union catholique des cultivateurs/Canadian Federation of Agriculture, the Heart and Stroke Foundation of Canada, the Canadian Council on Social Development, the World University Service, and Amnesty International Canada and Québec. The other case studies are mentioned directly in the text.

2 For example, trust can occur between individuals or groups, be social or abstract (i.e., concern an "absent" Other), institutional (structural arrangements), procedural (institutionalized practices), technological ("expert system"), existential or systemic ("ontological security") (Sztompka 1999: 41–5).

3 Cameron and Simeon (2009) show that in Canada there are separate unitary, unilingual, bilingual, regional, provincial, binational, confederal, and autonomous voluntary associations.

REFERENCES

Allport, G. 1954. *The Nature of Prejudice*. Cambridge, MA: Perseus Books.

Axelrod, R. 1984. *The Evolution of Cooperation*. New York: Basic Books.

Baier, A. 1986. "Trust and Antitrust." *Ethics* 96: 231–60.

Baldassari, D., and M. Diani. 2007. "The Integrative Power of Civic Networks." *American Journal of Sociology* 113, no. 3: 735–80.

Bashevkin, S. 1991. *True Patriot Love: The Politics of Canadian Nationalism*. Oxford: Oxford University Press.

Berger, C.R. 1986. "Uncertain Outcome Values in Predicted Relationships: Uncertainty Reduction Theory Then and Now." *Human Communication Research* 13, no. 1: 34–8.

Blacklock, C. 2009. "Managing Linguistic Practices in International Development NGOs: The World University Service of Canada." In *Language Matters: How Canadian Voluntary Associations Manage French and English*, edited by D. Cameron and R. Simeon, 136–73. Vancouver: University of British Columbia Press.

Breton, R., and D. Stasiulus. 1980. "Linguistic Boundaries and the Cohesion of Canada." In *Cultural Boundaries and the Cohesion of Canada*, edited by R. Breton, J. Reitz, and V. Valentine, 137–328. Montréal: IRPP press.

Cameron, D. and R. Simeon. 2009. "Language and the Institutions of Civil Society." In *Language Matters: How Canadian Voluntary Associations Manage French and English*, edited by D. Cameron and R. Simeon, 3–22. Vancouver: University of British Columbia Press.

Coleman, W. 1995. "Le nationalisme, les intermédiaires et l'intégration politique canadienne." *Politique et sociétés* 28: 31–52.

Coleman, W. and T. Mau. 2009. "French-English Relations in Comprehensive Business Associations." In *Language Matters: How Canadian Voluntary Associations Manage French and English*, edited by D. Cameron and R. Simeon, 3–51. Vancouver: University of British Columbia Press.

Cook, K., R. Hardin, and M. Levi. 2005. *Cooperation without Trust?* New York: Russell Sage.

Dryzek, J. 2005. "Deliberative Democracy in Divided Societies: Alternatives to Agonism and Analgesia." *Political Theory* 33, no. 2: 218–42.

Dufour, P. 2006. "Projet national et espace de protestation mondiale: des articulations distinctes au Québec et au Canada." *Revue canadienne de science politique* 39, no. 2: 315–42.

Duquette, M., and S. Dugas. 2009. "Two Voices for Human Rights: Amnesty International." In *Language Matters: How Canadian Voluntary Associations Manage French and English*, edited by D. Cameron and R. Simeon, 53–173. Vancouver: University of British Columbia Press.

Gagnon, A.-G., and J. Tully, eds. 2001. *Multinational Democracies*. Cambridge: Cambridge University Press.

Gambetta, D. 2000. "Can We Trust Trust?" In *Trust: Making and Breaking Cooperative Relations*, edited by D. Gambetta, 213–37. New York: Basil Blackwell.

Gillespie, A. 2008. "The Intersubjective Dynamic of Trust, Distrust, and Manipulation." In *Trust and Distrust: Sociocultural Perspectives*, edited by I. Marková and A. Gillespie, 273–89. Charlotte, NC: Information Age Publication.

Horowitz, D.L. 1985. *Ethnic Groups in Conflict*. Berkeley: University of California Press.

Howe, P., J. Everitt, and D. Desserud. 2006. "Social Capital and Ethnic Harmony: Evidence from the New Brunswick Case." *Canadian Ethnic Studies* 38, no. 3: 37–57.

Jenson, J. 1993. "Naming Nations: Making Nationalist Claims in Canadian Public Discourse." *Canadian Review of Sociology and Anthropology* 30, no. 3: 337–58.

Jenson, J., and R. Laforest. 2009. "From Biculturalism to Bilingualism: Patterns of Linguistic Association in the Canadian Council on Social Development." In *Language Matters: How Canadian Voluntary Associations Manage French and English*, edited by D. Cameron and R. Simeon, 121–35. Vancouver: University of British Columbia Press.

Kramer, R.M., and P. J. Carnevale. 2008. "Trust and Intergroup Negotiation." In *Blackwell Handbook of Social Psychology: Intergroup Processes*, edited by R. Brown and S.L. Gaertner. Oxford: Blackwell Publishing.

Laforest, R., and S. Philips. 2001. "Repenser les relations entre gouvernement et secteur bénévole: à la croisée des chemins au Québec et au Canada." *Politique et sociétés* 20, no. 2–3: 37–68.

Langlois, S. 1991. "Le choc de deux sociétés globales." In *Le Québec et la Restructuration du Canada: 1980–1992: Enjeux et perspectives*, edited by L. Balthazar, G. Laforest, and V. Lemieux, 3–108. Montréal: Septentrion.

Laponce, J.A. 1987. *Languages and Their Territories*. Toronto: University of Toronto Press.

– 1996. "Minority Languages in Canada: Their Fate and Survival Strategies." In *Languages: Cultures and Values in Canada at the Dawn of the 21st Century*, edited by A. Lapierr, P. Smart, and P. Savard, 78–83. Ottawa: Carleton University Press.

Lederach, J.P. 1998. *Building Peace: Sustainable Reconciliation in Divided Societies*. Washington: United States Institution of Peace.

Lemieux, V. 1973. "Le conflit dans les organisations biculturelles." *Recherches sociographiques* 14, no. 1: 41–57.

– 1998. *Les Coalitions: Liens, transactions et contrôles*. Paris: Presses Universitaires de France.

MacAllister, D.J. 1995. "Affect- and Cognition-based Trust as Foundations for Interpersonal Cooperation in organizations." *Academy of Management Journal* 38: 24–59.

Maclure, J. 2006. "On the Public Use of Practical Reason: Loosening the Grip of Neo-Kantianism." *Philosophy and Social Criticism* 32, no. 1: 37–63.

Manfredi, C. 2004. *Feminist Activism in the Supreme Court*. Vancouver: University of British Columbia Press.

Marková, I., and A. Gillespie. 2008. *Trust and Distrust: Sociocultural Perspectives*. Charlotte, NC: Information Age Pub.

McIntosh, T. 1999. "Organized Labour in a Federal Society: Solidarity, Coalition Building and Canadian Unions." In *How Canadians Connect*, edited by H. Lazar and T. McIntosh, 147–78. Montréal and Kingston: McGill-Queen's University Press.

McKnight, D.H., and N.L. Chervany. 1996. "Trust and Distrust Definitions: One Bite at a Time." In *Trust in Cyber-Societies*, edited by R. Falcone, M. Singh, and Y.-H. Tan, 27–54. Heidelberg: Springer-Verlag.

Meisel, J., and V. Lemieux. 1972. *Ethnic Relations in Canadian Voluntary Associations*. Documents of the Royal Commission on Bilingualism and Biculturalism, no. 13.

Mendelsohn, M. 2000. "Public Brokerage: Constitutional Reform and the Accommodation of Mass Publics." *Canadian Journal of Political Science* 33, no. 2: 245–72.

Möllering, G. 2001. "The Nature of Trust: From Georg Simmel to a Theory of Expectation, Interpretation and Suspension." *Sociology* 35, no. 2: 403–20.

Noël, A. 2006. "Democratic Deliberation in a Multinational Federation." *Critical Review of International Social and Political Philosophy* 9, no. 3: 419–44.

Pelletier, A., and M. Morden. 2012. "Linking Multinational Federalism and Civil Society: Theoretical Considerations and Examples from Canada." In *The Ways of Federalism and the Horizons of Territorial Autonomy in Spain*, edited by Alberto López-Basaguren and Leire Escajedo San Epifani, 619–36. Heidelberg: Springer-Verlag.

Putnam, R. 1993. *Making Democracy Work: Civic Traditions in Modern Italy*. Princeton: Princeton University Press.

– 1995. "Tuning In, Tuning Out: The Strange Disappearance of Social Capital in America." *PS: Political Science and Politics* 28, no. 4: 664–83.

Rousseau, D., S.B. Sitkin, Ronald S. Burt, and Colin Camerer. 1998. "Not So Different After All: A Cross-Discipline View of Trust." *Academy of Management Review* 23, no. 3: 393–404.

Seppanen, R., K. Blomwvist, and S. Sundqvist. 2007. "Measuring Inter-Organizational Trust – A Critical Review of the Empirical Research in 1990–2003." *Industrial Marketing Management* 36: 249–65.

Sheppard, B.H., and D.M. Sherman. 1998. "The Grammars of Trust: A Model and General Implications." *Academy of Management Review* 23, no. 3: 422–37.

Simeon, R. 2002. *Political Science and Canadian Federalism: Seven Decades of Scholarly Engagement.* Kingston: Institute of Intergovernmental Relations, Queen's University.

– 2009. "Associations in the Voluntary Health Sector: The Heart and Stroke Foundations of Canada and the Huntington Societies of Canada and Québec." In *Language Matters: How Canadian Voluntary Associations Manage French and English*, edited by D. Cameron and R. Simeon, 95–120. Vancouver: University of British Columbia Press.

Simeon, R., and D. Cameron. 2009. "Accommodation at the Pinnacle: The Special Role of Civil Society's Leaders." In *Language Matters: How Canadian Voluntary Associations Manage French and English*, edited by D. Cameron and R. Simeon, 174–86. Vancouver: University of British Columbia Press.

Sitkin, S.B., and N.L. Roth. 1993. "Explaining the Limited Effectiveness of Legalistic 'Remedies' for Trust/Distrust." *Organization Science* 4: 367–92.

Skogstad, G. 2009. "Canada's English and French Farm Communities." In *Language Matters: How Canadian Voluntary Associations Manage French and English*, edited by D. Cameron and R. Simeon, 52–73. Vancouver: University of British Columbia Press.

Smets, P., H. Wels, and J. van Loon, eds. 1999. *Trust and Cooperation: Symbolic Exchange and Moral Economics in an Age of Cultural Differentiation.* Amsterdam: Het Spinhuis.

Smith, M. 2004. "Segmented Networks: Linguistic Practices in Canadian Lesbian and Gay Rights Organizing." *Ethnicities* 4, no. 1: 99–124.

Stevenson, D., and R. Gilbert. 2009. "Municipal Associations." In *Language Matters: How Canadian Voluntary Associations Manage French and English*, edited by D. Cameron and R. Simeon, 74–94. Vancouver: University of British Columbia Press.

Sztompka, P. 1999. *Trust: A Sociological Theory.* Cambridge: Cambridge University Press.

Tajfel, H. 1974. "Social Identity and Intergroup Behavior." *Social Science Information* 13, no. 2: 65–93.

Taylor, C. 1994. *Multiculturalism*. Princeton: Princeton University Press.

Tjosvold, D. 1984. "Cooperation: Theory and Organizations." *Human Relations* 37, no. 9: 734–67.

Tully, J. 1995. *Strange Multiplicity: Constitutionalism in an Age of Diversity*. Cambridge: Cambridge University Press.

Turgeon, L. 1999. "La grande absente: La société civile au coeur des changements de la Révolution tranquille." *Globe: Revue internationale d'études québécoises* 2, no. 1: 1–20.

Uslaner, E.M. 2002. *The Moral Foundation of Trust*. Cambridge: Cambridge University Press.

Varshney, A. 2001. "Ethnic Conflict and Civil Society." *World Politics* 53, no. 3: 362–98.

Vickers, J. 2000. "Feminisms and Nationalisms in English Canada." *Journal of Canadian Studies* 35, no. 2, 128–48.

Weinstock, D. 1999. "Building Trust in Divided Societies." *The Journal of Political Philosophy* 7, no. 3: 287–307.

Wesinger, J.Y., and P.F. Salipante. 2005. "A Grounded Theory for Building Ethnically Bridging Social Capital in Voluntary Organizations." *Nonprofit and Voluntary Sector Quarterly* 34, no. 1: 29–55.

Wright, A., and I. Ehnert. 2010. "Making Sense of Trust Across Cultural Context." In *Organizational Trust: A Cultural Perspective*, edited by M.N.K. Saunders, D. Skinner, G. Dietz, N. Gillespie, and R.J. Lewicki, 107–26. Cambridge: Cambridge University Press.

Yamagishi, T., and M. Yamagishi. 1994. "Trust and Commitment in the United States and Japan." *Motivation and Emotion* 18, no. 2: 129–66.

PART THREE

Comparative Perspectives

11

Through the Mirror of Contingency:
Trust and Mistrust in Multinational States

Philip Resnick

Trust is a relative, rather than an absolute, matter. It is not common to all states, particularly ones whose civic culture is weak or non-existent, or where deep ethnic, racial, or religious cleavages prevail. Its absence has been widely apparent in places such as Kyrgyzstan, Xinjiang, Kashmir, Afghanistan, Sri Lanka, Chechnya, ex-Yugoslavia, Darfur, Somalia, the Congo, Rwanda, and Colombia – to evoke but a number of places where bloody conflicts or civil wars have occurred over the past two decades

Nor should we have any illusions about how frequently trust has been a norm in the West. Local identities preceded national ones everywhere. City folk had mentalities apart from country folk. The rich and the poor lived in separate worlds. Religious communities had strong motivations to distrust those outside their own faith group. Political ideologies bred their own disharmony. The result was frequent conflict – be it in the form of dynastic wars, religious wars, wars of ideas, or class or ethnic strife.

The origin of the modern state has rarely been a pretty story. Conquest was a key part of the equation; for example, the wholesale destruction or enslavement of subordinate peoples as in the history of European settlement of the new world. The emergence of strong central authority – so pivotally associated with the state – was usually a coercive, blood-stained affair.

But trust could come with the slow development of toleration. We know the chequered history of religious toleration in the Western world. This did not come easily or naturally to Catholics or Protestants in the aftermath of the Reformation and Counter-Reformation. The Inquisition presents one face of this; the Night of St Bartholomew massacre a second; Cromwell's conquest of Ireland a third; and the story does not really begin to improve until Enlightenment ideas begin to hold greater sway from the eighteenth century on.

The same is true with regards to toleration towards political opponents. The 1801 American presidential election marked the first example of a peaceful turnover of power from a ruling political party to its opposition in a democratically contested election. With time, this would become the norm as liberal societies became more democratic, and political parties contending for popular support came, however grudgingly, to accept the legitimacy of their opponents. Still, losers do not always accept winners when they sense that vital issues are at stake – the South's reaction to Abraham Lincoln's inauguration in 1861 is but one example of this. And not all political parties that have contested popular elections have subscribed to democratic norms – Communist and fascist parties in the first half of the twentieth century did not, and nor did the leaders of many post-colonial third world states.

The story repeats itself where multinational states are concerned. Trust did not come naturally where differences of language, custom, or shared history prevailed. The historical record can itself be a source of contention.

Is Belgian history the history of a single people with a common social life and a syncretic mixing of two cultures, as Henri Pirenne, the distinguished francophone Belgian historian of the early twentieth century, argued?

> Belgium, divided ethnographically between a Latin and a German race, and politically between France and Germany, is a "microcosm" of Western Europe. Its unity does not lie in a community of race as in Germany, or in the centralizing action of a hereditary monarchy as in England or France, but in the unity of its social life ... Our national culture is a sort of syncretism, where one finds, mixed with one another and modified by one another, the genius of two races. (1900: 10)

Or is it more accurate to see the Flemish and Walloons, with their two respective national outlooks so often at loggerheads with one another, as having quite different memories of the past and, therefore, outlooks on the present, as the Flemish historian Lode Wils suggests (1996: 339)?

In the Spanish case, one can point to conflicts in archaeology – between researchers in universities and centres who have a broader Spanish perspective, and professionals or amateurs attached to the archaeological departments of the autonomous governments, who are only interested in research that is nationalist-regionalist in character (Díaz-Andreu 1994: 211). One can contrast the exhibits at the Museum of Catalan History in Barcelona, highlighting a Catalan-based interpretation of events through the centuries, with the Royal Academy of History in Madrid and its insistence on the teaching of a single Spanish history. A Basque nationalist view of the broad nature of foral rights in an earlier period can be contrasted with Castilian centralists for whom the *fueros*, institutions of regional autonomy, were privileges granted by the sovereign crown (Keating 2001: 44–5). More generally, one can compare the single-nation view of Spanish history associated with conservative historians today with regionalist interpretations, and with left versions of the common history of Spain based on the coexistence of plural identities (Núñez 2001: 730–7).

In the Canadian case, one can contrast French Canadian/Québec views of history with those of English-speaking Canadians. Was the Conquest of 1759 a fatal curse or a new beginning? Were the 1837 Rebellions in Lower Canada primarily national in character, or were they part of the same quest for responsible government found in Upper Canada? Was Confederation essentially a pact between the two founding peoples or the creation of a new nation with a system of government modelled on Great Britain's? Similar differences characterize approaches to the hanging of Louis Riel, to the Manitoba and Ontario School Questions, and to the question of conscription during the two world wars. It is interesting to note that there is no simple agreement among history teachers in secondary schools in English Canada and Québec on what actually constitute the most important events in Canadian history. In a 2001 survey, anglophone teachers stressed events like Confederation, the two world wars, or the Charter; Québec francophone teachers gave lesser weight to such events, and greater weight than their anglophone counterparts to the discovery of Canada, the Conquest, or the post-1960 development of Québec nationalism (Dominion Institute 2001).

History plays a central role, not only between majority-type and minority-type national communities, but also within each camp. Alan

Bold, writing about Scotland, observes, "Scotland is still fighting old battles, still obsessed by the past, still trying to convert defeat into victory. Scotland is a country uniquely haunted by history. With so many defeats to contend with the Scots have gradually come to regard themselves as born losers" (1983: 11). For Colin Kidd,

> history rather than natural law or political theology derived from Scripture was the very backbone of political argument in early modern Scotland. Scottish history as ideology was multi-faceted and highly developed. Scotland's past provided material for the national origin myth; for national independence; for the religious nation's "chosen people" status; for pride in the caste of its aristocratic warriors who preserved freedom intact against foreign invaders and domestic tyrants. (1993: 27)

And for David McCrone, "Scotland has no shortage of history; indeed, it can be argued that it has too much" (1998: 59).

Language is often another key feature of national identity for members of minority or peripheral nationalities, one of the political geometries that shapes multinational states.[1] A Flemish dictum of the nineteenth century stated: "Language is the entirety of the people."[2] Somewhat similar claims could be made for Catalan. "Our language, the expression of our people, which can never be given up ... is the spiritual foundation of our existence," read an appeal by the Catalonian Cultural Committee in the 1920s (Fishman 1996: 160). "The Basque language must be the pillar of national consciousness," argued Sabino Arana at the end of the nineteenth century.[3] "*Nos institutions, notre langue, nos lois,*" read the motto of the French Canadian newspaper *Le Canadien* in 1831 (Lamonde 2000: 176).

Language becomes even more pivotal when it has been threatened with repression or actively repressed. In the Canadian case, the Durham Report of the late 1830s called for the assimilation of French Canadians into the English-speaking population of British North America; this threat was successfully resisted by generations of French Canadians and their political leaders, but not without sinking into the French Canadian collective consciousness. In the Spanish case, one can point to the long decades of dictatorship between 1939 and 1975, during which Franco insisted on "a national unity that is absolute with a single language, Spanish, and a single personality that is Spanish" (Tusell 1999: 151). This only reinforced the appeal of Catalan or Basque nationalism.[4] Similarly, Flemish was very much a secondary language to French in Belgium in the nineteenth century, securing an equal status only in the twentieth century. Much of the Flemish movement revolved around its promotion and defence (Hermans 1992).

Even languages that have been much weakened over time can play a symbolic role where the assertion of national identity is concerned. A Welsh activist acknowledges the fact that Welsh is no longer needed for purely functional communication in Wales, but sees it as having a structural role in "saving the separate identity of the Welsh as a People" (Jones, cited in Reicher and Hopkins 2001: 157). Gaelic may play something of a similar role in Ireland. The same is true for various aboriginal languages in contemporary Canada. And the same may be true for Basque, which is spoken by little over a quarter of the population in the Basque Country (as compared to the significantly larger number of Catalan or Galician speakers in their respective regions of Spain[5]), though language is still an important element of Basque national identity, especially for nationalists.

Members of one language group often have quite different memories and readings of history than members of another language group. This can lead to a sense on the part of minority nationalities of constituting a distinct society or people. This is reinforced by the desire for a strong territorial base, to better reinforce security for one's language (Laponce 1987). For the defence of a minority language in places like Flanders, Québec, Catalonia, or the Basque Country is at the same time a defence of the memories of the larger national community.

The possibility exists of turning multiple languages, identities, and memories into defining features of the larger state. Canada since the late 1960s has used official bilingualism as a unifying feature, helping to define Canadian identity vis-à-vis the United States. Flemish along with French are defining characteristics for Belgium. Spain in its post-Franco constitution recognizes its nationalities, regions, and its minority languages.[6] The recognition of distinct languages is not necessarily a zero-sum game, so much as an acknowledgement of the complex reality that makes multinational states what they are.

Nonetheless, a common state structure in multinational states is rarely the result of consent. It comes about because stronger cores defeat weaker peripheries, because overseas empire leads to the strengthening of central power, because the language and high culture of the court win out – despite manifold resistance – against provincial and regional identities. Never entirely, to be sure. But enough to allow centres to stamp state cultures with their mark. As the Spanish humanist Antonio de Nebrija, author of the first *Castilian Grammar*, noted in a letter to Queen Isabella in 1492, "language has always been the perfect instrument of empire" (la Rosa 1995). *A fortiori*, one might add, this has been true of the language of dominant nationalities within multinational states.

Mistrust is born of the very process by which multinational states come into existence. The mistrust is that of minority nationalities who find themselves in a subordinate position, politically, linguistically, or otherwise within newly structured nation-states. Scotland gave up its autonomous governing institutions through the Act of Union. The Catalans were defeated in 1714. Québec fell to the British in 1759. Flanders, despite its demographic supremacy, was very much the junior partner in nineteenth-century and early twentieth-century Belgium.

Need this mistrust be fatal? Obviously not, since the United Kingdom, Spain, Canada, and Belgium are still with us today – though of the four, Belgium and Spain seem to be holding together by ever-looser threads. Two key questions present themselves: (1) *By what means do patterns of trust come to be established and how do these break down?* (2) *Can values of shared citizenship permanently overcome the historical, linguistic, or regional bases for conflicting identities?*

INSTITUTIONAL ARRANGEMENTS

Federalism has been a key feature of the Canadian case. The compact theory of two founding peoples had tended to prevail in Québec versus a predominant view of territorial equality among the provinces that has prevailed in English-speaking Canada. Québec has enjoyed significant autonomy, though at key moments majority interests have trumped minority ones.

For an example, one need but refer to the conscription crises in Canada during the two world wars, with the majority English Canadians strongly supportive of conscription for overseas service and the minority French Canadians opposed. During World War I, two jibes directed at French Canadians by English Canadians were that French Canadians "enlist in retail and desert in wholesale" and are "the only known race of white men who quit."[7] "Where are your sons?" thundered the anti-conscription mayor of Montreal, Camille Houde, to his French Canadian supporters during World War II.

Still, accommodation has been the name of the game more often than direct conflict. One can refer to Québec's move to collect its own income tax in 1954; the Canada Pension Plan/Québec Pension Plan arrangement 1965; the Cullen-Couture agreement on immigration of 1977; the coexistence of official bilingualism federally alongside Bill 101 provincially, consecrating French as the official language of Québec; two referenda on Québec sovereignty; the Social Union Framework Agreement of 1999, with its Québec opt-out provision; and the November 2006 House of Commons declaration recognizing the Québécois as constituting a nation within Canada. All of these point to forms of special status for Québec, a de facto acknowledgement of Québec's distinct identity within Canada.

But mistrust has not disappeared. The rise of the sovereignty movement in Québec sparked English Canadian resentment. There was concern that escalating Québec demands from the 1960s on would excessively weaken the federal government. The turning down of the Victoria formula after Québec government approval in 1971, the refusal of Québec to accept constitutional patriation in 1982, and the use of the notwithstanding clause by the Bourassa government to overrule the Supreme Court judgment on language used on signs in 1988 were not well received outside Québec. At the time of the Meech Lake Accord, there was concern that, even if it had gone through, this would not dispel recurring Québec demands. Successive Québec referenda on sovereignty, in which sovereigntist governments chose the question and the rest of Canada was forced to stay on the sidelines, sparked anger about the survival of the country. Québec is often perceived as getting a larger share of federal expenditures through transfer payments than most other provinces, but not acknowledging as much.[8] And there is little sympathy for Québec's recurring desire to re-open constitutional debate when the rest of Canada sees this as a closed matter.

For its part, Québec, as the one majority francophone society in North America, has a *survival complex*, fearful of going the Louisiana route. Long-run socio-economic and demographic trends are not favourable to Québec, which is experiencing a declining share of Canada's population as economic power is increasingly transferred to western Canada, along with Ontario. Québec has been unable to constitutionalize its status as a distinct society/nation because of the English Canadian majority's refusal. Federal jurisdiction and the federal spending power place limits or encroach on Québec's ability to act in a variety of sectors. The Clarity Act passed in 2000 attempts to limit any future move to Québec sovereignty. There has been heated debate in Québec about reasonable accommodation of immigrants, sparked by potential threats that immigration could pose to Québec's predominantly francophone identity. Eternal vigilance is seen as the price of preserving Québec's distinctiveness. And with it come divided loyalties, far more divided than those one finds in the rest of Canada.

Aboriginal identities have been enhanced through sections 25 and 35 of the Charter and through successive Supreme Court judgements, most especially Delgamuukw. Confrontations between aboriginals and non-aboriginals like those at Oka, Québec, Caledonia, Ontario, and Miramichi, New Brunswick; the role played by Elijah Harper in torpedoing the Meech Lake Accord of 1990; overwhelming Cree opposition to the possible secession of Québec at the time of the 1995 referendum on sovereignty; ongoing and unresolved land claims in a province like British Columbia; road blockages in various provinces; disputes over fishing rights for natives as opposed to non-natives; the legacy of abuse of native children in residential schools – all bring home the complex and often conflictual relationship between aboriginal and non-aboriginal Canadians.

The regionalized character of Spain predates its imperial ascendancy. An anecdote regarding a sixteenth-century Spanish ruler, Charles V or Philip II, and Catalonia underlines the point.

> The entourage of the King arrived at a monastery on the outskirts of Barcelona and a servant was sent ahead to ask for lodging for the royal party for the night. When the servant knocked, he was asked who had sent him. "The King of Spain," he replied. "We know no King of Spain," the monk replied, and slammed the door shut in the servant's face. The servant reflected on the situation and knocked again. "Who is there?" came the reply from within. "The Count of Barcelona," replied the servant. This time the gates flew open to receive the rightfully designated ruler of Catalonia.[9]

The suppression of minority nationalities in the eighteenth, nineteenth, and large chunks of the twentieth centuries left a legacy of mistrust. Mobilization around language occurred in Catalonia during the Franco period, along with the birth of the radical separatist movement ETA and anti-Spanish violence in the Basque Country. The Statute of Autonomy was the Spanish road to routinizing more stable relations between majority and minority nationalities in the post-Franco period. This proved more successful in the short run in Catalonia than in the Basque Country, where ETA-led violence persisted for decades, only a minority of the population ratified the constitution of 1977, and the Basque National Party (PNV), with a strongly nationalist agenda, dominated the political scene until 2008.

Minority nationalities tend to push for ever-greater autonomy. The PNV asserted the right to hold referenda on sovereignty, something denied by successive central governments. The Catalan regional government advocated for a new statute of autonomy with greater recognition of its national status; however, the designation of Catalonia as a "nation" rather than a "nationality" in the 2006 Statute of Autonomy was ruled unconstitutional by Spain's Constitutional Court (Lazaro 2010).[10] The upshot was a march in the streets of Barcelona on 10 July 2010, encompassing between 500,000 and 1 million people (estimates vary), protesting this decision and asserting Catalonia's national character. Subsequently, the dominant party in the ruling CiU coalition in Catalonia adopted a separatist stance, demanding a referendum on sovereignty. In the Catalan elections of 2015, pro-independence parties achieved a majority in the regional parliament, though falling short of 50 per cent of the overall vote. After laborious negotiations, a pro-independence coalition government was formed. Conflict with the central government escalated in autumn 2017, with the Catalan Parliament voting for independence from Spain following a constitutionally illegitimate referendum on sovereignty and the central government suspending the Catalan government by invoking Article 155 of the Spanish Constitution. The election of 21 December 2017 saw independence parties again winning a majority of the seats in the Catalan Parliament, though falling short of 50 per cent of the overall vote. So the deep divisions within Catalonia and between Catalonia and Spain will continue.

The majority of Spaniards see Spain as a single, united country with autonomous regions that have roughly equal powers, save for the linguistic bilingualism of regions like Catalonia, the Basque Country, or Galicia. The balance of power held by minority nationalist parties in the federal parliament has in the past helped their regions secure concessions from Madrid. This in turn has sparked a counter-sense of mistrust by a majority of non-Catalan and non-Basque Spaniards about where minority national identities may be leading – for example regarding the rights of the Spanish-speaking minority in Catalonia. There have been mobilizations of millions in opposition to the violence of ETA in the aftermath of terrorist attacks in major Spanish cities. There was strong opposition in the rest of Spain to the referendum of 1 October 2017 initiated by the pro-independence Catalan government, and to the short-lived proclamation of independence by the Catalan parliament shortly thereafter. Nor would amending the Spanish constitution along more overtly federal lines, as the Spanish Socialist Party has proposed, necessarily resolve the situation. For Catalan nationalism has provoked an equally strong sense of Spanish nationalism on the other side, making any acceptable compromise so much more difficult to achieve.

The United Kingdom was consecrated by the Act of Union of 1707. Despite concessions to Scotland regarding its legal system, the Church of Scotland, and education, this marked the end of a Scottish Parliament for almost three centuries, and of Scottish political autonomy. The British Empire would act as a unifying force, with religion a key additional ingredient.

The political situation has shifted since World War II. There has been a weakening of Conservative, Unionist forces north of the border, especially in the aftermath of the Thatcher regime. The Scottish National Party (SNP) has grown in importance, and Labour in opposition threw its support behind the devolution movement, culminating in the referendum of 1997 and the establishment of an autonomous Scottish Assembly. Thrust and counter-thrust has characterized the relations between Labour and the SNP within Scotland, and between Scotland and England, with the SNP eventually supplanting Labour as Scotland's ruling party. The upshot was the holding of a referendum (with the agreement of the UK government) on 18 September 2014 on whether Scotland should become an independent country; 55.3 per cent voted against, 44.7 per cent in favour.[11] But Scottish nationalist sentiment still runs strong, and the results of the 23 June 2016 UK referendum on EU membership, in which English voters supported the victorious Leave side by 53.4 per cent but Scottish voters supported Remain by 62 per cent, makes the possibility of a second Scottish referendum on independence "highly likely," to cite Nicola Sturgeon, the Scottish First Minister.[12] Though this may be less true now that the SNP's share of the popular vote declined dramatically in Scotland in the June 2017 British election.

In reaction to Scottish nationalism, there are recurrent complaints about the treatment of English north of the border. There has also been greater prominence given in England to the flag of St George, as opposed to the Union Jack. Wales represents a weaker case for minority nationalism, with a stronger English presence as a share of population than in Scotland (only a bare majority of the population voted for devolution in 1997). Still, there has been an overall weakening of the sense of British identity as reflected in polling surveys.

The British Social Attitudes 23rd Report discovered fewer people willing to volunteer "British" as the best way of describing themselves. Between 1996 and 2006 the proportion describing themselves as British had become a demographic minority, declining from 52% to 44%. Though "Britishness has long been no more than a secondary identity both in Scotland and Wales," the most dramatic trend was for it to become a secondary "identity" in England as well. "Already relatively weak in Scotland and Wales, Britishness now appears to have lost some ground in England to a sense of feeling English instead." In the same decade, Britishness as the primary identity of residents in England had declined from 59% to 48%. (Heath 2007: 11–13)

Belgium in good part was historically defined by what it did not want to be: a southern province of the Netherlands as it had been between 1815 and 1830, or a de facto province of France, as during the Napoleonic period. But this turns out to have been an insufficient basis for forging a strong common national identity. Francophones dominated throughout the first century of the country's existence, with greater industrialization in Wallonia and the attraction of the French language for upper-class Flemish, even in Flanders. Religion was an additional dividing factor – Flanders more traditional, clerical, Wallonia less so. Politically, Flanders was more conservative, Wallonia more liberal or socialist.

Warfare engendered its own collective memories. In the Belgian case, the Germans favoured the Flemish over the Walloons, through their so-called *Flamenpolitik*, both in World Wars I and II. This left differing memories of these events. For a Flemish novelist, Gerald Walschop, who was a young Flemish activist in 1918, "activism divided us more profoundly than it is possible to understand today. We had to choose between Flanders and Belgium, two homelands that had been equivalent in our eyes until then, and which, to our horror, had suddenly become irreconcilable enemies" (qtd in Wils 1996: 222). For a future Belgian Liberal senator, Maurice Despret, himself a Walloon: "The Germans (in Flanders) did what the population desired ... It is the modest provincial bourgeoisie – the shopkeepers and lower-level functionaries – that supports the Flemish movement, along with younger elements of the lower clergy" (qtd in Wils 1996: 223).

During World War II, greater support for the German occupier could be found in Flanders than in Wallonia. This sparked further division, for example, over the collaboration of Leopold III with the Germans, as well as during the subsequent referendum over his abdication of 1950, with Flanders favouring the king and Wallonia opposing him. As Lode Wils observes, "Half a century after World War II, it seems that the politics of the German occupation has left a time-bomb. Not only in Yugoslavia and Czechoslovakia, but also in Belgium" (1996: 337).

The politics of language and regional identity have come to increasingly permeate the entire political system. One can point to the bitterly divisive coal strike of 1960, the battle over the University of Leuven/Louvain in the mid-1960s, the battle over Fleurons, and more recently over Brussels-Halle-Vilvoorde, a suburb located on the outskirts of Brussels in Flanders with a significant francophone population with political rights, such as to French schools and the ability to vote for French (as opposed to Flemish) political parties. Such conflicts speak to the strongly territorial sense of linguistic identity among the Flemish, which in turn has led to the increasing federalization of the country. Such conflicts have also led to the collapse of successive Belgian governments, and to the recent rise of N-VA, the New Flemish Alliance headed by Bart de Wever, with secessionist leanings.[13] The political system is approaching paralysis; the politicians were unable to form a stable government for a full year and a half after the election of June 2010. There is little trust by the Flemish of Walloons, who are seen as sponging off the prosperity of Flanders given the much higher unemployment and social service expenditures in Wallonia than in Flanders; and little trust by Walloons of the Flemish, who are seen as intransigent and intolerant to French-language speakers in the Greater Brussels area.

Multiple variables can shape the majority-minority relations in the four countries under consideration. Economic growth versus decline;

the historical track record; the degree of elite accommodation; tolerance for ambiguity and compromise on the part of both minority and majority populations; the degree of polarization of political parties along the unity/autonomy/independence spectrum; and the existence of political parties with a nationalist agenda in sub-state nationality regions – for example, the Scottish National Party, the Parti Québécois, Junts per Catalunya and ERC in Catalonia and the PVN in the Basque Country, and the N-VA in Flanders.

When ideological and economic cleavages overlap with nationality differences, these intensify the debate. Examples include Lucien Bouchard playing the social equity card against Ottawa, and governments like that of Mike Harris in Ontario, engaged in major fiscal cut-backs at the time of the 1995 Québec referendum; the rise of Scottish nationalism and support for devolution in reaction to the neo-conservative policies of Margaret Thatcher; or the rich region/poor region dimensions of the Flemish-Walloon conflict.

COMMUNITY (OR COMMUNITIES) OF DESTINY

The idea of shared citizenship evokes notions of a shared community of destiny. This can be cemented through shared experiences – be they of triumph or defeat. One thinks of the rise of the Spanish or British empires and the cementing of a sense of common affinities amongst the constituent nationalities of their respective states. "The Basques found an important role in the Spanish Empire in America ... They were conquistadors and colonizers, navigators, theologians and jurists, evangelizers, sailors, soldiers, and secretaries of state" (Fusi 2006: 17). The British empire, for Linda Colley, became "the means by which the union between Scotland and rest of Great Britain was made real" (1992: 132).

Religious solidarities can play a role – *limpieza de sangre* (purity of blood) directed against *conversos* and *Moriscos* in Spain, Portugal, and Hispanic America, or Protestantism as a unifying creed in the settlement of British North America and the development of the British Empire.

Economic interests are also important. Belgium as a whole benefitted from the exploitation of the Belgian Congo. Railway expansion and the opening of the west had a salient nation-building role to play in the Canadian case.

Wars can be a unifying factor, especially when thinking of battles like Trafalgar, Waterloo, the Peninsular War against Napoleon, World

War I, and World War II. Conversely, as noted above, these can also constitute negative moments that challenge the unity of the state when internal divisions are reinforced by conflict, as seen in Belgium and Canada, or when minority national sentiments are suppressed, as in the aftermath of the Spanish Civil War.

Is there a single community of destiny linking the members of multinational states? Such sentiments are often hostages to ghosts from the past – resentments over unfair treatment, nostalgia for a fate that could have turned out differently – such as Wallace and Scotland, or the Battle of Québec. They lead to a form of bracketed identity, with constant references to the distinct destiny of the minority nationality within that of the larger ensemble. The upshot can be communities of destiny, rather than a single community of destiny.

How overlapping are these destinies? This has been the subject of intense division within sub-state national communities. For me, a salient feature of all the multinational cases we are concerned with here is the profound ambiguity of allegiance within these sub-state national communities. For members of majority nationalities, there is little conflict between one's identity as an Andalusian and a Spaniard, a British Columbian and a Canadian, or an East Anglian and a Briton. For minorities, the cleavages are more acute, with a range of identities from *exclusively* or *mostly* Catalan or Scot or Québécois to *equally* Catalan and Spaniard, et cetera. This is where the real divergence lies between those whose nationalism veers towards independence and those whose nationalism does not. There is enough of a residual sense of shared destiny amongst those who speak of overlapping, rather than exclusive, identities, to maintain the hinge that binds the larger state structure together. Yet there is a greater ambiguity to this sentiment – a sense of multiple allegiances rather than a single national one – that stands in contrast to that which prevails in the majority community. Hence, there is a shifting balance in the relations between these communities, and a tug-of-war for loyalty as between secessionist nationalist movements – PNV, JpC and ERC, SNP, PQ – and those who oppose secession.

A period of imperial meltdown may also heighten internal nationalist tension. The generation of 1898 expressed Spanish disillusionment with defeat abroad in a very palpable way, reflecting on "the bitter melancholy of a grand past."[14] A notable radicalization of Spanish nationalism occurred in the decades that followed (de Riquer 1994: 298–9). For their part, members of Spain's peripheral nationalities could have a quite different reaction to the same event. "A Catalan nationalist movement seized the opportunity presented by the crisis of the Spanish state (divided between the war with the United States and the loss of Cuba, its last American colony) to build a strong sense of identity on the basis of the recognition that Spain was the state and Catalonia the nation" (Folch-Serra 2001: 162).

Once the British Empire entered into decline after World War II, a notable weakening of Scottish identification with Britain took place. As the Scottish nationalist Neil MacCormick noted in a lecture to the British Academy: "The empire was, perhaps, the 'British thing' par excellence. Now it has gone, and now Europe is, as once before for Scots, far more a theatre of opportunity than a threat to identity" (MacCormick 1998: 143). Certainly the Scottish National Party has enjoyed far greater success in recent decades than was the case when the British Empire was a going concern.

Larger political questions regarding the relationship between nation and state, or between national identity and citizenship, remain unresolved. These are a good deal more complex than hard-line political nationalists might assert. Although committed supporters of minority-type nationalism aspire to political independence, as in Québec, moderate nationalists and non-nationalists do not, and retain a significant loyalty to Canada.[15] One thinks of the quip by the well-known Québec comedian Yvan Deschamps about "Quebecers want[ing] a sovereign Québec within a strong, united Canada." Scottish nationalists may dream of an independent Scotland; a majority of Scots over recent decades, and this as recently as the 2014 referendum, have rejected this.[16] Josep Ramoneda, the director of Barcelona's Centre of Contemporary Culture (CCCB), expressed what was for long the majority sentiment on Catalonia's status: "I am a Catalan, I am not a nationalist, but Catalonia is a nation" (Tusell 2003: 180). The largest single group of respondents to surveys in Catalonia has historically seen itself as Spanish and Catalan, preferring to not have to choose between the two.[17] This may have changed in recent years, with a hardening of support for Catalan independence, though it has not become the majority position as yet. Basque society, for its part, is split right down the middle between supporters and opponents of nationalist positions.[18] An in-depth study cites a cross-sample of Basque opinion that underlines the range of views to be found there. "It is the duty of every member of *Euskal Herria* to resist the destruction of the Basque nation." "I want to defend *Euskal Herria*. I want a free nation for us. Nationalism is what we need to keep our language, our customs, our way of living." "I think that clinging to nationalism as a proposal for the 21st century is a step backward." "*Euskara* is just one of many languages. My country includes all of humankind." "If violence is the price that we Basques have to pay for independence, I am not going to pay it" (Davis 1997: 61–88).

In his *Representative Government*, John Stuart Mill famously argued that the existence of different nationalities within the same country, especially if their members read and spoke different languages, would make it next to impossible to have the united public opinion necessary to make representative government work (1968: 361). This turns out to have been unduly pessimistic, as the survival of Belgium, Canada, or Spain would attest. But the citizens of such states may have to accept a greater degree of ambivalence in their interactions with one another across linguistic and cultural lines than might be true for the citizens of states who have developed a more unitary type of national identity.

A key factor that differentiates Belgium from the three other states that we have been examining has to do with the fact that in the Belgian case, the sub-state national community with the strongest sense of nationalist grievance – the Flemish one – happens to constitute a majority of the population. As a majority, with memories of a period when it was subordinated to the francophone community, it has a sense of empowerment that leads it to take much harder positions than is the pattern in the three other states. In those states, minority nationalities can only go so far in securing their goals, be the goal constitutional recognition as a distinct society in the case of Québec, or recognition as "nations" in the case of Catalonia or the Basque Country. Majorities, who have profited most from the development of the larger shared state and dominated its key institutions, may show a willingness to accommodate minority interests, albeit never in a fashion completely satisfactory to hard-line minority nationalists.

But when the majority has the reflexes of a minority, as in the Flemish case, it can pursue its larger objectives with greater success. Peterjan Gijs, a Leuven architect, explains the reason for disenchantment with Belgium amongst some of his Flemish-speaking compatriots: "Some of my friends ... believe that the francophones of Belgium have never made the effort to understand us."[19] The Flemish have pushed for an ever-greater weakening of the central government, an end of social transfers to Wallonia, and a hardening of language boundaries – this, when the international boundaries of Belgium have largely vanished under Schengen. The underlying logic of Flemish nationalism is ultimately confederal, rather than federal. Belgium, under such an arrangement, would cease to be a shared community of destiny, becoming two communities of destiny with only limited interests to share – and with Brussels as a dangling capital of uncertain status between them. Something of a *coquille vide* (an empty shell) as opposed to a reasonably unified state with a sense of shared solidarity amongst its citizens.

Belgium may be the canary in the mine when it comes to distrust in the relations between sub-state nationalities within multinational states. There is no certainty that Canada, the United Kingdom, or Spain may not encounter similar quandaries in the future. Canada has had its own close encounter with the possibility of Québec secession on at least two occasions, and a number of confrontations with First Nations over treaty and fishing rights. Poll results suggest quite different desiderata for the future between Québec and the rest of Canada.[20] Spain has had the ETA to remind it of where deeper forms of distrust by members of minority nationalities can lead, and more recent conflict with Catalan nationalists over Catalonia's continuing links with Spain. And English-Scottish resentments have their own ways of bubbling to the surface: for example, over an anti-English jibe by Scottish tennis player Andy Murray back in 2006, and over larger questions, such as the United Kingdom's continuing links with the European Union.[21]

My conclusion is that contingency is an inevitable element in the mix that keeps multinational states together. The actions of dominant sub-state nationalities towards subordinate sub-state nationalities, be they in the past or in the present, are mirrored in the behaviour of those same sub-state nationalities subsequently. And shared institutional arrangements are only as secure as the trust that binds the populations of the relevant country together over the long term.[22]

NOTES

1 For the use of the term political geometry in relationship to multinational states, see Hossay (2002: 29–31).

2 "*De taal is gens het volk.*" Cited in Wols (1996: 330). See also Hossay (2002: chapter 4).

3 Sabino Arana, founder of the Basque National Party at the end of the
   nineteenth century, cited in Izquierda (2000: 56).
4 "Suppression breeds opposition, and there is a long history in Catalonia
   of protest and resistance to centralist policies which has helped to maintain Catalanism alive" (Hoffmann 1993: 53).
5 A poll by the Centro de Investigaciones Sociológicas from 1995 shows
   only 28 per cent of residents in the Basque Country with a speaking
   knowledge of Basque versus 79 per cent of the residents of Catalonia with
   a speaking knowledge of Catalan, and 89 per cent of the residents of
   Galicia with a speaking knowledge of Gallego (cited in *Le Courrier
   International*, no. 486, 24 February–1 March 2000).
6 Article 3 of the 1978 Spanish Constitution reads:
   1 Castilian is the official Spanish language of the State. All Spaniards
      have the duty to know it and the right to use it.
   2 The other languages of Spain will also be official in the respective
      autonomous communities, in accordance with their Statutes.
   3 The richness of the linguistic modalities of Spain is a cultural patri-
      mony which will be the object of special respect and protection.
7 The *Orange Sentinel* and the *Manitoba Free Press*, cited in Meisel
   (1998: 98).
8 "Since 2000 Quebec has been increasingly dependent on federal transfer
   payments, such as equalization, to fund its social programs ... In less
   than a decade annual federal transfers to Quebec grew by $7.4 billion ...
   Quebec is more dependent on Ottawa's willingness to fund its social programs than any province outside the Maritimes" (Vaillancourt 2010: 77).
9 This anecdote was related to me by Xavier Arbos Marin, dean of the
   Faculty of Law, University of Gerona.
10 See Julio M. Lazaro in *El Pais*, "El Constitucional aprueba un recorte
   moderado que permite aplicar el Estatuto," 28 June 2010.
11 See "Scottish Independence Referendum, 2014," *Wikipedia*, https://
   en.wikipedia.org/wiki/Scottish_independence_referendum,_2014.
12 See the following BBC articles from 24 June 2016: "EU Referendum
   Results" and "Brexit: Nicola Sturgeon Says Second Scottish Independence
   Vote 'Highly Likely.'"
13 See a recent declaration by Bart de Wever, whose Nieuw-Vlaamse-Alliantie
   is part of the current right-wing Belgian coalition government: "Belgium is
   a failed nation – the failure of a national project, the greatest failure since
   the disappearance of Czechoslovakia and Yugoslavia." *Le Monde*, "Les
   conflits sociaux ébranlent l'exécutif belge," 31 May 2016.
14 The poet Antonio Machado, cited in Tusell (1999: 117)

15 For example, in a 1996 Québec poll, 68 per cent of respondents agreed with the statement "I am profoundly attached to Canada," as opposed to 32 per cent who did not (Pinard 1997: 340).

16 See Keating, *Support for Constitutional Options, Scotland, 1975–2000* (2001: 61, figure 2), showing support for Scottish independence from less than 30 per cent of respondents to most surveys taken over twenty-five years.

17 A 1996 poll by the Centro de Investigaciones Sociológicas showed that 36.5 per cent of respondents saw themselves as equally Catalan and Spanish, the largest single group in this survey of Catalan attitudes towards Catalonia and Spain (McRoberts 2001: 165).

18 Núñez (2001: 740) speaks about approximately equal numbers of those who identify with Spanish or with peripheral nationalism in Catalonia and in the Basque Country.

19 *Libération*, 12 June 2010; our translation.

20 See articles in *Le Devoir*, 7–8 May 2010, highlighting the results of an extensive poll done by Pierre Drouilly for the Bloc Québécois and *Intellectuels pour la Souveraineté* on the twentieth anniversary of the failure of the Meech Lake Accord, showing far greater identification of Canadians outside Québec than of Québec respondents with the federal government, and continuing disagreement between the two on any wholesale transfer of additional powers to Québec. On the other hand, a CROP poll in October 2015 showed diminishing support for Québec independence, especially among the young, though two-thirds of the latter identified themselves as Québécois first and foremost. *Journal de Montréal*, "La souveraineté en perte de vitesse," 28 October 2015.

21 See BBC, "Profile Andy Murray," 2 July 2010; and BBC, "Brexit: Nicola Sturgeon Says Second Scottish Independence Vote 'Highly Likely,'" 24 June 2016.

22 Aughey (2010: 27) reaches a fairly similar conclusion when analyzing the debate about the possible break-up of Britain: "Reviewing the evidence from Scotland, certain trends in national identity seem to imply the break-up of Britain and yet 'the relationship between national identity and support for independence is sufficiently weak' that such a deduction could not be easily drawn ... The future is uncertain."

REFERENCES

Aughey, Arthur. 2010. "From Declinism to Endism: Exploring the Ideology of British Break-Up." *Journal of Political Ideologies* 15, no.1: 11–30.

Bold, Alan. 1983. *Modern Scottish Literature*. London: Longman.

Colley, Linda. 1992. *Britons: Forging the Nation, 1707–1837.* New Haven: Yale University Press.

Davis, Thomas C. 1997. "Patterns of Identity: Basques and the Basque Nation." *Nationalism and Ethnic Politics* 3, no. 1: 61–88.

de Riquer, Borja, and Enric Ucelay-Da Cal. 1994. "An Analysis of Nationalisms in Spain: A Proposal for an Integrated Historical Model. In *Nationalism in Europe Past and Present*, volume 2, edited by Justo Beramendi, Ramon Mais, and Xose Nunez, 275–301. Universidade de Santiago de Compostela, Lugo.

Díaz-Andreu, Margarita. 1994. "The Past in the Present: The Search for Roots in Cultural Nationalism; The Spanish Case." In *Nationalism in Europe Past and Present*, volume 1, edited by Justo Beramendi, Ramon Mais, and Xose Nunez, 199–218. Universidade de Santiago de Compostela, Lugo.

Dominion Institute. 2001. *History Teachers Survey.* http://www.dominion.ca/English/polls.html.

Fishman, Joshua. 1996. "Language and Nationalism." In *Nationalism in Europe 1815 to the Present: A Reader*, edited by Stuart Woolf, 155–70. London: Routledge.

Folch-Serra, Mireay, and Joan Nugue-Font. 2001. "Civil Society, Media, and Globalization in Catalonia." In *Minority Nationalism and the Changing International Order*, edited by Michael Keating and John McGarry, 155–78. Oxford: Oxford University Press.

Fusi, Juan Pablo. 2006. *Identidades proscritas: El no nacionalismo en las sociedades nacionalistas.* Barcelona: Seix Barral.

Heath, A., J. Martin, and G. Elgenius. 2007. "Who Do We Think We Are? The Decline of Traditional Social Identities." In *British Social Attitudes: The 23rd Report; Perspectives on a Changing Society*, edited by A. Park, J. Curtice, K. Thomson, M. Phillips, and M. Johnson, 1–34. London: Sage.

Hermans, Theo, Louis Vos, and Lode Wils, eds. 1992. *The Flemish Movement: A Documentary History 1780–1990.* London: The Athlone Press.

Hoffmann, Charlotte. 1999. "Language, Autonomy and National Identity in Catalonia." In *Whose Europe? The Turn towards Democracy*, edited by Dennis Smith and Sue Wright, 82–8. Oxford: Blackwell.

Hossay, Patrick. 2002. *Contentions of Nationhood: Nationalist Movements, Political Conflict, and Social Change in Flanders, Scotland, and French Canada.* Latham: Lexington Books.

Izquierda, J.-M. 2000. *La question basque.* Brussels: Complexe.

Keating, Michael. 2001. *Plurinational Democracy: Stateless Nations in a Post-Sovereignty Era*. Oxford: Oxford University Press.

Kidd, Colin. 1993. *Subverting Scotland's Past*. Cambridge: Cambridge University Press.

Lamonde, Yvan. 2000. *Histoire sociale des idées au Québec*. Montréal: Fides.

Laponce, Jean. 1987. *Languages and their Territory*. Toronto: University of Toronto Press.

la Rosa, Zhenja. 1995. "Language and Empire: The Vision of Nebrija." *The Loyola University Student Historical Journal* 27: 27–32.

MacCormick. Neil. 1998. "The English Constitution, the British State, and the Scottish Anomaly." *Scottish Affairs* 25, no. 2: 129–45.

McCrone, David. 1998. *The Sociology of Nationalism*. London: Routledge.

McRoberts, Kenneth. 2001. *Catalonia: Nation Building without a State*. Toronto: Oxford University Press.

Meisel, John, Guy Rocher, and Arthur Silver, eds. 1999. *As I Recall/Si je me souviens bien*. Montreal: Institute for Research on Public Policy.

Mill, John Stuart. 1968. *Representative Government*. London: Dent.

Núñez, Xosé-Manuel. 2001. "What Is Spanish Nationalism Today?" *Ethnic and Racial Studies* 24, no. 5: 719–52.

Pinard, Maurice, Robert Bernier, and Vincent Lemieux. 1997. *Un combat Inachevé*. Montréal: Presses de l'Université du Québec.

Pirenne, Henri. 1900. *Histoire de Belgique: Des origines à nos jours*. Brussels: La Renaissance du Livre.

Reicher, Steve, and Nick Hopkins. 2001. *Self and Nation: Categorization, Contestation and Mobilization*. London: Sage.

Tusell, Javier. 1999. *España, Una Angustia Nacional*. Madrid: Espasa.

– 2003. "Historia de una Relación." In *Cataluña-España: Relaciones políticas y culturales*, edited by Xavier Antich, Angel Castiñeira, and Joaquim Colominas, 177–90. Barcelona: Icaria.

Vaillancourt, François, and Mathieu Laberge. 2010. "Quebec: Equitable Yes, Sustainable No." *Inroads*, no. 26: 74–83.

Wils, Lode. 1996. *Historie des nations belges*. Brussels: Quorum.

12

Identity and Political Trust in Multinational Democracies: The Cases of Québec and Catalonia

Réjean Pelletier and Jérôme Couture

"The democratic ideal now reigns unchallenged, but regimes claiming to be democratic come in for vigorous criticism almost everywhere. In this paradox resides the major political problem of our time." This paradox of contemporary democratic life opens Rosanvallon's work, *Counter-Democracy* (2008: 1), as he describes the erosion of citizens' trust in their leaders and political institutions.

This same paradoxical observation also dominates in an article by Catterberg and Moreno (2005: 31), when they write: "Today, the number of societies ruled by a democratic government is larger than ever. Paradoxically, our results show that political trust, understood as citizens' confidence in political institutions, has declined in new democracies during the last two decades and does not seem to have increased in the established ones either."

Many authors have analyzed the decline in trust among citizens, not only with respect to politicians, but also with respect to key political institutions like governments, parliaments, and political parties. According to Pippa Norris (1999a: 21), "The general diagnosis ... confirms that there has been an erosion of public support for the core institutions of representative government, including parties and parliaments in recent decades." In the same volume, Miller and Listhaug (1999: 204) believe that the "empirical evidence dating back to the early 1970s reveals a trend toward growing distrust of government institutions in a number of countries."

Focusing more specifically on American political life, Hetherington (2005: 1) adds: "declining political trust has had such profound effects on American politics that, in many ways, it has defined the American political landscape over the last several decades." Finally, Russell Dalton's observations (2004: 1) are more pessimistic and raise further concerns: "Contemporary democracies are facing a challenge today ... the challenge comes from democracy's own citizens, who have grown distrustful of politicians, sceptical about democratic institutions, and disillusioned about how the democratic process functions."

Yet political trust – more specifically, trust in the political institutions that govern societies – is an essential element for the smooth functioning of modern democracies. When a low level of trust exists, political decision-makers face major constraints that often prevent them from acting. When trust is high, they have more room to manoeuvre, to adopt and implement policies designed to solve specific problems (Kamarck 2009). Citizens who trust their leaders and political institutions are thus more likely to perceive political decisions as acceptable and to comply with them than citizens who do not share such trust.

Moreover, if institutions have low levels of legitimacy, we cannot expect citizens' trust in them to be strong. If the fundamental values and norms that they defend do not coincide with our own, trust in them cannot be high. This is why a low level of political trust that lasts for some time should cause concern, potentially signalling the low legitimacy of political institutions or the non-acceptance of certain norms and values that they defend or represent.

However, not everyone shares this vision. According to some, a new generation of "critical citizens" (Norris 1999a) or "post-materialist citizens" (Inglehart 2008) should force political decision-makers to react to citizens' demands in a more attentive and receptive manner, thereby helping to improve the democratic political system. At the same time, leaders of political institutions should get used to citizens more intently monitoring and examining their work.

Exploring different forms of counter-democracy, Rosanvallon (2008: 23) sees in them "a sort of *counter-policy*, which relies on monitoring, opposition, and limitation of government powers, the conquest of which is no longer the top priority of government opponents." Next to the people-electorate, we find the people-monitor, people-veto, and people-judge. Without wanting to settle this debate, in which contradictory but also complementary visions compete, it is important to point out that, while the exercise of control and opposition are both essential to the functioning of a democratic system, trust is just as essential as a source of support and legitimacy for decision-makers and political institutions.

POLITICAL TRUST

The Two Dimensions of Political Trust

To begin with, it is important to distinguish between interpersonal trust, or the trust we have in others, and trust with respect to political institutions. As Hardin (2006: 69) points out, citizens cannot trust the government in the same way that they trust other citizens. Here, we are focusing on political trust, even though many studies based on the notion of social capital (Putnam 1994, 2002) have successfully established a link between the two.

However, we should note that when they assess trust in political *institutions*, citizens probably refer to the *actors* who inhabit the institutions and carry out actions undertaken in the name of those institutions. Thus, trust in the provincial or federal government cannot be dissociated in the Canadian parliamentary system from the trust people have in whoever is the prime minister at the time (including by comparison with other prime ministers they have known). The same applies to parliaments, the public service, and the courts, the "raw" knowledge we have of which is most often the product of the media or discussions with friends and family. This raw knowledge is then filtered and shaped according to a number of factors, such as personal knowledge and experience acquired over the years, or one's interest in politics, partisan leanings, social environment, level of education, age, dominant values, political community, and so on: everything, in short, that combines to gradually mold a citizen.

In the tradition of the work developed by Easton (1965), political trust can be compared to a reservoir of (diffuse or specific) public support that makes it possible for actors in roles of authority to achieve certain objectives through the imperative allocation of resources, especially via the adoption and implementation of public policy. Political trust then makes it possible for allocation of resources requests, or "inputs," to be transformed by the system into public policies, or "outputs," thus impacting the level of support people have in the political system. From this perspective, trust equates to an individual's willingness to support public policy proposed by political leaders (Warren 1999). From an *instrumental* perspective on political trust, this is what allows actors to achieve their objectives, since the population supports them and rewards them with their trust.

A contrario, other authors argue that political trust finds its origin outside of the political sphere. Fukuyama (1995) suggests that political support is more closely related to a community's "will to live together." More precisely, he links trust to the social capital that can develop in a dynamic civil society. Such a civil society, beyond the state, is the source of a national culture and its set of traditions, which flow from family, religion, community solidarity, or a "will to live together," and translate into common values shared with others. In this sense, political trust linked to this form of support represents a level of endorsement of a society's central values. It is a *normative* perspective on political trust. In other words, political support would be, to a large degree, determined by individuals' level of trust in relation to other members of the community and their adherence to societal norms that are foundational to a shared identity. This form of support for the community then cultivates political trust. A satisfactory definition of political trust should therefore incorporate these two dimensions of trust.

Balme, Marie, and Rozenberg (2003) also base their analysis on this twofold dimension of trust. Envisaging political trust as "the product of a reciprocal relationship between the governors and the governed," they first emphasize the relationship between the preferences of citizens and the actions of authorities, which we previously referred to as the *instrumental* dimension of political trust, or the relationship between "public actions' performance, and citizens' political demands" (2003: 435; our translation). Second, they link trust to the relationship between "knowledge and political evaluation" (2003: ibid.), which we have translated as the *normative* dimension of political trust. This normative evaluation can be based on various criteria, such as the principles and values that guide us.

From their analysis, Balme, Marie, and Rozenberg conclude that "the two initial perspectives explaining contemporary distrust in politics, that of poor performance with respect to public action and that of a values crisis, finally have to be combined in the interpretation" (2003: 458; our translation). They add that "overall trust requires a dual feeling that the public action has been performed appropriately and that norms have been met" (ibid.). This is also consistent with Hardin's terms (2006: 70) when he distinguishes between the two dimensions of political trust (especially with respect to government): "competence to perform what one is trusted to do and motivation to perform." If these two dimensions – competency and motivation – are combined in a negative manner, trust will then be at its weakest.

We can also see this dual dimension of political trust from another angle. Indeed, the concept of trust is essentially relational: A trusts B, who has to prove worthy of that trust. Translated into the political sphere, this relationship takes the following form: individuals give their trust to an institution that could possibly betray them. If an institution (or a political player) is not trustworthy, we cannot expect that the level of trust will be high. Trust is thus not unconditional. It is given to specific institutions in specific areas. It therefore flows from an individual judgment concerning the potential that an institution is worthy of its mission.

Levi and Stoker (2000), Hetherington (2005), and Hardin (2006) attribute two dimensions to this potential. On the one hand, there is an assessment of the *capacity* (in the sense of aptitude or ability), or motivation, of a political institution to act in the interests of those who place their trust in it. At this level, the assessment concerns norms defended by the political institution (for example, protecting public interest), or is related to a judgment about the *legitimacy* of the institution (for example, the legitimacy of an institution in a multinational federation). Indeed, if citizens feel that a political institution is not legitimate, how can they trust it? In this sense, the legitimacy that a political institution is acknowledged as having can be a source of trust in it, whereas the absence of legitimacy can be a source of distrust of the institution. Such an assessment of capacity corresponds to the *normative* dimension of political trust.

On the other hand, the assessment can also be related to a judgment about the institution's *competency* in areas where trust is attributed – areas like economic performance or the fulfilment of electoral promises. At this level, judgments concern the quality of the institution's actions. Competency corresponds to the *instrumental* dimension of political trust. In summary, the expression of trust is based on individuals reflecting on their political experiences. The concept of trust in political institutions makes it possible to measure how political institutions and actors have performed with respect to the normative and instrumental expectations of citizens and whether they have thereby merited the trust being placed in them.

The Dynamics of Political Trust

Hetherington (2005: 66–7) uses the "babysitter" analogy to highlight the causal dynamics surrounding political trust in relation to the concept's two dimensions. It is expressed in the following terms:

> Any new parent can tell you that deciding on a babysitter is difficult business. Your child is precious, and this decision carries a high degree of risk. If you choose poorly, the consequences could be catastrophic. Hence you need to have significant trust to leave your baby with another person. In all likelihood, you will choose someone that you have had some previous experience with, whether it be a friend, or, more helpful for my purposes, someone who has done other work for you in the past.

Trust plays two roles in the choice of a babysitter. On the one hand, it plays a role in evaluating their ability to do the work. Thus, it is easier to leave your child in the hands of someone you already know than in the hands of a stranger. On the other hand, the evaluation of the person's competency will determine your trust that the person will do the work a second time. Indeed, a person who has been entrusted with a task and has fulfilled their mission in a satisfactory manner will have better chances of being rehired.

We can thus distinguish two sets of factors that determine political trust in line with the dimensions described above. The first factors relate to an assessment of the capacity and legitimacy of political institutions, and can be associated with *cultural* theories. Such theories postulate that dominant public philosophy or central values exist with respect to political institutions and are transmitted by socialization (Norris 1999b). Thus, the themes of ideology (left-right), social capital (Putnam 2000), post-materialism (Inglehart 1997, 2008), and the meaning of *national identity* (in both unitary and multinational states) are features that can explain deeply anchored differences between levels of trust. Here, we are interested in the relationship between national identity and political trust, and not in verifying all these cultural theories, which would go far beyond the scope of this text.

Table 12.1
Theoretical framework

Dimensions of trust	Indicators	Variables
Normative	Capacity-legitimacy	National identity
Instrumental	Competency	Government performance

.The second factors are related to the competence of political institutions, which we can associate with theories about government *performance*. Theories related to government performance postulate that trust is not a stable phenomenon. It changes with citizens' demands and a government's fulfilment of electoral promises (Norris 1999b: 218). Therefore, trust reflects citizens' level of satisfaction with government. Themes such as economic performance (McAllister 1999) and government responses to the salient social issues, which Hetherington and Rudolph (2008) also call "priming,"[1] would be determining factors for the level of political trust, and would above all explain short-term fluctuations in trust (which does not prevent us from analyzing specific issues, e.g., the economy, over the long term).

Table 12.1 summarizes the framework for theoretical analysis, based on the two dimensions – normative and instrumental – of political trust.

How Can Trust Be Measured?

Some authors study political trust in relation to many institutions taken separately. However, there is an endogenous relationship between these variables (Chanley, Rudolph, and Rahn 2000), in the sense that trust in these different institutions co-varies in accordance with events. Thus, some authors argue that political trust should not be understood as uniquely linked to government (Levi and Stoker 2000).

In the same sense, we consider it appropriate to measure political trust in relation to more than the government alone. We will thus proceed in two different ways: first, by comparing the specific level of trust in government, and then by comparing general political trust in relation to a set of political institutions (such as political parties, the public service, and the courts) that are associated with the central governments in Canada and Spain. It is not possible to obtain exactly the same data for both countries, but we have attenuated this problem by constructing an index (alpha) with a strong congruence in both cases. The elements forming this index for each country can be found in the tables.

NATIONAL IDENTITY AND MINORITY NATION

In Search of National Identity

National identity has been at the heart of much recent research related to European integration. Some have wondered whether national identity is an obstacle to European integration (Carey 2002) or whether citizens of the European Union feel that European integration threatens their national identity (McLaren 2004). Others, basing their reflection on Putnam's social capital theory, wonder whether the ethnic heterogeneity in Europe affects trust not only with respect to other ethnic groups living within national borders, but also with respect to members of one's own ethnic group, which has become more diverse (Gerritsen and Lubbers 2010).

The present text is not guided by these approaches to national identity research. Instead, we will ask whether, in multinational societies, the minority national identity has an impact on political trust, defined here as trust in political institutions.

Bhikhu Parekh (1995: 255–7) has identified four different meanings of "national identity." The first associates identity with difference, with what distinguishes us from others, which he considers to be insufficient as a notion. The second associates national identity with self-knowledge, with the conception one has of oneself as an entity or political community, which Parekh feels overlooks other factors that shape identity. The third associates national identity with the political entity's values, goals, and commitments, which simply makes identity a shared undertaking and translates into a rationalist vision.

Parekh favours the fourth meaning of national identity: namely, national identity as an internal structure and set of central organizational principles that constitute a polity. "National identity refers to the way a polity is constituted, to what makes it the kind of community it is" (1995: 257). However, from his list of everything that constitutes national identity, we can conclude that, in the end, this broader conception of identity includes the three others in one form or another.[2]

More important to us is the way in which Parekh links the cultural dimension (the shared way of life) and the political dimension (the shared mode of conducting its collective affairs) in the identity of a society organized in a territorial manner, while highlighting the fact that such an identity is both cultural and political. "A territorially organized society is both a cultural and a political community ... Its cultural identity lies in the character of its shared way of life, its political identity in the way its political life is constituted" (1995: 260).

We focus above all on the political dimension of national identity, while being aware that it also has a major cultural dimension. In other words, national identity rests on the existence of a community that is linked by "blood and belonging"[3] and based on sharing the same land, culture, historical symbols, economic resources, political rights, and, ideally, political institutions. In this sense, the concept of a minority nation as defined by Kymlicka is very useful for understanding the minority's form of national identity, or "the way its political life is constituted." In both of the cases being analyzed, the minority nation has its own political institutions that act as constituting elements of the minority's identity and political life.

Kymlicka (1998: 2) defines a minority nation (or national minority) in the following way: "By 'national minority' I mean a historical society, with its own language and institutions, whose territory has been incorporated (often involuntarily, as in the case with Québec) into a larger country." In addition to the Québécois, his examples include the First Nations in Canada, and the Catalans, Basques, and Flemish in Europe. These communities consider themselves to be separate nations because they have had to struggle to survive and not be assimilated into the majority nation (ibid.). The concept of minority nation thus refers to those whose territory has been incorporated into a larger whole, and who have a national identity based (among other things) on language, history, culture, and institutions.

We prefer the term "minority nation" to "national minority" because it highlights the fact that the minority nation cannot be defined as a sub-category of the majority nation, as the metaphor of concentric circles (or Russian dolls) could lead one to suppose. That metaphor inappropriately describes the reality. It is obvious that all Québécois are Canadian citizens and included in the Canadian state, but they do not all have the feeling of belonging or of being included in the "Canadian nation." In other words, it is important to distinguish between inclusive shared citizenship, and a nationality (in the sense of belonging to a nation) that may or may not be shared.

The metaphor of overlapping circles is more appropriate for this reality because it makes it possible to maintain an exclusive majority national identity or an exclusive minority national identity, or two overlapping identities. This is the case for the Québécois in Canada and the Catalans in Spain.

In order to describe these different realities, some have also used the concept of nested nationalities (Miller 2001: 304) or nested identities (Keating 2001: 46), while keeping in mind that "national identity can exist at more than one level" (Miller 2001: 306). However, how should we understand the minority nation and overlapping identities? As Keating (2001: 45–6) points out,

> in places like Scotland and Quebec, there is a whole range of attitudes, from those who consider themselves exclusively Scottish or Québécois, to those (very few in number) who consider themselves exclusively British or Canadian. In between are a diminishing number who consider themselves Canadian or British, and Québécois or Scottish as a subset of this; and a growing number who consider themselves primarily Scottish or Québécois, with Britain and Canada seen more as instrumental identities than as primary ties. These are all territorially based national identities.

How Should National Identity Be Measured?

Some make a distinction between self-identification and shared identity (Festenstein 2009: 283). The first appeals to a sense of solidarity, shared goals and projects, or even the emotional weight related to national belonging. The second refers to language, culture, and shared beliefs. While our survey is based on self-identification (how one defines oneself), it is difficult to dissociate it from an identity shared with others on the basis of a common language, culture, or history – factors that are often at the foundation of shared solidarity and common collective undertakings.

From our point of view, the central problem is knowing whether the majority nation encompasses the minority nation or nations. If members of the majority nation say they include all citizens in the country, do all members of the minority nation share the feeling that they belong to a single central political community? In order to answer this question, surveys have often used the way that members of the minority nation define themselves, which has also been called the Moreno question after the person who popularized it. This question usually has five possible answers, from identification with only the majority nation or only the minority nation (single identity), to various forms of identification with both the minority and majority nations (double identity).

However, the following problem then arises: How should these different categories be grouped? In reference to his first works, Luis Moreno (2007) brings out the "dual" aspect of national identity or "composite nationality" in relation to this question. According to him, more generally, the problem is that of the compatibility of "the sub-state/ethno-regional identity and the nation/state identity " (502). His research showed that identity duality exists in Scotland (this was shown by grouping together the three categories concerning double identity), but that it was far lower than the identity duality of the Catalans.[4]

Others, such as David McCrone (cited in Moreno 2007: 507), have insisted more on "regional identity" (or, perhaps we should more precisely say, the identity of the minority nation) by grouping together the first two categories, thereby showing that Scottish identity was stronger than British identity. Taking the example of Québec in the Canadian federation, this way of doing things consists of grouping together, on one side, the two groups that define themselves first as Québécois, and, on the other side, the two groups that define themselves first as Canadians, and finally, between these poles, positioning a third category of people who define themselves as *equally* Québécois and Canadian. This way of grouping is based on the idea that one definition of nationality (Québécois or Canadian) dominates the other in two clearly differentiated groups, while in the third group people cannot choose between membership in one nation or the other, since they place them on the same footing. This is the most usual way of doing it. However, this grouping raises the following problem: among those who define themselves first as Québécois, how can we make a distinction between those who refuse to define themselves by double belonging (i.e., they are first and foremost Québécois), and those who accept double belonging (i.e., they are first Québécois but also Canadian)? The same problem arises for those who define themselves primarily as being Canadian.

This is why we have chosen a different approach. While it is partly in accordance with Moreno's initial concerns about double identity,

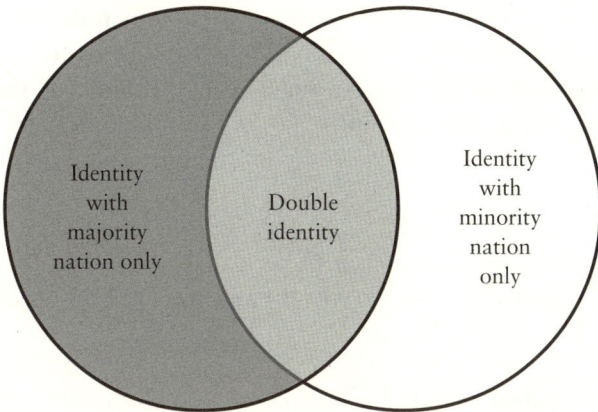

Figure 12.1 Identification with majority or minority nations by individuals belonging to the minority

we focus less on that aspect, and more on the opposition (with respect to political trust) between single belonging and double identity. More precisely, we concentrate on *single* belonging, expressed in the form of Québécois only or Canadian only, in contrast with *double* identity, in whatever form or combination (some place the emphasis on being Québécois first, others on being Canadian, and others put both on the same level since they are unable to rank them). It is thus the opposition between single and double identity that interests us here.

In other words, identity is a measure of attachment to a community of reference. The attachment determines individuals' expectations of, and support for, policies adopted by the central government. In a multinational context, an individual belonging to the minority may identify more with the country that is the larger political unit, or more with the minority nation that is the polity included in the country, or with both communities at once (see figure 12.1).

By conducting statistical analyses of political trust, we found that differences are more marked when we use this second form of grouping, affirming our approach.[5]

Proceeding from these theoretical considerations, we plan to answer the following general question: Among members of the minority nations of Québec and Catalonia, does the way one defines oneself – by a single or double identity – have an impact on trust in central political institutions and in the minority nation's institutions?

The distinctions we established above make it possible for us to posit two hypotheses. Indeed, individuals strongly identifying with a minority nation would have stronger recognition needs than other individuals. Among other things, they would judge as less legitimate the political institutions identified with the central government.

Hypothesis 1: Individuals identifying *uniquely* with the minority nation would have less trust in the central government than would other individuals, and, conversely, they would have more trust in the minority nation's government.

Hypothesis 2: Individuals identifying solely with the minority nation would have less trust in the different political institutions associated with the central government than would other individuals.

How Should Government Performance Be Measured?

The effect of public policy on government performance has been a major concern in political science (McAllister 1999). Studies have focused mainly on the role of the economy. For example, it has been demonstrated that governments perceived as delivering economic well-being and prosperity are more likely to be re-elected (Lewis-Beck 1990; Fiorina 1981). Among other things, the government's position on political issues would be a determining factor for the level of trust. Most studies on the link between preferences in public policy and trust in institutions have used Downs's model (1957). These studies place the emphasis on the difference between individual preferences and subjective evaluation of the government's position based on the line drawn between the left and the right (Miller 1974; King 1997; Miller and Listhaug 1998).

However, Dalton (2004: 143) questions this very broad conception of the link between preferences and trust in institutions.

> We suggested that a conversation with a typical citizen in California, Paris, or Sydney would find agreement on the poor policy performance of government. If one pursued the conversation, however, I think certain differences would appear. You both might agree that government is performing poorly, but when you talk about specifics you would probably find that you have different policy examples in mind. While one person is concerned

with the government's shortfalls in social programmes, the other might feel that not enough is being done to protect the environment, or that taxes are too high, or that government is not correctly dealing with globalization issues.

According to Dalton (2004), government performance should be analyzed by looking at its work on societal issues first. Hypothesis 3 conveys this perspective on the relationship between government performance and political trust. However, there are a number of measures of government performance. Among other things, measurements vary from one database to the next. We suggest indicators of satisfaction with government performance for Québec and Catalonia that measure satisfaction with the government's work in relation to *specific* issues. The indicators and coding of this variable can be found in the appendix.

Hypothesis 3: The more satisfied an individual is with government performance, the more trust he/she will have in public institutions.

DATA

Our data comes from two major sources. Data on Québec and Canada comes from our own surveys of Canadians (aged eighteen and over), and from similar surveys done in Spain and Catalonia.[6]

RESULTS

First, it is important to establish distinctions between the majority and the minority, especially in countries where one of the communities clearly dominates, as in Canada and Spain. As Miller notes (2001: 305): "Whereas people who belong to one of the minor nationalities will typically endorse a dual identity, those belonging to the numerically dominant group are likely to identify themselves nationally only with the inclusive units." If this is the case, we can expect that trust in central political institutions would be stronger among those who identify with the majority nation than those who belong to the minority nation. Since the minority nation is concentrated in a specific territory (this is one of Kymlicka's criteria; see also Keating 2001: 44), we are going to use a *territorial* criterion to distinguish the minority from the majority – that is, Québec from Canada and Catalonia

Table 12.2
Trust in the central government among members of a majority or minority

Minority/majority	Level of trust	
Canada	Canadian federal government	
	2005	2010
Québec	1.16	1.12
Canada outside Québec	1.40	1.35
F	28.80***	9.24**
Gamma	-0.21	-0.15
Spain	Spanish central government	
	1999	2007
Catalonia	1.13	1.39
Spain not including the historical communities[1]	1.49	1.40
F	27.85***	0.11[NS]
Gamma	-0.36	-0.02

* $p < 0.05$; ** $p < 0.01$; *** $p < 0.001$; NS: Not significant

1 Spain not including Catalonia, the Basque Country, and Galicia.

Sources: Our survey (2005, 2010); Spain World Values Survey (1999, 2007).

from Spain. The majority will thus be defined as Canadians outside Québec, and, in Spain, by the Spanish outside the three historical communities (Catalonia, the Basque country, and Galicia).

Table 12.2 shows the findings on trust in the central government, according to whether the respondent belonged to the minority or the majority. Our hypothesis is only partly verified. As we expected, the Québécois have less trust in the central government than the majority: the differences between the two groups are statistically significant, both in 2005 and in 2010, with a moderate gamma. This was also the case in Catalonia in 1999, where the difference between the Catalans and other Spanish people (excluding the three historical communities) was significant and had a stronger gamma in Spain than in Canada. However, this was not the case in 2007: at that time, Catalans had the same amount of trust in the central government as other Spaniards. How can this situation be explained?

We think that the most plausible explanation is related to the government in power at the time of the survey. In 1999, the People's Party (PP), a right-wing party, had been in power in Spain since March 1996, with a weak majority. Even though it was governing with the support of the Basque Nationalist Party and the Catalan CiU, the PP was not supportive of decentralizing powers to the autonomous communities. Instead, it advocated a strong central government – a position unlikely to rally the support of a majority of Catalans. In 2007, the Spanish Socialist Workers' Party (PSOE), led by Prime Minister Zapatero, had been in power since 2004, and Spain had been experiencing a period of great economic prosperity during its rule. Moreover, the PSOE had also won the elections in Catalonia in November 2003. Finally, it was during this period, in 2006, that a stronger autonomous status for Catalonia was accepted by the Zapatero government, and was submitted to a referendum in June in which the "Yes" side won with 73.9 per cent of the votes (but with a low voter turnout of 49 per cent). All of these events combined to clearly increase Catalans' level of trust in the central government. The level of trust then matched that of other Spaniards in the 2007 survey, whereas the difference between the two was greater in 1999.

Beyond this initial view of political trust within a minority nation, we need to further analyze such trust in relation to central and regional institutions, this time taking into account *identity* – single or double – among members of the minority nation. We expect that those who have a single minority identity will have less trust in central institutions than other people, and greater trust in the institutions of the minority nation. Tables 12.3 and 12.4 show such trust felt by the Québec and Catalan minority nations with respect to the central government (Ottawa and Madrid), and with respect to governments representing the minority nation (Québec City and Barcelona).

We can draw a few general conclusions from these tables. First, the findings confirm our initial hypothesis that individuals who identify uniquely with the minority nation have less trust in the central government than other individuals. This is especially the case in Québec, in both 2005 and 2010, and partially in Catalonia (it was the case in 2009, but not in 2006 for the reasons mentioned above). Inversely, the same individuals with single identities (Québécois or Catalan) always have more trust in the minority nation's government than they do in the central government. This is verified in both Québec and

Table 12.3
Québec minority trust in the central and minority governments

Identity of the minority nation	Level of trust		
Québec 2010	Trust in the federal government	Trust in the provincial government	Mean difference
Québécois only (96)	0.73	1.15	-0.42***
Double identity (199)	1.31	1.17	0.14*
Canadian only (52)	1.46	1.16	0.30*
F	20.84***	0.02	16.09***
Gamma	-0.43	-0.02	-0.42
Québec 2005	Trust in the federal government	Trust in the provincial government	Mean difference
Québécois only (135)	0.58	0.73	-0.15*
Double identity (277)	1.38	1.34	0.04
Canadian only (39)	1.37	1.22	-0.15
F	50.82***	30.85***	-3.67*
Gamma	-0.57	-0.44	-0.20

* $p < 0.05$; ** $p < 0.01$; *** $p < 0.001$

Source: Our survey (2005, 2010).

Catalonia. The differences are statistically significant and stronger in 2009–10 than in 2005–06.

The findings also allow us to draw a second conclusion: the group that defines itself as having a *double* identity usually has more trust than the other two groups in the central government and in the regional government, although the findings for this were stronger in 2005–06. It was no longer the case in 2009–10: at that time, it was only those who defined themselves uniquely in terms of their membership in the majority nation who had more trust in the central government. The latter finding is more consistent with our expectations.

Finally, among those who agreed to define themselves, there was a slight drop in the percentage who identified themselves only as Québécois (29.9 per cent in 2005 and 27.7 per cent in 2010), but a strong increase in those who identified themselves as Canadian only (8.6 per cent in 2005, but 15 per cent in 2010). In Catalonia, however,

Table 12.4
Catalan minority trust in the central and minority governments

Identity of the minority nation	Level of trust		
Catalonia 2009	Trust in the Spanish government	Trust in the Catalan government	Mean difference
Catalan only (195)	1.02	1.41	-0.39***
Double identity (803)	1.33	1.54	-0.21***
Spanish only (88)	1.47	1.46	0.01NS
F	19.19***	3.37*	16.71***
Gamma	-0.27	-0.10	-0.28
Catalonia 2006	Trust in the Spanish government	Trust in the Catalan government	Mean difference
Catalan only (101)	1.52	1.64	-0.12*
Double identity (1482)	1.54	1.67	-0.13***
Spanish only (161)	1.39	1.32	0.07
F	3.49*	15.22***	6.14**
Gamma	0.11	0.19	-0.12

* $p < 0.05$; ** $p < 0.01$; *** $p < 0.001$; NS: Not significant

Source: Institut de Ciències Polítiques i Socials (2006, 2009).

there was a major rise – threefold, in fact – in the number of people who identified themselves as Catalan only (5.8 per cent in 2006 against 17.6 per cent in 2009). However, we should not forget that double identity, no matter how the identities are ranked, was always much stronger than single identity, especially in Catalonia, but also in Québec.

It seems more interesting to go beyond this initial level of analysis focusing on trust in government, which is always more sensitive to day-to-day political realities, such as decisions made and policies adopted. In order to do this, we have created an indicator composed of a *set* of political institutions at the central level (there is a strong match between these institutions in Canada – alpha 0.81 and 0.76, respectively – and in Spain – alpha 0.70 and 0.72), and we have sought to measure the influence of *identity* on trust in this set. However, the

Table 12.5
Trust in central political institutions

Minority nation		Political trust index		
Québec	(N)	Supreme court, army, federal public service, federal political parties, federal parliament, federal government		
Alpha	0.76	2010	0.81	2005
Québécois only	(92)	1.25	(125)	0.99
Double identity	(185)	1.54	(261)	1.56
Canadian only	(47)	1.57	(33)	1.39
F		9.35***		46.20***
Gamma		-0.26		-0.44
Catalonia	(N)	Courts, army, central government, political parties		
Alpha	0.72	2009	0.70	2006
Catalan only	(165)	1.00	(88)	1.19
Double identity	(654)	1.25	(1255)	1.32
Spanish only	(71)	1.28	(135)	1.26
F		16.46***		3.59*
Gamma		-0.23		-0.01

* $p < 0.05$; ** $p < 0.01$; *** $p < 0.001$

Sources: Our survey (2005, 2010); Institut de Ciències Politiques i Socials (2006, 2009).

available data does not allow us to create such an indicator for the political institutions of the minority nation itself.

Table 12.5 shows trust in this set of central institutions, taking *identity* into account within the minority nation. The findings are consistent with those we obtained in the preceding tables. Trust is always lower, as our second hypothesis predicted, among those who identify only with the minority nation, in both Québec and Catalonia. In 2005–06, trust was higher among those who shared a double identity, but in 2009–10 it was higher among those identifying uniquely with the majority nation. In all cases, the differences were statistically significant.

To put this in different terms, with respect to trust in central political institutions, there was little difference between those with double identity and those who identify with the majority nation only, especially in 2009–10. Those who defined themselves as belonging only to the minority nation were clearly differentiated from the other two groups since they had much less trust in central political institutions, which is consistent with our expectations. These findings also show that in Québec there was an increase in trust in central institutions from 2005 to 2010 among those who identify themselves only with the majority nation (and also that there were more people who defined themselves as having a single Canadian identity). In Catalonia, we saw a reduction in trust in central institutions from 2006 to 2009 among those who only identify with the minority nation (and growth in the number of those with single Catalan identity).

In summary, no matter how we consider central political institutions (as the government or as a set of institutions), we find that *identity* always influences trust in those institutions.

One last question remains: does the normative dimension of trust, which we measured using identity here, provide a better explanation for trust in central political institutions than the instrumental dimension measured by government performance? To answer this, we will use a regression analysis controlling for socio-economic variables (age, sex, level of education) and, following Pippa Norris (1999: 218–21), for the situation of *winner* or *loser* in the last election, which is part of the instrumental dimension of trust. We will also add *interest* in politics (which does not, according to our findings, have a statistically significant effect) and the *language usually spoken* (which also does not have a significant impact, except in Catalonia in 2009 – we will come back to this). As we indicated in hypothesis 3, satisfaction with government performance should improve trust in political institutions. This should also be the case for those who are "winners" on the political level.

Another important factor has been added to the normative dimension: *cynicism*. It can be defined as the belief or perception that others (political actors or institutions) are motivated only by their own interests or by the interest of a few major players, rather than by the general interest (see also Hardin 2006: 63–4). In this sense, cynicism (or the indicator used to define it empirically) is not sufficient to define trust, because it is only the negative side of trust (in other words, distrust). Likewise, the opposite of cynicism can also be part of trust, but only partially.

Table 12.6
Index of political trust (OLS method)

	Québec				Catalonia			
	2005		2010		2006		2009	
	b	t	b	t	b	t	b	t
Constant	2.06	17.04***	1.85	12.61***	1.32	30.55***	1.27	24.44***
Sex (1 = male)	0.02	0.48	-0.06	-1.02	-0.05	-1.90	-0.04	-1.34
Age (1 = 45&+)	-0.07	-1.53	-0.10	-1.77	0.02	0.58	-0.04	-1.33
Education (1 = University)	0.05	1.08	0.07	1.15	-0.04	-1.29	-0.04	-1.06
Language usually spoken (1 = French or Catalan)	-0.10	-1.66	0.03	0.38	-0.04	-1.32	-0.10	-2.78**
Interest in politics	0.07	1.39	-0.03	-0.52	0.00	0.16	-0.00	-0.10
Government performance	0.29	5.10***	0.32	4.66***	0.40	14.34***	0.53	11.66***
Winner (1 = voted for the ruling party)	0.20	3.51***	0.29	3.70***	0.12	4.24***	0.13	3.87***
Cynicism index	-0.29	-6.55***	-0.22	-5.17***	-0.18	-5.76***	-0.11	-2.95**
Minority identity only	-0.36	-6.16***	-0.16	-2.32*	-0.11	-2.08*	-0.14	-3.00**
Majority identity only	-0.07	-0.78	0.20	2.07*	-0.00	-0.08	-0.06	-1.03
N	393		295		1460		856	
Adjusted R^2	0.38		0.27		0.20		0.23	

* P < 0.05 ** P < 0.01 *** P < 0.001

Sources: Our survey (2005, 2010); Institut de Ciències Politiques i Socials (2006, 2009).

Table 12.6 is instructive in a number of ways. First, we can point out that the instrumental dimension measured by government *performance* has a strong *positive* effect on those who express trust in central political institutions. This applies to both minority nations that we studied, especially in Catalonia. This is consistent with the conclusions of other authors, such as McAllister (1999), who analyze government performance in different countries. In this respect, we can add that, within a minority nation, the group with double identity is larger and usually demonstrates greater trust in central political institutions. This has an impact on the overall findings.

We should also note that being a winner (having voted for the governing party) has a significant positive impact on trust in central political institutions in both Québec and Catalonia. This factor can be associated with government performance in the sense that citizens may be all the more satisfied with the work done by the party in power if it is the party that they voted for in the preceding election. These two factors (performance and being in a winning situation) thus exert influence in the same direction, and have major positive impacts on trust in political institutions.

Moreover, as we might expect, those who identify *uniquely* with the minority nation have *less* trust in central political institutions. This was the case in Québec in 2005, when this factor and cynicism were stronger than all the others, including trust in government performance. In Catalonia also, the relationship goes in the expected direction with respect to minority identity and cynicism. Indeed, we should note that *cynicism* was always the strongest explanatory factor for distrust, except in Catalonia in 2009 when Catalan identity was the most important. It should also be noted that in Québec in 2010, another explanatory factor was identification with the *majority* nation only, which, as we expected, had a positive impact on political trust. However, the overall effect of identity was the same in 2010 as in 2005.

With respect to socio-economic variables in Québec, the oldest have the least trust. This was also the case in Catalonia in 2009. In contrast, those with the highest level of education in Québec had the most trust, whereas in Catalonia they had the least. However, in all cases the findings were never statistically significant. We therefore cannot take them into account as explanatory factors since there were others that were stronger.

Overall, we can identify the following profiles, only taking into account statistically significant factors. These profiles are very similar in Québec and Catalonia, and are verified for the two periods studied:

- In Québec, those who are satisfied with government performance and who voted for the governing party show the greatest trust in central political institutions; those who identify themselves as Québécois only and those who are cynical have less trust or express greater distrust in such institutions. This profile was verified in both 2005 and 2010 (with a major clarification concerning 2010, mentioned in the conclusion below).

· In Catalonia, those who are satisfied with government performance and who voted for the governing party have greater trust in central political institutions; those who identify uniquely as Catalan and those who are cynical have less trust. This profile was verified both in 2006 and in 2009 (but here also some clarifications are required concerning 2009).

CONCLUSION

From this set of findings, we can draw four broad conclusions. First, trust in central political institutions (the government or a set of institutions) is lower among those who identify *only* with the minority nation, but they have greater trust in minority nation institutions (the government). This finding is consistent with our expectations and does not really shock us. The opposite would have been very surprising.

As we have shown, the single-identity group has specific forms of behaviour that distinguish it clearly from the other two groups. Having less trust in central political institutions, it is probably the group that is most ready to question the political structures of the central government, favouring greater autonomy or greater political sovereignty for the minority nation. This is therefore the group that poses the greatest threat to the central government. As Keating notes (2001: 46), national identities "may compete, in which case there is a potential for conflict." This is the case here since the conflict between the two identities is now resolved: the identity of the minority nation is the only one claimed, and it excludes membership in the majority nation.

At the same time, in the absence of the political changes that they desire, it is probable that these citizens, who define themselves uniquely through their membership in the minority nation, are becoming increasingly cynical towards central political institutions in the sense that they do not believe that these institutions serve the general interest or the minority nation with which they identify. This could explain why these two factors (cynicism and single minority identity) are identifiers of strong political distrust. These two characteristics are found in both Québec and Catalonia.

Second, *double identity* rallies the greatest number of people in the two minority nations studied here – approximately three out of four Catalans and six out of ten Québécois. With respect to trust in central political institutions, those who identify themselves as having a double identity resemble those who identify uniquely with the *majority* nation, except that sometimes they express greater trust. They seem satisfied with both their dual belonging and the political institutions that govern them, at both the central and regional levels. For them, the political arrangements, whether in the form of greater autonomy or federation, merit their trust. This has already been noted by Keating (2001: 46), who writes that national identities "may be nested, in which case the problem is less acute, and can be accommodated through federal arrangements."

Moreover, these nested identities and nationalities do not flow from ambiguous thinking or conflicted membership feelings. As Miller points out (2001: 304), those with a split identity "think of themselves as belonging both to the smaller community and to the larger one, and they do not experience this as schizophrenic, because their two identities fit together reasonably well." Given the preceding results on political trust, central government leaders of multinational states should accept and recognize this double identity, which is a source of trust, instead of opposing or ignoring it.

Third, by analyzing trust in the central political institutions of these two multinational states, we find that the normative dimension of trust related to *cynicism* (closely followed by *minority identity* in 2005) is stronger than the instrumental dimension and other explanatory factors in Québec; while the *instrumental* dimension related to the government's performance is more important in Catalonia, compared with other explanatory factors, including identity. The instrumental dimension is more closely related to economic events and ruling governments, and as such is more susceptible to variations over time than identity or even cynicism, which are based on individuals' more deeply anchored values. In this sense, the situation in Québec would be more problematic for the Canadian federation than that of Catalonia for Spain.

Finally, recent changes have occurred (2009–10) in these two multinational countries. In Catalonia, single identification with the Catalan nation (which is growing) and use of Catalan as an everyday language were stronger in 2009 than in 2006 as explanatory factors for greater distrust in central political institutions. In other words, in recent years,

Catalan identity has become a more important element in Spain's political trust-distrust dynamic.

In Québec, by contrast, the opposite has occurred. In 2005, single Québec identity and cynicism were major explanatory factors for distrust. In 2010, the situation had changed greatly: cynicism (related also to government integrity issues, especially in Québec) was clearly greater, and single identification with the Québec nation played a smaller role. Moreover, there was a new factor in Québec: those who identified themselves as Canadians only, who were a bigger group than in 2005, expressed (statistically significant) greater trust in central political institutions. In short, cynicism became a more important explanation for distrust and single identification with the Québec nation became less important, owing to a new factor in 2010: sole identification with the Canadian nation. However, as we pointed out above, the *overall* impact of the identity factor on political trust was the same in 2010 as in 2005. We will have to wait and see whether this trend will continue or even increase in the future, which would certainly change the political face of Québec and Canada.

APPENDIX

CODING

1. POLITICAL TRUST INDEX

Québec
Question:
   Now I am going to name some organizations in Canada. For each of them, please tell me whether you have a great deal of confidence (3), some confidence (2), little confidence (1) or no confidence at all (0) in them.
Institutions: Federal political parties, Supreme Court, army, federal public service, federal government, federal parliament.
Operating definition: (political parties + Supreme Court + army + public service + government + parliament)/6
Scale (0–3)
Catalonia
Question:
   Now, thinking about Spain's political institutions, please use the 0 to 10 scale to indicate how much confidence you have for each

of the following, where 0 means no confidence and 10 means a great deal of confidence.

<u>Institutions</u>: Courts, central government, political parties, army
<u>Operating definition</u>: ((courts + government + political parties + army)/40) x 3
Scale (0–3)

2. PERFORMANCE

Québec
<u>First question</u>:
  What is, according to you, the most important issue facing the federal government today? Is it ... reducing the debt, improving social programs, improving health care, creating jobs, reducing taxes, fighting crime, maintaining national unity, or improving the environment?
<u>Second question</u>:
  With respect to this issue, is the government doing... very well, fairly well, not very well, or not well at all?
<u>Coding</u>: 1 = very well or fairly well; 0 = not very well or not well at all.
Catalonia
<u>Question</u>:
  How do you qualify the general management of central government? Very well, fairly well, neither well nor badly, fairly badly, or very badly.
<u>Coding</u>: 1 = very well or fairly well; 0 = neither well nor badly, fairly badly, or very badly.

3. WINNER

Québec
<u>Question</u>:
  Which party did you vote for in the last federal election in June 2004?
<u>Coding</u>: 0 = the opposition or abstention; 1 = the Liberal Party (2005) or the Conservative Party (2010)
Catalonia
<u>Question</u>:
  Who did you vote for in the last general election?

<u>Coding</u>: 0 = the opposition or abstention; 1 = the PSOE/PSC (2006 and 2009)

4. IDENTITY

Québec
<u>Question</u>:
> How do you define yourself? Would you say you are... first and foremost Québécois; first Québécois, but also Canadian; both Québécois and Canadian; first Canadian but also Québécois, or first and foremost Canadian.

<u>Coding</u>: 0 = first and foremost Canadian, and double identity; 1 = first and foremost Québécois

Catalonia
<u>Question</u>:
> Which, if any, of the following best describes how you see yourself? Catalan not Spanish, more Catalan than Spanish, equally Catalan and Spanish, more Spanish than Catalan, Spanish not Catalan.

<u>Coding</u>: 0 = Spanish not Catalan & double identity; 1 = Catalan not Spanish

5. CYNICISM

Québec
<u>Question</u>:
> Now I am going to read four assertions. For each of them, please say whether you agree strongly, mostly agree, mostly disagree, or strongly disagree:
> (1) In general in Canada, politicians are ready to lie to get elected.
> (2) In general in Canada, elected officials quickly lose contact with the people.
> (3) In general in Canada, governments do not care much about what people like me think.
> (4) In Canada, all the federal political parties are pretty much the same; people don't really have any choice.

<u>Operating definition</u>: (Question 1 + Question 2 + Question 3 + Question 4)/4

<u>Coding</u>: Index (scale from 0 to 3, where 3 means very cynical and 0 means not cynical)

Alpha 2005: 0.69; 2010: 0.75

Catalonia

Question:

What is the main feeling you have about politics?

(1) Enthusiasm

(2) Commitment

(3) Interest

(4) Indifference

(5) Boredom

(6) Distrust

(7) Irritation

Coding: 0 = 1 to 3; 1 = 4 to 7

NOTES

1 "We demonstrate that people decide how much they trust government based on the problems they think are important at any given point of time, a process we broadly define as priming" (Hetherington and Rudolph 2008: 498).

2 "It [national identity] includes the central organising principles of the polity, its structural tendencies, characteristic ways of thinking and living, the ideals that inspire its people, the values they profess and to which its leaders tend to appeal, the kind of character they admire and cherish, their propensities to act in specific ways, their deepest fears, ambitions, anxieties, collective memories, traumatic historical experiences, dominant myths and collective self-understandings" (Parekh 1995: 257).

3 This is the title of a work by Michael Ignatieff (1993).

4 Double identity is still very strong in Catalonia, as can be seen from tables 12.4 and 12.5 below.

5 We conducted two other regression analyses that confirmed our initial choice. The first uses the "classical" form of grouping (which involves grouping together those who are first and foremost Québécois with those who are first Québécois but also Canadian): this solution is the least efficient one because this variable does not appear on the statistical level. The second involves no grouping and thus uses all five categories. This way of doing things works well, but gives more or less the same results as those found in table 6 (the single identities come out) in addition to making the table needlessly heavy.

6 The surveys, conducted by Léger Marketing, were funded by the Social Sciences and Humanities Research Council of Canada (SSHRC) in 2005 and by the Québec Secrétariat aux Affaires intergouvernementales

canadiennes (SAIC) in 2010. The first was done in October–November
2005 (N = 2,007 respondents with 500 from Québec), and the other
in March–April 2010 (N = 1,500 respondents with 400 from Québec).
In both cases, the data was weighted according to gender, age, region,
and language. The data for Catalonia and Spain was taken from two
sources: a survey conducted by the Institut de Ciències Politiques i
Socials in 2006 (N = 2000) and another in 2009 (N = 1,200) in
Catalonia only, and the findings of the 1999 World Values Survey in
Spain and Catalonia (N = 2,064, of which 175 were from Catalonia)
and 2007 (N = 1,200, of which 192 were from Catalonia).

REFERENCES

Balme, Richard, Jean-Louis Marie, and Olivier Rozenberg. 2003. "Les
motifs de la confiance (et de la défiance) politique: Intérêt, connaissance
et conviction dans les formes du raisonnement politique." *Revue internationale de politique comparée* 10, no. 3: 433–60.

Carey, Sean. 2002. "Undivided Loyalties: Is National Identity an Obstacle to European Integration?" *European Union Politics* 3, no. 4:
387–413.

Catterberg, Gabriela, and Alejandro Moreno. 2005. "The Individual Bases
of Political Trust: Trends in New and Established Democracies." *International Journal of Public Opinion Research* 18, no. 1: 31–48.

Chanley, Virginia A., Thomas J. Rudolph, and Wendy M. Rahn. 2000.
"The Origin and Consequences of Public Trust in Government: A Time
Series Analysis." *Public Opinion Quarterly* 64, no. 3: 239–56.

Dalton, Russell J. 2004. *Democratic Challenges, Democratic Choices:
The Erosion of Political Support in Advanced Industrial Democracies.*
Oxford: Oxford University Press.

Downs, Anthony. 1957. *An Economic Theory of Democracy*. New York:
Wiley.

Easton, David. 1965. *A Framework for Political Analysis*. Englewood
Cliffs, NJ: Prentice-Hall.

Festenstein, Matthew. 2009. "National Identity, Political Trust and The
Public Realm." *Critical Review of International Social and Political
Philosophy* 12, no. 2: 279–96.

Fiorina, Morris P. 1981. *Retrospective Voting in American National
Elections*. New Haven: Yale University Press.

Fukuyama, Francis. 1995. *Trust: The Social Virtues and the Creation of
Prosperity*. New York: Free Press.

Gerritsen, Debby, and Marcel Lubbers. 2010. "Unknown Is Unloved? Diversity and Inter-population Trust in Europe." *European Union Politics* 11, no. 2: 267–87.

Hardin, Russell. 2006. *Trust*. Cambridge: Polity Press.

Hetherington, Marc J. 2005. *Why Trust Matters: Declining Political Trust and the Demise of American Liberalism*. Princeton: Princeton University Press.

Hetherington, Marc J., and Thomas J. Rudolph. 2008. "Priming, Performance, and the Dynamics of Political Trust." *The Journal of Politics* 70, no. 2: 498–512.

Ignatieff, Michael. 1993. *Blood and Belonging*. Toronto: Viking.

Inglehart, Ronald F. 1997. *Modernization and Postmodernization: Cultural, Economic and Political Change in 43 Societies*. Princeton: Princeton University Press.

– 2008. "Changing Values among Western Publics from 1970 to 2006." *West European Politics* 31, no. 1–2: 130–46.

Kamarck, Elaine C. 2009. "The Evolving American State: The Trust Challenge." *The Forum* 7, no. 4, article 9.

Keating, Michael. 2001. "So Many Nations, So Few States: Territory and Nationalism in the Global Era." In *Multinational Democracies*, edited by Alain-G. Gagnon and James Tully, 39–64. Cambridge: Cambridge University Press.

King, David. 1997. "The Polarization of American Parties and Mistrust in Government." In *Why People Don't Trust Government*, edited by Joseph S. Nye, Philip D. Zelikow, and David C. King. Cambridge: Harvard University Press.

Kymlicka, Will. 1998. *Finding Our Way: Rethinking Ethnocultural Relations in Canada*. Toronto: Oxford University Press.

Levi, Margaret, and Laura Stoker. 2000. "Political Trust and Trustworthiness." *Annual Review of Political Science* 3: 475–507.

Lewis-Beck, Michael S. 1990. *Economic and Election: The Major Western Democracies*. Ann Arbor: University of Michigan Press.

McAllister, Ian. 1999. "The Economic Performance of Governments." In *Critical Citizens*, edited by Pippa Norris, 188–203. Oxford: Oxford University Press.

McLaren, Lauren M. 2004. "Opposition to European Integration and Fear of Loss of National Identity: Debunking a Basic Assumption regarding Hostility to the Integration Project." *European Journal of Political Research* 43, no. 6: 895–911.

Miller, Arthur. 1974. "Political Issues and Trust in Government." *American Political Science Review* 68, no. 3: 951–72.

Miller, Arthur, and Ola Listhaug. 1998. "Policy Preferences and Political Distrust: A Comparison of Norway, Sweden and the United States." *Scandinavian Political Studies* 21, no. 2: 161–87.

– 1999. "Political Performance and Institutional Trust." In *Critical Citizens*, edited by Pippa Norris, 204–16. Oxford: Oxford University Press.

Miller, David. 2001. "Nationality in Divided Societies." In *Multinational Democracies*, edited by Alain-G. Gagnon and James Tully, 299–318. Cambridge: Cambridge University Press.

Moreno, Luis. 2007. "Identités duales et nations sans État (la Question Moreno)." *Revue internationale de politique comparée* 14, no. 4: 497–513.

Norris, Pippa, ed. 1999a. *Critical Citizens: Global Support for Democratic Governance*. Oxford: Oxford University Press.

– 1999b. "Institutional Explanations for Political Support." In *Critical Citizens*, edited by Pippa Norris, 217–35. Oxford: Oxford University Press.

Parekh, Bhikhu. 1995. "The Concept of National Identity." *Journal of Ethnic and Migration Studies* 21, no. 2: 255–68.

Putnam, Robert D. 2000. *Bowling Alone: The Collapse and Revival of American Community*. New York: Simon and Schuster.

– ed. 2002. *Democracies in Flux: The Evolution of Social Capital in Contemporary Society*. New York: Oxford University Press.

Putnam, Robert D., with R. Leonardi and R.Y. Nanetti. 1994. *Making Democracy Work: Civic Traditions in Modern Italy*. Princeton: Princeton University Press.

Rosanvallon, Pierre. 2008. *Counter-Democracy: Politics in an Age of Distrust*. Cambridge: Cambridge University Press.

Warren, Mark E. 1999. *Democracy and Trust*. New York: Cambridge University Press.

13

Trust and Distrust in the Belgian Federation

Kris Deschouwer

ONE BELGIUM, TWO STORIES

We can tell two stories about Belgium. The first is positive and optimistic. It says that Belgium is a nice place to live. Its annual per capita GDP – over $40,000 according to the International Monetary Fund (IMF) – places it in seventeenth place among the richest countries in the world: higher than Spain and Germany, but behind the Netherlands (tenth) and Luxembourg (first). Belgium has an efficient and especially generous social security system. The benevolence of the welfare state is based on a solid economy and easy access to world markets for its products. Belgium's capital is also the capital of the European Union (EU) and the North Atlantic Treaty Organization (NATO), which attracts many services to Brussels, giving it and Belgium a strong, internationally recognized image.

Belgium is moreover a country where cultural and territorial divisions have been dealt with peacefully. Of course, there has sometimes been very strong tension between the north and the south, but it has never come close to violent confrontation or civil war. Every time tension has really escalated, the political class has managed to find a way out. Indeed, Belgium's political elite has demonstrated an incredible degree of creativity, developing subtle compromises between demands that have seemed *a priori* irreconcilable. It is thus an enviable success. In Canada, where a quite similar territorial and linguistic conflict divides the country, there have been many attempts to reform the political system, although half a century of discussions on the status of Québec have not resulted in any significant constitutional change (Jans 2001). In Cyprus – where, unlike in Belgium and Canada, the conflict between the two communities has sunk into violence and created deep mutual hatred – the quest for new political institutions able to reunite the island has sparked a keen interest in Belgium and everything that has come to be known as the "Belgian model" (Emerson and Tocci 2003). This term refers to a territorial division establishing homogenous communities and power-sharing mechanisms for issues that are still managed jointly. Indeed, this approach has made it possible for Belgium to channel and sort out relations between the two linguistic communities (Deschouwer 2009a).

However, we can also tell a different story about Belgium. Belgium has been able to settle its territorial conflict peacefully, but the arrangements are constantly subject to domestic challenge. Periods of significant tension have ended with compromises, but every compromise has later been disputed. Periods of calm and stability have occurred, but sooner or later they have always been followed by another crisis, with every new crisis making us more aware that existing political institutions might not be able to contain the next one. As in San Francisco, where people know that the city is built on a major fault line and where from time to time they feel that the foundations beneath their feet are giving way, we are expecting the Belgian "Big One." Yet, this does not prevent Belgians from living well and feeling comfortable. All in all, the territorial conflict is not as terrible as all that, and is not life-threatening. Health and financial security are more important to Belgians than the way the government is organized today (Deschouwer and Sinardet 2010).

This twofold history, with its ups and downs, is also reflected in changes to the trust that Belgians have in their political system. Since 1975, the Eurobarometer has been questioning the inhabitants of the EU member states on how satisfied they are with the way democracy functions in their country. The data for Belgium is presented in figure 13.1. The fluctuations are truly impressive.

The first serious drop was at the end of the 1970s and beginning of the 1980s. Between 1978 and 1981, there were no less than eight governments, all confronted with the fact that the Flemish and the French-speakers each wanted radically different state reforms, and were proposing equally different approaches to the economic crisis. Obsessed by these discussions, these ephemeral governments completely lost interest in public finances, which drifted out of control. It was at that time that the foundations were laid for the public debt

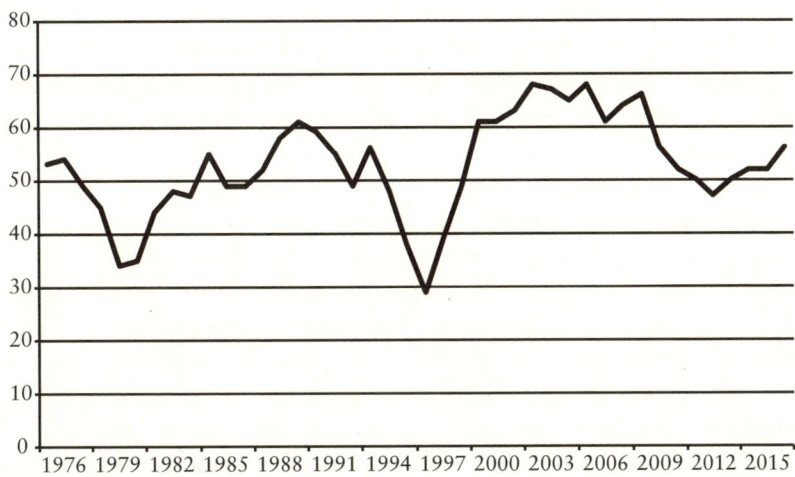

Source: Eurobanometer

Figure 13.1 Percentage of Belgians who say they are "satisfied" or "very satisfied" with the way democracy operates in Belgium

to skyrocket to 130 per cent of the GDP by the end of the 1980s. The consequences of this *malgoverno* are still being felt today, and this will continue for at least another generation (Heylen and Van Hecke 2008).

Nonetheless, the following governments managed to find a successful compromise that was enshrined through constitutional reforms. Belgians thus regained trust in their political system. This return of trust was however interrupted in 1985. That year, Brussels was hosting the European Cup final soccer match between Liverpool and Juventus. The event turned into a tragedy, and forty people died when charging fans knocked over a wall at Heysel Stadium. It was rapidly revealed – following work done by a Belgian Chamber of Representatives' commission of inquiry – that the high number of victims was largely due to the federal and local authorities' mediocre organization, combined with an absence of appropriate communication between police forces. The ability and performance of public authorities had been seriously inadequate (T'Hart and Pijnenburg 1998). The leaders of the Belgian Football Association stepped down, though the minister of the interior's refusal to do the same sounded the government's death knell.

A second serious low followed in 1991, and lasted until 1997: less than 30 per cent of Belgians said they were satisfied with the way their country was functioning. The decline was marked by a series of events, all of which strengthened Belgians' perception that the state was unable to operate correctly. First, there were the results of the 24 November 1991 election, known as "Black Sunday." Against all expectations, the Vlaams Blok, a radical right-wing populist party, which was also demanding the independence of Flanders, won 10 per cent of the vote in Flanders. It took over one hundred days to form a new government. The success of the radical right was generally interpreted as a protest vote and an expression of discontent, a rejection of the political class, and a bright red warning signal indicating that a rift had occurred between citizens and politicians. This was thus a challenge to the basic characteristics of the Belgian system: a strong dose of partitocracy; large-scale patronage; a myriad of parties and opaque, laborious processes for forming coalitions; the constant presence and return to power of Christian Democrats and socialists, even though they were losing elections; the holding of multiple offices by politicians; and a long retinue of legal proceedings. Proof of some of these aspects came when various scandals broke related to the suspicious funding of political parties. Highly placed politicians in the two socialist parties were obliged to step down. The final blow occurred in 1996, when in the summer the criminal pedophile Marc Dutroux was arrested and two young girls were freed from his basement, where others had previously died. Although such horrible events unfortunately occur in many countries, in Belgium they led to renewed questioning of the government's ability to do what was needed. The police had visited the house before, but had not discovered the hidden part of the basement where the two kidnapped girls were imprisoned. The information held by the national police had not been shared with the local police, and vice versa. As in the Heysel tragedy, the political consequences proved dramatic.

The Dutroux case – in which the fate of innocent children hung in the balance – sparked the largest public protest ever seen in Belgium: 300,000 Belgians took to the streets for the White March (Rihoux and Walgrave 1998). The purpose was to provide support for the children's parents, but also to tell the political elite that things had to change. The latter message, however, proved difficult to decode. The demonstrators were wearing white and carrying white balloons and umbrellas, but their slogans did not convey any concrete demands. Nevertheless, deep discontent and a desire for change became apparent. The concrete reforms inspired by the White March included the creation of Child Focus, an especially efficient organization that organizes searches whenever a person is reported missing. The court system was reformed so that political parties would have less say in the appointment of judges, and victims would be better protected and have easier access to information. The various police forces were merged into a single integrated Belgian police force.

Trust in Belgian institutions then began to grow, peaking in 2003. At the time, a new coalition of liberals, socialists, and greens shared power, and tensions between the north and south were well under control. A constitutional reform was negotiated in 2002, without any real conflict. A new Belgium was born. Prime Minister Guy Verhofstadt resolutely affirmed his confidence that he would transform Belgium into a model state. He said that he was convinced that his new, original approach would make protest votes melt away. However, in 2003, and then again in 2005, Vlaams Blok – now rechristened Vlaams Belang (Erk 2005) – registered its greatest number of votes ever.

In 2003, a reform of the electoral system instituting provincial ridings brought back into the foreground the old question of the Brussels-Hal-Vilvorde riding – straddling the Flemish and Brussels areas – and the boundaries of Brussels (Govaerts 2007). The Flemish Christian Democrats, who had until then spearheaded all of the state reforms, formed an electoral alliance with the Flemish nationalist party the N-VA, and promised that longstanding Flemish demands would finally be fulfilled if they came back to power. French-speakers were horrified to see the gradual radicalization of Flemish positions. On 13 December 2006, the RTBf French-language public television station interrupted its usual programs to announce – as a stunt – that the Flemish parliament had just declared independence and that the king had fled abroad. If we are to believe the survey conducted by the RTBf itself, many viewers were taken in by the hoax, in which a number of Flemish and French-speaking politicians had participated. In panic, people went to the Royal Palace to express their support for Belgium and the king. Suddenly, the end of Belgium no longer seemed like a strange demand from the insignificant or troubling political parties in the north, but a real possibility – even though the "Bye-bye Belgium" scenario, with a line of cars blocked at the border of Flanders, was pure fiction.

The 2007 federal parliamentary elections were strongly marked by urgent demands from the Flemish parties and by francophone fears in the face of the prospect of a new dismantling of Belgium. After the elections, it still took six months to form an interim government. Once again, the trust of Belgians in their political class was crumbling. After ten years of stability and strong trust, Belgian political foundations were quaking again. This time, fear of the "Big One" was being expressed more strongly than ever. Since there was no agreement on state reform or the fate of the Brussels-Hal-Vilvorde riding, new (preterm) elections were held in 2010, resulting in the N-VA becoming the largest party in Flanders and Belgium.

THE PEAK OF DISTRUST

Citizens whose trust in the political system is declining or significantly fluctuating reveal a potential threat to democratic legitimacy. However, what about a lack of trust among members of the elite? Challenges to the foundations of a political system are not very surprising when they come from parties opposed to the Establishment. This said, one of the weaknesses – one of the problems – of Belgium is that support from elite groups is also structurally lacking in the system. Today's Belgian state and the principles on which it is based are the results of many laborious compromises, which have required a good dose of creativity. Among the principles, the most important is the sharing of power – the obligation to govern together at the federal level. However, for that to function properly, decision-makers themselves have to believe in the system at least a little bit, accept the compromise that prevailed when it was created, and agree that there is a need to make further compromises in the future.

Unfortunately, there are often red lights indicating the opposite. On various occasions, French-speaking parties have tried to challenge the way that the francophone minority in Flanders is treated, which they have seen as much too restrictive. They persuaded the Council of Europe to send a rapporteur to the areas around Brussels to see that, in Belgium, francophones in Flanders are not recognized as a national minority. In fact, Belgium has not ratified the Framework

Convention for the Protection of National Minorities, which, in Article 5, provides that signatory countries shall

> undertake to promote the conditions necessary for persons belonging to national minorities to maintain and develop their culture, and to preserve the essential elements of their identity, namely their religion, language, traditions and cultural heritage [and] refrain from policies or practices aimed at assimilation of persons belonging to national minorities against their will and shall protect these persons from any action aimed at such assimilation.

The arrangement established in favour of French-speakers in the Brussels region – language facilities in six municipalities – is clearly much more limited, but it is the result of a compromise that combines the demands of both linguistic groups concerning language use and territorial boundaries.

There have been a number of attempts on the Flemish side to limit, as much as possible, the implementation of language facilities. While initially the inhabitants of the municipalities in question could register as French speakers and have public authorities send them all information in French automatically, the Flemish government has asked local authorities to systematically send the information in Dutch and to limit the sending of French translations to only those citizens who have explicitly requested them. The normal discourse on the Flemish side has also consisted in saying that, in reality, the facilities are nothing more than an interim mechanism, and that they will have to be abolished in the near future.

French-speaking politicians perceive Flanders as a bulldozer seeking to make all of its territory uniform. When emotions are unleashed, terms such as "ethnic cleansing" are even heard. As for Flanders, it sees the demands of francophones as a perpetual attempt to speak their language when and where they want, in disregard of the fact that in Belgium language-use is now defined on the basis of territory. Thus, Flanders behaves as if it were a threatened community that has to protect its linguistic integrity. Neither of these two communities is able to accept the consequences of the compromise.

Many countries experience political tensions that can be described as conflicts between the centre and a periphery (Lipset and Rokkan 1967). An elite that builds the state is challenged by groups from areas that are not, and refuse to be, fully integrated into the state and its overall identity. Historically in Belgium, the periphery meant Flanders, which challenged the linguistic identity of the country. Today, Belgium is composed of two peripheries, and it no longer has any centre. For both sides, the centre means a place where the other community also lives, an area where that community is perceived as dominant. The elite has no confidence in the system because the system is perceived as being more advantageous for the other (Deschouwer 2009a, 2009b).

UNEASY CONSOCIATION

The Belgian federal system is a consociative federation (Seiler 1997). Its central level requires the sharing of power and gives each partner a veto. In other words, at its federal level, Belgium acts more like a confederation than a federation. Constitutionally speaking, Belgium is obviously not a confederation. That would suppose that it is the union of different sovereign states, rather than a single state. However, the rules and procedures for making decisions at the central level require nothing less than a political agreement between the leaders of the two linguistic communities. Certainly, the decisions of the federal parliament are taken by a simple majority vote, but any issue of some importance requires a double majority. In a parity-based government, it is always indispensable to come to a consensus when launching legislative initiatives and making them concrete.

Thus, the Belgian federation is not only consociative, but also bipolar (Deschouwer 2009b). The unanimity rule applies to decision-making that involves only two partners. In fact, this is another reason why the rule has to be consensus. When there are only two partners, there is no other choice. However, this number does not really favour the harmonious sharing of power.

> A multiple balance of power among segments of a plural society is more conducive to consociational democracy than a dual balance of power or a hegemony by one of the segments, because if one segment has a clear majority its leaders may attempt to dominate rather than cooperate with the rival minority. And in a society with two segments of approximately equal size, the leaders of both may hope to win a majority and to achieve their aims by domination instead of cooperation. (Lijphart 1977: 55)

Once a two-partner consociative system has been established, we find the poor conditions described by Lijphart, and they are powerful sources of frustration.

Belgium's bipolarity has been carried over into virtually all of its institutions and organizations. In this regard, the most important – the most crucial – aspect lies in the party system. Division of the national parties is the inevitable consequence of differences of opinion between the north and south on the principles and components of the Belgian government. This scission has had a significant impact on the functioning and legitimacy of the system precisely because the divided parties arrangement has to operate in a context in which the sharing of power is compulsory (Verleden 2009).

Escalating electoral competition is normal in democracies, just as it is normal in multiparty systems to find a certain degree of mismatch between campaign promises and the major options retained when coalitions are formed. In the Belgian system of divided parties, electoral promises address two different and perfectly distinct electorates. It is thus not easy to meet expectations. Elections are in principle a good opportunity to gain a rapid understanding of what is going on in society, to measure the importance of other claims and the dynamics that convey them, and to evaluate the trends and shifts in voices between competing parties. However, if each party restricts itself to one half of the territory, it will not really be possible to read the results of elections or to interpret them. It will also not be possible to take expectations into account. Consequently, the results are not read and interpreted at the Belgian national level, but only at the level of the federated entities. Elections produce two results, and so the formation of a government has to try to meet the expectations of the two different results, and sometimes even different trends. For a very long time, the quasi-natural response to the two different electorates took the form of a coalition between Christian Democrats, well-established in Flanders, and socialists, well-established in Wallonia.

The impact of divided parties on democratic legitimacy, and on the democratic obligation to be accountable, are also of major importance when political institutions themselves are at the heart of the debate. The parties of each linguistic community are very inclined to promise a state structure that would cater to the dominant vision and perception of things in their own linguistic community. No one will contradict such proposals, except for the parties of the other linguistic community, which communicate only with the voters in their own community. The advent of the system of divided parties has been the end of most incentives towards moderation. Yet, clearly, decisions concerning state structure, the distribution of jurisdictions, the status of regions and communities, the status and boundaries of Brussels, the meaning and interpretation of language facilities, the scope of fiscal and financial autonomy, and redistribution all have to receive the consensus of the leaders of the linguistic communities. The gap between electoral promises and promises that have been kept is enormous. In bipolar Belgium, with its system of parties and public opinion divided in two, elected politicians wishing to govern at the federal level first have to solve the problems that they have created themselves. This is the reason for the long, laborious negotiations and incredibly complex compromises that can be read and interpreted differently in the north and in the south.

This illusion of unilateralism is striking. We also find it in the attempts of the two language groups to defend a more "normal" functioning of democracy at every opportunity. Consociative logic excludes the exercise of majority power. Yet, majority power is a much easier technique to explain than the need to compromise with a minority, particularly when voters receive political proposals from only one of the two communities. Indeed, there are clear, visible majorities in Belgium. The Flemish are a majority in Belgium, and are thus inclined to defend their claims by telling their voters that, in a real democracy, the will of the majority has to be respected. French speakers are a majority in the Brussels area, and are thus inclined to assert that the seats reserved for the Flemish in the Brussels parliament and the parity within the Brussels government represent an unacceptable overrepresentation of the minority. French speakers are in the majority in several Flemish municipalities around Brussels. This leads them to defend the principle that they have the complete right to decide, for example, the conditions according to which language facilities are to be offered to the inhabitants of those towns. Majority democracy is much easier to defend and explain than consociative democracy, with its subtle balances and mutual vetoes that reduce the majority to silence.

NEW INSTITUTIONS AND DECISION-MAKING ABILITY

The elements that make Belgium difficult to govern are far from new. In this precarious context, Belgian political institutions have already definitively demonstrated that they are able to contain tension when really necessary. Some time has often been required to solve territorial and linguistic problems, and in budgetary terms, the price has been high. However, in the end, it has probably been worth it. Other divided societies have proven less able to control tensions related to identity and territorial claims.

It is thus important to ask to what degree, in the future, the Belgian political system will still be able to govern a divided Belgian society. The question is relevant, given that the context today and going forward is not perfectly identical to the context of the 1970s and 1980s. The basic ingredients of the conflict remain the same, and the basic rules for finding solutions – power sharing and a mutual veto – remain unchanged. That said, there have been a number of developments that could, in the future, make governing Belgium even more complicated. This is not without irony, since it is precisely the institutions that have been set up to manage the divided society that could throw a hammer into the works. The Belgium of the past, the one that made it possible to find a way out of deadlocks, was a unitary country. The Belgium of today and tomorrow is a federal state, and certain aspects of this federal state do not make it easier to govern.

One of the crucial differences between the former Belgium and the new federal Belgium is that there are now a number of power centres. In the unitary Belgium, the centre of power and the place where all policies and reforms were decided was the national government. The formation and survival of the national government required a formal agreement between the two linguistic groups. If there was none, all of Belgium's politics slowly became completely paralyzed. The more time that was needed to find a solution, the more dramatic the lack of a solution became. Thus, the lack of an agreement between the two linguistic groups led to "general policy paralysis" (Jans 2001). The pressure then became so intense that politicians were forced to find creative compromises, which made it possible to break the stalemate for a while.

In today's federal state, power is obviously no longer concentrated in a single government. There are several governments of the federated entities, which have broad powers and competencies. The power to define and change federal institutions has still remained in the hands of the federal government and parliament. Nonetheless, when no solution has been found at that level, the consequences are much less serious. The result is no longer general policy paralysis, but only the

lack of a solution for the problem in question. Policies controlled at
the regional or community level can be pursued without any problem.
Of course, the absence of a functioning federal government does create
problems over the long term, but the political history of Belgium
since 2007 shows that it is possible to survive for quite a while with
a government that limits itself to dealing with current business. The
pressure to form a new one is not very great, and a community that
really desires to have a claim upheld cannot brandish the threat of
complete policy paralysis to force the other community to come to
the bargaining table.

There is also an international dimension that reduces pressure.
Belgium is a member of the European Union, which means that many
powers – in particular those defining the rules of economic and financial
exchange – have been transferred to a higher level, out of the
hands of the Belgian government. In the 1970s and 1980s, when the
Belgian government showed signs of weakness and an inability or
reluctance to manage its financial policy, speculative attacks on the
Belgian currency could translate into extremely strong pressure to
come to a compromise. Today, the Belgian franc has disappeared and
been replaced by the euro. Belgium is anchored in the (mostly) safe
waters of Europe, and for precisely this reason it has become less
imperative to solve Belgian problems. Belgium can tolerate much
longer periods of instability than before. In constitutional matters, it
has thus lost its decision-making ability.

In the new federal Belgium, it might be possible to keep constitutional
negotiations out of the central framework and shift them to
an inter-governmental forum. This might be a good way to shelter
the federal government from virtually any pressure, but it in no way
strengthens its ability to find a solution. First, we never manage to
come to a clear agreement on which governments have the right to
sit at the bargaining table. Flanders argues for a dialogue between
two *communities*, while French speakers want the *regions* – and thus
Brussels as well – to be full partners at the table. Next, the rules for
making decisions – whether there are two or three partners – do not
change. Only consensus and the elimination of veto rights can lead
to an agreement. Finally, if inter-governmental negotiations fail, there
is no consequence beyond simply the failure itself, and the frustration
of those who wanted them to succeed. However, there is no means
of applying pressure to force an inter-governmental forum to come
to a decision at any price. The very fact that Belgium has become a

federal state – following attempts to contain and appease tensions between the linguistic communities – has considerably diminished its ability to manage the tensions better.

Having several power centres is one of the consequences of introducing a federal system in Belgium. Another consequence of federalism that has affected the ability to make decisions is the way that elections are held at these different levels. This electoral logic interacts with the system of divided parties. At first, it was possible to attenuate the effects of elections at different levels by holding all of the elections on the same day, and in particular by forming congruent coalitions and ensuring that there were the same government parties at all levels (Deschouwer 2009c). This also meant that the federal and regional elections could not develop any specific dynamics.

The different election terms – every five years for regional elections, and every four years for federal elections – were designed to give the elections their own flavour. However, two correlated factors explain this system's failure. First, to a large degree, the parties have chosen to nominate the same candidates for both elections. Senior political officials are always well placed on the candidate list, but they do not necessarily occupy the seat to which they are elected. After each election – whether regional or federal – the parties now redistribute their cards within the governments they participate in. Naturally, this choice is related to the fact that there is no party covering the entire territory. Even if the candidates were different and the campaign themes were chosen carefully to correspond with the competencies required at the level of government being voted on, the parties would nonetheless continue to offer voters the same choice, and the results would always be read and interpreted at the same level.

The separation of the elections since 2003 has not introduced more differentiation, but it has further weakened the ability to make decisions. Government coalitions at different levels have become less and less congruent. This has resulted in a new type of conflict in the Belgian federation: conflicts between governments. Inter-governmental tensions are not new, but congruent coalitions make it possible for the parties in power to control them. When coalitions are not congruent, conflicts between governments are always also conflicts between parties. This is something that does not help to establish trust between partners in a coalition.

Thus, the separation of federal and regional elections institutes a sort of *permanent election campaign* in the system. As soon as elections approach, all the parties mobilize their troops. Each election outcome has consequences for all of the governments. Every coalition is constantly made up of parties preparing to ask people to vote for them. It is not very easy to form a coalition and keep it alive in a context in which the next elections are never far away.

At the federal level, this has proven truly problematic. If all parties hesitate to take initiatives, fearing that they will be punished by voters in the next regional elections – which will occur sooner or later during the coalition – then their willingness to find compromises, especially on constitutional issues, dwindles away. This explains the deadlock. Once again, the advent and establishment of a federal Belgium reduces the government's decision-making power.

Moreover, another factor weighs on this ability. It is not related to federal institutions but to more general social change in both the north and south. As always, election outcomes are perceptibly different in the two regions, but elections have become more unpredictable. The two forces that used to dominate in the north and south, respectively the Christian Democrats and the socialists, have lost their positions as leaders. In other words, they are no longer virtually certain to serve in the governments of their regions and in the federal government. Losing only a small percentage of the votes can make all the difference. Another element that adds to the limited willingness to play the consociational game at the federal level is the increased competition in each of the systems of Belgian parties. Coming to a compromise means accepting a settlement that is noticeably distant from what one has promised voters, but voters always punish rapidly, given that every election mobilizes the same voters for the same parties on each side. Since the lack of a solution is not sufficiently troublesome to pressure those confronting one another into coming to a compromise, in the new federal Belgium periods of crisis and stalemate can be much longer and more serious than they ever were in the former unitary Belgium. The federal solution is now part of the problem.

QUO VADIS?

Two stories are told about Belgium (Peters 2006). The first is the story of a prosperous European country that has been able to solve its identity-related conflicts by creating institutions that accept differences and make it possible to limit the scope of the tensions generated by the conflicts. The second is a story of a country that often does not believe in itself, in which distrust reigns. People's attitudes toward the political system shift between great trust and deep suspicion. The elites do not err on the side of excessive trust either. The new Belgium is very far from ideal for the two linguistic groups. Both are frustrated by the other's veto right. Moreover, the new federal institutions and increased competition within the two systems of parties provide little incentive – perhaps even none at all – to be accommodating.

So, where is Belgium going? Each political crisis amplifies the fears, and hopes, that it will be the last: that the regime will not manage to regain control, and Belgium will come to an end. This supposes that if there is no agreement, there is still the possibility that we will be able to find, once and for all, a solution to the difficult quest for constitutional reform. It supposes, in other words, that there is an easy way out. This belief, or the fear that the country might be dismantled, is a useful illustration of the illusion of unilateralism favoured by federal institutions. It is the felt conviction that since Belgium cannot be as we wish, whatever comes after Belgium will eradicate the sources of frustration. This assumes that it is possible to be finished with Belgium without having to find an agreement on its components or how boundaries should be drawn between lands. Can Belgium be split into two linguistic communities with Brussels attached to Flanders? This is very unlikely because it would mean that Brussels's population would prefer – in time of major tension – to join Flanders instead of Wallonia. Could Belgium be replaced by a Flanders without Brussels and a Wallonia that would include Brussels? It is improbable. If Flanders were not to claim Brussels, or need it, Belgium's structures could be much less complicated. Both communities see Brussels as their city – their capital – and this is what explains the creation of the twofold federation, with both regions and communities. Many different types of territorial organizations can be imagined for an "après-Belgium," including defining Brussels as a European "District of Columbia," but each scenario entails that existing regions and communities would lose something that they have sought and obtained (even if only partially) in Belgium.

Of course, it is possible to imagine the end of a country. History teaches us that territory can be divided. Is not the very creation of Belgium the fruit of a break with the Kingdom of the Netherlands (Witte et al. 2005)? However, dismembering Belgium and dividing its land, economy, and public debt between the newly created entities is certainly not an easy way to solve the problem. It would require a compromise that would not have the advantage of being vague and ambiguous enough to enable both sides to claim a kind of victory. There is no simple means of governing Belgium, just as there is no easy way out. What more is needed for a political class to protest its distrust of a system in which it finds itself trapped?

Governing Belgium will never be easy. It is diabolically complicated to rule a divided society. A balance constantly has to be maintained between conflict and compromise, fear and hope, satisfaction and frustration, distrust and trust. However, Belgium has proven – so far – that it is a balance that can be maintained.

REFERENCES

Deschouwer, K. 2009a. *The Politics of Belgium: Governing a Divided Society*. London: Palgrave MacMillan.

– 2009b. "La dynamique fédérale en Belgique." In *Le fédéralisme en Belgique et au Canada: Comparaison sociopolitique*, edited by B. Fournier and M. Reuchamps, 65–72. Bruxelles: De Boeck.

– 2009c. "Coalition Formation and Congruence in Multi-Layered Systems: Belgium 1995–2007." *Regional and Federal Studies* 19, no. 1: 13–35.

Deschouwer, K., and D. Sinardet. 2010. "Langue, identité et comportement électoral." In *Les voix du peuple: Le comportement électoral au scrutin du 10 juin 2009*, edited by K. Deschouwer, P. Delwit, M. Hooghe, and S. Walgrave, 61–81. Bruxelles: Editions de l'ULB.

Emerson, M., and N. Tocci. 2003. *Cyprus as Lighthouse of the East Mediterranean: Shaping Re-unification and EU Accession Together*. Brussels: CEPS.

Erk, J. 2005. "From Vlaams Blok to Vlaams Belang: The Belgian Far-Right Renames Itself." *West European Politics* 28, no. 3: 493–502.

Govaerts, S. 2007. "Bruxelles-Hal-Vilvorde: Du quasi-accord de 2005 à la procédure en conflit d'intérêts." *Courrier hebdomadaire du crisp*, no. 1974: 5–40.

Heylen, W., and S. Van Hecke. 2008. *Regeringen die niet regeren: Het mal-governo van de Belgische politiek*. Leuven: Lannoo Campus.

Jans, M.T. 2001. "Leveled Domestic Politics: Comparing Institutional Reform and Ethnonational Conflicts in Canada and Belgium (1960–1989)." *Res Publica* 43, no. 1: 37–58.

Lijphart, A. 1977. *Democracy in Plural Societies: A Comparative Exploration*. New Haven: Yale University Press.

Lipset, S.M., and S. Rokkan. 1967. *Party Systems and Voter Alignments*. New York: Free Press.

Peters, B.G. 2006. "Consociationalism, Corruption and Chocolate: Belgian Exceptionalism." *West European Politics* 29, no. 5: 1079–92.

Rihoux, B., and S. Walgrave. 1998. *L'année blanche: Un million de citoyens blancs*. Brussels: Éditions Vie Ouvrière.

Seiler, D. 1997. "Un système consociatif exemplaire: La Belgique." *Revue internationale de politique comparée* 4, no. 3: 601–24.

T'Hart, P., and B. Pijnenburg. 1998. *Het Heizeldrama: Rampzalig organiseren en kritieke beslissingen*. Brussels: HD Samson.

Verleden, F. 2009. "Splitting the Difference: The Radical Approach of the Belgian Parties." In *Territorial Party Politics in Western Europe*, edited by W. Swenden and B. Maddens, 145–66. London: Palgrave MacMillan.

Witte, E., E. Gubin, J.P. Nandrin, and G. Deneckere. 2005. *Nouvelle histoire de la belgique: 1830–1905*. Bruxelles: Complexe.

14

Trust between Party Elites in Consociational Federations: The Case of Belgium

Dave Sinardet and Niels Morsink

Trust is a much-discussed concept in social science, and has been looked at from many perspectives, be it sociological (Lewis and Weigert 1985; Misztal 2001), philosophical (Baier 1986), managerial (Rousseau et al. 1998), or otherwise. The political science literature on trust largely concentrates on horizontal trust between citizens and vertical trust between citizens and the government (Lenard 2007: 314; Oskarsson 2010). Horizontal trust between political party elites is however a largely overlooked subject, although it can be an influential factor in political life, mostly in coalition systems and more particularly during government formation. Lupia and Strom (2008: 54), for instance, mention it as one of the exogenous contextual factors in bargaining to form a coalition. Trust can also be a relevant factor after coalition formation, as it can play a role in government stability by assuring all parties that everyone will defend the coalition agreement to their rank and file, stick to it, and not leave the government once their own objectives are fulfilled.

While trust between party elites is therefore important in coalition systems in general, this is certainly also the case in federations (and even more so in federations with coalition systems). In federations, not only do differences between parties have to be dealt with, but also differences between political representatives of different regions, cultural groups, and so on. This means that additional differences in interest have to be bridged. As Simeon and Conway (2001: 361) argue, federal institutions in themselves are not a guarantee for easing over a divide, as other factors need to provide integrative counterweights to a centrifugal tendency within federations. Trust between party elites can play a significant role in this respect.

Trust between party elites seems even more crucial in federations with a consociational mode of decision-making. These are often established in so-called divided societies, where trust between groups is generally low (Lenard 2007: 312; Zucker 1986: 82). Moreover, in consociational democracies, the role of party elites in bridging these societal divisions (and lack of trust) is crucial. Nevertheless, even the literature on consociationalism is rather silent about the role of trust between party elites.

This chapter will try to fill this gap. First we will look into the precise relation between consociational theory and trust. Do consociational mechanisms enhance or deteriorate trust? Is trust between party elites necessary in consociational federations or can consociational mechanisms replace trust? Next, we will look into the relation between consociationalism and trust by focusing on the Belgian case and more specifically on the political crisis around the negotiation of a sixth state reform. One of the causes of the crisis has indeed been attributed to a lack of trust between the different party leaders of the north and south of the country. We will suggest that consociational mechanisms do not seem to enhance trust between party elites in Belgium, and that, in the absence of trust, they may even lead to paralysis.

TRUST AND CONSOCIATIONAL FEDERATIONS

Trust

Trust is the willingness to be vulnerable and interdependent, because of positive expectations that the other will follow a certain set of norms (Rousseau et al. 1998: 395). These expectations depend on the potential cost of trust as well as the reputation of the trustee. The set of norms relevant in the field of trust between party elites involves a preference for collective welfare over individual welfare, a willingness to come to a compromise, and loyalty to the federal level of government. We distinguish between institutional-based trust and relational trust. We interpret the concept of institutional-based trust (Zucker 1986) as the expectation that people in a certain institution (e.g., job) will follow a certain set of norms. Trust is thus based on the institution, not on the person. For instance, we trust that the fire department will extinguish a fire, not because we trust individual firefighters, but because we trust the institution. Relational trust is different because the positive expectations are limited to specific persons and do not extend to the institution. Distrust results from disappointments or betrayals attributed to the person's or the group's character (Lenard 2007: 316).

Positioning oneself in a vulnerable position logically implies risk. If the potential cost connected to this risk is low, one will trust the other even if there is not much reason to do so, such as, for example, when asking for directions. However, if the potential cost linked to this risk is too high, one will not trust the other even if there is a reason to trust them (Gambetta 1988: 395; Cook, Hardin, and Levi 2005: 80). An important element is reputation. The reputation of the trustee is crucial in estimating the risk of the trustee to not fulfil an agreement. Hence the truster will be more willing to trust the trustee if he has positive information about his reputation (e.g., to compromise to form an agreement) (Dasgupta 1988; Zucker 1986: 60). We will look into the question of whether consociational mechanisms in federations enhance trust, or can even replace trust. First we will make explicit what is understood by consociational federations.

Consociational Federations and Party Elites

Consociational theory, as primarily developed by Lijphart (e.g., 1969, 1977, 1999), is considered a model of conflict management for "divided" or "plural" societies. While originally developed to explain how specific states in Western Europe remained politically stable despite deep societal divisions, it gradually became a normative theory (Andeweg 2000: 516–17). The types of divisions being studied also evolved: while originally mostly associated with socio-economic or ideological cleavages, consociational theory was soon broadened to also include territorial or cultural divisions. Lijphart (1999) became an advocate of consensus democracy, which he considered to be the type of democracy most suitable for deeply divided societies.

Political elites, and more specifically party elites, play a crucial role in this model, as they are supposed to act as the main pacificators. Lijphart (1969: 216) first defined consociational democracy as "government by elite cartel designed to turn democracy with a fragmented political culture into a stable democracy." Indeed, consociationalism is a system of "elite-accommodation" or power sharing between elites, who play a key role in building bridges between subcultures in society because they are aware of the destabilizing danger that subcultural segmentation entails in the absence of an agreement (Wolinetz 1999: 226; Deschouwer and Luther 1999: 246). Members of a group are represented by elites of the same group, and the latter are supposed to build bridges to the elites of the other group(s) to create political consensus; in so doing, they are supposed to pacify disagreements in society as a whole (Lijphart 1977). Moreover, interaction on the mass level is generally discouraged because it is supposed that in divided societies mass interaction could lead to conflict. The emphasis is on the attitude of party elites who are supposed to act as "prudent leaders," and on their conflict-resolving techniques, which could include a proportional division of power, jobs and means, veto power, and strong autonomy (Wolinetz 1999: 226).

These techniques can rest on a consociational tradition. However, we agree with the suggestion of Magnette and Papadopoulos (2008: 5) that, when speaking of consociationalism, it is not enough to have "a particular style of consensual politics," because it also must be "consolidated by a particular institutional architecture designed to ensure the preservation of the vital interests of the composing segments of these societies." This is achieved by non-majoritarian institutions, which ensure that political power rests on as large a majority as possible, with the inclusion of representatives from at least the different relevant segments or groups in a given society. The basis of the system is that decisions are taken by consensus and that no single group can make decisions on important matters without the other(s). According to Lijphart (1981: 1), the majoritarian democracy is "the antithesis of consociational democracy." Consociational arrangements can therefore be defined as "institutions and procedures that encourage consensus rather than allowing the will of those who represent a simple majority of the population to prevail" (Pinder 2007: 9–11).

While Lijphart generally considers decentralisation and federalism as possible characteristics of consociationalism, many authors working on federalism nevertheless clearly distinguish federalism from consociationalism. While it is true that both are in part underpinned by the same logic of combining self-rule and shared-rule (Hooghe 2003: 80), Elazar (1987), for instance, sees consociationalism more as a process and federalism as more structural. According to Duchacek (1985), decisional modes in federal systems can vary on a continuum between consociationalism and majority rule. He does, however, link a consociational decision mode to confederations. Actually, Belgium, Switzerland, and (according to some) the European Union are generally considered to be the only political systems combining consociationalism with federalism (Magnette and Papadopoulos 2008: 5). However, according to Pinder (2007: 9–11), consociational arrangements are a staple feature of multinational federations, denoting federal states whereby at least one component is (self-) defined as a nation. This does not imply that consociational arrangements have to be developed as strongly in all multinational federations. It is argued that, for instance, the Canadian system also contains some of these features, such as the right of Québec to veto constitutional amendments. Earlier, Lijphart (1977) classified Canada as semi-consociational.

Because of the pivotal role of party elites in consociational federations, it logically seems important that they trust one another. However, one could also say that where consociationalism is strongly institutionalized, trust might be rendered obsolete. In what follows, we will look into this precise relationship between consociational democracy and trust.

TRUST, PARTY ELITES, AND CONSOCIATIONAL FEDERATIONS

Can Consociational Mechanisms Replace Trust between Party Elites?

First of all, as mentioned above, in consociational federations, the obligation for party elites of the different groups to decide through consensus is institutionalized. As this minimizes the risk of an unfavourable decision, one could argue that such consociational mechanisms simply render trust obsolete.

Cook, Hardin, and Levi (2005: 2) have indeed argued that trust is expendable and can be replaced by institutions encapsulating the interests of all actors. Axelrod (1984) has even argued that trust is not necessary for cooperation. It can emerge from the use of a tit-for-tat strategy in negotiations. This means that when one party cooperates, the other one will cooperate as well and vice versa. Thus trust can be the result, rather than the precondition, of cooperation. This hypothesis was criticized by Gambetta (1988), who argued that after a first disappointment, distrust can emerge, eliminating the willingness for further cooperation. A second critique is focused on political party strategies. Lijphart (2002) assumes that parties will seek a compromise because they want to transfer electoral power into governmental power. In the words of Müller and Strom (1999), he assumes political parties are policy-seeking or office-seeking. In contrast, Horowitz (2002) argues that political parties can be unwilling to reach a compromise, either because they fear losing votes in the next election or because they estimate that they can win votes by holding a hard line. As Müller and Strom put it, this means acting as vote-seekers.

We tend to agree that, in a consociational federation, the fact that one group is incapable of imposing decisions on another is one thing, but making decisions is another. Consociational mechanisms lower the potential cost linked to the risk of trusting, but this is not sufficient for effective policymaking, particularly in a consociational federation where decisions need to be made through consensus. Not all decisions can be detailed or implemented at the same time and not all daily government business is agreed collectively. Hence party elites still need to trust that other party elites will be loyal to the coalition and execute decisions faithfully. Consociational mechanisms reduce risk, but increase dependence between party elites as each one of them can block the whole governing process. As will become clear from the Belgian case, the danger of distrust concerning the strategy (i.e., vote-seeking or policy-seeking) of other political parties for hampering further negotiations should not be underestimated. The idea that consociational mechanisms cannot entirely replace trust does not mean *a priori* that they can't enhance it. This brings us to our next question.

Do Consociational Mechanisms in Federations Enhance or Deteriorate Trust between Party Elites?

There is no consensus on this aspect of the relation between trust and consociational mechanisms either. Some authors argue that trust between party elites is enhanced by consociational mechanisms. Three main arguments would support this.

First, in states, powerful incentives such as the rule of law, contract law, and independent courts reduce the risk of doing business. Similarly, we can reason that because groups are protected in a consociational democracy by their elite's veto power, they will be more willing to negotiate. As mentioned above, when the potential cost of risk is lower, trust is created more easily. In this way, "the threat of sanctions to protect each, make all better off" (Hardin 1996: 32).

Second, this obligation to reach consensus in consociational federations results in party elites deliberating on issues more often than in other systems. Most scholars believe that repeated contact results in relational trust which entails higher chances of successful negotiations (Williams 1988: 8; Sztompka 1997: 12; Reilly 2004: 8; Fearon and Laitin 1996). This is what happened in Belgium in the run-up to the Egmont agreement in 1977. Party presidents became a tightly knit group, getting so far ahead of their rank and file that the agreement eventually wasn't accepted by the latter. Weinstock (1999: 302) adds that trust can spread from cooperation in less sensitive policy areas to cooperation in more sensitive policy areas. Although he applied this logic to the trust of citizens in corporations or the government, it seems valid between political negotiators as well. Specifically concerning political elites, Luther (1999: 19) argues that once rival elites have established long-lasting cooperative behaviour, the efficacy and legitimacy of purely ideological language might decline, as it can be expected to reduce the scope for entering into required compromises. Thus, the creation of consociational mechanisms might increase trust.

Third, Weinstock (1999: 301) sees the devolution of competences as a way of avoiding distrust between groups within a divided society. He refers to it as "containment," breaking the link between A's capacity to reach a certain goal and B's capacity to inhibit A's reaching it. Group autonomy is obviously the essence of federalism, but is also identified by Lijphart (2002: 39) as an essential consociational mechanism. It can be argued that group autonomy avoids creating distrust between party elites because it eliminates potential conflict.

While some arguments can thus be put forward to argue that consociational federalism enhances trust between party elites, a number of authors argue the opposite, stating that institutionalizing distrust deteriorates trust because it communicates and reinforces this distrust (Rousseau et al. 1998: 399). First, it can be argued that consociational democracies cement conflicts by creating institutions around them. For instance, Braithwaite (1998) argues that the trouble with institutions that assume that people or business organizations will not be virtuous is that they destroy virtue. He cites a study that came to the following conclusion: retirement homes that were not trusted to comply with regulations actually complied less than when they were trusted to do so. Sitkin and Roth (1993: 369) state that "the literature suggests that attempts to remedy trust violations legalistically frequently fail because they paradoxically reduce the level of trust rather than reproducing it." They argue that "legal remedies" impose a psychological barrier between the two parties that stimulates formality and distance. Even Lijphart (2002: 54) admits that when consociational rules are laid down in formal documents, instead of just relying on informal agreements and understandings among group leaders, this does not tend to enhance trust: "My reading of the evidence is that informal rules generally work better because they reflect a higher level of trust among groups and group leaders." He seems to prefer an informal consociational culture, but argues that "when sufficient mutual trust is lacking and inter-group relations are highly contentious, there is probably no alternative to formal constitutional and legal rules to govern power sharing and autonomy in deeply divided societies." Consequently, one could see institutionalizing consociationalism as part of a vicious circle, where party elites try to remedy a lack of trust by institutionalizing consociational mechanisms, which in turn underlines the fact that this lack of trust creates distrust.

In addition, the tendency of consociational as well as federal institutions to essentialize identities is also a potential danger for relations of trust between elites. Even Lijphart (1977: 42) acknowledges that segmental autonomy increases the plural nature of an already plural society. Reilly (2004: 2) notes that, because ethnic identities tend to be invested with a great deal of symbolic and emotional meaning, it is tempting to use communal demands to attract votes. Hence "parties that begin by merely mirroring ethnic divisions help to deepen and extend them" (Horowitz 1985: 291). This polarization and reinforcement of communal demands provides party elites with incentives not to compromise, thus setting aside an essential part of the set of norms that parties are expected to follow. In this way, the institutionalization of identities and the consequent polarization can undermine trust.

In summary, we have identified several arguments supporting the view that consociational mechanisms *enhance* trust (by reducing the potential cost of trusting, creating relational trust, and avoiding distrust through autonomy), as well as several arguments supporting the view that consociational mechanisms *deteriorate* trust (by communicating a lack of trust and institutionalizing divided identities). We will now turn to the Belgian case to examine which of these arguments can be seen to play a role in practice.

THE BELGIAN CASE

The Consociational Core of the Belgian Federation

According to Lijphart (1981: 8), Belgium is "not just a complete example of consociational democracy: it is the most perfect, most convincing and most impressive example of a consociation." This makes it an ideal case to test the arguments stated above. Lijphart mostly refers to the institutional mechanisms that were implemented in the constitutional revision of 1970. This first Belgian "state reform" created regions and communities, the two types of entities Belgian federalism would be based on, while at the same time also institutionalizing a consociational logic to protect the French-speaking group and thus "pacify" the linguistic cleavage (for more details on why these mechanisms were introduced, see Sinardet 2010a: 351–2).

This logic rests on four elements. The first one is the building block and precondition for the other three: the division of all national MPs into two language groups, Dutch or French. Practically, every MP elected in the Dutch language region automatically belongs to the Dutch language group, and every MP elected in the French language region automatically belongs to the French language group. Those elected in the bilingual district of Brussels have the choice: the language in which they take their oath determines their group membership. German-speakers belong to the French language group. In other words, all "national" representatives will have to be either Dutch-speaking or French-speaking representatives. This is in line with the consociational premise that every group is represented by its own elites. The split of the three traditional national parties on a linguistic basis between 1968 and 1978 strongly reinforces this logic.

The three other elements are based on this division in language groups: the special majority law, the alarm bell procedure, and the linguistic parity in the council of ministers. A special majority law not only requires an overall majority of two-thirds of the MPs (as was already the case before constitutional revisions were made), but also a "double majority" in both legislative chambers: a simple majority in both language groups with the majority of the members of both language groups being present. This special majority is only required for a number of specific cases, stipulated in the constitution and all related to the execution of constitutional principles regarding institutional matters.

The "alarm bell procedure" prescribes that when at least three-quarters of a language group judge that a legislative bill could "severely damage the relations between the communities," they can "ring" the alarm bell by introducing a motivated motion. The parliamentary procedure is then interrupted and the proposal is sent to the Council of Ministers, which has thirty days to formulate a recommendation on the matter. Parliament is then invited to support the recommendation or possibly an amended proposal by the Council of Ministers.

This brings us to the mechanism introduced on the executive level: the Council of Ministers has to be composed of an equal number of Dutch speakers and French speakers, excluding the prime minister. It is also important – though it is only customary law – that the Council of Ministers makes decisions by consensus and not by majority vote. This implies a veto right for the two language groups and also for each of the parties, certainly if one takes into account that in Belgium the executive dominates the legislative branch and votes in parliament are often the consequence of a government consensus.

These four elements clearly show the consociational logic at work in the Belgian federation: a strongly institutionalized, anti-majoritarian model of conflict regulation based on consensus between elites representing their own language group, implying a mutual veto possessed by the two communities and an obligation to decide in consensus.

While the 1980s constitutional reform in Canada became less a prerogative of the elites or "men in suits" – because of the use of referenda, town hall meetings, and public conferences (Gagnon 2010: 240) – Belgian constitutional reform remains largely confined to party elites (Covell 1982: 452; Leton and Miroir 1999: 286). This has certainly been the case in recent decades. While in the 1960s mass protests were organized around the community conflict, this has hardly been the case in the recent decade, bringing the Belgian sociologist Luc Huyse to label Belgium's political troubles from 2007 onwards as "a crisis without a public" (quoted in Sinardet 2008). The question of whether these consociational mechanisms enhance or deteriorate trust between party elites is therefore all the more relevant.

Trust and Party Elites in Belgium

In Belgium's recent political history, a number of indications can be found in favour of the argument that consociational federalism would indeed enhance or at least not deteriorate trust. Indeed, the institutionalization of the consociational mechanisms described above does seem to have permitted, or at least not hindered, party elites in governing the country, and even in pursuing no less than six state reforms over a forty-six-year period. Consociational mechanisms seem, indeed, to have enhanced trust by reducing risk. On first inspection they seem to have enhanced (or again, at least not hindered) the trust that is needed to profoundly reform the country. In parallel, through the repeated interactions of party elites resulting from the obligation to come to consensus, relational trust seems to have been sufficiently present to make institutional reforms possible. It has been argued specifically that governing through mutual agreement has had the consequence of strengthening the contacts and mutual trust between party elites in Belgium (Witte, Craeybeckx, and Meynen 1997: 403). Indeed, the four state reforms between 1970 and 1993 were largely negotiated by the same parties: the Christian Democrats and socialists on both sides of the language border, to which generally smaller parties were added to form a majority. Even Flemish and Walloon nationalists participated in those state reforms and were integrated in the consociational negotiating culture. In 2002, the third of the classic party families, the liberals, took the lead in the fifth state reform.

These state reform agreements have all led to the further devolution of competences from the federal level to the regions and communities. This, indeed, seems to have led to containment (Leton and Miroir 1999: 345), as argued by Weinstock. The tensions on the federal level concerning a number of competences were (partly) solved by regionalizing these competences. This was the case, for instance, when these tensions were caused by an ideological dispute along community dimensions, with the political centre of gravity leaning more to the right in the country's north and more to the left in the south. When Wallonia's industry started to decline in the 1960s, left wing forces in the south – later followed by the Walloon wing of the socialist party – allied themselves with the Walloon movement to demand socio-economical regionalization that would combat the crisis with resolutely left wing policies. Such policies were difficult to pursue at the national level, where they had to work with the more right wing Flemish Christian Democrats. Similarly, since the 1990s, Flemish regionalization demands always came from the right of the political spectrum, with the conclusion being that a number of liberal reforms would be easier to pursue at the Flemish level rather than at the federal level. However, ideological discourse often simply hid differences in economical or electoral interest. An example of this is the regionalization of weapon export licenses. Flemish parties opposed the export of weapons from the Walloon factory of Herstal on pacifist grounds. In the end, the competence to grant export licenses was regionalized, though the Flemish policy hardly changed from what previously existed at the federal level. Nevertheless, devolution of competences did defuse community conflicts – or communitized conflicts – that existed about a number of issues at the federal level. Because of the pre-existing tensions surrounding the devolved competences, it seems that they didn't lead to opportunities of cooperation being missed. Rather, it seems that devolving competences, as Weinstock argued, avoided creating distrust.

However, the total picture is not quite so positive. It must be added that most of these reforms have occurred amidst a highly tense political atmosphere. Indeed, at different times, quite long periods of paralysis have preceded agreements on state reform. Between 1978 and 1981, Belgium had no less than six short-lived governments. In 1988, Belgium broke its own record of government formation longevity. That record was again broken in 2007 in attempts to negotiate a sixth state reform (194 days). In the period from 2010 to 2011, the world record for government formation longevity was even broken while trying to negotiate the same reform, which was finally concluded after 541 days.

The effects of consociational federalism diminishing trust, as described above, can also be seen in Belgium. Indeed, institutionalizing consociational logic also institutionalized the community divide, perpetuating tensions rather than pacifying them. The institutionalization of the community divide as a continuous source of tension is most apparent in the split of the Belgian political parties that only contest elections within their own linguistic community. Because parties only seek votes within their own linguistic community, they cannot lose votes by taking a tough stance in the defence of the linguistic community's interests. This gives parties on both sides of the language border disincentives to compromise, given that other parties from within the same group will be all too keen to point out the compromising party's abandonment of the group's interests. Hence, by organizing the institutional architecture according to the linguistic divide, relations between Dutch-speaking and French-speaking parties polarized the leading party elites, to the extent that they mutually believe that they might no longer operate according to a broader set of norms, hence reducing trust.

Moreover, there is a particularly perverse effect that is caused by the character of multi-level electoral politics, especially since the disconnection of federal from regional elections since the 2003 federal election (Sinardet 2010a: 363). The latter was explicitly done to grant the regional governments more autonomy. It can, however, incite parties who are not in the federal government to go even further in outbidding on community issues during regional campaigns, as they will not have to bear the consequences of their radical discourse after the elections; elections only concern the regional level. Moreover, if incongruent coalitions are formed, parties present in the regional but not in the federal government can even use their position to continue campaigning on the community issue from the regional government, putting pressure on the federal government. Hence, regional governments partly took over the role of sub-state nationalist parties by demanding more autonomy. This dynamic is part of what explains the years of crisis in Belgium around the issue of the Brussels-Halle-Vilvoorde electoral district split (Sinardet 2010a: 357–64). This dynamic, resulting from group autonomy, further forces party elites into breaking with the set of norms that serve as the basis for trust. This type of dynamic is reinforced by the Belgian media system, which is also organized linguistically. Rather than offering a balanced view on community issues, media tend to implicitly follow the political consensus of their own language community (Sinardet 2007). This reinforces the deterioration of trust brought about by the institutionalization of identities and group autonomy. Another problematic element is the lack of institutional-based trust. In the case of institutional-based trust, the positive expectations that someone will follow the required set of norms results from the reputation of the function or institution represented by this person, regardless of the specificities of the person involved. In the Belgian case, the beneficial consequences of institutionalizing consociational logic remained dependent on a specific set of persons, hence only creating relational trust. It was therefore all but structural, depending instead on the fact that parties and their elites were part of the same networks and formed a cartel of elites running the country. The problem is that either no or little institutional based trust seems to be created, because of the mutually reinforcing trust-deteriorating mechanisms of group autonomy and the institutionalization of identities. Each state reform completely disregarded cohesion at the federal level. This was not necessarily a problem for the maintenance of relational trust between party elites, as long as they could rely on the old networks described above. For instance, for a long period the Flemish and French-speaking Christian Democrats regularly had informal meetings (Martens 2006). However, centrifugal tendencies also had an influence on these networks. After eight years in opposition, between 1999 and 2007, the leaders of the Flemish and francophone Christian Democrats had hardly talked to each other about the state reform that they would have to negotiate together after the 2007 elections. Hence relational trust, which was pivotal due to the lack of institutional-based trust, diminished as well. Moreover, in part due to these centrifugal tendencies and in part due to other factors, new political parties emerged that had not been socialized in the classic political networks and the shared set of norms that form the basis for trust. This made the necessity of finding a compromise with elites representing the other language group less evident.

This leads to the conclusion that the combination of separate and institutionalized identities (forcing parties into a role defined by their belonging to a community), and the centrifugal effects of group auton-omy, reduced trust. Relational trust was created through repeated interaction and dialogue, but institutional-based trust was hampered by these centrifugal effects. How did this dynamic unfold during the negotiations leading up to the most recent Belgian state reform?

The Long and Winding Road to a Sixth Belgian State Reform

With its two separate party systems and electoral spaces, the 2010 federal election produced two distinct winners. In Flanders, the Flemish nationalist and separatist Nieuw-Vlaamse alliantie (N-VA; New Flemish Alliance) became the country's largest party, with 17.4 per cent of the votes in the chamber of representatives, which corresponds to 27.8 per cent of the votes for Dutch-speaking parties and a total of 27 out of 150 seats. Of the French-speaking parties, the PS (Socialist Party) was the uncontested winner, with 26 seats. Although a so-called government of national unity without the N-VA would be theoretically possible, the other Flemish parties at first did not want to exclude the uncontested winner of the elections.

The same goes for at least two of the other French-speaking parties with respect to the PS.

An important factor in understanding the 541-day period without a federal government in 2010–11 was that several parties refused to form a government before an institutional reform was agreed upon. Thus the risk of misplaced trust was even higher than during a regular government formation. In addition, the N-VA, being a relatively new party, did not have a reputation on which trust could be based.

Still, it was not wholly unreasonable to doubt that the N-VA would operate following the set of norms required for trust between party elites, for three reasons. The first is a historical one. The N-VA defines itself explicitly as a successor of the Flemish nationalist party Volksunie. The Volksunie had several successes but suffered a huge electoral loss after its participation in an institutional compromise in 1978 known as the Egmont pact (Leton and Miroir 1999: 113). More importantly, it split in 2001 because of a conflict over the Lambermont compromise (Sinardet 2010b). The radical part of the Volksunie that was fiercely against the Lambermont agreement went on to form the N-VA. In other words, the refusal of the fifth state reform agreement is one of the main reasons for the N-VA's existence. Second, ever since its conception in 2001, the N-VA has wanted an independent Flanders (N-VA 2001: 1), which makes other parties doubt its federal loyalty. Moreover, by portraying the federal government formation and the federal level in general as a failure, it could emphasize the inadequacy of the Belgian state, which probably contributed to a more widespread opinion in the electorate that there was inadequacy at the federal level, and also potentially enhanced future N-VA election results. Part of its discourse has always been that the federal level does not work structurally, because of the structural incapacity of Dutch-speaking and French-speaking representatives to agree on which policies should be pursued. Third, polls at that time indicated that the N-VA and the PS were regarded by voters as the only parties advancing significantly on the 2010 election results in their regions. Not compromising could therefore have been a vote-seeking strategy. As a result, there was a lack of positive expectations on the part of the other parties that the N-VA would be willing to compromise, and consequently a lack of trust. The low reputation might have been turned around by repeated interaction, creating relational trust between the party elites after several interactions. However, the hope for relational trust was crushed when the "gentleman's agreement" that N-VA president De Wever and PS president Di Rupo closed shortly after the elections was subsequently breached. Distrust emerged.

As a result of this distrust, no compromise could be found with the N-VA. Eventually, the traditional political parties (socialists, liberals, Christian Democrats), but also the greens, concluded an agreement on the sixth state reform. The traditional political parties went on to govern until the end of the term in 2014.

CONCLUSION

We looked into the precise relation between consociational theory and trust, exploring two questions: is trust a necessary requirement to reach consensus, or can consociational mechanisms replace the role of trust? And do consociational mechanisms enhance or deteriorate trust between party elites in consociational federations?

First, we elaborated on the question of whether consociational mechanisms can replace trust. Indeed, as elites of the different groups in society are "protected" against one another by mechanisms such as veto power, they would no longer need to trust one another. The potential cost of misplacing trust is low, as a group can always veto a decision. However, consociational mechanisms force them to come to a consensus in order to govern – but this does not mean that parties will come to this consensus. Trust is still needed for effective policy-making, let alone agreement on an institutional reform, where the potential cost is even higher. Authors such as Axelrod (1984) have argued that cooperation can emerge in a situation where trust is lacking by using a tit-for-tat strategy. However, this theoretical approach does not take into account the distrust that can prevent further negotiations in the real world.

We then turned to the following question: if consociational mechanisms do not replace trust, do they enhance or deteriorate trust? Based on the literature, we get a mixed answer. Some arguments suggest that they should be expected to enhance trust. The first is that consociational mechanisms enhance trust between groups because all groups feel protected by their veto power, and know that it is in the interest of the other groups to find consensus. The second argument is that, through repeated interactions between party elites, relational trust is created. The third argument is that group autonomy will impede distrust between party elites of these groups, because policies where compromise is difficult are avoided by devolving competences. However, others argue that consociational mechanisms have quite the opposite consequences for trust between party elites: they institutionalize separated identities and communicate the lack of trust between these identities, which in turn stimulates centrifugal tendencies. In addition, group autonomy creates institutional, often electoral, incentives for an antagonistic attitude.

We then looked at which of these arguments were supported by the evidence offered in recent decades using the Belgian case. While it is indeed possible to find support for the three arguments that trust is enhanced in consociational federations, as well as support for the conflict-reducing potential of devolution, the dominant dynamic in Belgium rather seems to support the argument that consociational mechanisms do not enhance trust, owing to unintended consequences of group autonomy. We saw in the Belgian case that only relational trust was created between the elites and that the more structural institutional-based trust seemed absent. This might be because the institutionalization of identities, an essential aspect of consociational-ism, imposes on party elites the role of defender of group interests. This leads other party elites to doubt whether they will still follow the appropriate set of norms, which include a willingness to compro-mise or a preference for collective over individual welfare and federal loyalty. This doubt lowers trust, which might in turn lead to regional-izing more competences. Regionalization enforces the institutionalized identities even further, lowering trust. This vicious circle culminated in the new nationalist and separatist party (N-VA) becoming by far the largest party in the Flemish region. Their arrival led to a break-down of trust, because of uncertainty as to whether this party would operate according to the appropriate set of norms, with several indi-cations suggesting that it would not. All hope for repeated contacts leading to relational trust became obsolete, after a perceived breach of trust between both central actors. In the end no compromise with the Flemish nationalist party could be found. This led to an agreement between the traditional parties and the Green Party. The traditional parties would go on to govern until the end of the term even though they could be perceived as the losers of the election. The Belgian case thus seems to show that consociational mechanisms cannot replace trust between party elites, and that they even seem to diminish trust by institutionalizing groups with separate identities and providing electoral incentives to pander to these identities.

REFERENCES

Alen, A. 1990. *België: Een tweeledig en centrifugaal federalisme*. Brussels: Ministerie van Buitenlandse Zaken.

Andeweg, R. 2000. "Consociational Democracy." *Annual Review of Political Science* 3: 509–36.

Axelrod, R. 1984. *The Evolution of Cooperation*. New York: Basic Books.

Baier, A. 1986. "Trust and Antitrust." *Ethics* 96, no. 2: 231–60.

Braithwaite, J. 1998. "Institutionalizing Distrust, Enculturating Trust." In *Trust and Governance*, edited by M. Levi and V. Braithwaite, 343–76. New York: Russell Sage Foundation.

Cook, K.S., R. Hardin, and M. Levi. 2005. *Cooperation without Trust?* New York: Russell Sage Foundation.

Covell, M. 1982. "Agreeing to Disagree: Elite Bargaining and the Revision of the Belgian Constitution." *Canadian Journal of Political Science* 15, no. 3: 451–69.

Dasgupta, P. 1988. "Trust as a Commodity." In *Trust: Making and Breaking Cooperative Relations*, edited by D. Gambetta, 49–73. Oxford: Blackwell.

Deschouwer, K. 1999. "From Consociation to Federation: How the Belgian Parties Won." In *Party Elites in Divided Societies: Political Parties in Consociational Democracy*, edited by K. Luther and K. Deschouwer, 74–108. London: Routledge.

Deschouwer, K., and K. Luther. 1999. "Prudent Leadership to Successful Adaptation? Pillar Parties and Consociational Democracy Thirty Years On." In *Party Elites in Divided Societies: Political Parties in Consociational Democracy*, edited by K. Luther and K. Deschouwer, 244–65. London: Routledge.

Deschouwer, K., and D. Sinardet. 2010. "Identiteiten, communautaire standpunten en stemgedrag." In *De stemmen van het volk: Een analyse van het kiesgedrag in Vlaanderen en Wallonië op 7 juni 2009*, edited by K. Deschouwer, P. Delwit, M. Hooghe, and S. Walgrave, 75–99. Brussels: Brussels University Press.

De Winter, L., A. Timmermans, and P. Dumont. 2000. "Belgium: On Government Agreements, Evangelists, Followers and Heretics." In *Coalition Governments in Western Europe*, edited by W.C. Müller and K. Strom, 300–56. Oxford: Oxford University Press.

Fearon, J.D., and D.D. Laitin. 1996. "Explaining Interethnic Cooperation." *The American Political Science Review* 90, no. 4: 715–35.

Gagnon, A.-G. 2010. "Executive Federalism and the Exercise of Democracy in Canada." In *Federal Democracies*, edited by M. Burgess and A.-G. Gagnon, 232–51. London: Routledge.

Gambetta, D. 1988. "Can We Trust Trust?" In *Trust: Making and Breaking Cooperative Relations*, edited by D. Gambetta, 213–39. Oxford: Blackwell.

Good, D. 1988. "Individuals, Interpersonal Relations, and Trust." In *Trust: Making and Breaking Cooperative Relations*, edited by D. Gambetta, 31–49. Oxford: Blackwell.

Hardin, R. 1996. "Trustworthiness." *Ethics* 107, no. 1: 26–42.

Horowitz, D.L. 1985. *Ethnic Groups in Conflict*. London: University of California Press.

– 2002. "Constitutional Design: Proposals versus Processes." In *The Architecture of Democracy: Constitutional Design, Conflict Management and Democracy*, edited by A. Reynolds, 15–37. Oxford: Oxford University Press.

Lenard, P.T. 2007. "Trust Your Compatriots, but Count Your Change: The Roles of Trust, Mistrust and Distrust in Democracy." *Political Studies* 56, no. 2: 312–32.

Leton, A., and A. Miroir. 1999. *Les conflits communautaires en Belgique*. Paris: Presses Universitaires de France.

Lewis, J.D., and A. Weigert. 1985. "Trust As a Social Reality." *Social Forces* 63, no. 4: 967–85.

Lijphart, A. 1969. "Consociational Democracy." *World Politics* 21, no. 2: 207–24.

– 1977. *Democracy in Plural Societies*. New Haven: Yale University Press.

– 1981. "The Belgian Example of Cultural Coexistence In Comparative Perspective." In *Conflict and Coexistence in Belgium: The Dynamics of a Culturally Divided Society*, edited by A. Lijphart, 1–13. Berkeley: University of California.

– 1999. *Patterns of Democracy: Government Forms in Thirty-Six Countries*. New Haven: Yale University Press.

– 2002. "The Wave of Power-Sharing Democracy." In *The Architecture of Democracy: Constitutional Design, Conflict Management and Democracy*, edited by A. Reynolds, 37–55. Oxford: Oxford University Press.

Lupia, A., and K. Strom. 2008. "Bargaining, Transaction Costs and Coalition Governance." In *Cabinets and Coalition Bargaining: The Democratic Lifecycle in Western Europe*, edited by K. Strom, W.C. Müller, and T. Bergman, 51–85. Oxford: Oxford University Press.

Luther, K. 1999. "A Framework for the Comparative Analysis of Political Parties and Party Systems in Consociational Democracy." In *Party Elites in Divided Societies: Political Parties in Consociational Democracy*, edited by K. Luther and K. Deschouwer, 3–20. London: Routledge.

Magnette, P., and Y. Papadopoulos. 2008. "On the Politicization of the European Consociation: A Middle Way between Hix and Bartolini." *European Governance Papers* (EUROGOV-C-08-01).

Martens, W. 2006. *De Memoires*. Tielt: Lannoo.

Ministerie voor Binnenlandse Zaken. 2010. *Verkiezingen 2010: Zetelverdeling in de Kamer*. Accessed 1 October 2010. http://www.elections2010.belgium.be/nl/cha/seat/seat_CKR00000.html.

Misztal, B. 2001. "Trust and Cooperation: The Democratic Public Sphere." *Journal of Sociology* 37, no. 4: 371–86.

N-VA (Nieuw-Vlaamse alliantie). 2001. *Beginselverklaring*. Accessed 1 October 2010. http://www.nva.be/files/default/nva_images/documenten/beginselverklaring0.1.pdf.

Oskarsson, S. 2010. "Generalized Trust and Political Support: A Cross-National Investigation." *Acta Politica* 45, no. 4: 423–43.

Reilly, B. 2004. *Democracy In Divided Societies: Electoral Engineering for Conflict Management*. Cambridge: Cambridge University Press.

Rousseau D., S. Sitkin, R. Burt, and C. Camerer. 1998. "Not So Different After All: A Cross-Discipline View of Trust." *Academy of Management Review* 23, no. 3: 393–404.

Simeon R., and D.P. Conway. 2001. "Federalism and the Management of Conflict in Multinational Societies." In *Multinational Democracies*, edited by A.-G. Gagnon and J. Tully, 338–66. Cambridge: Cambridge University Press.

Sinardet, D. 2007. "Wederzijdse mediarepresentaties van de nationale 'andere': Vlamingen, Franstaligen en het Belgische federale samenlevingsmodel." PhD thesis, Universiteit Antwerpen, Antwerp.

– 2008. "Belgian Federalism Put to the Test? The Belgian Federal Elections of 2007 and Their Aftermath." *West European Politics* 31, no. 5: 1016–32.

– 2010a. "From Consociational Consciousness to Majoritarian Myth: Consociational Democracy, Multi-Level Politics and the Belgian Case of Brussels-Halle-Vilvoorde." *Acta Politica* 45, no. 3: 346–69.

– 2010b. *Institutional Reform In Belgium: An Analysis of the Political Dynamics behind the Lambermont State Reform of 2001*. Hagen: Fern Universität.

Sitkin, S.B., and N.L. Roth. 1993. "Explaining the Limited Effectiveness of Legalistic 'Remedies' for Trust/Distrust." *Organization Science* 4, no. 3: 367–92.

Sztompka, P. 1997. *Trust, Distrust and the Paradox of Democracy*. Berlin: Wissenschaftszentrum Berlin für Sozialforschung.

Watts, R. 1998. "Federalism, Federal Political Systems, and Federations." *Annual Review of Political Science* 1: 117–37.

Weinstock, D. 1999. "Building Trust in Divided Societies." *The Journal of Political Philosophy* 7, no. 3: 287–307.

– 2001. "Vers une théorie normative du fédéralisme." *Revue internationale des sciences sociales* 167, no. 1: 79–87.

Williams, B. 1988. "Formal Structures and Social Reality." In *Trust: Making and Breaking Cooperative Relations*, edited by D. Gambetta, 3–14. Oxford: Blackwell.

Witte, E., J. Craeybeckx, and A. Meynen. 1997. *Politieke geschiedenis van België*. Antwerpen: Standaard Uitgeverij.

Wolinetz, S. 1999. "The Consociational Party System." In *Party Elites in Divided Societies: Political Parties in Consociational Democracy*, edited by K. Luther and K. Deschouwer, 224–43. London: Routledge.

Zucker, L.G. 1986. "Production of Trust: Institutional Sources of Economic Structure, 1840–1920." *Research in Organizational Behavior* 8: 53–111.

Contributors

DARIO CASTIGLIONE teaches political theory at the University of Exeter. His main research interests are in the history of political thought and democratic theory, and in particular the relation between political and civil society. His publications include *Constitutional Politics in the EU* (Palgrave, 2007) and a number of edited volumes, such as *The Handbook of Social Capital* (Oxford, 2008), *The Language Question in Europe and Diverse Societies* (Hart, 2007), *The Making of European Citizens* (Palgrave, 2006), *The Culture of Toleration in Diverse Societies: Reasonable Tolerance* (Manchester University Press, 2003), and *The History of Political Thought in National Context* (Cambridge, 2001).

JÉRÔME COUTURE has a PhD in political science from Laval University, where his thesis was about municipal elections in Canada. He is currently a SSHRC postdoctoral fellow at the INRS-UCS (Institut National de la Recherche Scientifique, Urbanisation, Culture, Societé). He has co-authored several papers on political trust in multinational states with Rejean Pelletier. He is a specialist in quantitative methods, which he has been teaching at Laval since 2010. He was a municipal elected official in the Québec City region from 2005 to 2013. He is also a member of the laboratory on local elections (LABEL).

KRIS DESCHOUWER is a research professor in the Department of Political Science at the Vrije Universiteit in Brussels. His research and publications deal with political parties, elections, political represen-tation, regionalism, federalism and consociational democracy, and Belgian politics. He is the author of *The Politics of Belgium: Governing a Divided Society, 2nd Edition* (Palgrave, 2012).

DIMITRIOS KARMIS is an associate professor in the School of Political Studies at the University of Ottawa. His research interests include citizenship, cultural pluralism, immigration, federalism, dialogic democracy, university transformations, and the history of political thought. He has published in many edited volumes and journals, including *Studies in Social Justice*, *The Tocqueville Review*, *Ethnic and Racial Studies*, *Cahiers de l'idiotie*, *Politique et Sociétés*, and *Canadian Journal of Political Science*. He has also co-edited a number of volumes and journal issues, including *Défaire / Refaire l'université* (*Cahiers de l'idiotie*, 2015), *Ceci n'est pas une idée politique: Réflexions sur les approches à l'étude des idées politiques* (Laval, 2013), *Du tricoté serré au métissé serrée? La culture publique commune au Québec en débats* (Laval, 2008), and *Theories of Federalism* (Palgrave, 2005).

JEAN LECLAIR is a professor in the Faculty of Law at the Université de Montréal. His teaching and research interests include legal theory, Canadian legal history, constitutional law (federalism and fundamental rights), and Aboriginal legal issues. He was one of the four Pierre Elliott Trudeau Foundation fellows for 2013. Some of his most recent publications relating to federalism are "Envisaging Canada in a Disenchanted World: Reflections on Federalism, Nationalism, and Distinctive Indigenous Identity" (*Constitutional Forum constitutionnel,* 2016), "Military Historiography, Warriors and Soldiers: The Normative Impact of Epistemological Choices," in *Essays on the Constitutional Entrenchment of Aboriginal and Treaty Rights*, edited by P. Macklem and D. Sanderson (University of Toronto, 2016), "'Daddy, Is the Sky Higher Than the Ceiling?': Roderick Alexander Macdonald's Federal Epistemology and Ontology," in *The Unbounded Level of the Mind: Rod Macdonald's Legal Imagination*, edited by R. Janda, R. Jukier, and D. Jutras (McGill-Queen's, 2015), and "Le fédéralisme: Un terreau fertile pour gérer un monde incertain," in *Fédéralisme et gouvernance autochtone / Federalism and Aboriginal Governance*, edited by G. Otis and M. Papillon (Laval, 2013).

PATTI TAMARA LENARD is an associate professor in the Graduate School of Public and International Affairs at the University of Ottawa.

Her current research focuses on the moral question raised by migration across borders, multiculturalism, trust and solidarity, and democratic theory. Her work has been published in a range of journals, including *Political Studies*, *Journal of Moral Philosophy*, and *Review of Politics*. Her first book is titled *Trust, Democracy, and Multicultural Challenges* (Penn State, 2012).

NIELS MORSINK studied political science at the University of Antwerp, Université Capitole 1 in Toulouse, and Marmara University in Istanbul. He worked for three years as a junior researcher at the University of Antwerp, mostly on federalism, interest groups, and the European Union. Since September 2014 he has been a voluntary researcher at the Public Governance Institute focusing on interest groups and the European Union, as well as Turkish politics and political theory.

GENEVIÈVE NOOTENS is professor of political science at Université du Québec à Chicoutimi. She is the author of *Désenclaver la démocratie: Des huguenots à la paix des braves* (Québec Amérique, 2007), *Souveraineté démocratique, justice et mondialisation* (Liber, 2010), and of *Popular Sovereignty in the West: Polities, Contention, and Ideas* (Routledge, 2013). She has co-edited *Contemporary Majority Nationalisms* with A.-G. Gagnon and A. Lecours (McGill-Queen's, 2011), *Dominant Nationalism, Dominant Ethnicity: Identity, Federalism and Democracy* with A. Lecours (Peter Lang, 2009), and *Le cosmopolitisme: Enjeux et débats contemporains* with Ryoa Chung (Presses de l'Université de Montréal, 2010). She has published papers in *Nations and Nationalism*, *Contemporary Political Theory*, and *Global Constitutionalism*. She also has chapters in several edited books, including *National Cultural Autonomy and Its Contemporary Critics* (Routledge, 2005), *After the Nation?* (Palgrave, 2010), *Political Autonomy and Divided Societies: Imagining Democratic Alternatives in Complex Settings* (Palgrave, 2012), and *Minorities and Territory: Rethinking Autonomy as Strategy* (Oxford, 2015).

DARREN O'TOOLE is an associate professor in the common law section of the Faculty of Law at the University of Ottawa. His teaching and research focus on Canadian politics, the history of political and juridical ideas, Aboriginal law, and critical Indigenous legal studies. He has primarily published in the areas of the Indigenous rights of the Métis of Manitoba and Ojibwe legal orders. He is a descendant of the Bois-Brûlé from Waabishki-mishtadim Mashkodeng (White Horse Plains) in Manitoba.

ALEXANDRE PELLETIER is a PhD candidate at the University of Toronto and a Fellow at the Trudeau Centre for Peace, Conflict and Justice at the Munk School of Global Affairs. His research focuses mainly on civil society, ethnic politics, and religious conflict in Indonesia and Myanmar. His previous works on Canada have been published in the *Canadian Journal of Political Science* (2014) and *Quebec Studies* (2012), and his current works on Southeast Asia have been published in *Nationalism and Ethnic Politics* (2017) and *South East Asia Research* (2017).

RÉJEAN PELLETIER is a fellow of the Royal Society of Canada (Academy of Social Sciences). He was a professor in the Department of Political Science at Université Laval until his retirement in 2009. Recognized as a specialist in Québec and Canadian politics, his main research interests are federalism, political institutions, political parties, women in politics, and political trust. Author of more than 100 articles in scientific reviews and edited books, he recently published *Le Québec et le fédéralisme canadien: Un regard critique* (Laval, 2008), edited *Les partis politiques québécois dans la tourmente* (Laval, 2012), and co-edited (with Manon Tremblay) *Le parlementarisme canadien, 5th edition* (Laval, 2013).

PHILIP RESNICK is professor emeritus in the Department of Political Science, University of British Columbia. He has been a visiting fellow at the Australian National University and in 2002–03 held the chair in Canadian Studies at the University of Paris III – Sorbonne Nouvelle. His publications include: *Letters to a Québécois Friend*; *The Masks of Proteus: Canadian Reflections on the State*; *Towards a Canada-Quebec Union*; *Thinking English Canada*; *Twenty-First Century Democracy*; *The Politics of Resentment: British Columbia Regionalism and Canadian Unity*; *The European Roots of Canadian Identity*; *The Labyrinth of North American Identities*; and, most recently, a collection of poetry entitled *Footsteps of the Past*.

DAVID ROBICHAUD is an associate professor in moral and political philosophy at the University of Ottawa, and a member of the Groupe de Recherche Interuniversitaire sur la Normativité (GRIN). His current research projects include work on linguistic justice, (dis)trust in diverse societies, and normative justifications for taxation. He has recently published papers in the *Cambridge Companion to Language Policy*, CRISPP (*Critical Review of International Social and Political Philosophy*), *Philosophiques*, *The Journal of Multicultural and Multilingual Development*, and in many edited volumes. He is the author (with P. Turmel) of *La juste part* (Atelier 10 and Les liens qui libèrent). He is also co-editor (with H. De Schutter) of *Linguistic Justice: Van Parijs and His Critics* (CRISPP and Routledge, 2016), and (with D. Anctil and P. Turmel) of *Penser les institutions* (Laval, 2013).

FRANÇOIS ROCHER is a professor of political science in the School of Political Studies at the University of Ottawa. His research interests include constitutional politics, Canadian federalism, Québec national-ism, and the management of ethnocultural diversity. He has published widely in these areas. His publications include *Guy Rocher: Entretiens* (Boréal, 2010) and *Immigration, diversité et sécurité: Les associations arabo-musulmanes face à l'État au Canada et au Québec*, with Micheline Labelle and Rachad Antonius (Université du Québec, 2009). He recently co-edited *Essential Readings in Canadian Politics and Government, 2nd Edition* (2015); *Le nouvel ordre constitutionnel canadien* (Université du Québec, 2013); *The State in Transition: Challenges for Canadian Federalism* (Envenire, 2011).

PETER RUSSELL was a professor of political science at the University of Toronto from 1958 to 1996. He published mainly in the area of constitutional politics, native politics, and the legal system. His most recent works are: *Recognizing Aboriginal Title: The Mabo Case and Indigenous Resistance to English-Settler Colonialism* (University of Toronto, 2006); *Two Cheers for Minority Government* (Emond Montgomery, 2008); the third edition of *Constitutional Odyssey: Can Canadians Become a Sovereign People?* (University of Toronto, 2013); and *Canada's Odyssey: A Country Based on Incomplete Conquests* (University of Toronto, 2017). He is a former president of the Canadian Political Science Association and the Canadian Law and Society Association. He is the founding principal of the Senior College, University of Toronto.

RICHARD SIMEON (1943–2013) was professor emeritus in political science and law at the University of Toronto (1991–2010). In 2010, he was awarded the Daniel J. Elazar Award by the American Political

Science Association for his contribution to the study of federalism and intergovernmental relations. He taught at Queen's University (1968–1991), where he was director of the Institute of Intergovernmental Relations (1976–1983), and had also been a visiting professor in several universities, including Harvard and Cape Town. His work focused on the design of institutional structures and political accommodation in divided societies.

DAVE SINARDET is a professor in the Department of Political Science of the Free University of Brussels (VUB). He is also a professor at the Université Saint-Louis in Brussels. His research concentrates on federalism, nationalism, consociational democracy, political communication, and multilingual polities. He published in many readers and journals including *Party Politics* (Acta Politica), *Governance*, *Pouvoirs*, *Revue française d'études constitutionnelles et politiques*, *Regional and Federal Studies*, *West-European Politics*, *Government and Opposition*. He is also an expert on the Belgian state reform process, as well as on Belgian politics in general. He is a columnist and an active participant in public debate.

JEREMY WEBBER is dean of law at the University of Victoria. He held the Canada Research Chair in Law and Society at the University of Victoria from 2002 to 2014, and in 2009 was appointed a fellow of the Trudeau Foundation. Prior to joining UVic, he was dean of Law at the University of Sydney, Australia, and professor of law at McGill University. He has written widely in the areas of constitutional law, Indigenous rights, federalism, cultural diversity, and constitutional theory. He is the author of *Reimagining Canada: Language, Culture, Community and the Canadian Constitution* (McGill-Queen's, 1994) and *The Constitution of Canada: A Contextual Analysis* (Bloomsbury, 2015).

Index

Aboriginal and treaty rights, 120–8, 169, 173, 175–7, 180

Aboriginal peoples. *See* Indigenous peoples (or nations)

accommodation, 178, 210, 243, 248–76, 285, 286, 291, 351

assimilation, 94–100, 142, 156–7, 282, 337

asymmetry: constitutional, 177, 187, 193, 194, 197, 203, 230; of power, 9, 10, 141, 161

attitude(s), 19; antagonistic, 364; towards Catalonia and Spain, 297n17; of distrust, 92; akin to doubt and cautiousness, 27–8; epistemological, 225–6; of faith, 21–2; of hope and confidence, 21–2; towards others, 25, 27; of party elites, 351; positive, 136; racist, 118; reflective, 235; "Socratic," 236; of suspicion and cynicism, 27–8

autonomy: cultural, 156; group, 253, 265, 351, 354–5, 363–4; individual, 28–30, 211; provincial, 142, 144–9, 161n5, 168, 171–2, 174–5, 179–80, 184–5, 194–5, 202n16, 219, 227–31, 241n26, 284; regional, 281, 287, 291, 322–3, 340, 360

Baier, Annette, 22, 70, 105, 249, 262, 348

Banting, Keith, 32, 52

Basque Country, 281–3, 287, 291–4, 296n3, 297n18, 308, 314, 315. *See also* Spain

Belgium: and confederation, 338; federal elections, 336, 343–4, 360–1; federal government, 338, 360, 362; federal level, 338, 340–2, 344, 359, 361–2; federalization of, 10, 290; linguistic issues, 9, 11–12, 284, 290, 294, 331–47, 356–64. *See also* Brussels; consociation; federal loyalty; Flanders; veto; Wallonia

bilingualism. *See* language rights

Bill 101. *See* Charter of the French Language (Québec)

Bloc Québécois: as the expression of the binational vision, 195; motion on Quebecers forming a nation, 183–4, 202nn19–20; possible coalition government depending on, 132;

methodological nationalism, 231–2;
as minority nations, 308; and mon-
isms, 213; and power asymmetry,
161; resistance, 286, 295; and sections 25 and 35 of the Canadian
Charter, 286. *See also* Aboriginal
and treaty rights; Inuit; Metis;
Royal Commission on Aboriginal
Peoples
individual autonomy. *See* autonomy
individualism: versus collectivism, 176–
8, 180–1, 192–3; liberal, 224, 235;
methodological, 212–13
intergovernmental agreements, 172,
186–7
Inuit, 120–6. *See also* Aboriginal and
treaty rights; Indigenous peoples (or
nations); Metis; Royal Commission
on Aboriginal Peoples

Keating, Michael, 281, 297n16, 309,
313, 322–3
Kymlicka, Will, 32–4, 38, 44, 52, 90,
177, 308, 313

language rights, 286; in Belgium, 337,
340, 356–7; Canadian Charter of
Rights and Freedoms, 153, 169–70,
176–7, 193, 200n7; of French
Catholic minorities in Canada, 120,
147–50, 162n6, 162n8; interpretation of, 10, 179–82, 189, 203n33;
Official Languages Act (1969), 256;
in Spain, 287, 296n6. *See also*
Canadian Charter of Rights and
Freedoms; Charter of Human Rights
and Freedoms (Québec); Charter of
the French Language (Québec)
Lenard, Patti, 3, 5–6, 27, 68–86,
348–50

Lévesque, René, 88, 94, 102–5, 108n17,
130, 158, 176, 190
Liberal Party of Canada, 151, 169–70,
183–4, 195, 199n2, 202n20, 238n5,
325
Liberal Party of Québec, 104, 153,
239n10
Lijphart, Arend, 338–9, 350–56
Locke, John, 28

Mahé v Alberta (1990), 180
Meech Lake Accord (1987), 92, 168,
172–5, 177–90, 192–4, 196–7; and
Aboriginal peoples, 124, 173, 286;
distinct society clause, 172–3, 179–
84, 195; failure of, 130, 155, 159,
166–7, 173, 175–6; post-failure
adoption through constitutional
practice, 175–91; Québec's five conditions leading to, 104, 109n20. *See
also* Charlottetown Accord (1992)
Metis, 120–27, 147. *See also* Aboriginal
and treaty rights; Indigenous peoples
(or nations); Inuit; Royal
Commission on Aboriginal Peoples
Mill, John Stuart, 69, 294
Miller, David, 33–41, 44, 45n4, 61, 63,
309, 313, 323
mistrust (as distinct from distrust), 40;
as central to democracy and compatible with trust, 86, 105–6; and federalism, 11, 211; forms of, 6, 86–7;
as it relates to distrust, 5–6, 27–8,
107n11; as it relates to trust, 20, 86,
92–3, 105–6; reservoir of, 102; rise
of the society of, 86. *See also*
counter-democracy; vigilance
monism, monist(ic), 11, 210–47
Montesquieu, 102, 219
Mulroney, Brian, 104, 108n17, 125, 166